PHALLIC FRENZY

Ken Russell and His Films

JOSEPH LANZA

First published in Great Britain 2008
by Aurum Press Ltd, 7 Greenland Street, London NW1 0ND
www.aurumpress.co.uk

Published by arrangement with Chicago Review Press, Inc, Illinois.

Interior design: Sarah Olson

A catalogue record for this book is available from the British Library.

ISBN 978 1 84513 373 3

10 9 8 7 6 5 4 3 2 1

2012 2011 2010 2009 2008

Printed by Cromwell Press, Trowbridge, Wiltshire

Mixed Sources
Product group from well-managed forests and other controlled sources
www.fsc.org Cert no. TT-COC-2082
© 1996 Forest Stewardship Council
FSC

CONTENTS

ACKNOWLEDGMENTS

My warmest thanks to David Litofsky, Leonard Pollack, and Barry Sandler for their help, encouragement, supplies, and conversations through this ordeal by fire.

I would also like to thank the following friends, associates, and institutions for their generosity, assistance, encouragement, and resources: Iain Fisher, Paul Jensen, Thomas Kenny, Jim Meehan, savagemessiah.com, Jay Schwartz, TopFoto, the Museum of the Moving Image (Astoria, New York), and the Museum of Television and Radio (New York City).

Thanks to my editor, Yuval Taylor.

And my special thanks to Ken Russell for his help, inspiration, permissions, and for sending me a homemade copy of *Hot Pants*.

PINOCCHIO'S PECKER

Ken Russell's phallic frenzy always reverts to two events in his youth, both of which occurred in cinemas. The first happened when he went to see *The Secret of the Loch*, a very British film from the early 1930s about a Scottish town all in a twist when

> "He's a lovely monster, isn't he, Ken Russell?"
>
> —*Michael Powell*

the legendary Loch Ness monster appears. Russell recalls in his memoirs that it was a plucked chicken with a prominent beak, but it was actually an iguana, enlarged with primitive special effects to suggest a Behemoth. Little Kenny took one look at this terrifying creature's jutting head with its dangling, testicular neck skin and bolted out of the theater.

The follow-up trauma happened in his early teens, when he went to see Walt Disney's *Pinocchio*. He elaborates in his autobiography: "I had never enjoyed a film more. And as I watched Pinocchio's stiff little pointed nose grow and grow, so my enjoyment grew with it. And so did my willie. Something else was moving around my crotch. It was a man's hand. I couldn't believe it. How had it got there? And why? I became aware of a shadowy presence in the next seat."

Cringing at the forbidden delights this groping Geppetto offered, Russell fled the theater once again and stayed away from cinemas for a spell. But the sensations of danger and forbidden joy lingered to inform much of his life and art. In Russell's surrealistic interpretative mind, the creature in the movie, the mysterious stranger's groping paws, and the doll's growing nose formed one vast dragon that he, like a mythical Siegfried caught in a Freudian nightmare, has time and again attempted to subdue, slay, and even seduce. His childhood memories suggest the landmark impressionistic study *Leonardo da Vinci*, in which Sigmund Freud traced da Vinci's artistic gifts to the artist's own recollection of being an infant in a cradle and having a vulture swoop down to spank his lips

1

with its tail. Russell's creative life is, similarly, the product of what Freud calls a "disfigured reminiscence," rife with exciting conflicts between the horrific and the erotic, the neurotic and the visionary, the puerile and the profound.

When he finally picked up a movie camera sometime in the 1950s, Russell set out to explore his mind's watery depths. His search has continued for over four decades, with his "willie" the thematic maypole. Around it, he has wrapped stories of love, hate, death, religion, politics, and the fragile role of art in a world where commerce and mass media co-opt and castrate the creative spirit at every juncture.

"All of Russell's work," the *New York Times*' Stephen Farber wrote in the early 1970s, "his BBC documentaries and his feature films, reveal a terror of mental and physical disintegration. In his films, death has a shocking, visceral immediacy; his career can be seen as a continuing struggle to find an imaginative vision that will be powerful enough to ward off the terrible stench of decomposing flesh." Russell appears to try to take control of this threatening natural order by making it appear fake, transforming the primordial ooze into gaudy, glossy objects from discount stores, and making alienation so alienating that he can purposely induce snickers instead of sobs.

Even though most critics consider *Women in Love* one of the tamer of Russell's works, which accounts for its 1969 Best Director Oscar nomination and a Best Actress Oscar for Glenda Jackson, many of its subjects have haunted subsequent Russell projects. Lawrence's story is perfect for summarizing Russell's courtships and inevitable conflicts between the sexes; his conflicted sympathies with homosexual relationships; his so-called love of nature and his phobias about its slimier side; his desire to tell a serious story while simultaneously slipping into farce; his love of art and his penchant for destroying art's mystique; his battle between visceral, irrational sensations and the more intellectual approach to life that Lawrence once derided as "sex in the head"; and spells of anger, pessimism, and even nihilism that belie his frustrated love of life. All of these themes contain a welter of contradictions that inspire rather than handicap his narratives: a kind of bizarro world where nothing is what it seems and where the director's passions and neuroses are a vital part of his stories.

The Devils, Russell's most controversial and harshest work, takes these themes further. It casts Oliver Reed as a womanizing priest who gets his comeuppance when an adoring mother superior (Vanessa Redgrave) exacts revenge for his rejection by accusing him of rape. She feigns demonic possession, submits to a public exorcism (a euphemism for a public enema), and inspires her nuns to use a giant crucifix for their orifice-plugging orgies. But the colorful depravity, much of which was censored out and only recently restored, has the effect of a Hieronymus Bosch painting, capturing in its excess a religious allegory about lost souls and eternal hell. Also, in the spirit of Aldous Huxley's novel on which it's based, *The Devils* links religious corruption to sexual repression and the lust for political power—all executed in an often-schizoid directing style that mixes spiritual depravity with physical comedy.

The deaf, dumb, and blind boy in *Tommy* might be sexless, but he's still threatened with syringes, fire hoses, and an array of invasive instruments. When submitting to mind-altering drugs, Tommy Walker (Roger Daltrey) envisions his death: a skeleton with a snake writhing out from his pelvis. Even amid the film's carnival atmosphere, exaggerated acting, and childlike, flighty atmosphere, *Tommy* conveys an underlying terror, particularly with the subject of child abuse lording over the otherwise cartoonish proceedings. Russell might simplify the movie's message by saying it's about the death of innocence and the triumph of commerce, but something about *Tommy* suggests that the shimmering and often-campy world of artifice offers another kind of mysticism. The film's fans tend to remember Ann-Margret's flashy jewelry and makeup, the vibrant colors of the pinball arcade, the maniacal acting, the garish costumes and choreographed hysteria, and the final crowd scene full of drugged-out and menacing 1970s youth. Such images and sounds overwhelm the rather anticlimactic ending, when Tommy finds redemption by diving back into the waters where he was conceived.

The *New York Times'* Vincent Canby, who hated *The Devils* for what he called its "clanking, silly, melodramatic effects," paid *Tommy* a backhanded compliment, begrudgingly admitting it's "the movie that proves that there are times when too much may be just about right, when overindulgence approaches art. . . . *Tommy* is to movies what a juke box is to furniture. It is not something you'd want to live with every day but it's kind of fun when you go out."

In *Lisztomania*, Daltrey returns as the lothario composer Franz Liszt, who attracts screaming fans and struts like a sex idol on the stage. He smiles during one dreamlike interlude as his trouser snake rises to twelve feet, but he screams all the way to the penile guillotine, paying the price for his Faustian pact with a power-hungry princess who promises him fame in return for his soul. "Russell's gimmicks may be crazily burlesque," Jack Kroll wrote in *Newsweek*, "but they burlesque historical truth. Liszt was the first great international superstar, lionized by a public that was already marshaling itself into what has become the mass audience of today's mass culture."

Valentino, an underrated masterpiece for which even Russell has expressed feelings ranging from disdain to ambivalence, casts Rudolf Nureyev as the silent screen's Latin lover. But instead of the dark, mysterious, and relentlessly erotic screen image, Valentino emerges as a combination buffoon and Hollywood martyr. In one grueling scene, "the Sheik" spends a night in the slammer.

A sadistic prison guard, apparently curious and jealous about "the eighth great wonder of the world" Valentino supposedly has between his legs, forces the star to urinate in his pants while a gaggle of whores and drunks and a snaggle-toothed masturbator torment him more. Russell films this scene in an apparent fit of inspired anger; fortunately, he fought off the studio's attempt to nix it. It remains one of the most brilliant, uncompromising, and disturbing moments ever to show up in a mainstream feature.

Then there are all those eels, lizards, and snakes that saturate Dr. Jessup's (William Hurt) hallucinations in *Altered States*, or the menacing boa constrictor in *Gothic* that keeps haunting Mary Shelley (Natasha Richardson) on the night she conceives her novel *Frankenstein*. And there's that menacing solid steel electric dildo that the randy Reverend Shayne (Anthony Perkins) wields in *Crimes of Passion* to terrorize the prostitute he also wants to save. *The Lair of the White Worm*, Russell's drollest British film offering, is one drawn-out phallic parlor game: a guiltless pleasure for those who like their sensationalism with wit. The movie belches out crucifixion nightmares with skewered nuns and rapacious Romans a vampire seductress whose fangs castrate a Boy Scout and a slithering, carnivorous creature deep in a cave's bowels that waits for sacrificial victims. With this, Russell includes dialogue that at times resembles an amalgam of Noel Coward and Oscar Wilde; there's even a metamessage in which the film's semi-hero, the smug and stiff-upper-lipped Lord D'Ampton (Hugh Grant), represents the last gasp of British aristocracy in the Thatcher era.

In addition to the aforementioned stars, Russell worked with such acclaimed actors as Alan Bates, Ed Begley, Gabriel Byrne, Michael Caine, Leslie Caron, Richard Chamberlain, David Hemmings, Karl Malden, Helen Mirren, Jack Nicholson, Julian Sands, and Kathleen Turner, not to mention such rock superstars as the Who, Elton John, and Tina Turner. These players helped Russell make some of the most daring, original, disturbing, blissfully distasteful, and beautifully photographed films of all time.

Through the years, Russell has earned laurels and barbs. He's been called the "Wild Man of the BBC," "the enfant terrible of British cinema," and a "fish and chips Fellini." There's even a possibly apocryphal story about Russell and Fellini encountering each other in Italy outside a movie studio. Russell tells him he's considered the Fellini of the North, while Fellini replies he's considered the Russell of the South. But Fellini's excesses usually exude a more lightheartedly Italian regard for love and luxury. In *Roma*, for instance, when he has priests rollerskating on a catwalk in a Vatican fashion show, Fellini satirizes the clergy with prickly affection.

In contrast, when Russell portrays Cardinal Richelieu in *The Devils* as a shrew in red silk, getting wheeled around inside a church fortress lined with steel bars, he regards the papacy with a much more caustic, and uniquely British, irony. Russell has often claimed that many of his films are Catholic in nature, but he appears to hate Catholicism as an institution. And for all his garishness and his reputation for making movies for crazy people, Russell exceeds Fellini as an organized storyteller; his inspired lunacy works best when he has a tight script to complement his mania. Russell's best films are, as a result, easier to follow, less sloppy, more deviant, and more edgy than Fellini's.

Many times, the negative responses to Russell's films reveal the critics' biases and hang-ups; often they inadvertently make Russell seem appealing to the kinds of viewers—and there are many—who like such films. Depending on who reads Penelope Gilliatt's scathing review of *The Devils*, her words might be an incentive to run to the theater or grab the video: "The epileptic rhythms of the editing are revved up with a score that might be program music for the onset of psychosis." Who needs a press release when a bad review can be this enticing?

Then take the chronically anti-Russell Pauline Kael, who drags along her aesthetic baggage whenever she wags her erudite finger in the director's face. In one breath, she dismisses both *Women in Love* and one of Michael Powell's finest films, claiming that Russell "makes Lawrence's period romantically *exotic* the way a movie like *Black Narcissus* was exotic, so even when he's most effective it's a fruity falsification of Lawrence's work." She gets nastier with her review of *The Music Lovers*, calling Russell's enthralling take on the life of Tchaikovsky "baroque vulgarity" and accusing him of being "one of the most reckless movie directors who have [sic] ever lived."

Confronted with *Savage Messiah*, Russell's relatively kink-free offering about the Vorticist sculptor Henri Gaudier, Kael snaps: "[Russell] garbles until there is no base of truth left in a situation; his volatile mixture of bombast and venom and parody isn't an exaggeration of anything we can recognize; we no longer know what world we're in. That's why, at a certain point in a Ken Russell movie, I always say to myself, 'The man is mad.' But it's why those who adore his movies say, 'He's a genius.'"

Stephen Farber, on the other hand, appears to be among those adorers that got Kael riled. His review of *The Music Lovers* recognizes that Russell "has abandoned himself to his subject, and his dynamic baroque style of shooting and editing draws us boldly into scene after scene. The imagery is as lush and intoxicating as the music. At moments, Russell achieves a kind of cinematic synthesis, a dizzying, disorienting experience in which all senses—visual, aural, even tactile—seem to blur."

Life's Richard Schickel, with some reservations, credited Russell as "one of the most exciting talents to appear in some time." Dilys Powell, in London's

Sunday Times, called him, with some fondness, "an appalling talent." The tag stuck with many, including film historian John Baxter, who used it for the title of his 1973 book on Russell that includes a priceless appraisal: "Like the sorcerer's apprentice in his beloved *Fantasia*, Russell has the power and knows the spells, but lacks the master's insight that would allow him to understand and control the creatures he summons up. And though his creations are often appalling, even to himself, he would rather not know how to control them, for fear that with knowledge would come a crippling impotence."

Decades later, Russell would continue to fight these creatures. But in an age of multiplexes, entertainment

An Appalling Talent Ken Russell John Baxter

Ken Russell poses on the set of *The Devils*—from the cover of John Baxter's pioneering book.

conglomerates, bottom-line movie producers talking down to audiences, and bean counters, all reaching for the lowest common denominator with hollow heroes, generic scripts, talent-packaged stars, and audience-sampled content, Russell flipped his middle finger to the movie industry and, with a digital camera, retreated to a parallel world: a thatched cottage at his home in England's New Forest district that he had converted into a makeshift movie studio in order to tell stories his way.

If detractors dismiss him as nothing but a dirty old man with a penis fixation, Russell has only to remind himself that he's in good company. In 1915, when D. H. Lawrence published *The Rainbow* (which Russell later adapted), a reviewer from London's *Daily News* described the novel as "a monotonous wilderness of phallicism." Russell is also a lot like François Rabelais, the sixteenth-century French satirist and scholar, whose *Gargantua and Pantagruel* he once tried filming. Rabelais, also deemed blasphemous, seasoned his observations on theology, love, and art with phallocentric images.

Ken Russell's movies offer both brazen sensationalism and food for thought; they horrify yet inspire. Even during moments when the plot drags or the foils between good and evil get too simplistic, viewers plugged into Russell's nervous system can count on continual jolts of sound and vision that few directors can pack with such command. Through it all, Russell maintains a simultaneously impish and intellectual sense of humor. And a man so willful and consistent about being "vulgar" and "excessive" at the expense of "decorum," and who has done so in most cases without any regard to what is "fashionable" or even "bankable," needs and deserves an appraisal that values his quirky aesthetics.

Unfortunately, too many critics have discounted Russell's excesses from a template more apt for assessing a film by John Ford or François Truffaut. But support for Russell has surfaced from various places. "Russell's films are often coarse, symbol-ridden, pretentious, and confusing," Ephraim Katz wrote in *The Film Encyclopedia*, "but there is always a sense of excitement about them and a creative energy that makes the release of each an event eagerly awaited with curious anticipation." One of the very best observations beamed from an unexpected source: the *Catholic Film Newsletter*, a publication from the U.S. Catholic Conference's Department of Communication, that stamped the "Condemned" seal on *The Devils* and later *Valentino*, but had some enthusiasm for *Lisztomania*. According to its writer Michael Gallagher, "To accuse Russell of excess when he is working in this area, however, is very much like accusing Rubens of sensuality."

Through the years, Russell has written extensively and hilariously about his life, loves, loathings, exploits, and theories of great cinema. But his words have appeared as a scrambled mosaic. If anything, his life invites a more linear story, told (or at least interpreted) as a Rake's Progress full of epiphanies and misadventures. The following narrative is impressionistic and picaresque, a tale of a man-child who struggles in the forest primeval with a go-for-the-gonads approach to storytelling. It is a madcap tale full of wild ideas, surreal situations, and a cavalcade of equally colorful personalities. And it comes from an author who admits his own biases, who favors Russell's flights of fancy, and who even gets therapy out of watching Russell at his harshest and "weirdest."

This is a story about how Ken Russell romances the Freudian joystick by loading his movies with paradoxical themes: clashes between the body and the spirit, the inane and the sublime. Russell is the cinema's true rogue, a human moviola who pisses and ejaculates tales of gods and devils, love and lust, sex and death, inspiration and melancholia, and the increasingly fuzzy boundaries (which he has helped to blur) between art and the hypercommercialism that gave birth to the music video.

"Understatement never won a war," Russell once declared, "and most of my films are about war."

THE LAIR OF THE BLACK MAMBA

Henry Kenneth Alfred Russell was born on July 3, 1927, in Southampton, England, a quiet seaside town that became a major military transport station as well as World War II's front line. The Romans had their Clausentum settlement there; ancient coins, jewelry, and bones from as early as the Pleistocene period occasionally surface.

Russell's childhood memories begin and end in explosions. First, his movie projector combusted in a tangle of nitrate film, a conflagration of metal and acetate which nearly set fire to the house and assumed, for Russell, the epic grandeur of a Cecil B. DeMille disaster. Then there was World War II, when the German Luftwaffe squirted bombs over England, and a much-loved relative succumbed to a wartime blast.

In his autobiography and various interviews, Russell describes his young self as a sensitive, aspiring artiste, spending great amounts of time alone, estranged from his peers and siblings, and looking to his mother for support. Boyhood memories of his brother, Ray, five years his junior, appear to register as little more than a few wrestling matches. Ken's parents—Henry and Ethel (née Smith) Russell—represented such warring factions in his personality that they became for him almost mythical figures. This might explain why he has avoided using their first names in his recollections, referring to them as simply "Dad" and "Mum."

Besides Mum, Russell's company was usually Muriel Codd, whom he called "Aunt Moo," and his beloved, free-spirited cousin Marion. "She had a very strange imagination too," he recalls of Marion, "and we would create all sorts of weird and wonderful adventures together. She was also a tomboy and anything I could do she could do better. I was a bit jealous of her and completely mad about her."

Just a year younger, Marion Russell embodied the sweeter side of his childhood, when he gnawed on Mars bars and pored over *Rainbow* comics. She was boyish, with her blonde hair in a bob, freckles, blue eyes, and a smile that Russell says he "could never place until I saw it years later on Botticelli's *Primavera*. And she was blessed with an ease of movement and gesture that seemed almost choreographed in its perfection."

On those days when he waited for a visit from his boyish Botticelli to no avail, Russell spent afternoons sitting up in his backyard conker tree daydreaming. Mum was always there to take her impressionable lad to the shops or nurture her own inner imp by accompanying him to movie after movie. "If anything sustained her and thousands like her," Russell recalls about a frustrated Mum coping with an indifferent Dad, "it was not the example of saints and angels from the Holy Bible, but their Hollywood counterparts. Not Saints Peter and Paul but Peter Lorre and Paul Muni. I think Mum would have gone mad without the movies."

Life beyond Mum, however, was more and more taxing, especially at school. When evaluating the effect his schoolmates and masters had on his daily life, Russell conjures memories of puddles that would form after a rainy day. He'd look down into them, see clouds in the reflection, and fancy that the world inside this "magic mirror" was much more enchanting than the actual sky. "I lived on the street where no children ever came," he told Colin Wilson in a 1973 television interview, "and my world was made up of heroes and heroines of the silver screen." He affirms in his autobiography that movie houses were a sanctuary: "I lived in the dark."

One of Russell's magic mirrors was the Hollywood musical. When craving romantic adventure, he looked to Dorothy Lamour in particular to throw him a lifeline. He watched *The Fleet's In* over and over again, memorizing the dialogue, so that one day he might impress his screen idol when she adorned him with leis and led him along the pink sands. But Westerns, especially anything with William Boyd, bored him to tears. As for Continental cinema, G. W. Pabst's 1933 version of *Don Quixote*, starring the Russian opera basso Fyodor Chaliapin, goaded his inner critic. For him, the movie was "corny, undramatic, and boring," but the orchestral score impressed him enough to inspire a lifelong love of classical music.

Russell recalls another indelible time, when Mum took him to see the 1930 clinker *Puttin' on the Ritz*. It featured Harry Richman as a vaudevillian who, following what would become a predictable story in countless other pictures, lets success fill his head and alcohol rot his brain. By the time Richman performs Irving Berlin's title song, the lavish sets are vaudeville with *delirium tremens*: creepy buildings with eyes and claws bearing down on a corral of equally creepy minstrels. For an adult, this scene is disturbing enough; for a child, it can provoke abject terror.

Less charitable about homegrown films, Russell claims that the term "a British picture" had insulting implications in those early years. He remembers Mum and Aunt Moo griping over the newspapers at the paltry choices. They especially hated the *Old Mother Riley* series, in which the homely actor Arthur Lucan dressed up as an even homelier Irish washerwoman and dragged viewers into one shopworn pratfall after another. Perhaps the ladies' prejudices sent little Kenny alone to see *The Secret of the Loch*, an idiosyncratically British movie that plods along until an idiosyncratically British monster steals the show.

Mum and Aunt Moo were being a bit unfair with their anti-British movie slant. Into the 1930s and early '40s, England was offering some unique and fairly risqué films that sometimes surpassed Tinseltown's formulaic gloss, and could be considered precursors to Russell's roguish style. Even otherwise innocuous family viewing could get bizarre and indecorous. Gracie Fields, the grand matron of wholesome, offered Depression-era favorites with such titles as *Sing as We Go* and *Look Up and Laugh*. Along with a sprightly supporting cast, she would suddenly break into song at the oddest moments. Her elaborate productions and mob choruses could make an otherwise mawkish musical livelier and loopier.

The British were also adept at putting their unique dottiness into horror and melodrama. Around 1936, just after Boris Karloff reprised his Monster role in James Whale's *Bride of Frankenstein*, he went back to England to star in *The Man Who Changed His Mind*, which Robert Stevenson directed for the Gainsborough Studios. The story, merging horror with droll humor, proved to be among Karloff's most eccentric performances: a mad scientist who performs electronic brain transplants between humans and monkeys.

There was also the villainy of Tod Slaughter, a cloak and dagger villain who made nastiness an obscene pleasure. "Tod Slaughter, yes!" Russell cheers at just the mention of his name. For Russell and many other fans, Slaughter had supreme screen charisma: he laughed maniacally, chewed up scenery shred by shred, and loved corrupting and then offing pretty waifs while sneering such lines as, "You wanted to be a bride, my dear Jessica, did you? So, you shall be: a bride of death!"

Sadomasochism was fun to watch, but prettier pictures seduced him outside the cinema, when he and Mum spent afternoons going to High Street for tea and chocolates. There, they would hear a ladies' string trio perform ditties like "Tea for Two" at the Cadena Café. Next would be a stroll along Canal Walk, an alleyway that he remembers as "the Kasbah of Southampton." To him, it was an exotic paradise, fit for an Albert W. Ketèlbey soundtrack with exotic instruments from "foreign lands" and sentimental melodies fit for a tourist's packaged paradise. "It was Aladdin's fairytale," he writes in his autobiography. "Baghdad come to life, a place of magic carpets and wonderful lamps where you might be ambushed by Ali Baba and the forty thieves or help Sinbad rescue the captive princesses calling on high from the sultan's palace."

But reality, usually in the form of some adversarial male figure, kept creeping in. One fascinating case involved St. George's, a school he attended just around the corner from his home. He remembers it primarily for its Gothic-style, stained-glass windows and the ritual of singing "See Me Dance the Polka at the Penguin Polka Ball" in unison with his classmates. But sinister vibrations hovered when a new headmaster took over and conducted classes at his house.

"I was only about eight or nine," Russell remembers, "but even I felt a strange undertone. He was quite a tough guy, the new headmaster, with a terrifying collection of canes and I'd seen some of the older boys, sixteen-year-olds, walking around in very smart uniforms. I thought, God, that looks great! Why are they dressed like that?"

Having the temerity to ask, Ken soon found out that the boys who made it to the fifth form had the privilege of joining the headmaster as members of Oswald Mosley's Fascist Blackshirts. Russell recalls the ensuing spectacle: "Every Sunday they used to march up and down the High Street in Southampton. I can even remember Mosley coming down, and they had a parade and were inspected. There was stone-throwing; a riot. Then the school suddenly disbanded."

The other problem was closer to home. Mum was all kookiness and sunshine, but Dad was usually coldness and cruelty. Strict and perhaps a bit self-loathing, Dad had abandoned a much more daring life as a ship's detective during Prohibition and was reduced to selling shoes like the rest of his family. But he swallowed his pride, conformed to family expectations, and took it out on those household members nearest his footrest. "Mum and Dad didn't get on," Russell told the *Times* of London years later. "They argued. Love was a scarce commodity in Mum's life. She took me to the cinema nearly every day and I'd complain: 'You said there wasn't going to be any love in the film and they're kissing already.'"

Dastardly Dad also seemed to vent his rages when taking Ken on sporty outings: "My father was a distant figure who took delight in scaring my mother and I in a weird way. He roared his head off as he forced us to dig for ragworms, which are a foot long with thousands of legs, to use as fishing bait. Otherwise, he didn't have much fun in life." Russell also describes this King Ragworm as a creature "with hands all the way along his body, and the top of his head opens and two great pincers come out and snap at you. And when you break him to bait your hook blood spurts out, and pus and slime, and a terrible smell. We had to bait our own hooks, putting our hands into this mess, and to this day I hate worms."

Responding to such fatherly love, Russell would forever be on the lookout for snakes or other incubi hiding in corners. He believed one lurked in an empty and seldom-entered spare room. He tried avoiding it, but one day he tempted fate by wandering in, recoiling at what he found behind a cupboard door: "It was an octopus with an elephant's trunk. I fully expected it to grab my ankle and drag me into the darkness. I fled. At night the fearsome monster joined the ghostly giant at the end of the bathroom corridor to haunt me in my dreams. I started using the garden lavatory rather than pass the spare room to get to the one upstairs, and it wasn't long before my parents noticed."

Like an archaic headshrinker throwing a lunatic into a snake pit, Dad took Kenny by the hand, guided him to the dreaded spot, threw open the cupboard doors, grabbed the monster by the neck, and waved it in the boy's face: "It seemed to writhe like a creature trapped in its lair on the ocean floor, throwing up a cloud of dust as camouflage. Its glassy eyes flashed with malice. The ribbed trunk swung towards me. I shuddered, tore myself away from my father's grasp, and ran." When the scary dust cloud settled, Kenny saw nothing but an old gas mask, a souvenir from a kit bag that his maternal grandfather retained from the Great War.

Even a ride in the family car could detour to *Dante's Inferno*. Russell recalls a return drive from a vacation and hearing the hissing of serpents in the back seat. Dad stayed quiet and collected, while Ken lifted his feet and, in a helpless, crouching position, screamed to get out. Dad kept driving, calling his boy a coward and informing him that the hissing was just a twenty-four-volt battery with its leads connecting. "Ever a practical man," Russell recounts, "he must have seen my story as a childish attempt to hide my fear of a harmless phenomenon. To him the idea of a couple of deadly snakes hissing away on the back seat of his car was beyond his comprehension, whereas to me it was always a possibility, one I hope to realize one day in a film."

Russell's phobia of reptiles intensified a few years later when, on a summer outing during his stint at a nautical college, he took a dare from a gal pal named Elsie and bared his little white worm. But this attempted rite of passage in the dirty old woods turned into another encounter with the Leviathan. As the girl gently groped him, something else stirred. "A crackle of twigs," he writes. "I froze for a moment, thinking of the housemaster. Guiltily I pulled away, gasped, and looked up. Towering above me was a big, big black man in the uniform of the U.S. Air Force. The girl withdrew her hand with a giggle. They both looked at my gym pants which my erection had turned into a fairy's bell tent. She gave a shrill laugh. It deflated fast. The airman guffawed, then with a flick of his wrist loosened his fly and released something that swung down in front of my face like a big black mamba. I ran and ran and ran and never ran through that wood again."

Russell faced other monsters, such as the one he remembers in a preposterous story involving a boyhood acquaintance: "I remember he lived in a Gothicky-looking house with a rather sinister garage which had a gorilla locked up inside. I hadn't seen *King Kong*, but my parents told me about it and of course I'd seen the poster. Well, one day he pushed me into the garage and locked me up with the gorilla. I was terrified. The garage was pitch-black, and I was convinced the ape was breathing down my neck. It probably accounts for a lot."

Russell had happier social interactions when he converted his garage into a cinema and invited folks to share with him the Betty Boop and Felix the Cat cartoon loops he got as a Christmas present. Later, he added extension arms to his clunky Pathescope Ace 9.5mm hand-cranked projector and started renting feature length movies from a local drug store. Though born the same year the talkies came alive, Russell felt a kinship for the desperate language of silent films, mainly Fritz Lang's German Expressionism in *Die Nibelungen* and *Metropolis*.

Unlike the thing in *The Secret of the Loch* that terrified him, Fafnir the dragon in *Siegfried*, the first part of Lang's *Die Nibelungen*, inspired him. He loved the movie's netherworld of dragons, ogres, giants, and dwarfs. He would also inherit Lang's approach to character and style: the larger-than-life settings, exaggerated mannerisms, and facial gestures. This is most apparent in a scene when irony threatens the otherwise solemn tone: the manly Amazon Brunhild challenges the fey King Gunther to feats of Norsk valor that are outlandish enough to prompt sacrilegious thoughts of Lang snickering from behind the camera.

Lang would also be a role model. He was the man with the discerning eye, the martinet with the monocle and the jodhpurs, who presided over his movie sets like a tyrant, brandishing a riding crop and pushing the extras around. Russell too would carry a crop to some of his film sets; he too would bark orders and sometimes frighten the cast and crew. His films would also traverse Lang's netherworld, where a director's mad passion sometimes blurs the line between tragedy and travesty.

Thanks to a shellac gramophone record he found in his Christmas stocking, Russell augmented Lang's vision

Siegfried and the dragon from Fritz Lang's *Die Nibelungen*.

with musical soundtracks. Scoring *Siegfried*'s encounter with the dragon, he drowned out the staccato sounds of the Nazi Blitz overhead with a heroic march by Edvard Grieg. To accompany the scary moment in *Metropolis*, when the evil Dr. Rotwang unveils a robot wench programmed to wreak havoc on workers in the city of the future, Russell had only to flip the record over for trumpet blasts from Sir Arthur Bliss's "March of Things to Come."

Looking back, Russell appreciates the grotesque comedy. How lurid to be enjoying the movies about Nordic prowess that Hitler and Goebbels also drooled over. Even then, Russell felt a twinge of guilt and donated any proceeds he collected on his garage shows to the Spitfire Fund for England's war machine. "I have to confess," Russell would write, "that some of my happiest memories involve those shows in Dad's garage, where the irony of the situation—in which the songs of Siegfried rained down fire from above, as their heroic Aryan ancestor destroyed that evil fire-breathing dragon—totally escaped me."

Siegfried slew his dragon, but Russell was no match for the Jabberwockys that teemed in his home terrain and in his mind. He sometimes thought he was so secure during those Sundays, when the family went to Highcliffe, rented bungalows, gamboled in waist-high grass, and contemplated buttercups. But there were still those seasides, where conger eels snapped, and woodlands, where serpents hissed: "Highcliffe was our weekend haven for six months of the year. I remember it raining only once in the entire decade, and that was the day I was scared nearly out of my skin by a giant adder in the glen." But Cousin Marion, like a Botticelli superhero, came to his rescue.

Other "slithy toves" from the lower kingdom waited at the edge of the world to snatch up insolent dreamers. In 1940, Marion, so full of grace but always venturing into forbidden places, became Russell's ultimate war casualty: the victim of a landmine explosion. Looking some thirty years back on the day his uncle stormed into the house and cried, "Marion's dead," Russell confessed that it was the moment when his romantic ideals also went kaput: "And suddenly that was the end—of everything."

THE LOST LAMOUR

As a boy, Ken Russell took walks to St. Denys, an old Victorian-style railway station where he'd stand on a lattice bridge over the tracks, waiting to catch a glimpse of the London-bound locomotive. That iron horse speeding along those silver rails represented for him a journey to the unknown, an escape from a house where the parents bickered and open affection was rare. He recalls a time at age ten, when he snuck out to St. Denys in the moonlight. The moment the red signal flashed to green, he grabbed onto the latticework as the bridge started rattling, and the steam resembled a friendly ghost flying closer: "It was coming, coming fast, it was nearly upon me. I was dead over the track but never more alive. My blood felt as if it were racing the train, the last few yards took on the space of a delirious eternity."

> 'Twas on the Good Ship Venus,
> Egad! You should have seen us;
> The figurehead was a whore in bed,
> The mast the skipper's penis.
>
> —*This and later stanzas are from the old Pangbourne sea shanty "The Good Ship Venus," as Ken Russell rendered them in his 2006 short film of the same name.*

By the lucky age of thirteen, however, Russell got tired of waiting for the silver bullet. Each time, it flashed by and shot white clouds in his face before speeding off on the undertow. This always left him feeling exhilarated for a few moments and then abandoned. He had to scheme a real escape from war-ravaged Southampton to an exotic land, where the rooms weren't damp and Dorothy Lamour danced. Still smitten over the dusky screen star of *Aloma of the South Seas* in the brown body makeup, he got desperate enough to send Lamour love letters and receive photos with her dubiously authentic signature.

This was not enough: he had to somehow geographically unite with her—in spirit if not in body: "I got books from the library on the islands of Polynesia and drooled over the soft-focus pictures of blue lagoons and saronged maidens climbing trees for coconuts. So when my father suggested I went away to a nautical school like my cousin Roy, I jumped at the idea."

In 1941, Russell entered the Royal Navy College at Pangbourne, a regrettable and irreversible decision. Now, he realized the waters teeming with congers looked nothing like his South Sea utopia. Worse, he was faced with sex-crazed mates he feared might latch onto him for lack of anything softer. Not even the shaking of metal he experienced while crouched in bomb shelters could match the horrific impact when "row upon row of metal bunks rattled to the rhythm of mass masturbation."

Russell's bunkmates often took their sexual frustrations out on him: "I spoke with a typical Southampton accent, so automatically I was subjected to the most unremitting attack and ridicule. I had to go up and say, 'Russell HKA 157 *Sir*,' at some ridiculous weekly identity parade, but because my *A* sounded like an *I* I was sent up unmercifully." The cadet leader also publicly ridiculed him and incited other senior cadets to grab him by the lanyard and twist until he had a crimson streak across his collar. They would accuse him of having B.O. and "throw me, fully clothed, into a stinking bog."

One day, the cadet leader discovered a five-pound note had vanished from his pocket. His eyes immediately leapt on Russell; so did his cane. Though his rump was striped with red welts, Russell still managed to plant it on the seat at a cinema in nearby Reading, where he'd sneak off to catch variations on *Stage Door Canteen*. He broke such bounds for about three years and got "caned unmercifully upon my return."

> *The captain had a daughter,*
> *Forever in the water;*
> *You could hear the squeals of the conger eels*
> *Around her sexual quarter.*

The canings and the verbal abuse could have emerged from some Dickens or Melville tale, but Russell could find no literary or cinematic equivalent to what housemaster "Handy" had in store. Russell recalls that, along with a speech impediment, Handy "had big feet and bore more than a passing resemblance to Frankenstein's monster as played by Boris Karloff."

Once the lights went out each night, and the no-talking policy kicked in, Russell lay in terror at the thought of the monster's arrival. In his autobiography, he remembers getting pulled out of his bunk and into the office, where

Handy confronted him with a sheaf of drawings depicting female nudes and forced him to admit to owning them. Russell also re-creates Handy's anatomy lecture: "You're living in a f...f...fools' paradise, Russell. There's no slit there, it's more ... more like an open sewer of stinking flesh, eels, sea anemones hidden in a bush of sli...sli...slimy hu...hu...hair and sometimes there's blu ...blu...blood that smells like...sm...smell my f...fi...fingers. Smell tha ...that?"

Handy held a crumbled beef bullion cube to Russell's nose before stuttering, "Drop your pajamas. P...pu...please. I...I'm not go...go...going to h...hurt you." Russell closed his eyes and quivered. But the slimy shaft he feared might impale him turned out to be a measly finger, rubbing what felt like Vaseline over his caning sores. Thanks to the divine intervention of a whistling teakettle, Handy's hands went no further. He ordered Russell to pull up his pajamas and declared, "When you grow up y...y...you will realize that life is a f...f...fools' paradise. Do you under...understand me?"

Russell hobbled back to his bunk and to visions of his Lost Lamour's soft dark hair flowing in the tropical breezes one moment and morphing into a Gorgon's head of squirting lampreys the next. His bunkmates' nightly wanks got even more excruciating.

But life among the wankers wasn't all misery. They gladly took part in one of his very first projects: an amateur silent movie called *The Maiden and the Monster*, for which Russell was the writer, director, and star. Pivotal scenes involved an elaborate chase sequence where Russell, sporting a top hat and curly moustache, plays a villain who hits beggars and covets the girlfriend of the story's hero. When his character gets arrested, he escapes by battering his warden with a large sausage (a satire on the inedible ones the college served). He then arrives at a wedding altar to whisk away the heroine, whom Russell recalls was played "by a boy named Bird whom everybody had a crush on." Russell and the heroine flee down a hill, ditch the crowd, and find a shed in the middle of the woods. This amateur adventure in what Freudians would call castration anxiety ends when Russell, knowing his pursuers will soon gain on him, throws open the shed doors to release a giant monster who makes off with the girl after pulverizing Russell and his rival.

As he continued sneaking out for spectacular picture shows, Russell also developed a yen for Betty Grable's Technicolor extravaganzas. They stirred him to stage for the college a ninety-minute salute to American movie musicals called *Thank Your Lucky Tars*. "The shows the cadets put on were mostly dull affairs," Russell brags, "but when *I* directed a show, it was lively, because I dressed them all up in drag and made Carmen Mirandas out of them." The show included numbers like "Jet Black and the Seven Giants," featuring what was for pasty Pangbourne the novelty of a black entertainer. He also included a Latin American number with the plumpest member of the division dressed as a tutti-frutti dame and singing, "Amor, Amor, Amor."

To Russell's delight and surprise, his mates enjoyed impersonating ladies. Russell too stopped longing for Lamour and *became* her, donning a sarong, singing "Aloha-ee," and sneaking a cheeky thrill by blowing the commander a kiss. He remembers someone named Robin Lee-Smith, the only mate he could call a pal, as one of the many Carmen Mirandas: "With the aid of a pineapple, a pair of platforms, and a borrowed dress augmented in the right places by a couple of rolled-up rugger socks, Robin was the Brazilian Bombshell to the life. And when he rolled his hips and his baby blues and sang, 'Do you want my heeps to heep-na-tise you?' many hearts in the audience fluttered and many hands crept into many trouser pockets, and they weren't counting change."

Pangbourne College's first drag show was a huge success, the metal bunks continued shaking, and it looked as if life at the nautical college had finally paid off. But the rigors of the sea were inessential compared to the practice he got in staging the outlandish and gangly choreography that would later be among his cinematic trademarks.

> *The chippy was Benjamin Gleem,*
> *He built a wanking machine;*
> *On the ninety-ninth stroke, the bloody thing broke,*
> *And whipped his bollocks to cream.*

As the war was ending in the summer of 1945, Russell was just seventeen. A glutton for punishment, he joined the Merchant Navy as an apprentice sixth officer, on board the *Queen of Rataroa*, an eleven thousand–ton merchant ship heading for Lamour's South Seas. But crossing the Atlantic to make a cargo stop in Sydney, Australia, would prove nauseating in more ways than one. Bad enough he was constantly getting seasick; Russell had to abide the ship's captain, the master of the *Rataroa*: a short, squat, bowlegged bastard with Scottish red hair, a foul temper, and the complexion of a raw pork chop.

"Bligh of the *Bounty* was kindness in comparison," Russell writes. When the captain wasn't showing off by standing naked on his hands, he would bark orders that sounded like, "Rah, rah, re, rah!" Russell would respond, "Aye, aye, sir! Could I trouble you to repeat that?" The meeker Russell appeared, the madder the Scot got as he clenched his red fists, focused his beady eyes, and raised his voice. Fortunately, the ship's third mate, who had a sadistic streak of his own, decoded the captain's rant. What sounded like a hyena in heat turned out to be a crotchety crank yelling such banalities as "Lower the boats" or "Get me a cup of tea."

The "Old Man," as the crew called him, was also fearful of Japanese attacks. While the rest of the world was rejoicing on V-J Day, he forced his minions to keep watch for up to eight hours out of the twenty-four, waiting for the enemy to rise from the waters like the Loch Ness monster or plummet kamikaze-style from the sky. And when not watching through his porthole for attack submarines, the Old Man veered his sights on young Ken's gams.

"Dorothy Lamour had nothing on me when it came to legs, I promise you," Russell recollects, "and the sight of me standing there with my back to him in my short white shorts and my short white ankle socks and those gorgeous bronzed legs, shifting languorously from one foot to the other, day after day in the tropical heat, must have got too much for him."

By now, the Old Man's porthole went from being a paranoid's lookout post to a peep-show slot, as the heavy breathing emitting from it got louder and faster. No surprise when the Old Man soon issued another edict: during the off-duty hours, Ken had to shield his tempting flesh with heat-inducing fatigues. Through it all, Russell's whimsies over Lamour got eclipsed for good by thoughts of jumping ship the moment the *Rataroa* docked at Brisbane.

But Ken stayed on, looking out at the Pacific through binoculars. The Old Man watched too, trying to quell his desires with spite by assigning Ken such grueling duties as cleaning condensation off a locker room's walls. Russell recalls a gyrocompass inside the locker room that sounded like "a howling scream, more human than mechanical, as if the Old Man's repressed hysteria had found a voice, a voice that I could never shake off by night or by day."

As the inclement weather turned the *Rataroa* into a vomit comet, the sailors slipped and slid in their regurgitated lunches. All the while Russell, with headphones attached to a radio receiver, tried taking navigation orders transmitted in a code that seemed more the brainchild of a sadistic soda jerk than a naval official.

According to Russell, the guy who "dreamed up that code must have had a really sick sense of humour for in the circumstances they were the most nauseating words imaginable: chocolate cream, Turkish delight, mint cream, fudge sundae, marzipan coffee whirl, cherry malt liqueur. Every time a sickly message crackled into my headphones I threw up, and by the time I managed to stagger across the bridge to the third officer, all was confusion, including the words I was spewing up."

The third officer was also up to mischief as he routinely checked his codebook and screamed against the wind for Russell to verify whether the proper code was cherry fudge delight, chocolate mint cream, or cherry malt liqueur.

Ken could stand no more: "Keep your stinking chocolate. I've had it." He then pelted him with the headphones, went below to his bunk, and risked a court martial for vacating his post.

"By rights I should report you to the Old Man," the third officer declared. "He'd probably hang you by the yardarm as a deserter . . . You need a good lesson, my boy." But when the fleet reached its Panama destination, Russell was puzzled: so far, no showing up, no flogging, and no simulated rape. The third officer even had lifeboats tossed out from the ship to allow the sailors to get nearer the harbor for a better view. But Ken's boat remained stationary.

Standing confused and in a clean white suit, Russell toppled over as his boat knocked against the ship's hull. The third officer chuckled from above before shouting, "Now!" Russell recalls a fresh deluge of cherry fudge delight and chocolate mint cream, only this time from the bad end of the alimentary canal: "I'd been maneuvered underneath the main sewer pipe. The derisive laughter of the crew added to my humiliation but did not complete it. . . . When we were hauled on board an hour later the sun had baked me dry. I had turned into an artifact and smelt like one too. No matter how much I showered, I stank for days and days. I never deserted my post again, though I was sorely tempted."

Russell finally broke down and jumped ship (as he sometimes recounts) or got dismissed (as he claims on other occasions). Mum and Dad, to whom he now returned with bowed head, were livid. But they showed more compassion when a doctor concluded that Russell suffered from an anxiety neurosis—a fitting diagnosis for a young man who, after his throes at sea, got closest to living his tropical fantasy by roasting under the sun in dung. But then the farthest Lamour ever got to an actual island paradise was via a Paramount studio backlot.

"All these films I'd seen of the South Seas were probably better, really, than the South Seas, and so I became totally immersed in Hollywood fantasy. . . . If I couldn't live in a fantasy world in the South Seas, I'd better make my own."

MUSIC FOR A MENTAL BREAKDOWN

"**N**avy life was too monotonous," Russell once wrote, "too mind-sapping. Even if I had been on a decent ship, I realize I wouldn't have stuck it for long. I was glad the ship was bad, otherwise I might have tried to make a go of it just to please my parents, who'd spent all their money on this bloody education and fitted me out with all these expensive nautical kits. When I arrived home with a trunkful of stuff they asked, 'What's up?' and when I said, 'I'm not going back,' they couldn't believe it."

Mum and Dad kept pushing him to sell shoes, but Russell preferred to wander about the war-ravaged Southampton streets, catching a movie or two at the few cinemas that survived the bombs. He even considered going into the movie industry and made several trips to London, knocking on the doors of such studios as Ealing, Gainsborough, and Pinewood.

Each studio received him with the same cold and patronizing response, relegating some underling to inform him that there weren't even any jobs sweeping floors or making tea. "The only person who gave me any encouragement was Michael Powell. He wrote me a long letter saying he couldn't help directly but that it might be easier if I could get into the photographic stills department. I tried that and nothing came of it. So I found myself hanging around the house again."

For months, Ken Russell was human furniture: "I stayed on the settee," he recalls in his autobiography about his mental breakdown, "staring at the empty fireplace with the bees buzzing around my head. I stayed there day after day. Apart from bed and ablutions, I never left the settee."

Monsters still vexed him; even mundane household items like the Hoover vacuum cleaner morphed into serpents. The Hoover hissed in his ear, competing only with the buzzing bees and Mum's carping voice. Then, one day a slow and tender melody wafted from the radio.

"I became conscious of an incredible kind of beauty," he later wrote, "the existence of which I had never dreamed. Even the bees stopped to listen and became as entranced as I. Mum too fell silent and switched off the Hoover. I wished the music would never end. When it did I was weeping. The announcer gave the particulars of the recording. I got up. Mum's mouth fell open."

Recharged, Russell hopped on his bicycle to the local record store, where a slice of supernatural shellac landed in his hands: Solomon (the stage name of Solomon Cutner) and the Hallé Orchestra's recording of Tchaikovsky's Piano Concerto no. 1 in B-flat Minor. He went back home to listen again to the lush, beautiful melody that finally got his carcass off the cushion.

Instead of souring at room temperature like a glass of milk, he now propelled himself into the air and around the house. When Pavlova danced, audiences reacted with waves of love and awe, but Russell pirouetted across the floor in the spirit of Isadora Duncan, dancing with more conviction than grace. Tchaikovsky and Stravinsky blaring from a Deccola radiogram at maximum volume were ideal therapy: "I used to race to the top of the stairs and leap to the bottom, then swing from the landing to crash down in the hall. It lasted thirty minutes, and at the end of it I felt absolutely great."

Mum and Dad were leery about their son's new outlet, especially when they came home to find prized objects either broken or in disarray. Matters got worse when Mum came home with a neighbor and discovered him dancing naked to Stravinsky's *The Rite of Spring*. She and Dad gave him an ultimatum: he had to either grovel at his father's shoe store or risk his life in the Royal Air Force (RAF).

•

In 1946, after getting turned down for a job as a movie studio tea boy (a rite of passage for many budding British directors), Russell shirked the horrible home life for more military misery. He filled out his required national service by enlisting in the RAF. Never blending with his macho mates, he was again ridiculed for talking funny and got pelted with remarks like, "What d'you think you are, Russell, a fucking ballet dancer?"

While he found a niche as a radio engineer, a fucking ballet dancer he tried to become. He met a sympathetic mate named Bert Woodfield, a "merry fat sailor who loved to dance about to classical music." Together, they ran a "music circle" to spin 78s from two turntables, blaring the likes of Stravinsky over loudspeakers to edify the crew. They had the most fun when Bert started teaching Russell the steps to Tchaikovsky's *Swan Lake*, with Russell as the Swan Queen.

Bert also gave him some good advice, which he took when he left the RAF two years later. He went to London, rented a room in a boarding house, and joined Bert at the Hampstead Ballet Club. At twenty-one, Russell included ballet among several artistic aspirations. When his wallet thinned, he got a job at an art gallery on Bond Street. He impressed the proprietor by pretending to love the paintings of the postimpressionist and posthumous Jack the Ripper suspect Walter Sickert, even though he really hated them. After working there for about six months, he failed to sell a single painting and was shown the gilded door.

Russell in the RAF.
(Courtesy of Ken Russell)

"I thought: Christ, these are *real* bohemians," Russell recalls of those London days. "I suppose I was a bit of a bohemian myself in a way and was probably one of the first people to grow my hair long and wear a cloak since Oscar Wilde. Big deal! I used to get chased and stoned and bloody well thumped. It was 1948."

When Russell sought a career in photography, the RAF was not on his side. Its education officer appraised his talents by writing, "Would make an excellent picture framer." He considered working at a furniture factory in Shepherd's Bush, but the sight of a gigantic, intimidating clock at the main gate reminded him too much of the macabre scenes from the workers' catacombs in Fritz Lang's *Metropolis*.

He still wanted to leap like Nijinsky and continued with the Hampstead Club. But his teacher—a former chorus boy for the dance company of Nijinsky's mentor and lover Sergei Diaghilev—was too wrapped up in his own bygone fantasies to take real interest in his amateurs. Russell, already in his twenties and a late bloomer, was also one among precious few male dancers in the field, the one qualification that secured him a scholarship to attend the International Ballet School in South Kensington. There, he studied under Michael Strosigiev from St. Petersburg's Imperial Mariensky Ballet—a mad Russian whose knowledge of English was limited to about one word.

"The audition was a nightmare," Russell recalls. "Everyone else was dressed in the school uniform—black tights, black ballet shoes, and black leotards—but I was in khaki shorts and white gym shoes. I couldn't even keep up with the exercise at the barre, which lasted forty-five minutes . . . I couldn't begin to do even the most simple things." But he could jump high, a talent that at least got him accepted.

If the sea made him sick, the dance floor made him Judy to Strosigiev's Punch: "He used to beat me mercifully with a very hard stick on the buttocks," Russell later told music historian John C. Tibbetts, "shouting, 'Shoemaker! Shoemaker!,' which I gather is the worst Russian swear word you can possibly utter. Hence, my interest in sadomasochism!" The situation was almost on a par with the brutal relationship between Anton Walbrook's tyrannical dance impresario and Moira Shearer's ballerina in the Michael Powell–Emeric Pressburger film, *The Red Shoes*, which came out about this time.

Little girls studying for the barre might have idolized Shearer's ballerina as she danced nonstop in slippers that seemed demonically possessed, but others (particularly some film critics) were aghast at seeing her white stockings covered in blood after the carping Walbrook (supposedly based on Sergei Diaghilev and his dictatorial relationship with Nijinsky, his protégé) drives her to a suicidal leap onto a railway track.

The squeamish and the snooty found the movie's graphic detail gratuitous and tasteless; Russell loved it. "I was there for the very first performance along with a dozen other fans in an otherwise empty cinema at ten o'clock in the morning at the Odeon, Haymarket. I sat there for two complete screenings, and have seen it at regular intervals ever since."

Raging Russell couldn't fill Nijinsky's dainty slippers. After spraining his ankles several times and finally getting booted out for exuding no "classical" poise after all of those free lessons, he realized his dreams of a graceful *pas de deux* with gravity were doomed.

•

Russell now approached life as if it were a dilettante's funhouse. One of its warped hallways led to the boys' dressing room for a touring company of *Annie Get Your Gun*. He had a difficult time telling which female impersonators were preparing for *Annie* and which for a production called *Soldiers in Skirts* being staged at the theater next door. As the boys donned their wigs and high heels, and bitchy remarks ricocheted across the room, Russell joined the gaggle.

This first bout with musical comedy lasted just a few weeks before the production company faced bankruptcy. "I loved being on stage, even though I didn't have much to do. I was an Indian, a ringmaster, and in the opening number played a pretty boy with a straw hat, blue and white striped blazer, and tight white ducks. Except for myself, none of the chorus took it seriously. There was a song that began, 'The stagecoach is coming down the hill,' and everyone was supposed to peer over the footlights watching its approach, its attack by Indians, and final rescue by Buffalo Bill. Well, they'd been doing it for about four years and they never looked anymore. They were all too interested in the talent in the front row they might pick up afterwards."

Russell tempted fate with yet more dance auditions, eventually getting a stint with the British Dance Theatre. There too he had a demanding instructor, an intense Jewish woman from Central Europe, who wanted her students to express the agonies of hard working peasants and their ancestral communion with the soil. Russell debuted with "Born of Desire," a piece requiring proletarian interpretations of Grieg's "Death of Ase" from *Peer Gynt*. This academy was also doomed for the poorhouse.

At a job performing for seaside resort shows with the London Theatre Ballet, he met Terry Gilbert, the future choreographer for several of his films. Russell milked the part of Dr. Coppelius in a production of *Coppélia* for all it was worth, interpreting the character not as an eccentric toy maker but as a mad manipulator with German Expressionist excesses reminiscent of Werner Krauss's evil mesmerist in *The Cabinet of Dr. Caligari*: "I terrified matinee audiences in every southern seaside resort in England in 1949!"

Soon the London Theatre Ballet also faced bankruptcy, but he lucked into traveling to Oslo after a successful audition for the Norwegian Ballet. During rehearsals, though, Russell started developing a Quasimodo stoop after having to hold up a plump ballerina. Once again, dancing did not become him; he was more at home when the company rerouted him to a play a doll in yet another production of *Coppélia* that toured through Scandinavian villages to little avail. A stage castaway with a sunken morale, he drifted back to London.

Taking a stab at being an actor, Russell perused the trade magazines before passing an audition for the Garrick Players of Newton Poppleford in South Devon, reading out the parts to Act 2 of Oscar Wilde's *Lady Windermere's Fan*. But the first night he was to perform, he faced what would be several brushes with his sexual identity: "I was supposed to be an ordinary chap in the play who comes in and says something like, 'Can I make a telephone call?' But I had these eyelids painted purple and green with black and silver lines sweeping back to my ears. The others looked at me and thought; oh, he's one of *those*."

Russell tried lowering the volume on his makeup but still muffed up when donning armor for *When Knights Were Bold*, overacting as a decrepit old man for a part in Act 2 that required a man of only forty. Russell recalls the final performance in a park "to an audience of about three people, braving it out in the drizzle." Alas, what seemed to be Ken's Curse fell on that company as well: it too folded.

●

A failing romantic, lonely, and in perpetual poverty, Russell needed a new muse, someone who could comfort him in his garret squalor. He happened onto H. S. Ede's *Savage Messiah*, the biography of the French Vorticist sculptor Henri Gaudier. During the peak of his career, Gaudier was roughly Russell's age, struggling to survive during the coarse days of the early twentieth century. Gaudier aspired to be an artist but wasn't above being an artisan as well. He also had a belligerent personality that made him a pariah in polite society. His work, often portraying bodies folded up in anguished, defensive postures, reflected his angst.

Gaudier spent his last five years in the company of Sophie Brzeska, a Polish writer almost twice his age. They were two mercurial personalities in a platonic relationship; they often fought like husband and wife yet inspired each other. Propelled by the great events, Gaudier joined the World War I effort. He got killed at the Western Front trenches in 1915; the high-strung Brzeska eventually perished in an insane asylum.

Savage Messiah had no happy ending and a loose structure consisting partly of Ede's commentary but mostly of letters Gaudier wrote to Brzeska. But Russell loved Gaudier's fulminations on the true meaning of art: the need for the struggle, bravery in the face of uncertainty, and the virtues of exaggeration. He elaborated to Reverend Gene D. Phillips, who wrote a monograph on Russell in the late 1970s: "I was impressed by Gaudier's conviction that somehow or other there was a spark in the core of him that was personal to him, which was worth turning into something that could be appreciated by others. I wanted to find that spark in myself and exploit it for that reason."

Through the rough times with the roaches tapping on the plates and mice traipsing across the floor, Russell found strength in Gaudier's bohemian struggle. Gaudier once wrote, "Thus, with big strokes, boldly. Don't be frightened, make mistakes, as many as you like, but all the time draw very, very strongly." This became the Ken Russell credo.

CATHOLIC SPACE CADETS

5

"I was a moronic innocent," Ken Russell remembers, "not interested in girls until I was twenty-five and met my first wife, Shirley Kingdon, when we were photography students. She was an elfin beauty, like Audrey Hepburn; she filled the horizon for me."

It was 1953. Russell, though just in his mid twenties, was among the oldest students attending East London's Southwest Essex Technical College and School of Art in Walthamstow. He also claimed to have been the "oldest student in London learning the basics of photography." He borrowed a few quid from Dad and thrived on a diet of "rice, porridge, gooseberries, and Heinz vegetable soup—it had letters in it then—that I brewed on a Bunsen burner in the darkroom."

On photo shoots, Russell would dress his subjects in Victorian period costumes and dedicated one to the horror fashions of Charles Addams's *Monster Rally* illustrations. But once he accumulated a meaty portfolio, he had trouble convincing agencies of his worth—a problem he attributes not to his camera skills but to his eccentric fashion sense. Far from being the elegantly attired dandy expected from all aspiring Cecil Beatons, he donned slapdash suits and clomped around in brogans.

Russell as a young photographer. *(Courtesy of Ken Russell)*

Shirley Ann Kingdon, a London stockbroker's daughter who chose a more artistic route as a student in the college's fashion department, proved his ideal model. But in this tony atmosphere, where one wouldn't expect anything less than "classical" for background music, Ken and Shirley initially encountered one another under the easy-listening strains of Robert Farnon's "Journey into Melody," a light but haunting tune that sprinkled down from the hall's P.A. speakers.

Born March 11, 1935, Kingdon developed a gift for sartorial niceties when in her teens. Later, she would be affectionately called "Second Hand Rose" because she had a knack for finding the most regal robes from any given era in the most common of thrift shops. Her mentor was designer and historian Doris Langley Moore, who went on to establish the Museum of Costume in Bath. While Shirley dressed out of step for an urban girl with designs that more conservative fashion editors would find loopy, Ken was insufficiently Bond Street—far too casual with his sport shirts, jeans, and often tussled hair. Happy to be an eccentric duo, they cultivated their outré look through the years.

Melvyn Bragg, who would work later work with Russell on various television productions, remembers Ken and Shirley as "this sly, mischievous, way off-center pair; hippy before hippies, maverick before mavericks." Russell's future costume designer Leonard Pollack first met them in the early 1970s. "When I saw a picture of Ken and Shirley together from a program for *The Boy Friend*, with Shirley looking very independent in her bobbed haircut and Ken looking very flamboyant in his jewelry, they seemed less like an ordinary husband and wife and more like the marriage of two great artists. In other words, I thought he was gay and she was a lesbian. They both laughed when I told them."

Ken and Shirley would spend some of their most splendid moments along the dusty old cast-off stores and antiques shops along Portobello Road. There, at modest prices, they acquired a vast wardrobe that would come in handy when they collaborated on their first movies. For now, they concentrated on black and white photographic dream worlds. Russell recalls having Shirley stand on the Yorkshire moors dressed as Charlotte Brontë: "I photographed her on the couch where Charlotte had died, walking over the tombs of her sisters in the churchyard with Charlotte's own hat, tramping across the moors in the sort of shoes they would have worn, which made one realize that they would have been waterlogged after two minutes on that soggy grass."

•

For many years, Shirley was Russell's costume designer. She would earn Oscar nominations for the 1920s-style outfits she designed for Russell's *Women in*

Love and for recapturing the 1920s in Michael Apted's *Agatha*. But in these early lean times, she and Ken were enamored with photo essays. One Ken did for *Illustrated* magazine demonstrated various ways to use the pogo stick.

Russell in the 1950s was apparently a much shier man than the brazen fellow he'd become in the late '60s. For example, in the fall of 1954, he missed a great photo opportunity. On a plane from Paris to Madrid, he claims he was sitting next to Audrey Hepburn and Mel Ferrer, both of whom were on their honeymoon. The press had been speculating about this Hollywood romance, but Russell seemed the only one on Earth at that moment who could confirm the elopement with a photograph.

"When I arrived in Madrid airport," he confessed to *Amateur Photographer* magazine in 2005, "the address system was screaming out my name. It was my agent on the phone telling me to give my film with the picture of the couple on to the next pilot going back to London. 'I didn't want to disturb them. They looked so happy together,' I told him. I knew I was a failure. I had the hottest couple in the world cuddling up next to me and I'm taking pictures of the clouds."

But Russell made an impressive photo essay a year later, after Shirley's friend Josie Buchan introduced him to the Teddy Girl circle. In the 1950s, the Teddy Girls, like the Teddy Boys, were a byproduct of Britain's postwar malaise; once Russell focused his old Rolleicord camera on them, they contrasted beautifully with London's leftover bombsites.

Russell was old enough to remember the war yet young enough to understand the alienated gangs of postwar teenagers. They skulked about like stray cats among the rubble still crumbling from Hitler's blitz just as food rationing finally came to an end.

Teddy Girl at bombsite
(Courtesy of Ken Russell and TopFoto)

In the early to mid-1950s, British teenagers had yet to even find their feet with rock 'n' roll, content instead to dance to Ted Heath and His Orchestra's "The Creep." This was the era of the "angry young men," but Russell was also interested in the angry young women.

The term *Teddy Boy* referred to the youth fad of wearing Edwardian-style mockups. It was more than just a fashion statement; it also ultimately led to the violent feuds between Mods and Rockers of the early 1960s (dramatized in the film *Quadrophenia*). The Teddy Girls especially represented something about London life that haunted Russell: the notion that Britain's prowess in the world had gone flaccid after peacetime. In these belligerent and sad faces, he saw lost souls shut out from the norm. Working in assembly lines and clerical offices by day, they donned unorthodox attire to assert some kind of identity.

So in January 1955, Russell set out to photograph these misbegotten youth, focusing on London's working class environs of Walthamstow, Poplar, and North Kensington. Some of Russell's Teddy Girl pictures appeared in the June 4, 1955, issue of *Picture Post*. Androgynous and dazed, they stared amid the bomb blights and other signs of urban decay with a look of loss and petulance. They also tried to make a show of strength by leering behind the armature of men's suits, matching polka dot clutch bags and gloves, cameo brooches, and sometimes turbans. Some even had their hair combed back in a style soon championed by the likes of James Dean. They toted umbrellas that were always closed.

"He was just another photographer," a former Teddy Girl named Shine, who showed up in several Russell photos with her twin sister, reminisced to the *Sunday Times Magazine* in 2003. "He took photos of us and that was the last we knew of it. We didn't know he was going to do anything with them. We thought it was a laugh."

•

Though perhaps not as contentious as Henri Gaudier and Sophie Brzeska, Ken and Shirley celebrated the glories of art amid modest surroundings. In 1956, they borrowed a 16mm Bolex movie camera and scrimped about £100 (including all of Ken's savings) to make a short film entitled *Peepshow* that addresses problems of art and identity—not with a serious, heady, "Bergmanesque" style but rather as a German Expressionist slapstick comedy. To get an antiquated look, Russell scrawled subtitles over fences and sidewalks, while the score consisted of tunes pounded out on a rinky-dink pianola.

The story revisits themes from the Dr. Coppelius tale as well as Russell's never-seen Pangbourne monster movie. With some allusions to J. J. Peachum's beggars scam in Brecht and Weill's *The Threepenny Opera*, the story involves a group called the Bogus Beggars that learns to limp and grovel to collect money from passersby. They encounter an old magician (Norman Dewhurst), who opens a box to expose a life-size doll (Shirley) in white face makeup and moppy blonde wig—a yin version of Cesar the somnambulist from *Caligari*. As the doll comes to life, and the ersatz cripples invade the premises, *Peepshow* becomes a crazed procession of dancing and chasing until the old magician toots his clarinet and leads the Bogus Beggars like a pied piper into a river before hobbling merrily away with his reanimated daughter into London's fog.

The most important star of *Peepshow* is the frail, bearded gentleman playing the old magician with the bewitching clarinet. Norman Dewhurst became Russell's friend and fellow tenant at a Bayswater Road boarding house. A civil servant with theatrical ambitions, Dewhurst started playing a real-life pied piper by luring Russell into his esoteric belief that science-fiction films, with their extraterrestrial super-beings and epilogues imploring world peace, were modern-day religious texts. He was a recent Catholic convert who brought Russell into the faith just before *Peepshow* got finished. Russell says that he was especially intrigued when Dewhurst claimed, "We eat God."

Russell met Dewhurst on an awkward occasion when they battled over who would get to use the boardinghouse bathroom first. Russell recalls Dewhurst (whom he mysteriously calls "Morton Lyndhurst" in his autobiography) as "short and frail with a lantern jaw, wispy beard, and thick horn-rimmed glasses, and he was definitely coming off worst in the struggle until suddenly he produced a crucifix from beneath his pajamas and held it up before him with all the bravura of a Hollywood priest confronting Dracula. I was so startled that I stepped back. A second later he was inside the bathroom and bolting the door in my face. This was my first intimation of the power of Rome!"

Part of Russell's conversion from the Church of England to the Church of Rome was physiological. At the time he met Dewhurst, Russell was suffering from an addiction to snuff that he acquired during his ballet manqué days. Starting at a modest two tins a month but moving onto more frequent sniffs and harder stuff, he got to a point when he would wake up at various intervals in the night, groping at his bed table for a fix of Dr. Rumney's Mentholyptus blend. Eventually, he couldn't let ten snuff-free minutes elapse without trembling. But once Russell received Dewhurst's sign of the cross and heard about the intergalactic path to deliverance, he was on his way to recovery.

One day, before boarding a bus at Victoria Station, Russell happened upon a three-foot high plaster replica of the Tichborne Madonna with child. He was really too broke to afford the thirty guineas it cost, but he bought it anyway, lugging the statue to the top of a double-decker bus while reaching for his tin of Dr. Rumney's with a shaking hand. Still unable to get the tin opened once he got back to his Bayswater place, he attributed his addict's frustration to the statue's divine intervention.

"When I was young," he recalled to the *New York Times* in 1972 a year after coming out with *The Devils* (what many consider his most blasphemous film), "I didn't really know where I was going, but as soon as I came into the faith, my work, my philosophy, gained direction. Except for *The Boy Friend*—a pathetic event—all my films have been Catholic films, films about love, faith, sin, guilt, forgiveness, redemption. Films that could only have been made by a Catholic."

●

For Russell, the notion that the Savior could transubstantiate his essence into bread and wine seemed infinitely more mystical and meaty than the Church of England's finger-sandwich approach to salvation. But even more sensational motives came into play. Dewhurst, as Russell explains, "had the knack of making the New Testament sound like amazing science fiction." Years later, in his filmed autobiography for England's *South Bank Show,* he described Dewhurst turning him into "a Catholic space cadet" by introducing him to a teenage nun who lived on Portobello Road.

Amid bizarre paintings of winged astronauts and what Russell recalls as "a print of the virgin space mother hovering above St. Peter's in Rome, surrounded by seven heart-shaped UFOs of shining silver," the space sister gave a persuasive sermon that, in movie terms, sounded like a hybrid of *King of Kings* and *Queen of Outer Space*: an almighty spaceman made the universe and also manufactured people in his image. But the people malfunctioned the way mass-produced items self-destruct with blown circuits or defective parts. Seeing what a mess he'd made, the supreme spaceman assigned his only son to descend onto the planet and make repairs, imbuing people with otherworldly potential that would allow them to repair themselves whenever their circuits went askew again.

The woman's words were comforting, fantastic, and very 1950s: Klaatu could have given a similar sermon as an intergalactic prince of peace at the foot of his flying saucer in *The Day the Earth Stood Still.* "Then she gave me an awesome communications system called a rosary," Russell recalls, "which sent coded messages to the great spaceman himself. The countdown began. I gripped the rosary and beamed the message: my cosmic journey had begun."

"I've rejected a lot of Catholicism since," Russell told John Baxter in 1973, "but I feel that if I hadn't gone through that catharsis I would still be unsure. I was vague and sentimental before I became a Catholic, but sentimentality went out the window. I may still be nostalgic, but a basic core of irony has crept in. It's easy to be swayed by sentiment from getting at the truth, to be driven off course by an easy way out. The thing the faith taught me was that there is no easy way out. The Church of England, the little I had to do with it, was all vague, like Christ holding the lantern at the door in Holman Hunt's 'The Light of the World,' whereas in the Catholic church he's shining a searchlight in your face. You can't make excuses if you're a Catholic. You either go to confession and communion once a week and try to lead a better life, or you don't; you accept certain things or you don't. What I got out of it was a very hard philosophical toughness."

But Russell never had any political fealty toward the Catholic Church; being Dionysian in most sexual matters, he despised its reactionary morality. Far from taking on the orthodox credo, Russell incorporated a personalized Holy Trinity to fuel his artistic pursuits: the ever-forgiving sci-fi Christ joined the tortured Tchaikovsky and the fevered Gaudier. So, before his Tichborne Virgin collected dust in the cellar and he realized he was trading in a physical addiction for a spiritual one, Russell made his version of Catholicism a form of cosmic theater. This was a modern, metaphysical space opera onto which he could layer Biblical lore, cinematic epic, cheeky comedy, and variations on Lang's *Siegfried*—a movie that, alongside *The Secret of the Loch*, stuck to him like psychic flypaper.

Russell wanted to celebrate his newfound faith that year with a satire on the life of Saint Christopher, which would have taken place in the Victorian Era. But without needed backing from the British Film Institute, he scraped up only enough cash to make a short film about a hero in shining armor who saves townsfolk on a bicycle rather than a horse. In *Knights on Bikes*, filmed in 1956, Russell cast himself as the do-gooder, jousting on two wheels with a villainous geezer in a wheelchair who absconds with a princess. Russell's hero also battles men in black tights who, instead of swords, wield umbrellas painted over with human faces. When the time arrived to finish the film, however, Russell didn't have a prayer: the man who owned the equipment neither came back to see the first rushes nor returned with the camera.

∎

Ken and Shirley married in February 1957, the same year that Russell went behind the camera again to make another redemptive narrative. *Amelia and the Angel* is a short, quaint piece about a child's misadventure. Mercedes Quadros, the nine-year-old daughter of a Uruguay ambassador, agreed to play Amelia provided Russell alleviated her Rolls-driven doldrums by taking her for spins through London in his car at reckless speeds. Mercedes's long dark hair and large, probing eyes made her ideal for the part of the young ballet dancer who commits the sin of stealing a pair of prop wings from her school play.

Inspired by some of Jean Cocteau's films, Russell also cites as an influence Albert Lamorisse's 1956 short *The Red Balloon*, about a little boy who triumphs over adversity while traversing Paris's filthy and sometimes mean streets. Amelia's story begins with children prancing about the ballet floor in white costumes. White wings flit in the foreground, giving an ethereal flickering effect that contrasts with menacing close ups of a frenetic dance teacher (Helen May)—another nasty martinet—ordering her charges about.

The offscreen narrator informs us that these are five little angels, with Amelia "the least angelic of them all." Amelia thinks "all boys were horrid little beasts," especially her hooligan brother (Nicolas O'Brien), who steals her stolen wings, treks over to a nearby playground, and while gyrating hysterically on a swing, breaks them.

Scoring Amelia's frantic quest along the London streets to find another pair, Russell provides no heavenly church choirs or even space music, preferring melodies on what sound like circus calliopes gone awry. Amelia encounters strange characters, even a winged dog, but at last finds salvation in a white-robed, bearded artist (Elisha Manasseh) who resembles one of the Apostles. He climbs up a long ladder in his studio and—after spending some mysterious moments out of camera range—descends like an angel of mercy with the right pair of wings, sending a redeemed Amelia running gaily into the horizon.

Mercedes Quadros finds redemption in *Amelia and the Angel.*

Like *Peepshow, Amelia and the Angel* is childlike and wholesome, the kind of family-friendly fare that might win over the BBC, which he was by now hoping to court. But the BBC was initially cold to both films when he submitted them for approval. He thought that perhaps he should make a film with a little more edge. For the time being, Russell got moral support from a member of the Catholic Film Institute, with whom he soon flew to France to embark on his first documentary: the 1958 film *Lourdes.* He took a 16mm camera to the famous shrine where Saint Bernadette, though the grace of the Blessed Virgin, supposedly cures the sick and comforts the weary.

Russell pairs music from Benjamin Britten's *The Prince of the Pagodas* with images of afflicted pilgrims arriving from all over the world, lying prostrate for the pope's blessing and assembling for the procession of the Blessed Sacrament. But like all good stories (even documentaries), there must be a conflict: "This is also Lourdes," a narrator intones with *Mondo* movie irony, as the camera cuts to phalanxes of souvenir rosaries, plaster statuettes of holy figures, record albums capturing the oohs and aahs of previous miracles, Bernadette bidets, and other paraphernalia offered to the throngs at benevolently calculated prices—all with the backdrop of neon night lights.

While trying to get the film approved, Russell noticed his faith in the Faith starting to wither: "We showed it to the BFI and they weren't particularly impressed. We showed it to the Catholic people and they were horrified. Visually Lourdes is a pretty grotty place, a sideshow of terror, like Belsen. They had never thought of that, obviously. Finally it did go out through the Catholic Film Institute library service, minus the sequence satirizing the commercial side of Lourdes. . . . That to me was symptomatic, and has been ever since, of the church's attitude to the presentation of religion on film. Unless it's a laudatory, anaemic, mealy-mouthed, simpering piece of work with no blood in it at all, they're terrified."

Still, the immersion in saints, sinners, and healed believers afforded Russell—an aspiring altar boy trapped in a thirty-two-year-old body—some kind of miracle. After Norman Swallow, an assistant head of films at BBC-TV, screened *Amelia* to supervisor Huw Wheldon, Russell got one of the network's most coveted jobs. He replaced John Schlesinger (who ascended to directing big time features) as a resident filmmaker for the BBC's acclaimed biweekly arts program *Monitor*. "*Amelia* had all the signs of having been shot on lavatory paper," Wheldon later told John Baxter. "It was also romantic, eccentric, and in many ways not at all my cup of tea, but whatever else it was, it was neither predictable nor cliché-ridden, and so I thought I would see the author."

6

PATHOGRAPHER'S PROGRESS

In Ken Russell's early BBC days, biography was more like strict documentary. There was no place for metaphors or speculative drama. The network's purists felt such tactics were synonymous with the kinds of exaggerations Henri Gaudier championed and that Russell yearned to create. So, Russell kept a humble exterior while secretly plotting to subvert the BBC's codes of propriety.

"Ken was different in every way from what he is now," Russell's BBC boss Huw Wheldon reflected in the early 1970s on working with Russell in the late '50s and early '60s. "To start with, he was virtually wordless. He was shy and quiet. Quiet in *every* way: his clothes, his haircut, his countenance. A little watchful, but silent and extremely modest. I couldn't make head nor tail of him, partly because he wouldn't help me. He didn't say *anything*. He just looked at me."

When Russell finally started offering his own ideas—a film about the Teddy Girls and one about Albert Schweitzer playing Bach's music to lepers in the African jungle—he drew predictably cold responses. Wheldon did not want to alienate those sagging viewers snuggled by the hearth who would be put off by anything off-color. Russell had more luck with such middlebrow offerings as a salute to comedian Spike Milligan (1959), bios of dramatist Shelagh Delaney (1960) and artist Antonio Gaudi (1961), and a look at the late 1950s and early '60s craze for guitar music (1960).

Many of Russell's BBC projects between 1959 and 1962 had nostalgic and at times melancholy moods. *A Bedlington Miners' Picnic* (1960) followed workers in a Northumberland colliery who take their minds off drudgery in the pits by staging a brass band competition, riding on a carousel, and risking more mental depression by listening to lectures about "the morality of socialism" during a rainstorm. Russell would return to the same environs a few years later to film the mining town in *Women in Love*, disheartened to find the place in further decline. In 1962, he (along with Humphrey Burton) revisited rougher memories of World War II in *Lotte Lenya Sings Kurt Weill*. At one point, this fifteen-minute short has Lenya in a leather overcoat, performing "Moritat" from *The Threepenny Opera* to rear projections that depict Germany as it morphs from Weimar Era indulgence to Nazi brownshirts burning books and smashing Jewish delicatessen windows.

•

Under a vigilant Wheldon, Russell also explored a subject dear to him: the lives of composers. This is when the BBC brass started to give him grief. The network's philosophy went more or less as follows: depicting the lives of historical personages, especially those immortalized in the *Encyclopædia Britannica*, required strict verisimilitude. There could be no heady interpretations, no fancy narrations or reenactments, and especially no actors. Even traces of an actor's hands or feet were considered perversions of the truth.

When Russell did *Poet's London* (1959), the BBC balked at his request to use a child actor to represent a young John Betjeman. If he wanted to portray an artist at work, he could only use photographs, old movies, or newsreel footage. It was, in short, a recipe for dreary viewing that Russell had to challenge. He eschewed the assumption that the past is immune from speculation or even surrealism.

Russell was already irked at Norman Swallow's June 1959 memo, which specified that any efforts to use actors for historical figures "would be much more effective if the people concerned were *suggested* rather than literally seen." Yet for the June 18, 1961, broadcast of *Prokofiev: Portrait of a Soviet Composer*, Russell defied Wheldon's "fictionalization" phobia by including the hands of someone other than the actual composer at the piano. There were four hands, to be exact: young Prokofiev and his mother.

Then came the controversial moment when Russell used an actual actor for Prokofiev. The plan was to have him appear for a moment, but the BBC still insisted this would be a historical ruse. Russell had to compromise: Prokofiev's portrayer could only appear as a voiceless reflection in a muddy pool. A hand here, a spot of leg there, perhaps a fraction of a chest, and at last a face peering through muck—petty details compared to today's countless "dramatic reenactments," but the BBC saw them as revolutionary steps.

Russell and Wheldon continued to bump heads about creative decisions. As John Baxter, who interviewed Wheldon at length, writes, "Wheldon never tamed Russell—may never have wished to, seeing in him much of himself. Certainly they could be brothers in their habit of enfilading a topic with words,

Russell contemplating his art with the BBC's Huw Wheldon.
(Courtesy of Ken Russell)

Russell's barrage of images matched by Wheldon's cavalry charge of argument, rhetoric, and descriptive gesture."

Of the many Russell films during the early *Monitor* period, *Elgar* is often touted as the big breakthrough. Classed with Britten and Purcell as England's greatest composers, Elgar fell out of favor through the years: he became a symbol of the nation's now outmoded empire days, remembered for writing patriotic tunes that a more disillusioned generation deemed too chauvinistic.

But Russell felt a personal connection to the subject. Elgar too came from lower middle class origins, the son of a tradesman who at times had to curtail his creative pursuits when pressured to work for his father's business. He too suffered bouts of poverty trying to survive and despondency trying to create. Elgar was also a Roman Catholic.

Elgar was relatively subdued, the tone respectful and elegiac, and the information plentiful. At last, the BBC relaxed its rules against using actors for biographical films, but they still had to appear as landscape figures in medium and long shot. And they still couldn't speak. Russell even got to use four different actors, each representing a vital phase in the composer's life.

Still, Wheldon's temperate voice-over narration dominated such memorable moments as the opening shots of a young Elgar riding his father's white pony along the Malvern Hills (one of the composer's favorite haunts). The scene is so tasteful, so picturesque, and so conservatively wrought. It also pushed the BBC boundaries because the incident never

Young Elgar rides on the Malvern Hills.

really happened. But it got the spirit of Elgar down sufficiently as it played over his *Introduction and Allegro for Strings*.

Russell did try adding some spice to the porridge. As with his homage to Prokofiev, he juxtaposes music with brutal war images. This time it is Elgar's *Pomp and Circumstance March No. 1* ("Land of Hope and Glory"), which he wrote around the time of the Boer War, accompanying both re-created and stock footage of World War I casualties that Russell got from the Imperial War Museum: barbed wire battlefields, maimed soldiers, war prisoners, and acres of military graves.

Wheldon sniffed at this because he felt Russell was adding too much editorial comment and presupposing Elgar's beliefs. He recalls, "And on this Ken and I, as we frequently did, had what you might call an editorial row. He remembers this as only a small thing, but it was actually awful, lasting days on end. There was a time when I didn't want to talk to Ken, who was in the cutting room, and was very anxious to keep out of his way. . . . The result of that argument was a compromise: the war sequence, including 'Land of Hope and Glory,' was cut exactly in half."

Even with half of his battleground carnage still intact, Russell looks back on *Elgar* as too whitewashed. The scenes where Elgar strolls with his future wife Caroline Alice Roberts (whom he married in 1889) along shiny fields of grain, riding donkeys on a hillside beacon, or picnicking by a glistening lake struck him as too sentimental. He'd later lament: "The film was all too lovely, like a TV commercial for the Malvern Hills! I was perhaps too much in love with the man's music to see what really produced it. If I were to remake the film, I would be far truer to the man and his struggle than I was the first time. I would show the darker side of his life as well as the lyrical, colorful side."

Even amid *Elgar*'s stately splendor, its pomp, circumstance, and academic piety, there are Russellscopic signs—hints of the director's divine madness taking shape. Russell vents through an amusing scene inside a lunatic asylum, where Elgar led a resident band and had his first stint as a conductor. With an unsteady camera and extreme close-ups of inmates playing in an

The asylum scene: a twinge of Russell madness in an otherwise tame film.

orchestra, Russell exposes eyes that are slightly asymmetrical and expressions that are more than slightly maniacal. The technique is understated, for Russell at least, but he still shows a world askew.

Russell also got a chance to splurge on some of his newfound Catholic mania. When the soundtrack plays one of Elgar's favorite pieces, *The Dream of Gerontius*, the tip of Malvern Hills where he rode his pony in the beginning now converts into a makeshift Calvary, with Russell slowly zooming in on a crucified Christ looming over the English countryside. Wheldon, a Welsh Presbyterian, was wary of Russell's Catholic addiction and insisted on keeping the landscape as free of crucifixes as possible.

Elgar premiered on November 11, 1962, the occasion being *Monitor*'s hundredth program. The BBC, which back then rarely repeated programs, aired it again not long afterward and then two more times during the 1960s. Shortly after *Elgar*'s first broadcast, British viewers responded to a poll and named it their all-time second-favorite TV program, at least up till then. The film continues to garner praise, but for Russell it was merely the first, and modest, salvo in a war against strict verisimilitude.

"In my research," Russell later reflected, "I found a lot of things that didn't square with this conception, so I had to leave them out. There are three main things missing: his relationships with other women around Malvern, his preoccupation with suicide, and his friendship with Jaeger, his music publisher and friend, which is highly romantic."

There was also a morbid side to Elgar's story: his chronic ailments, worries about finances, long bouts of no inspiration followed by creative spasms, and thoughts of suicide. Wheldon does at least provide one of the composer's more jarring quotes: "I see nothing in the future but a black stone wall against which I am longing to dash my head."

With his 1964 film about Béla Bartók, Russell got closer to being a historical impressionist as he portrayed the exiled Hungarian composer facing his last years holed up in a New York City apartment. To drive home the oppressive urban atmosphere, Russell crams Bartók (Boris Ranevsky) into a noisy New York subway train before having him trudge toward the camera down a long, antiseptically white tube tunnel among indifferent passersby. Enthusiastic responses got predictably peppered with accusations that Russell was again being distasteful toward a musical icon. Even with its prickly touches, however, *Bartók* still has the innards of a conventional documentary, especially with Wheldon's prim and proper narration.

While seeking to unleash that inner demon that would eventually flout just about all of the rules that Wheldon tried to impose, Russell was also building up a family—a process about which he was sometimes ambivalent. Ken and Shirley produced five children. *The Guardian* later quoted Russell likening these off-spring to "spots before the eyes, too many and too close together." They received special names: Xavier Francis (1957) named after two saints, James Paul (1958) after two popes, Alexander Huw (1959) after Alexander the Great and the great Mr. Wheldon, Victoria (1963) after a dowdy queen, and Toby (1964) after a pet dog. As Russell recalls, "The only time I remember playing with them was during filming, which started at a very early age and was treated as a game."

Two of his offspring, Xavier and Victoria, showed up in 1965's *The Debussy Film*. This time, the actors talked, and Russell contrived a more complex approach to storytelling, partly because of budget constraints. The necessary nineteenth-century period costumes and decor were too expensive, so he bypassed having to use them too much by creating a frame story about a present-day acting troupe doing a film about Debussy. In the process, he created an impressionistic interpretation of the Impressionist composer's life.

With scriptwriter Melvyn Bragg, who would become one of his chief collaborators, Russell intended this as a theatrical feature. But the BBC liked the film-within-a-film novelty and took it on. Better yet, since the story revolved around actors portraying Debussy and the other historical figures, Russell also sidestepped all those nagging BBC rules against "cheating" with reenactments.

To pull off this narrative coup, Russell employed two consummate scenery gobblers, two unforgettable faces so passionate about prancing and prating before the camera that Russell would employ them again and again.

The first, Vladek Sheybal, was a native of Poland. He had the long nose and the round, probing eyes of a lemur but also exuded Continental suave—in the tradition of leering but likable character actors such as Peter Lorre and Mischa Auer. Sheybal would go on to portray the savvy gay artiste in *Women in Love* and the whimsical Hollywood mogul in *The Boy Friend*, but here he had a great start playing both the director and Debussy's demonic mentor Pierre Louÿs.

Debussy, on the other hand, required someone daring and brooding. Oliver Reed, nephew to director Sir Carol Reed, had had his first lead in the 1961 Hammer horror *The Curse of the Werewolf*, as a blond lycanthrope with eyes larger than his teeth. Imposing, scowling, sullen, a runaway from home, a high school dropout, a one-time bouncer at a Soho nightclub, and an aggressive toper, Reed also had a low, ominous voice that, when raised to angry decibels, could startle horses and make even the deaf flinch.

Russell, at home watching the telly with Shirley and the kids, discovered Reed in a more staid setting: as one of several panelists deciding the fate of pop songs on the British television show *Juke Box Jury*. To Russell, he looked so much like Debussy that, even when Reed came in to the director's office to show off the chin scar he recently got in a bar scuffle at the wrong end of a broken bottle, he saw nothing irregular in his face that could deprive him of a part for which Reed was destined.

Russell was now brazen enough to abandon the hagiographic approach of *Elgar* and opted to present Debussy with all the rough edges. A recurring theme in Russell's bios is the male artist who browbeats and often destroys the lives of those who devote themselves to him, usually females. Debussy appears here as a brilliant composer but also as a lazy, obnoxious sponger who cannot stop talking and who bullies his meal tickets.

Structurally, *The Debussy Film* has a hypnotic style that reflects Debussy's music, which the film's narrator declares "came out of his long daydream." As Russell asserts, "There are some points in the film, I think, where it doesn't matter if it's the director talking to the actor or Louÿs talking to Debussy—passages of intentional ambiguity."

"TV audiences are asleep in the armchairs," Russell once observed when explaining his outré techniques. "It's a good thing to shake them up, if only to reach for the phone." More than Russell's previous works, *The Debussy Film* calls attention to the aesthetic and political decisions involved in making this kind of a televised drama. Certain that a movie about a highbrow composer needed extra oomph to seduce the viewers' waning attention span, Russell made his most provocative scene come at the beginning, dramatizing Debussy's *The Martyrdom of St. Sebastian* (which he wrote as background music to Gabriel D'Annunzio's play) by depicting an ecstatic blonde (Jane Lumb) in a T-shirt, surrounded by a bevy of equally beautiful blondes in T-shirts shooting arrows into her.

This interpretation is anachronistic (Lumb could pass as a cover model for *Cosmopolitan*) and by prevailing tastes vulgar, but it startled many viewers who might otherwise change the channel if the story threatened to get academic. When asked why he depicted St. Sebastian as a woman, Russell responded: "D'Annunzio wrote it for a woman; don't ask me why, I'm just being faithful to the author's concept."

Russell turns his arguments with Wheldon about factual detail into an

Russell overseeing "The Martyrdom of St. Sebastian" in *The Debussy Film*. (Courtesy of Ken Russell)

inside joke. When making up Debussy's bon vivant mistress Gaby Dupont (Annette Robertson) as a fin de siècle nymph, who seduces a lethargic Debussy by fondling a white balloon and dancing to the strains of "Prelude to the Afternoon of a Faun," Sheybal—as the director—verifies, "They did play with balloons! I checked it!" Here, Robertson evokes a sylph gamboling about in a 1960s deodorant commercial, but Russell gave her a complete makeover in his next film, casting her as a midget in male drag for the role of the surrealist Alfred Jarry in *Always on Sunday* (1965), his tribute to the artist Henri Rousseau.

The Debussy Film also indulges in the musical anachronisms that Russell would toy with in his next two BBC films. Brash contemporary pop songs compete with Debussy's softer, more introspective work. A cocktail jazz version of "It Might as Well Be Spring" plays in the background while Sheybal's director explains to Reed's actor how Debussy adapted some of his pieces from paintings, poems, plays, and even the jig. While at a party, Reed's actor can't get his mind off acquiring the right "motivation" for his role, so he breaks the festivities by taking the Kinks' "You Really Got Me" off the turntable and puts on Debussy's *Dances Sacred and Profane*. But Dupont, now emerging in the movie as a femme fatale, reacts by launching into a strip tease, throwing her underpants onto the record player's tone arm, and doing all she can to throw Reed's meditative mood off-kilter.

As the story progresses, Russell makes it obvious that the existential pangs Debussy experiences are also applicable to the actor that Reed portrays. "It wasn't actor Oliver Reed portraying Debussy," Russell explained to John C. Tibbetts, "it was Oliver Reed portraying himself preparing to play the part of Debussy. This conceit allowed me to examine the very process of making a biopic."

Even in what appear to be Debussy's more triumphal moments, Russell never really frees him. Debussy marries his patron Emma Bardac (Iza Teller), has his only child, Claude-Emma or "Chou-chou" (Victoria Russell), and as Wheldon's narration indicates, "the listless drifting of garret life was over"; but Russell belies this serenity. As Debussy tries a relaxing swim, his *La Mer* inundates the soundtrack; the camera meanwhile moves farther and farther back until the composer is just a lonesome dot in a vast ocean—a tiny plaything that the gods plan to alienate and depress even more.

Debussy's slide into oblivion starts when Louÿs, his most ardent friend and patron, decides to marry and asks him to compose a wedding march that should be "pompous, lustful, and ejaculatory in character." But the newly minted Mrs. doesn't like him, and with wifely power being so strong and often destructive, Louÿs dismisses Debussy. Without a patron and with his work rejected, Debussy naturally gravitates to the patron saint of ungratified desire: Edgar Allan Poe, or more specifically, Poe's character Roderick Usher.

The composer essentially *becomes* Usher: bereaved, isolated, and obsessed. As with Elgar and Bartók, Russell again proves a master at portraying his protagonists as solitary figures pitted against a threatening landscape drained of meaning. Here, Debussy's final thoughts dwell on Gaby Dupont and Lily (Penny Service), the two women who almost killed themselves over him.

"Most of the people I've dealt with in films have quite dispassionately sacrificed someone in their way who misunderstood them," Russell admits to John Baxter. "It's not nice but that's how it works. The end of the film, the music from his unfinished opera *The Fall of the House of Usher*, with Debussy alone in the castle and his ghostly mistresses—whom he drove to attempted suicide—rising up, was an analogy of the lost romantic ideal he had destroyed by his disregard for people. You can be an egomaniac up to a point, but in the end it can destroy you, or your work, or both."

The Debussy Film turned out to be a movie that BBC officials thought they'd never make, let alone broadcast. It pissed many of them off, including Wheldon, who resorted to the censorship he had previously avoided by excising a lesbian kiss between two of Debussy's girlfriends. Wheldon tried rationalizing his Presbyterian prudery by telling Russell, "This is the best thing you've done in matching music to meaning, but it's *too* good." Still, Wheldon let the rest of the film pass, providing that it clarify matters with the subtitle: "Impressions of the French Composer." This disclaimer wasn't enough for the outraged Debussy estate. After the film's broadcast on May 18, 1965, it tried preventing all subsequent airings.

As Wheldon stressed again in 1972, "For the first two or three years Ken remained on the whole very quiet, very attentive. That abrasive exterior that is now apparently known in Ken as a public figure didn't come out in any full sense until he left the BBC. His manner was singularly quiet, gentle, and modest, but at the same time he was totally determined and always pent up with new ideas."

Russell had crossed the line, and there was no turning back. He was at last getting his personality across on film and apparently didn't even have to throw tantrums. In just six years, he had turned the heads of the previously conservative BBC—an institution that Russell would hail as "the only truly experimental film school that Britain has ever produced."

ART WITH A CAPITAL T

Like every good Catholic, especially one fresh to the faith and excited about its rituals of guilt and redemption, Ken Russell felt a need to atone. With all his talk about art and artists, he was now being tempted to become a media whore. The root of his sins lay in the television ads he worked on—jobs that gnawed at his conscience but also helped him cultivate a punchy, attention-grabbing style that would inspire some of his best films.

Russell would continue to harp both in his films and many interviews on a heaven-and-hell conflict between art and nature versus commercialism and artifice. He spoke about this to John Baxter in the early 1970s: "Talking of commercialism, I've been guilty of my fair share of that myself. I did a number of TV commercials in the early and mid-'60s—about twenty, I suppose. Black Magic chocolates; that was a bad one. Half a dozen for Galaxy chocolate bars, all slow-motion things shot in Rome. I did Horlicks, baked beans, though I drew the line at cancer-killing cigarettes. But I thought that even the apparently harmless ones were immoral and doing me as much harm as everyone else, so I stopped."

The art versus commercialism canard was already potent in his first feature film, *French Dressing* (1963), about a dreary English seaside resort town that is desperate for a boost in tourism. The solution: organize a film festival and, in the spirit of the French with their chesty Bardots dancing naked in fountains, import a Brigitte Bardot look-alike from the Continent to give the event pizzazz. It's "Art—with a capital *T*," as one character describes this ploy to merge a media strumpet with the art of *le cinema*.

The film's premise, as well as its narrative style, was nothing new to British comedies. There was droll dialogue with physical farce in the *Carry On* series and its permutations. And before Richard Lester helped redefine pop films with

A Hard Day's Night, several odd musicals revolved around Cliff Richard: the pop idol would sing songs (usually by the team of Ronald Cass and Peter Myers), while a gaggle of teenagers (who often looked well into their twenties) leapt into giddy dances and slapstick skirmishes. Russell was, in fact, slated to direct Cliff Richard and the Shadows in what would become the cult hit *Summer Holiday*, but bailed out and left the job to Peter Yates.

Summer Holiday's producer Kenneth Harper, along with Cass and Myers, masterminded *French Dressing*'s parody of such Jacques Tati films as *Mr. Hulot's Holiday*. With run-of-the-mill material and two main stars, James Booth and Roy Kinnear, who were standard comedic players accustomed to pat routines, Russell had expectations to fulfill and predictable ruts to avoid. So, if the story called for something silly, Russell would make the silliness more aggressive. And at times, what is supposed to be escapist entertainment takes on a macabre edge. Unfortunately, Booth and Kinnear tend to weigh the story down with performances too earnest for Russell's surrealistic irony.

James Booth and Bryan Pringle contemplate aesthetics in *French Dressing*.

Booth plays a frustrated deck chair attendant while Kinnear is his bumbling fat pal also down on his luck. One day they come upon the film festival idea and sell it to the town's pompous and prissy mayor, played to the hilt by Bryan Pringle (who would be just as prissy a few years later in *The Boy Friend*). The mayor, though full of puffed-up propriety on the surface, is a randy geezer who cranks away (suggestively) into a nudie peep show viewfinder in his office when no one is looking.

To offset all of this masculine angst, there is Judy (Alita Naughton), a pert American brunette and aspiring journalist who dresses like a sailor and complains to all the horny men about how sex is overrated. She nonetheless plays along with the scam as they all conspire to lure Françoise Fayol (Marisa Mell)—the ersatz Bardot—to be the festival's tart of honor.

Russell took the opportunity to exploit several angles: a satire on Anglo-French relationships and the ludicrous publicity putsches that often go into international film festivals, a few jabs at the pretentiousness of the French new wave, and the issue that would haunt Russell time and again—that queasy affinity between art and business. As one of the film's buttoned-down commentators, played by real-life British TV and radio announcer Robert Robinson, reports: "The publicity men, who are the chaps who run film festivals, think that an event is cultural if it's foreign, and even more cultural if it's wearing a bathing costume."

More than just an amusing plot, *French Dressing* is a relentlessly frantic romp with discernible Russell touches, especially the silly dances contrasted with genuinely scary surprises. Preparing for the festival, the characters stage a "Monster Gala Carnival Fancy Dress Competition," get decked out in animal costumes, and reel around a skating rink. Russell includes lots of frantic running and romping in quick-cut montages, characters screaming dialogue over each other, and an onslaught of sight gags orchestrated to Georges Delerue's often-manic score.

Eager to work with Delerue after hearing his work on Truffaut's *Jules and Jim* and *Shoot the Piano Player*, Russell was so enamored with his music that he followed this feature by directing a BBC tribute called *Don't Shoot the Composer*. Russell also intended it as a satire about a BBC film unit that attempts a serious documentary. And while parts of his tribute are judicious and respectful, he lets loose when Delerue practically pounds on the piano keys like a lunatic.

With Delerue's help, *French Dressing* has an equally nutty energy. Russell fans will likely notice eerie auguries. The clerical gags of *The Devils* and *Crimes of Passion* already surface as Françoise Fayol masquerades as a nun to escape the press, only to end up wielding a cigarette and flashing her thighs to the shock and salivation of photographers. When the festival finally shows Fayol's latest work, Russell relishes the opportunity to lampoon the *nouvelle vague* with a film-within-the-film called *Pavements of Boulogne*, in which the star gyrates with exaggerated eroticism while her greasy boyfriend fondles her with a knife in his hand. In the end, a riot ensues in the theater, fists fly, and the gigantic image of Fayol's lusty lips almost come out from the screen to devour the crowd.

The most Russellscopic moment occurs early on, when Booth and Kinnear romp along a beachfront in Torquay in search of their star. They instead encounter inflatable lady dolls in bikinis that line the streets and pile up on the shore. After a peevish Fayol plows through her plastic look-alikes in a sport convertible, she joins the rest of the gang in a joyous spleen-venting ritual by setting fire to them. Delerue's eerie music complements their dance around the conflagration, while images of the plastic heads, legs, and rumps melt into gray goo.

Several years after the film's release, Russell confessed to John Baxter a bizarre childhood dream that he recalls experiencing "with a mixture of terror and welcome": "Three different kinds of gray material were passing before my face. There was no beginning to the material. There was no end. . . . I found when they were burning those plastic dummies in *French Dressing* I felt very uncomfortable when I saw it again on TV. It was connected with the dream, in the same way as the plague pit scene in *The Devils*. After seeing that scene in *French Dressing*, I felt a bit sick. I didn't mean it to be like that, but I found my flesh beginning to creep."

●

By the autumn of 1965, Wheldon had left his *Monitor* post. Russell's BBC work became part of a new program called *Omnibus*, for which he worked between 1966 and 1970. Among his first major efforts was *Isadora Duncan: The Biggest Dancer in the World*.

Despite interviews in which he lauds the purely artistic over the crassly commercial, Russell's best films reveal someone who takes a perverse delight in watching the two extremes mesh—and *Isadora* is one of his most strident examples. Of all his television work, *Isadora* is his most accomplished, his most madcap, his most ambitious in merging image with music, and his most complex in portraying, while not being afraid to lampoon, the life of someone he deeply admires. This is where his ongoing theme about art being a thing of both glory and vulgarity is most vibrant: the more Isadora pontificates about the greatness of art, hers especially, the more she looks like a buffoon. Her every gesture aimed at inspiring the world to creatively careen—particularly her dream of leading five hundred in a dance to Beethoven's Ninth Symphony—appears more futile as her message tires, her public wanes, her money disappears, and her looks fade.

Through Isadora, Russell explores, celebrates, and yet masochistically derides artists' roles in the world. And since Isadora comes so close to representing an earlier Russell, who sincerely aspired to flounce and pirouette like Isadora, the director also satirizes himself. In this film and many others, Russell twists in a paradox. On the one hand, he lampoons art that goes commercial; on the other, he exposes how even artists like Isadora, who refuse to compromise or succumb to Mammon, can still end up unwitting creatures of self-parody.

Russell begins with an approximately thirty-second encapsulation of Isadora's life in the frenetic style of the "News on the March" segment that Orson Welles used to sum up Charles Foster Kane. The montage includes cops chasing Isadora's naked body around a stage, Isadora gyrating like a mad flapper atop a grand piano before pushing it out of a fourteen-story hotel suite, a one-legged man (a Russell cameo) running to rescue her from a seaside suicide attempt, the silhouette of the driver who accidentally drove a car into the Seine and drowned Isadora's two children, the blood-covered farewell love poem that her psychopathic Russian poet husband left while slashing his wrists before hanging himself, and finally Bugatti (Sandor Elès)—the film's fictional name for the real racecar driver Benoît Falchetto—who screams, "I killed Isadora!" after his wheel catches Isadora's scarf and chokes her. (Some sources claim Falchetto drove an Amilcar, not a Bugatti, when Isadora was killed.)

Like Welles, Russell proceeds to fragment and reanalyze the official story. To help him along, he includes Sewell Stokes among Duncan's final friends and most esteemed biographers, who wrote *Isadora Duncan: An Intimate Portrait* and also contributed to Russell's script and dialogue. Stokes gives an account of the dancer's life while sitting under an umbrella in Chelsea Old Church, among the gravestones where Isadora slept during her early penniless days: "I suppose Isadora led the most sensational life of any woman who has lived in this century. . . . She was warm-hearted, she was lovable; she was exasperating."

In one early scene, Russell stresses Isadora's reckless inventiveness by juxtaposing her dance with footage from the sterile, godlier-than-thou women in Leni Riefenstahl's *Olympiad*. Unlike Riefenstahl's Hellenic eye candy, Isadora's performance is raw artistic ambition with sincere but cloddish results. "The extract from the Olympic film showed her as she saw herself," Russell reflects, "in a romantic Hellenic aura, a slim backlit silhouette against the sun, hands upraised in a libation to the gods. But she wasn't that at all. I thought Vivian Pickles caught the vulgarity of Isadora very well."

Russell had already worked with Pickles on *Diary of a Nobody*, based on George and Weedon Grossmith's madcap comic novel. And although she is British, Pickles speaks more like an American than an American. She is brash, bold, naughty, and still affecting enough to get viewer sympathy, no matter how overbearing her character, how capricious her flirtations, how ill advised her attempts to turn a fleeting crush into an artist manqué, or how "uncontrolled and uncommercial," as critics claimed, her dancing seems.

"Since Isadora's life was so pathetic and tragic," Russell told interviewer Gene D. Phillips, "I tried to lighten the material at times. For example, I used the old Betty Hutton recording of 'The Sewing Machine' from the 1947 Hollywood film *The Perils of Pauline* on the soundtrack when Isadora is falling in love with Paris Singer, the sewing machine manufacturer."

Isadora looks progressively clownish as she tries waking a mostly dead world. For Isadora, as for Russell, dancing—even if it's bad dancing—is a means of redemption. "To tell the truth," he confesses in his autobiography, "dialogue scenes often bore me. The body is so much more expressive than the tongue—on film anyway. There's a lot of dancing in my work—or perhaps I should say choreography—and if the actors aren't making patterns, the camera is usually doing it for them."

With her ambitions turning into one farce after another, Isadora's failures are an indictment against the world. Almost everyone she meets is a drunken egomaniac, a gigolo, a sycophant, or, in the case of Paris Singer (Peter Bowles), an ineffectual hypochondriac who looks upon her as an exotic pet. Singer sets her up in a South Devon mansion, what Stokes's narration calls "a fascinating mausoleum of commerce and bad taste." On their wedding night, he gives her a huge gold box; she opens it to find six female harpists dousing her with song. In thanks, Isadora vows to dance along to their music through the night. But when Singer eventually falls asleep, Isadora hurls a glass of champagne in his face.

"Life in the Singer castle takes on the grandeur of Orson Welles at his most grand," the *New York Times'* John J. O'Connor wrote when *Isadora* aired in America on the NET Playhouse, "with conversations echoing in the great halls all the way down to the indoor pool."

Isadora has a few graceful moments, but they are usually tainted with tragedy. To the gentle sounds of Erik Satie's *Three Gymnopedies* as background, she makes a ritualistic farewell by the waters where her two children plunged to their deaths. Soon enough, however, she becomes more and more of a disillusioned tippler, her once-adoring public practically yawning in her presence. As the narrator declares, "She was just another drunken American showing off."

The French snub her efforts to build a dancing school, so she goes to Moscow for aid after the Soviets invite her as a "fellow revolutionary." But on her arrival at a train station, only a flock of starving children greet her. Unbowed, she leads the kids not to some morose Soviet march but to John Philip Sousa's "Stars and Stripes Forever." Thriving on potatoes and champagne, she sets up her dance academy in a "gutted Tsarist palace."

The Russian excursion intensifies when she meets Sergei Yesenin (Alexi Jawdokimov), the Russian poet and epileptic drunk who disrupts parties, destroys furniture, assaults women, and ruins Isadora's chances of an American comeback. When she goes to the States for a tour, Russell pairs scenes of her on stage, dancing frantically to Tchaikovsky's "March Slav," with Sergei stealing silverware and unfurling a Soviet flag outside an American hotel. Isadora's audience, by now whipped up into an anti-Red frenzy, boos her. She alienates the crowd even more by baring her breasts and inciting the cops to swoop her off the stage. Predictably, Isadora and Sergei get deported.

"Certainly Isadora," Stokes wrote in his biography, "except when she was dancing or heard music, was more miserable than any little dancer in the back row of the ballet." Russell dramatizes this emotional meltdown as Isadora finds the Soviet audiences just as deaf to her pleas for financial assistance. "Art is so much greater than government," she insists, but the huge portrait of Stalin lording over her indicates that she's preaching to an intellectual gulag. She leaves Moscow, gets swindled in Germany, and shows up in various European spots where ardent fans taunt her with lavish but ultimately unsatisfying recitals in her honor.

Russell is in his glory when Isadora attends a teatime garden party. A troupe of girls clad in Grecian tunics honors her influence with a ham-handed tribute to the ancients, replete with flowery wreaths and the flighty sounds of Ethelbert Nevin's "Narcissus." The music starts as a lush orchestral arrangement but morphs into the type of organ solo associated with silent cinemas and skating rinks as the recital gets clumsier. When the girls present her with a token of their appreciation, Isadora, looking gaunt and ghostly, mutters, "I lay this wreath on the grave of my hopes."

Soon, the tragic strains of "Liebestod" from Wagner's *Tristan and Isolde* accompany her screams inside a speeding car: "Faster! Faster! This is the way to die!" She settles in Nice, attends parties, gets drunker, lapses into flapper dances, and flirts with more potential gigolos. She reduces herself to an older and puffier version of *French Dressing*'s Françoise Fayol, using whatever is left of her feminine wiles for some illusion of acceptance.

During a photo shoot, Isadora even assumes tarty poses while pontificating again about great art. An effeminate photographer (Murray Melvin) snoots an air of indifference as Isadora prates: "When my body moves, it's because my spirit moves it." "If my art is symbolic of any one thing, it's symbolic of the freedom of women." "My body is the temple of my art. I expose it as the shrine of a worship of

Vivian Pickles as Isadora Duncan.

beauty." Then, Russell cuts to a rude close-up on her face, smudged with eye makeup and predating the Alice Cooper school of cosmetology, as she declares, "Age is only self-hypnotism."

When Bugatti, her inadvertent assassin, appears from behind a partition to liven up the atmosphere, he ignores her request for Beethoven or Wagner and puts on a recording of "Bye-Bye, Blackbird"—the quintessential giddy pop tune of its time. She dances—gauchely—nonetheless, unaware that in just a few moments it would be the soundtrack to her death. This was the kind of music Isadora loathed. Stokes quotes her ranting against "the frivolous caricatures and symbols of sex which are found in such dances as the fox-trot and Black-Bottom." His biography also has her taking the music personally: "And this jazz music! It's like America laughing at me." "Bye-Bye, Blackbird" (considered jazzy at the time) was, therefore, an ironic swansong.

Russell does make some concessions to Isadora's immaculate ideal: a vision of her leading her five hundred children to Beethoven's Ninth. But Russell cuts right back to a closing shot of her strangled head jerked back, blood oozing from her mouth, and "Bye-Bye, Blackbird" still grinding away in the closing credits.

"She was just a great person and that was her art," Russell would say. "God knows what her dancing was like. Pretty terrible, I imagine. But that doesn't matter. She affected and moved and meant a great deal to a lot of people. Everyone who saw or came in contact with her came away a bit different, even Mother Russia and Father Stalin."

Isadora, The Biggest Dancer in the World has the intelligence, the occasional compassion, the habitual sadism, and the heady goofiness that would character-ize Russell's best features. Karel Reisz's 1968 film *Isadora*, which stretches the story for over two and a half hours, is notably similar in parts to Russell's film. This is due to Melvyn Bragg who, serving as the screen adapter and coscreen-writer (with Clive Exton), might have assimilated some of Russell's version through osmosis. Reisz, like Russell, calls Isadora's fatal driver "Bugatti" and also closes with "Bye-Bye, Blackbird."

Reisz also uses Stokes's biography as a plot source, but he doesn't appear to share Russell's instinctive lifeline to Duncan's zany energy. Maurice Jarre's score is lush and often rapturous, the budget is vast, the colors are often vibrant, the Grecian location shots where Vanessa Redgrave dances as Duncan are in a soft focus, but the pacing is languid, Redgrave's performance often seems strained and too much like a British woman trying to be an American, and Reisz cap-tures none of Russell's manic energy.

In contrast, *Dante's Inferno*, about the life of Dante Gabriel Rossetti, has an alluring theme, inspired lunacy, and comic moments, but it's also a bit of a mess. "Russell is more affectionate with her than he is with Rossetti," Richard Schickel wrote with appreciation for *Isadora*, "but again there is that note of ambiguity that is always present in his work. Must I—must we—take this crazy lady seriously at every moment? Isn't there always a touch of the absurd in the artistic enterprise? And isn't the most significant thing about her the fact that she revealed it more openly than most other artists?"

HEAVEN, HELL, AND A WATERFALL

"**M**y heart pounded, my blood raced, I caught my breath, my eyes widened, my hair stood on end, an unseen orchestra played a tremendous chord. Only clichés can describe what no one has ever been able to portray—a vision of God."

Thus Ken Russell summarizes his life-changing epiphany when he first knelt at the feet of Skiddaw—a seven-mile mountain range in Cumberland, also called the Lake District, in northwest England. Many of Russell's precursors were equally smitten. John Ruskin set up house there, while Samuel Taylor Coleridge called Skiddaw "God made manifest."

All this sounds so holy and clean, but the circumstances in which Russell discovered Skiddaw are less angelic. While researching *Dante's Inferno*, which dramatizes the poet and Pre-Raphaelite champion Dante Gabriel Rossetti's inspiration and damnation, Russell discovered that Rossetti, at the end of his tether and prone to drinking bouts over his wife Elizabeth Siddal's death, vacationed in the Lake District, where he and his mistress Fanny Cornforth brandished gin bottles instead of rapiers in a lovers' duel. So, in the process of traveling to one of the district's hilltops, popularly known as Golden Howe, for an authentic touch, Russell changed his life. His commitment to Catholicism already shaky, Russell found in Skiddaw and its environs a religion based more on pagan nature worship.

Skiddaw also became for Russell "a place of enchantment, that can transform itself into Norway, Switzerland, or Bavaria at the sound of a clapperboard." It would later show up as a backdrop for a campy fantasia in *The Boy Friend* and spiritual renewal in *Tommy*, but watching how Skiddaw, with its surging Lodore Falls and vast Derwentwater Lake, appears in *Dante's Inferno*, viewers might suspect that this natural marvel could also be a vegetative abyss.

Skiddaw, through Rossetti's cerebral filter, transforms from a symbol of Heaven to a hellhole as he spirals downward with no signs of redemption.

•

Dante Gabriel Rossetti, the notorious English painter-poet who numbed his senses, thumbed his nose at aesthetic proprieties, and plumbed the poetic excesses of love and death, looked too deeply into the chasm one day and saw the future: the face of Ken Russell leering back at him. Had this really happened, it might explain why Dante destroyed so much of his compromising correspondence and other written material that he feared might fall into the hands of what he called a "biographic devil."

In *The Art of the Pre-Raphaelites*, author Elizabeth Prettejohn writes that the artists comprising this ornery batch of nineteenth-century English eccentrics whom Rossetti commandeered "were so determined not to repeat a pose from past art that they were obliged to twist their figures' bodies into bizarre configurations." The same could be said of Ken Russell, especially in the final years of his BBC spate, when his campaign to wrest the fickle television audience's attention span got more gnarled.

By 1967, viewers inured by caped crusaders and Hammer horror were too overstimulated to take in something as precious as a movie about some long-dead poet unless it had lots of bells and whistles tailored not only to get their attention but to scare their pants off. Rossetti's ghost wasn't the only quaking entity: the BBC's Huw Wheldon, traumatized by the macabre treatment of Debussy, shuddered at this next Russell offering, especially since it was now apparent that Russell was committed more than ever to hammer home his stories with cathartic, expressionistic punches.

Bryan Forbes planned to make his own version of *Dante's Inferno*, but the director famous for such arty yet salable 1960s dramas as *The L-Shaped Room* and *Séance on a Wet Afternoon* didn't think a story about the Pre-Raphaelite Brotherhood had promise. He sent Austin Frazer, a young scriptwriter still committed to the project, to a receptive Russell. "Why he [Forbes] thought it wouldn't be commercial I just could not understand," Russell recalls. "A man digging up his wife's remains to get a book he buried with her? It screams commercial."

With artistic inspiration and the moxie of a self-appointed press agent, Russell embarked on one of the darkest, most obsessive, and at times most untidy outings of his BBC career. *Dante's Inferno*, while concentrating on the wanting and wanton life of its title character, focuses also on the other painters and writers with whom he banded in 1848 to debunk an academic art world too preoccupied with aristocratic portraiture, dark brown hues, and the overbearing influence of the painter Raphael. It was perfect for Russell's ends, offering what he called "an ambiguous story" that "gives one more scope for suggesting things rather than saying them: that's what I like doing."

The actors portraying Rossetti's gang were also Russell's gang, since many were friends from Ken and Shirley's early days in the London art scene. They include Russell's Catholic Coppelius Norman Dewhurst as the dreamy-eyed and willowy Edward Burne-Jones. Arguably the film's most powerful player is Christopher Logue, a poet, playwright, and friend to Samuel Beckett who, under the nom de plume "Count Palmiro Vicarion," wrote a pornographic novel in the 1940s entitled *Lust*. He takes on the role of Algernon Charles Swinburne, the poet and pleasure-seeker noted for his melodious celebrations of masochism.

Russell assembles these characters to help him celebrate Skiddaw's splendor. Nature, for them, was not the sometimes ugly and impoverished world of their contemporary England, but some majestic hodgepodge drawn up from ideals about the Middle Ages. The results of their endeavors were paintings with otherworldly colors and poems—and so much sensual mysticism that one critic derided them as a "fleshly school of poetry."

Russell was lucky enough to find actors who bear uncanny resemblances to the real people: Judith Paris looks incredibly like Dante's wife Elizabeth Siddal, just as Iza Teller resembles Dante's sister Christina Rossetti. The painter, utopian philosopher, and sometimes wallpaper designer William Morris, whose mane of dark, curly hair earned him the nickname "Topsy," was by several accounts as athletic, mercurial, and often silly as Andrew Faulds portrays him. And Oliver Reed, with his large melancholy eyes, is close to the real Rossetti.

Russell is less faithful, however, to literary hagiography. All the textbook palaver about the Brotherhood's poetic visions and spiritual unions often comes across as verbal window dressing; the artists tend to present themselves more as pompous windbags, a Brotherhood of the Bollocks that has all the vision and vanity that Russell often finds in artists. And again, Russell compounds the laughs with pop music, offsetting the characters' preciousness with the anachronistic strains of Albert Ketèlbey's 1920s tune "In a Persian Market" and jumping ahead into the Hollywood '40s with Irving Berlin's "There's No Business Like Show Business."

Like his Debussy, Reed's Rossetti is convincing as a creative man who barely flinches at the thought of using women and ruining their lives. Reed, as Russell describes him, "is a physical actor and spends more time wrestling naked than in polite conversation at the dinner table." He had no time for drivel about Method and motivation. All he needed was dramatic shorthand: an emotive thermostat that the director could set for him at will. Since most of Reed's performances depended on degrees of sullenness and wickedness, both men agreed that before each scene, Russell would indicate: "Moody One," Moody Two," or "Moody Three," each depending on the degree of brooding or bellicosity required.

As expected, Reed's interpretation of Rossetti makes the poet come off as an inwardly torn maniac who could be boyishly affectionate one moment and cruel the next. Siddal, his tortured soul mate, is just a lower-class girl working in a milliner's shop before she's corralled into Rossetti's rat pack. She is also strapped with an eating disorder and laudanum addiction, conditions that worsen as Rossetti's alienated affections and constant philandering drive her to madness.

The Rossetti-Siddal conflicts are apparent in the film's very first scene, one reminiscent of the grainy and timeworn look of such silent horror fare as Robert Wiene's *The Cabinet of Dr. Caligari* and F. W. Murnau's *Nosferatu*. Russell grabs television viewers with an image few would ever forget: Rossetti's hand yanking open a coffin and riffling around Siddal's rotting corpse to retrieve a volume of his poetry that, in a half-hearted gesture of love, he had buried with her. Now that it has amassed monetary value, he wants it back.

Russell follows this with another of his apocalyptic conflagrations. Rossetti's heady hooligans attempt to overthrow the Royal Academy of Art, tossing academic paintings into a huge bonfire and sputtering out anarchist epithets. Spilling over from *French Dressing*'s burning blow-up dolls, the gray goo of Russell's nightmares saturates the blaze as Dante looks into the fire: he imagines Siddal as Joan of Arc, standing in the flames with a raised sword and calling him into oblivion.

Dante Rossetti (Oliver Reed) pays a graveside visit to his wife in *Dante's Inferno*, filmed in England's Lake District.

Dante's sister Christina, who initially comes across as arrogant and possessive of her brother, emerges as a more sympathetic character. She develops sisterly concern for Siddal's mental and physical corrosion. But Dante also dotes on Siddal as a brother to a sister; he spends more time attending to her and agreeing, however reluctantly, to her asexual demands.

Unfortunately, Dante does not even begin to share Siddal's high regard for chastity and instead wanders in search of a wifely substitute. One of the women he seeks is Fanny Cornforth (Pat Ashton), a stocky, gutter-mouthed Cockney wench. Dante attempts to paint her but seems to have more fun romping with her in the fields to the soundtrack's skating rink organ rendition of the 1960s tune, "Cuando, Cuando, Cuando."

Richard Schickel, who expressed enthusiasm for the aspects of Russell's work that many of his peers might deem too scary, found *Dante's Inferno* both repulsive and fascinating, especially Russell's interpolations of songs from another time and place: "The anachronism jars, it is in dubious taste—and yet the daring of the moment is almost literally breathtaking. One cannot help responding to the spirit of a director who will try such a stunt. And in the context of television at this moment that spirit seems to me more significant than the breach in good form it produced."

To make the story more complicated, Russell assigns the bulk of the narrative, and perhaps the movie's viewpoint, to Swinburne—the true sybarite and sexual experimenter who makes the rest of the pack look like prudes. Logue's curt and erudite tone suggests Alastair Cooke mouthing artistic appraisals while suppressing a belch. This is most apparent during a fantasy sequence when the Brotherhood assumes shining armor. Swinburne summarizes their fight against what they fancy as bourgeois respectability: "Then came there forth the full noble knights to take up arms in the name of art, against the dragons of iron and steel called *progress*."

"I think this says quite a lot about ideal love clashing with reality," Russell observes about *Dante's Inferno*'s ultimate message. "It's also a film about death, about physical and moral decay. The Pre-Raphaelites cut themselves off and tried to create something from the decay of the industrial revolution, and they only succeeded in doing what Debussy did, incarcerating themselves in an atmosphere of nightmare which destroyed them."

As the story unravels, nature looks less like a healing horizon of mountains and clear rivers and more like the grave, teeming with slimy creatures and penile monstrosities. Rossetti starts withering when, in another drunken stupor, he collides with his prized menagerie of wombats, worms, and other beasts. He initially crashes into some birdcages, but when he falls to the ground and a python crawls across his face, the artist sets out on his demented journey toward Siddal's grave seven years after her demise from a laudanum overdose.

Before the film retraces the tale from Siddal's crypt, Russell moves the story a bit forward, as Charles Augustus Howell (David Jones), Rossetti's shady art dealer, shows up with a lizard in his hand and a case that holds the moldering book of verse that Dante became a ghoul to retrieve (in real life he assigned the ghastly task to someone else). And like a glib and slippery player who would have fit well in Andy Warhol's circle, Howell offers some cold comfort by reminding Rossetti that copies of the poems will "sell like hotcakes."

Russell turns the Lake District into a mirror of Rossetti's soul, as the landscape appears to alter with the poet's moral demise. The region exudes picture postcard beauty in the beginning when Rossetti takes Siddal there to propose marriage. But the waters look more frightening once Rossetti and Siddal return there as spouses. And the area eventually takes on the pallor of Poe's "sepulcher by the sea" as Siddal's coffin rests on the rocks. The rivulets that once looked so refreshing and romantic seem unearthly as her cadaver reaches out to grab the stolen book out of her husband's hand.

The story takes another macabre turn with the appearance of Miss Jane Burden (Gala Mitchell), the Pre-Raphaelite wild card who marries William Morris but ends up wooing Dante. Janey leaves a lasting impression as she stares into the camera with a gaunt and grave expression, blank yet quietly demonic. In real life, she was the subject for Rossetti's *Study for Pandora*, but in the film she looks more like Edvard Munch's *Madonna*. Siddal, keen to prevent Janey's intrusion, calls her "the black-headed bitch."

When the cuckolded William Morris also quakes before Skiddaw's spell before exiling himself to Iceland, the Lake District hills seem as if they are impervious prison walls. And the Derwentwater Lake resembles the river Styx leading to oblivion when Janey, with arms stretched out in a boat, departs from Dante's life; she registers no emotion when he cries, "Don't leave me!"

Near death, Dante returns to the district, walking in solitude and wallowing over "the lost days of my life." The trees are almost indistinguishable from his gnarled body's black silhouette, and the once-beautiful river almost drowns him. He literally fights the waters with his fists, while the women he had loved and exploited flash in his mind. By now, Russell's "God made manifest" looks more hellish than ever, as Rossetti walks beside the silhouette of a dead tree before exiting with his muse and the bottle of chloral that he now needs to help him through his sleepless nights.

Ironically, Russell's limited budget prohibited him from using color film for a story about painters renowned for their inventive hues. But the limitation worked in his favor. He brought out the look of a classic black and white horror film, made his heavenly Lake District resemble a region of Transylvania, and still managed to close with the calliope strains of Vincent Youmans's "I Want to Be Happy."

COLD DAYS IN PURGATORY

"I know it's heretical for a film director to even think about it," Russell writes, "but I'll be glad when the last cinema has been turned into a bingo parlor, and films are seen under optimum conditions in the home." He held this animosity from 1967, when the London premiere of his second feature film, *Billion Dollar Brain*, turned out to be a technical disaster.

Russell squirmed in his seat next to its producer Harry Saltzman when reel three began without sound. With the already fickle audience getting testier, and the blare of catcalls and clapping getting louder, Russell scrambled to find the projectionist. He had to travel from the usherette who thought he was being fresh to the theater manager's empty office; from there, he went to the commissionaire, who guided him out of the cinema's swing doors and instructed him to go down an alley to the theater's fire escape and up along the rooftop until he found what Russell recalls as resembling "a brick shithouse." After rapping on the door four times, Russell finally faced the culprit.

"I thought it was a bit quiet for a Bond film," the elderly projectionist responded with noisome nonchalance. Besides messing up Russell's big night, he also got his secret agents confused; this was not a Bond thriller at all. And as he nonchalantly put down his copy of *Playboy* and flicked the switch for the sound, the projectionist proceeded to mess up the Panavision.

It was within this absurd and unreceptive atmosphere that Russell introduced one of his least appreciated but more intriguing early works. *Billion Dollar Brain* is the third in the series of spy movies based on the secret agent from Len Deighton's novel *The Ipcress File*. When United Artists mogul Saltzman (who worked with Albert R. Broccoli on the James Bond films) wanted to make Deighton's character into the anti–James Bond, he and the studio had to invent a name the author never provided. Saltzman and company dubbed him Harry Palmer, the dullest name they could find.

After Christopher Plummer turned down the role to pursue *The Sound of Music*, the part went to Michael Caine. Palmer is a more awkward, more vulnerable, somewhat nerdy agent who wears glasses, dabbles as a gourmet, prepares his own tea every morning, and usually sleeps alone. His field of espionage isn't even by choice; rather, he gets drafted into it because a stay in military stir for playing in the black market is the only other alternative. He is a new kind of antihero, or as Caine described him, "a spy's spy."

Though Palmer creates a new mold for the spy genre, the first two Harry Palmer films take a relatively conventional approach. Sidney J. Furie's *The Ipcress File*, released in 1965, has Palmer acting typically masculine and cocky. His environment, though hostile, still seems more within his control until enemy agents capture him. Bound, starved, shoved into a metal cage, and fed a diet of loud and creepy music, Palmer almost succumbs to the attempted mind control. The story is complex but unravels at a slow pace, with lots of overly audible footsteps, telephone gab, and too many interiors smudged in dull, brown hues. Even John Barry's theme has a post–*Pink Panther* pallor. Though *The Ipcress File* got great reviews and continues to be a cult item for many, Guy Hamilton's follow-up *Funeral in Berlin* a year later was drabber and less appreciated.

By the time Russell arrived to give Palmer a makeover, Caine was already exhausted with the role, even though Saltzman had him contracted to play it three more times. But Caine was so impressed after seeing *The Debussy Film* on *Monitor* that he was glad to have Russell as director. Saltzman agreed and tossed Russell a bone by promising to let him do his dream movie about the dancer Vaslav Nijinsky. They even took a side trip to Paris together to see Maurice Bejart's production of *The Rite of Spring*, but Saltzman, unimpressed by both the dancing and the music, nodded off. From then on, Nijinsky was on ice, but Saltzman hurried to get *Billion Dollar Brain* started and sent Russell and the crew over to frosty Finland.

For Russell, it was a second chance to establish himself as a serious feature filmmaker. But Deighton's novel didn't impress him. He also felt hamstrung by a genre that by the late 1960s had become exhausted. The idea of a semi-reptilian detective beset by a plotting world was so musty that Russell approached Harry Palmer the way he usually tackled potentially tedious projects: he rewrote and embellished the story with his quirks whenever possible, finding ways to grab the audience's attention.

The retiring Russell that Huw Wheldon described, the one who rarely spoke and got his way through passive-aggressive tactics, had by now ceded to a new Russell: one who was still socially reticent but now much less shy about sputtering his professional opinions. The tensions started when the producers racked their brains for a cinematographer to replace an aging and ailing Otto Heller.

Russell managed to insult Heller's replacement Robert Krasker by expressing distaste for his work on Sidney Hayers's *The Trap*, an adventure-romance from 1966 starring Oliver Reed and Rita Tushingham.

United Artists finally took the director's advice and hired Billy Williams, who worked with Russell on television commercials and would go on to photograph *Women in Love* and *The Rainbow*. Richard Rodney Bennett (who did the music for *Far from the Madding Crowd* that same year) provides a soundtrack with a chilly piano—an appropriately eerie and welcome change from the typically guitar-laden spy movie score. And title designer Maurice Binder, who created the memorable gun's eye view in James Bond's opening credits, supplies what at least back then looked like a space-age office with high-tech computer lights.

Russell recalls that when he and John McGrath collaborated on the screenplay, they "got down to the business of trying to insert some logic into the events while at the same time . . . throw[ing] in something that tickled our fancy." Oddball Palmer would get odder; the off-putting glacial atmosphere would look more like an alien planet.

When Palmer gets his assignment in Furie's film, there is much more exposition, much more conventional conversation—all done in an office with a portrait of the queen looming in the background. With Russell, Palmer's boss Colonel Ross (Guy Doleman) breaks into his ramshackle home, peruses the file of incriminating photos of philandering husbands Palmer keeps for his side business as a private eye, and spills a box full of Kellogg's cornflakes all over his floor. "You know, it's an extraordinary thing, but I have the feeling you don't like working for me," Ross later tells Palmer with British understatement.

Not an actor's director, Russell remedies his impatience with plot conventions by allowing the story's inanimate surroundings to compete with the characters. Otherwise innocuous public places become ominous, such as when Palmer goes to pick up a thermos containing eggs injected with a lethal virus in the locker of an airport terminal. Instead of offering comfort, the soothing strings from the piped-in music echo through the metallic corridors, calling more attention to the computerized voice that instructs him to head for snowy Helskini.

Filming in Finland, London, and England's Pinewood Studios, Russell rushes the story from locale to locale; at times, viewers might be confused as to where they are in this constant place and time shift. In Helsinki, Palmer thinks that the old friend assigned to receive the lethal thermos is on his side, but Leo Newbigen (Karl Malden) is really beholden to a mad Texas millionaire named General Midwinter (Ed Begley) who wants to defeat Communism, even if it means igniting World War III. Malden, whose screen roles have usually been cuckolds or fall guys, conveys greedy malevolence.

When Palmer goes to Latvia, Colonel Stok (Oscar Homolka), a pudgy Russian already introduced in *Funeral in Berlin*, pops in and out of the plot in an outlandish role: a Soviet good guy who unites with Palmer to save the world against the mad American tycoon.

This would be the last role for Françoise Dorléac, the sister of Catherine Deneuve, who died in a car crash in Nice before the film finished shooting. She plays Anya, the obligatory female interest, with whom something always goes wrong before she and Palmer get to consummate anything. But even though Anya is an ice princess, Russell includes her in one of the film's cuter touches. Russell, who had all along been contemplating a film on Tchaikovsky that would finally become *The Music Lovers*, begins a scene with one of his characteristic diagonal motions: from a psychedelic wall painting, down and across the room to Anya squeaking out a terrible rendition of Tchaikovsky's "None but the Lonely Heart" on the cello, while Harry and Leo sit among pop art furniture to discuss their plans.

While most spy films thrive on a calculating plot with a discernible beginning, middle, and end, Russell's contribution to the genre rests more on individual scenes that are florid, disorienting, and full of enough inside jokes to function independently of the larger story. When Palmer arrives in Helsinki to get his assignment, Russell makes an allusion to Carol Reed's *The Third Man*. In Reed's film, the "big wheel" where Harry Lime meets his pal is an enormous Ferris wheel; but when Palmer gets the same instructions, he finds instead a puny playground ride.

Palmer tries to talk to a Dr. Kaarna, a possible lead in discovering the source of the virus, but finds him bumped off in a rocking chair. An unlisted actor who looks like Russell in sunglasses and sprinkled with talcum powder plays the mysterious doctor, killed by a spine-piercing needle.

Russell also brings in some of his actor stable. Vladek Sheybal shows up as the sinister virus engineer Dr. Eiwort, while Alexi Jawdokimov and Iza Teller have cameos as Latvian gangsters smuggling contraband Beatles records while "A Hard Day's Night" (a segment cut out of the DVD release due to music licensing expenses) blares over a phonograph.

Russell adds another signature scene when Anya attends a hockey game, unaware that she just missed getting assassinated. Palmer, who knows that Leo is her would-be assassin and purposely missed because he is in love with her, joins her at the stadium. Just as he advises her that "some games are more dangerous than others," the camera puts an extreme close-up on a masked hockey player getting pummeled and then slammed against a wall. It's quick, scary, and helps the story along a progression that is at times more visceral than logical.

Russell's Palmer lacks the trickster impudence he had in *The Ipcress File*. He instead ambles from one nasty situation to the next, looking increasingly vulnerable. Russell, with his fondness for zooms, rushes into Caine's facial close-ups without warning, making the use of stunt doubles more difficult. Caine wound up doing many of his own feats, slipping into freezing water while leaping across ice floes, jumping from speeding trains, and braving gusts from a snow blower.

Compared to Furie, Russell is much more abrasive and likely to make viewers see a side to Caine and his character that is not so predictably smug. And each time he and Anya unite, something goes wrong, especially when she attempts to pierce his spine with the same long needle that felled Dr. Kaarna.

For this, Caine biographer Anne Billson has only praise: "What *Billion Dollar Brain* has, which the first two Harry Palmer films lack, is a dreamlike quality which lingers in the memory long after films with more meretricious plotting have faded." Billson also appreciates how the film subverts romantic expectations: "a fur-wrapped Dorléac leans over to kiss Palmer, but, stung by her treachery, he doesn't respond. Harry Palmer has been hurt. . . . For the first time, Palmer is showing signs of emotional distress. It is a pity that just as we are starting to suspect he is not as battle-hardened as he seems, the Palmer saga comes to an end, and we have to leave him there."

With a mood that is discordant from the start, and with constantly shifting geography, Russell takes the story in its most hysterical direction when the time comes to journey from the Arctic regions to a simulation of sultry Texas. This is the point in the film where those who have some sense of Russell's work are likely to see more of a stylistic continuity from *Billion Dollar Brain* to *The Music Lovers*, with *Women in Love* being somewhat of a lower-key anomaly.

Russell takes the story into overdrive with Midwinter's Texas barbecue and political rally, which packs more fire and brimstone than the flames in *French Dressing* and *Dante's Inferno*. The camera careens across throngs of revelers who seem drunk and happy one moment and malicious the next as their patriotic anthems get more cacophonous. Midwinter addresses his fans as they go from frolicking in a Texas-style square dance to participating in a cultic rite, with fascistic symbols and a bonfire for roasting portraits of Soviet leaders. Hellfire blazes behind him as Midwinter intones, "Oh Lord, I humbly accept the sword of leadership which thou hast thrust upon me."

The movie's centerpiece is its massive computer, which Midwinter operates to spin "enough inside information to program Soviet Communism right off the face of this Earth." He sends agents out to wreak havoc in enemy countries and plans to unleash the viruses onto the Russian army. Begley triumphs as the raving anti-Communist preacher and psychopath. Sweating under Russell's merciless close-ups, he warns Palmer that his arm is long and his vengeance is total.

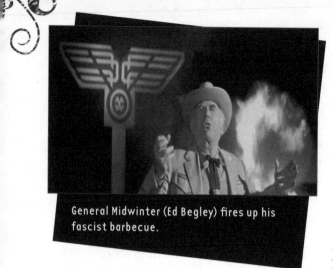

General Midwinter (Ed Begley) fires up his fascist barbecue.

Russell knew about President Lyndon Johnson but had scant knowledge about Texas or Texans. But when Colin Wilson interviewed him in 1973 for the CBS show *Camera Three*, Russell admitted being proud that it was "the first film . . . which showed American Texans as fantastic fascists." *Newsweek*'s Joseph Morgenstern echoed Russell's sentiments with his otherwise unenthusiastic and "pinko" review: "The only novelty worth mentioning is the gratitude we feel for the Soviets' cool competence in military affairs and their reluctance to be rattled by our lunatic fringe."

Russell remembers how "the script gradually became more and more anti-American and pro-Russian, in that the film deals with American interference in affairs which are not its concern. In this case it's Latvia . . . but for Latvia one could easily read Vietnam. I think it was the first anti-American spy film ever, and I'm told that many young people in America liked it for that reason, though it died the death in most places."

Once he learns that Newbigen has sabotaged plans to assassinate Anya, Midwinter interprets the treachery as a call to arms. He amasses his army: a phalanx of silver helmets converging in a grand battle on the icy Baltic that foreshadows the pinballs in *Tommy*. The epic battle takes place partly on a deserted airfield but also in Pinewood, inside a huge tank with polystyrene ice and piles of salt to simulate snow. Russell also cribbed from the closing of the "Battle on the Ice" sequence in Sergei Eisenstein's *Alexander Nevsky*, with Dmitri Shostakovitch's *Leningrad Symphony* as the blaring counterpoint.

Midwinter's helmeted army foreshadows the silver pinballs in *Tommy*.

Despite its engaging visuals and often-funny script, *Billion Dollar Brain* got a lackluster reception. *Variety* complained that Russell directed "with such abrupt speed that it doesn't make immediate sense in its own frivolous terms." Despite the less than glowing response, United Artists was still pleased. Saltzman even sent Ken and Shirley to the U.S.S.R. as British representatives for the Moscow Film Festival. The Russian authorities, however, thought this arty couple looked suspicious and held them in a temporary cell. "The whole trip was a ludicrous fiasco," Russell recalls in another of his life-imitating-art scenarios, "with us going from one bizarre situation to another; even more improbably than *Billion Dollar Brain.*"

Ken and Shirley had mixed feelings about being in Saltzman's court, especially when he invited them to join him and his wife at Montreal's Expo 1967. At dinner, the waiters kowtowed to Saltzman's every wish as he ordered the appetizer without anyone's consent. "You're at liberty to choose the next course," Russell remembers, "but he'll often say 'That looks good' and reach across to take half your food. Or say 'Try this' and ram a forkful of his own dinner down your throat. It's very funny for the first few months, then it begins to lose its flavor, and you see you're paying for your dinner by being courtiers."

Far from wanting to be a courtier, Russell wanted to direct. But he knew his next project wasn't going to be about Nijinsky. Even though Melvyn Bragg put together a script, and the recent ex-Royal Ballet member Christopher Gable was set to play the role, Saltzman insisted on Rudolf Nureyev. But when he and Russell met with the dancer in London to discuss the project over dinner, Nureyev demonstrated table manners as overbearing as Saltzman's.

As Russell recollects, "He was two hours late, arrived with a girl to whom he never introduced us, consumed vast quantities of vodka and caviar, and looked over our heads all the time." Worse, after dinner they trekked off to a Mayfair theater to view Russell's *Isadora*, but Nureyev detested the film, saying that Russell had desecrated a great icon. He said he would do the movie so long as Russell, the scriptwriter, and the designer were out of the picture.

Christopher Gable, meanwhile, still got his acting debut when Russell cast him in the 1968 BBC production *Song of Summer*, about the last days of the ailing composer Frederick Delius. Gable plays the young, idealistic, thin-skinned Eric Fenby, a Yorkshire lad and an aspiring composer who plays chess with his dad one day and goes into a near rapture when hearing Delius's music on the radio. He obsesses over the composer and is naive enough to think he's lucky when he gets the job as Delius's assistant. Fenby soon discovers his idol is a selfish tyrant as well as a musical genius. Like any sensitive soul foolhardy enough to play yes-man to an overweening—and dying—prima donna, Fenby edges toward a nervous breakdown.

Though another of Russell's low-budget, black-and-white television efforts, *Song of Summer* proved more promising for both Gable and its director, precisely because it managed to engage a healthy portion of England's viewership. The Russell-Nureyev-Nijinsky connection finally snapped. Russell bowed out of the project, unaware that Nureyev would get into his hair again almost ten years later. He at least felt some sense of accomplishment: he had turned Harry Palmer into an alien. He now wanted to make a movie about another kind of alien: Tchaikovsky. But first, United Artists put him through another trial by fire and ice: the honors of filming a four hundred-plus–page novel by D. H. Lawrence.

10
BLOWING BUBBLES

"I want to sit with my beloved in a field, with daisies growing all around us." So says Rupert Birkin, the leading character in Ken Russell's film of *Women in Love*, who is close in looks and temperament to his creator, author D. H. Lawrence. Rupert's sentiments, while twee by today's romantically underachieving standards, must have made Russell chuckle when, thanks to cinematic serendipity, a bee hovered near actor Alan Bates's face as he uttered these sweet, flowery lines. More significant is the fact that Rupert speaks these lines to Gerald Crich (Oliver Reed), the man he truly loves, who is too brutish to appreciate the overture. That's what much of *Women in Love* essentially is: a story of one man's unrequited love for another, albeit told in a roundabout and often oppressively "tasteful" manner.

Life wasn't always so sweet when Russell took on Lawrence. He no longer had to contend with Saltzman, but he had two new producers, Martin Rosen and Larry Kramer, the latter also the original script's author. Kramer, who would gain future fame as a novelist and gay activist, had purchased the rights to adapt the book into a screenplay. Other directors—Peter Brook, Jack Clayton, Stanley Kubrick, Silvio Narizzano—came up as contenders, but when United Artists insisted on Russell (his past connections to Saltzman certainly no hindrance), Kramer had to abide Russell's many revisions.

Russell admitted he had never read *Women in Love* and was not even conversant with Lawrence. He also said he was unimpressed with his literary forebear: "A lot of the book seemed pretentious and repetitive, and I left a lot of it out because films lasting twenty-four hours are frowned on by distributors and partly, as I say, because Lawrence simply repeated his theme about the separate-yet-united philosophy of love eight times over in different guises. I thought twice would be enough in the film for most people to get it."

When the final script arrived in his lap, Russell was miffed that Kramer got all the credit. He also wasn't thrilled when Kramer, especially during the casting process, kept referring to the project as *his* film. But after arguing with Kramer and others about being listed as cowriter, Russell was more or less browbeaten into taking the high road. He ceded his writing credit, mollified with the knowledge that, as director, he could still boss people around, throw fits, and exercise other prerogatives.

Even though scholar F. R. Leavis groaned in a letter to Larry Kramer that making the book into a movie was "an obscene undertaking," Russell got inspiration from other sources. Lawrence scholar Harry T. Moore noted that, by the mid-1920s, Lawrence himself was somewhat friendly to the idea of a cinematic adaptation. Critic George Ford likened Lawrence's novel to an intricate "court dance," where characters counterpoint one another. Such a choreographic theme was ripe for Russell, who would bring out intricacies in the film's main female characters through their flamboyant dance steps. "Perhaps I should have turned the whole thing into a musical," Russell later joked.

An English Anglophile, Russell delighted in scouting out great locations. He had a knack for the right spots and for collaborating with cinematographer Billy Williams to capture the beauty and mysteries of Derbyshire (Lawrence's native town) and Nottingham. While Shirley scrambled to approximate period costumes, Russell contacted the Royal Commission of Historic Monuments and examined its cache of photographs depicting just about every old building in England.

After *Billion Dollar Brain*, Russell was on friendly terms with Michael Caine and wanted him for the role of Gerald Crich, the brooding and doomed miner's son with a cold heart. But a vital scene when the two leading men wrestle in their birthday suits unsettled Caine. In a 2003 interview with American radio host Terry Gross on *Fresh Air*, he was upfront about the prospect of rubbing genitalia with another bloke: "Well, for a start, I turned down the thing because I won't appear stark naked in anything, you know? And the other thing, I couldn't imagine wrestling a naked guy, you know? I thought, 'So supposing I like this? I'll be in trouble.'" Oliver Reed, however, triumphed as Gerald, a part that allowed him to emphasize what he and Russell agreed would be mostly "Moody Three."

Alan Bates seemed fated to play Rupert, the well-oiled school inspector with poetic dreams. Kramer had been trying to get him the role, and Bates was so enraptured by Lawrence's work that he yearned for the part. Bates looked like Lawrence, especially when sporting the beard and spouting philosophical tidbits about love and landscape—observations and obsessions mouthed mostly from Lawrence's pen. But prickly Russell also makes Rupert one of the film's more annoying characters: so sensitive and philosophical one moment, so oblivious to the feelings of others the next. He is also a shrinking violet in his endeavor to win Gerald's erotic hand—a subtext that hazes in and out of the narrative, usually with too much subtlety.

Casting for the roles of the two lower-middle-class sisters who come of age—Gudrun and Ursula Brangwen—posed more of a conundrum. Jennie Linden emerged for the part of Ursula, but she had a Debbie Reynolds face that made her seem a bit too ingenuous at times. She could holler and exude beauty at the right moments, but Russell has subsequently wondered if she seemed younger than her actual character (she was, after all, the older sister) and too pert for the part.

Getting a good Gudrun was the biggest challenge. The novel describes her as "very beautiful, passive, soft-skinned, soft-limbed," but also having "perfect sangfroid and exclusive bareness of manner." Russell needed an actress with unconventional beauty who could martial these contradictory qualities and intimidate viewers at the same time, but Bette Davis was too old. But he soon found his young harridan.

Glenda May Jackson, who grew up on England's North West coast to a bricklayer dad and a barmaid mom, was a chubby overeater who gorged on biscuits and chips; she was also acerbic, resolute, and stubborn. Her parents, likely intuiting trouble, named her after Glenda Farrell, the American actress noted for her roles as pretty blonde wiseacres and hardboiled molls. A petulant schoolgirl cursed with acne and armed with a piercing intellect, she was also an avid reader. She could appreciate Shakespeare but was more a fan of popular culture, especially the movies. While Russell grew up devoted to Dorothy Lamour, Jackson admired the aquatic goddess Esther Williams and the "Queen of Technicolor" Maria Montez. But such Jezebels as Joan Crawford, Bette Davis, and Katherine Hepburn, who used claws more than glamour to hog the limelight, impressed her the most.

Jackson's history reveals a gal after Russell's heart. After teething her talents at the Royal Academy of Dramatic Art, she struggled with occasional repertory work. By 1963 she got a modest part in the stage production of Bill Naughton's sex comedy (later a famous Michael Caine movie) about a cad named *Alfie*—an experience she hated through all 194 performances. But her role as Siddie, one of Alfie's feminine conquests, impressed playwrights Peter Brook and Charles Marowitz. They invited her to partake in their Theater of Cruelty experiments, which they conducted under the tutelage of the Royal Shakespeare Company.

The Theater of Cruelty mutated from the imagination of French actor, poet, playwright, and theorist Antonin Artaud to celebrate primitive impulses. He enticed actors to forfeit logic and narrative conventions by going to absurd extremes of movement and sound. Frenetic behavior, violent impulses, hysterical incantation, misshapen gestures, and grunts were the divine delirium that he hoped would shock audiences out of their complaisance. His theater would, in his words, "bring the demons to the surface."

Marowitz was especially intrigued by what he called Jackson's "disconcerting presence," a quality that he, considering his love for Artaud, intended as a compliment. During her audition, she read aloud from a Dorothy Parker story and barely flinched when Brook made this request: "Now do that same piece again, but this time you're a woman who's just been committed to a mental asylum by her husband; and, in fact, she's not *really* insane and she's trying to convince the people who come to take her away that she is not insane, and, you know, you're in a straitjacket."

Jackson's affinity for projecting a lunatic personality on the stage was obvious in early 1964, when she joined the group for a revue. She chose Brook's *The Public Bath*, a short work in which she played Christine Keeler, who won notoriety through her bedroom romps with British defense minister John Profumo. After brandishing a whip for one of her kinkier clients, going on trial, and proceeding to take off all of her clothes in a prison bath scene, Jackson's Keeler soon changed into her opposite: the relentlessly respectable and recently bereaved Jacqueline Kennedy. Jackson played Jackie presiding at her husband's funeral, converting the bathtub into the president's coffin.

Though stage nudity in a public theater was still considered a crime in England, this was a private club. Jackson got kudos for being the first actress of importance to tread the boards in the buff and leave the theater free from police handcuffs. With what Marowitz called her "smoldering intelligence," she became the thinking person's nude, notwithstanding her self-description as a lady with "varicose veins, piano legs, and no tits."

Jackson considered these bouts of naked distemper artistic and intellectual acts. She got more extreme after accepting Brook's invitation to join the Royal Shakespeare Company and star as Charlotte Corday, Jean Paul Marat's murderess in Peter Weiss's *The Persecution and Assassination of Marat as Performed by the Inmates of the Asylum of Charenton under the Direction of the Marquis de Sade*. From 1964 to 1968, the award-winning play—abbreviated to *Marat/Sade*—mesmerized and stunned spectators. They got an extra jolt when Corday used her long hair, instead of a whip, to flagellate Sade.

When the play moved across the pond to Broadway, the atmosphere, as well as Jackson's psyche, got crazier. She started hating the production and expressed her disdain in the press. She dreaded the hysterics other cast members displayed in their dressing rooms: the mood of dread that overcame them as they endured night after night of what she described as "people twitching, slobber running down their chins, everyone preparing to isolate themselves from reality." Her future costar George Segal caught one of her performances and confessed that it "scared the Jesus" out of him.

Russell, however, knew nothing of Jackson as a stage nudity pioneer, or anything else about her, when meeting her for the first time. He remembers focusing only on her varicose veins, which he insisted she surgically remove. He at last tasted her talent after seeing her in Brook's 1966 film version of *Marat/Sade*, a performance Jackson herself confessed was "over-the-top."

Marveling at how her elfish face seethed from behind iron bars and how deftly she fondled a knife, Russell embarked on a professional relationship with a woman who now had smoother legs but promised a rocky road. And considering *Women in Love*'s themes of twisted heterosexuality and frustrated homosexuality, Jackson's frenzied love scenes and her unabashed nakedness served a purpose deeper than soft-core pornography. "I couldn't quite understand it," Russell would say. "Sometimes she looked plain ugly, sometimes just plain, and then, sometimes, the most beautiful creature one had ever seen."

With an ear for period music, Russell solidified the story with a melodic motif. He discovered that "I'm Forever Blowing Bubbles" was one of the most popular songs of 1920. Though in other films Russell shows a soft spot for anachronism, here the song fits the 1921 setting. It also summarizes the theme of broken dreams and illusions about art, spirituality, and, of course, unrequited love. "Nothing materializes! Everything withers in the bud," Gudrun gripes as she and Ursula watch a wedding from a graveyard's vantage point. The ugly aftermath of World War I also pervades the atmosphere, with a little girl holding up a sign reading "Remember Somme" and disoriented veterans popping in and out of the background.

Russell also fought against the potential stagnation that threatens filmed novels. One of his strategies was to impel some of the actors into almost constant dance dynamics. The ghost of Isadora Duncan hovers, primarily with Gudrun as the kind of girl who Russell claims would have aspired to be like Duncan: a free soul ousting custom and leaping to artistic heights. She flits about with ballerina gestures in several scenes; Rupert, in contrast, flounces like a clown when situations elude his control. Gerald, the earth father of the group, doesn't dance at all. Rarely does Ursula, who seems to ride along with Gudrun's dreams before derailing into a pudgy, wifely existence.

Beyond this foursome comes a more intriguing oddball: Hermione Roddice, whom Lawrence had based on Lady Ottoline Morrell, a famous society lady from the Bloomsbury circuit and a party-giver who assembled loads of talent under one roof, including the likes of Bertrand Russell and John Maynard Keynes. Hermione's part went to the dark and cerebral Eleanor Bron, who spurned a chance to play Emma Peel in *The Avengers* but looked enigmatic alongside the Beatles as an undercover mystic in Richard Lester's *Help!*

Hermione appears for the first time when discussing phallic botany with Rupert in a classroom. Rupert later reverses the sexual metaphor, embarrassing picnickers with words from a Lawrence poem about "the proper way to eat a fig

Hermione Roddice (Eleanor Bron) leads the dance of "Three Widows."

in society." He compares its "wonderful, moist conductivity towards the center" to the feminine privates. Hermione tries upstaging him by splitting it into four parts to savor the "glittering, rosy, moist, honeyed, heavy-petalled, four-petalled flower," but Rupert prefers "the vulgar way" and attacks it with a single gulp.

"And then the fig has kept her secret long enough," Rupert continues to recite from the Lawrence poem that Russell interpolated into the story, "So it explodes, and you see through the fissure the scarlet/ And the fig is finished, the year is over." Rupert uses the poem as a social weapon against an older woman sensitive enough to want him but too desperate to kick him away.

Rupert gets meaner when Hermione invites everyone to her manse for a "Greek ballet" recital. Liszt's thumping "Marche Funebre" accompanies her, Gudrun, and Ursula as they assume the roles of three widows. The heightened reality, outlandish gestures, and inspired gracelessness are pure Isadora: Hermione gets so carried away with the cadence that her fellow performers, as well as the guests, seem nervous that she might succumb to a paroxysm. But it never happens because Rupert, miffed at being relegated to the role of sheet music turner, cajoles the pianist to pass wind over Hermione's dreams by pounding out some raunchy ragtime.

Russell challenges viewer sympathy. Though she seems pretentious, Hermione makes a genuine if overwrought plea for affection from a man who talks a good game about love but wallows in solipsism. What follows is another example of Russell's moral dares: alone with Hermione, Rupert gives her a half-hearted apology. He then goes on to accuse her of being a power-hungry wench incapable of love; she reacts by grabbing a lapis lazuli paperweight and smashing it against his head. It's a cathartic moment: she nearly kills him, but the sound of Rupert's cracking skull offers delicious and warranted violence.

Isadora Duncan enters the story again when Gudrun and Ursula relax by a lakeside. The occasion is the Crichs' annual picnic, where Gerald's dad, a mining magnate (Alan Webb), placates with free food and booze the drones he exploits the rest of the year. Gudrun and Ursula, unfazed by matters of class or politics, want only to be artistes. So, they drift away from the crowd.

Ursula hums "I'm Forever Blowing Bubbles," while Gudrun propels herself into Duncanesque gyrations. But she breaks her mood when a flock of Highland cattle creep up toward her. "In most of my films I try to do the physically difficult bits first," Russell says with particular emphasis on Jackson's upcoming ordeal, "because it breaks down any preconceived notion the actor may have about his or her solipsist self-importance." Jackson, therefore, had to face the brood right away. The cattle, it turned out, were of a very tame species, which explains why her mad dance eventually scares them. She then falls with exhaustion at the feet of Gerald, who fancies he's arrived just in time to save her.

In the meantime, Russell builds all of the characters' doomed love with a parallel romance between Gerald's sister Laura (Sharon Gurney) and her new husband Tibby Lupton (Christopher Gable). As characters, they aren't allowed much personality: only gushy young paramours who dote on each other and, in their spotless union, unconsciously alienate lonelier onlookers. Their unbounded love proves futile once they go skinny-dipping in a lake and drown. The more reactive than rational Gerald tries plunging into the depths to retrieve them, but his father offers only ridicule. Probably not since James Dean whimpered before his stoic screen dad Raymond Massey in *East of Eden* did a father inflict such a stinging rebuff. From thereon, Gerald's psychological, and perhaps physical, impotence lingers through the story.

But Laura and Tibby's deaths have another meaning. The first time Rupert and Ursula attempt sex, frantically yanking off their clothes as the shaky hand-held camera imitates their pulsing glands, they end up as entwined as the bodies dredged up on the shore. The music is melodramatic and dire, as Russell again pops Rupert's philosophical bubble by making the aftermath of their intercourse seem flaccid and unsatisfying. "Must it be like this?" Birkin asks as they dress and prepare to greet the townsfolk hauling the corpses.

Signaling that Rupert and Ursula are turning into a Laurentian sham, Russell turns later to the gauzy allure of commercials. They approach each other naked and in slow motion: glistening hay (already used to questionable effect in *Elgar*) never looked so shiny, Georges Delerue's string orchestrations never sounded more lilting, and the camera is turned ninety degrees on its side. Even Lawrence's healing fields are not immune to this Russellscopic parody of television ads. One very nasty critic, oblivious to the joke, grumbled that this pastoral vignette "irresistibly suggests a shampoo commercial." This was Russell's point. But like Russell's other wry attempts at "kitsch," the visual effects are so striking that many viewers prefer to relish the cinematography instead of second-guessing his sarcasm.

●

Since the story is ultimately about Rupert's frustrated attempts to make love to Gerald, Russell had to finesse the now-notorious nude wrestling scene—a prelude to Rupert's verbal flirtation to Gerald on "two kinds of love," neither of them platonic. Film scholars and sexual theorists have waxed over the contours, colors, motions, and possibly the scent that this scene evokes. There was certainly never anything like it on the screen before: two males, entirely naked, locked in a combat yet subtly looking as if they're dying to taste each other.

Russell's original idea for the wrestlers was more in keeping with his "shampoo commercial" approach. Gerald and Rupert would be by a stream, locked together in a slow-mo struggle beside the moonlit water. But Reed, by now basking in the international acclaim as the roughhousing villain in *Oliver!*, stayed in character when he rapped on Russell's door one evening in a rage.

Reed threw his machismo weight the first time Russell approached him for the role. Russell, clad in a dandyish coat made of purple velvet, struck Reed as an amusing piece of work. Teasing the director, he noticed Russell's habit of wearing sandals to complement his shock of long hair and started nicknaming him "Jesus." "I know you're in there, Jesus," Reed screamed while pounding at the door of Russell's South Norwood home. "I saw your poofy candles through your poofy lace curtains. If you don't open up, I'll kick your poofy purple front door down."

Russell, trying to relax with Shirley before a warm fire, candlelight, and a plate of spaghetti Bolognese, recognized the terrifying voice. An inebriated Reed, dressed in a dinner jacket and flanked by his current girlfriend, barged through the door. Screaming that he refused to do the poofy wrestling scene "in the poofy moonlight on a river bank" and look like a poof in "a poofy commercial," he insisted that the bout take place, per Lawrence's novel, in the stately indoors—preferably a posh gentleman's hall fraught with trophies and other manly knickknacks.

"It's one thing to get away with it in a book," Russell countered, "and quite another to bring it off on the screen." But before the poofy Jesus could utter another word, Reed proceeded to demonstrate his tough love jujitsu. "And suddenly I was flying across the table, over the candles, and landing by the gas stove," Russell recalls. Prompted by the sound of Shirley's gasp and the potential clatter of smashed dinner china, Russell tried to escape by grabbing for the kitchen door key. But Reed threw him again, this time close to the fireplace.

Presented with an ultimatum—Reed's way or traction—Russell rethought the scene. He gave Reed his posh room—all decorated in gold leaf, an ambiance of shadows, the flicker of a medieval fireplace, and a colorful Edwardian carpet for a wrestling mat. For his part, Reed had to enhance the scene's aesthetics by losing some weight. Russell also prepared Bates for the physical abuse by putting him through judo lessons.

But with the wrestling shoot to illustrate the chapter that Lawrence simply titled "Gladiatorial" finally scheduled, Russell smelled reluctance. The once intrepid Reed now arrived on the closed set with a doctor's certificate that specified a sprained arm. Bates, whom Russell tried loosening up by having him tread naked through fir trees in front of over seventy gawking crewmembers, was only too glad to have "Gladiatorial" postponed. Sensing trouble ahead of time, Russell scheduled a standby scene in case the actors really did get cold feet (and more).

Soon, however, Reed's arm seemed fine, and both arrived on the set mysteriously self-assured. They disrobed, did their manly best, rubbed against each other's birthday suits, and were, as Russell describes them, "proud as peacocks." Russell assumed the lads were both good sports, but he got the real scoop from Reed's stunt man. As it happened, Reed and Bates were worried about who would out-protrude whom. So the stand-in arranged a priapic showdown, taking them to a pub the previous night and getting them soused on vodka. When they got relaxed enough to relieve themselves together in the outside toilet, the moonlight shone where the sun dared not: they at last saw that neither out-gunned the other.

According to Russell, "Oliver even began to make jokes about it, asking the continuity girl to check with a tape measure that nothing had changed between shots." He also claims Reed tried cheating by occasionally going behind a screen, trying to look a bit bigger. But when a blushing continuity girl witnessed him acting as his own fluffer, Reed didn't miss a beat and asked her to bring him a ruler.

The final showdown translates onto film into an encounter even fleshier than Lawrence had envisioned, when he wrote of "the swift, tight limbs, the solid white backs, the physical junction of two bodies clinched into oneness." Reed and Bates become grappling masses of muscle and might, their bodies thumping on the stone floor beneath the rug. They grit their teeth and push against one another yet betray body language suggesting that they yearn (at least for a moment or two) to meld into one man. When it's over, they lie side-by-side, panting and sweating in a similar position to the one Rupert and Ursula assume after their previous limp-noodle love scene.

Gerald soon ruins the fire-light ambiance by turning on an electric lamp—a signal that he does not want Rupert's romantic invitation to go any further. Despite Russell's desire to make it more, as he says, "ambiguous," the scene is unde-niably sexual and more than just "blood brotherhood." Con-sidering how he squealed like a buggered pig over the prospect of kissing another

Wrestlers (Oliver Reed and Alan Bates).

man dressed as a woman in the 1973 film *Triple Echo*, Reed handled Russell's "Gladiatorial" moments with aplomb.

Reed emerged from the three-day shoot with bruises and Bates with a dislo-cated thumb. But they were spared any further mutilation when John Trev-elyan, secretary of the British Board of Film Censors, left the scene intact, even with the male frontals in full view and all of the racy connotations. Trevelyan even described it as "one of the finest scenes I have ever seen in the cinema . . . It is time people adopted a natural attitude to the human body." Distributors also exploited the novelty of two guys depicted in a nude embrace for press releases.

For a man in his position, Trevelyan earned praised from directors like Rus-sell and Joseph Losey for being fair-minded. He determined what was "accept-able" to general public viewing without caving in to ultra-moralists and conser-vative pressure groups. Though he once prematurely stated, "The British people do not like dirty films, and they will never prosper," Trevelyan's tenure repre-sented for many directors a rational approach to an otherwise ghastly job.

In Argentina, however, when the censors got through snipping out the wres-tling, they left just the footage of Bates and Reed shaking hands, Gerald locking the door, and the two of them sweating next to each other on the carpet after the fact. These were excisions that, according to Russell, made the movie seem even more randy. The censors unintentionally attracted a hearty audience willing to line up around the block for "The Great Buggering Scene" that the missing footage implied.

The Reed and Bates match also sets up the story's equally potent cockfight between Reed and Glenda Jackson. In their first love scene, Russell intercuts their passion with quick shots of Gerald's dotty mother (Catherine Willmer) laughing during his father's funeral as she accidentally drops a trowel onto the coffin. Lawrence likened this love scene to a child cleaving to its reluctant and agonized mother's breasts, but Russell makes it more menacing: Mother Crich becomes a mind goblin, tainting her son's erotic urges with guilt as he keeps envisioning her barmy laugh while in Jackson's embrace. The spastic lovemaking turns out to be another dud. Afterward, Gudrun lies stuck under Gerald's spent body, a free spirit resisting his yoke as a clock's death chimes pound away before he finally wakes. A subsequent scene takes their relationship further into the abyss. Gerald responds to Gudrun's taunts with revenge sex, riding her rodeo style as if she were the white horse he gored with his spurs during an earlier exposé of his bestial nature.

On the set, Jackson had all sorts of problems: the stinking cattle, Reed's stinking garlic breath, the stinking cold, and not only Reed's but Russell's sometimes stinking attitude toward actresses and women in general. She also took objection to Lawrence's penchant for female servitude and was incensed when Russell, directing the revenge rape, insisted that she be on the bottom.

Jackson exuded masculine confidence, still reeling from her 1965 performance as Ophelia, for which Penelope Gilliatt, writing in the *Observer*, lauded her as "the first Ophelia I have seen who should play Hamlet." Even though Russell's scene called for her subjugation, she conceived ways of at least seeming physically dominant. "How could a beautiful, feminine girl like you emasculate a tough, rugged character like me?" Reed asked her on the set when his usual bravado failed. According to Jackson's biographer Ian Woodward, "Each recognized the other's strengths and weaknesses, and they maneuvered around each other like two powerful motorboats forced to compete in a narrow, dangerous waterway."

Not content to merely treat his actors as if they were the set furniture's fixtures, Russell also got into spells when he'd wrest control from the cameraman, thinking he would do a better job with a particular shot. Jackson also had to devise brilliant ways to conceal that she was pregnant during most of the shoot, even though her naked breasts in one scene appear to be in the ripening phase. She more or less gives it away when the narrative jumps to the Swiss Alps, and she lies in the snow after careening with Gerald, Rupert, and Ursula on a toboggan.

The story's switch to Switzerland is arguably the most intriguing part of the film. Here they meet up with Loerke, a homosexual German sculptor Vladek Sheybal plays to perfection. Loerke is the kind of ambiguous character who shows up in other Russell films: a deviant according to dull convention who, at least on the surface, seems a bit sinister. But like Hermione, he is the kind of outsider for whom Russell harbors empathy, and the character with whom Russell may secretly identify most. Loerke is the one who makes the most sense and seems to have a more solid view on the world. He also appears to have the keener perceptions about the people he meets, primarily Gerald, whom he regards as a gangly fool.

Loerke may seem played out and pretentious at first, but as his presence grows, he appears to be an artist in his social interactions as well as his craft. He is a catalyst, the only character strong enough to demonstrate how far apart Gudrun and Ursula have grown. When he invites the sisters up to his Swiss chalet to look at some of his artwork, Loerke shows off his equally enigmatic boyfriend Herr Leitner (Richard Heffer), who greets them naked from under the bed sheets. Leitner is very quiet and smiles with a knowing air as Loerke argues with Ursula about her pedestrian notions of art. He also wears his sexual deviance with pride, but Ursula responds with a smirk, rejecting Loerke along with his neoclassical notions of sculpture. Gudrun, however, is more sympathetic and finds in Loerke a soul mate.

Soon Russell takes the narrative into his comfortable world of manic music and exaggerated mannerisms that again recalls *Isadora*. When Gudrun and Loerke play dress up, in a scene based on Lawrence's reference about how they would get together and play at make believe like "marionettes," Russell also provides a coming attraction

Loerke (Vladek Sheybal) and his boyfriend Herr Leitner (Richard Heffer).

for his next feature film. Adorned with Cleopatra makeup and bobbing behind a phallic bedpost, Jackson is already playing Nina, Tchaikovsky's flustered wife in *The Music Lovers*, and Loerke is Tchaikovsky, grinding the composer's *Pathetique* Symphony on a gramophone. Loerke mimics the motions of the Trans-Siberian Express, where Russell will soon film Tchaikovsky gasping at Nina's naked body on their fateful honeymoon: the occasion when the composer's homosexuality is immutable and his love for his wife impossible.

In the meantime Gerald, unable to love either Gudrun or Rupert, takes a cheap shot by punching Loerke in the face and nearly strangling Gudrun to death. Dazed and wanting rest, he wanders into the forbidding snow for his eternal sleep. Gerald dying in the snow and an essentially unfazed Gudrun preparing to go off with Loerke to Dresden is a much more effective ending than the one Russell claims the initial script specified, when a fiercely independent Gudrun gallops with Gerald's white horse into the sunset.

Russell instead freezes on Ursula's shocked reaction when Rupert reiterates his claim that there are "two kinds of love." The ending implies that Ursula, with her baking and her knitting, is still not going to live quite as normally she had expected.

Gerald (Oliver Reed) and Gudrun (Glenda Jackson) have their final row.

Such critics as England's Alexander Walker and America's Judith Crist, who would go on to hate other Russell offerings, embraced *Women in Love*. Those who might later puke at *The Devils* took comfort in *Women in Love*'s humanistic touches, even though the movie, like the book, is fraught with doom.

More skittish critics expressed disdain. Pauline Kael used it to begin an ongoing tirade against Russell in *The New Yorker*, claiming that Russell's film "is purple because his idea of art is purple pastiche" and griping that "the experience of it is rather like Lawrence's accounts of bad sex."

Through the years, Kael's vendetta against Russell would become an ongoing gag, but others with nicer intentions probably goaded the director to get more outrageous. "Mr. Russell," John Coleman wrote in the *New Statesman*, "whose hazardous creations I continue to watch with close attention, sometimes appears not to care what he does as long as it's affecting. You might say he goes straight to the meat of the pathos. He should stop this."

If he even read Coleman's review, Russell obviously didn't take his advice. Many of his subsequent films made *Women in Love* seem tame and quaint. It might be considered among the films that English professors proudly show their students or that the more staid members of Britain's cinema establishment embrace. This is odd because Lawrence's inner struggle between sensual and spiritual halves complements the spasmodic, writhing style Russell would perfect in subsequent features. Jackson's winning the Best Actress Oscar and Russell's Best Director nomination legitimized *Women in Love*'s mainstream appeal even more.

In 1999, the British Film Institute tallied the results of a poll from directors, writers, distributors, critics, and others in the country's film and television industry to determine their favorite British movies of the twentieth century. *Women in Love* emerged on the BFI's Top 100 list. Russell finds the subsequent accolades bewildering because he doesn't count it among his very best films.

•

Women in Love's homosexual subtext has often either evaded or threatened the sensibilities of past Russell scholars. Joseph Gomez is anxious to "dispel any label of homosexuality which some viewers might attach to Gerald's relationship to Rupert." The Reverend Gene Phillips is also complicit in hiding behind Russell's statement (made at an earlier time) that "this is not a plea for a homosexual relationship." Instead, Russell uses phrases like "intimate relationship with each other that is different from, but which nevertheless complements, the heterosexual relationship that each has in his marriage" that sound too mealy-mouthed.

Ana Laura Zambrano also wrote something about symbols of "the feminine ideal" haunting the two men in mirrors so carefully placed on the set to surround them. For her, the reflections are like ghosts, "silently repudiating his philosophy until at least Rupert's own mirrored reflection epitomizes the futility of his search." There's at least one other way of interpreting the mirrors, however. Conceivably by having the two men inundated by their own reflections after the wrestling match, Russell hints there is deception afoot: what only seems to be a "normal" friendship between two men could have a deeper, erotic, maybe even more spiritual dimension, for which the women are mere distractions.

Movie critics see what they want to see; unfortunately, those hostile to homosexual love, especially between two men, have ruled the roost for too long. Their tenure is over! Why all the denial? Why are those on the cockblocker bandwagon so desperate to keep these two chaps from getting it on with one another either atop the Edwardian rug or in the Technicolor-ish hay? *Women in Love* longs for a healthier, less homo-hostile reading—one that understands how Rupert's search was futile only because the guy he wanted was a dunce incapable of reciprocating.

Penguin Books published an edition of *Women in Love* that contains a "Prologue," consisting of text that D. H. Lawrence intended for the first two chapters but removed. He might have felt pressured over misgivings that that book was, as he stated in a letter on May 1916, "beyond all hope of being published, because of the things it says." Much of it focuses on what he calls the "subterranean kindling" between Birkin and Gerald and is upfront about the story's beyond-platonic overtones. "They scarcely knew each other," Lawrence wrote of their meeting at a Derbyshire country house, "yet here was this strange, unacknowledged, inflammable intimacy between them. It made them uneasy."

Lawrence's Birkin has a spiritual regard for women, but men augment his spirit with a "hot, flushing, roused attraction":

> Why did not the face of a woman move him in the same manner, with the same sense of handsome desirability, as the face of a man? Why was a man's beauty, the beauté mâle, so vivid and intoxicating a thing to him, whilst female beauty was something quite unsubstantial, consisting all of look and gesture and revelation of intuitive intelligence? He thought women beautiful purely because of their expression. But it was plastic form that fascinated him in men, the contour and movement of the flesh itself.

When the DVD came out in 2003, Russell, after spending so much time straddling the fence over Rupert's message to Gerald, at last fessed up to the movie's ultimate theme when he closed his audio commentary: "People have said the film could be called 'Men in Love'; it equally could have been."

SONGS OF SUPERMAN

"Thus spoke Zarathustra," Nietzsche wrote, "and he left his cave, glowing and strong like a morning sun coming out of gloomy mountains." And so did Ken Russell ascend to the hills of his precious Lake District in the spring of 1969, his eyes glinting and hair flowing as he greeted the throng that gathered for the chance to be in his next television production, which he planned to shoot on the location in the summer.

> "I can't reconcile such hardness with such lovely music."
>
> —Eric Fenby, from *Song of Summer*

"Really, it's rather naughty to wear your hair on your shoulders at that age," someone exclaimed. Russell was true to the "Wild Man of the BBC" sobriquet as he speedily jotted down the names and addresses while Shirley measured for costume fittings the aspiring monks, nuns, nymphs, and Nazis. The film, *The Dance of the Seven Veils*, subtitled *A Comic Strip in Seven Episodes on the Life of Richard Strauss, 1864–1949*, would be Russell's next—and for quite some time last—BBC endeavor.

With bold strokes, Russell now refused to be respectable. He instead opted to do the anti-*Elgar*: a study in absolute caricature about a composer whose music he considered "bombastic, sham, and hollow." *Dance of the Seven Veils* portrays Strauss (Christopher Gable) as a chauvinist, narcissist, and appeaser, who ambled blithely through the First World War and then helped instigate events leading to the second by toadying up to the Third Reich.

Most of Russell's BBC docudramas mixed facts with speculation, but *Dance of the Seven Veils* plunges headlong into Henri Gaudier's "necessary exaggeration of the facts which helps to secure greater truth." He starts with Strauss conducting his famed tone poem *Thus Spoke Zarathustra*, based on Nietzsche's book, in the same silhouette that Disney used for Leopold Stokowski and Mickey Mouse in *Fantasia*. This is, however, the mild and stately part of the film. Soon Russell depicts Strauss as Nietzsche's Zarathustra, galumphing from the cave not as some Superman but as a Teutonic troglodyte, greeting the morning sun and confronting self-flagellating monks. Amid shouts of "Save them from their savior," Zarathustra is soon bound with rosaries while a gaggle of lecherous nuns molests him.

Poor Nietzsche. He'll always be tarred with Hitler's brush. Nietzsche's Superman (or Overman) was really meant to be a lonely soul, what Nietzsche called "the lightning out of the dark cloud of man," who overcomes earthly limitations and survives the death of God. But Russell presents the Overman as an underworld denizen, which many Nietzsche enthusiasts might call slander.

As Strauss conducts from a giant podium, Hitler (Kenneth Colley) seduces crowds with grand hand gestures. He also rides on Strauss's shoulders while the composer fiddles away. But Russell isn't content to make Strauss a Nazi by association; he also makes him a Nazi with a foot fetish who removes a strumpet's shoes and stockings before nibbling.

Now Russell's beautiful Skiddaw mountains are the backdrop to a combination of a Tyrolean utopia out of *The Sound of Music* and a Nazi picnic that accompanies Strauss's "Alpine Symphony." The sparkling Lodore Falls ejaculates behind Strauss and his white tunic–clad water sprites, while a harlot in a bright red wig reclines on a rock before doing another of Russell's prized Isadora Duncan impressions.

When the time arrives to play Strauss's "Domestic Symphony," Russell steps to the podium to conduct the orchestra, craning his neck to look below as Mr. and Mrs. Strauss thump in synch to the coming climax on their nuptial bed. But when Strauss conducts his *Rosenkavalier* to a silent movie, he commands the players to get louder and louder to drown out the screams as S.S. officers slice a star of David into an old Jew's chest.

As he filmed all this, Russell, like Zarathustra, beheld the multitudes, but he felt no glory. The summer

Strauss (Christopher Gable) carrying the weight of the Third Reich (Kenneth Colley) in *The Dance of the Seven Veils*.

weather in the Cumberland region was damp, rainy, and windy. He also felt ever lonely and misunderstood: such dismay, such unrest, and such a bunch of chronic complainers!

Phillipa Reid, a theater worker and wife of the poet David Wright, organized the auditions for this small rural area by getting word to an art college. Amateur actors, schoolgirls from a youth club, farmers, and hippies rolled in; not long afterward, Reid started hearing stories: "They've been shooting a religious orgy today," one of the participants shouted to her over the phone. "Nuns going berserk and raping monks. Nothing left to the imagination!"

"It's been dreary," bleated another actor. "We've spent twelve hours freezing in blouses and knee socks, marking up a mountain, shouting Sieg something or other."

"The most unprofessional bloody lot I've ever come across," yet another griped. "The makeup was this latex stuff. I was supposed to have been horribly wounded . . . I asked the makeup girl if this tomato ketchup had a name, and she said it was the very latest thing in blood. 'In fact,' she said, 'you're the first person we've tried it on . . . We call it Kensington Gore.'"

In the script, a cow was to be slaughtered. Russell and the crew planned to use a live one but kept a carcass on standby. Realizing the bovines were not the same color, the property man had to tint the dead one. But, as a sardonic Reid recalls, the live cow also posed a problem: "When the sacrificial blade was put to her throat, she may have been uncertain how far the entertainment industry went on these occasions. She wasn't going to risk it. She reared back, charged the director, and kicked his regulation canvas seat smartly from under him."

This slapstick surrealism surrounding *The Dance of the Seven Veils'* production ultimately nourished the movie's look and spirit. "I am eaten up with the image, with the way things look," Russell would say whenever confronted with questions about his motivation. But some mainstream critics cackled when Russell confronted them with a mere fifty-five minutes of edgy camp that made Fellini seem an underachiever by comparison.

John Baxter, who early in the 1970s managed to write what is some of the very best Russell criticism, states that Russell "attacks Elgar and Strauss for their subservience to the establishment, because he sees in himself the capacity to become what they were, obedient entertainers, and abominates the TV commercial rat race and Strauss's Nazism because the former's blunt visual assault and Strauss's barbaric emotionalism, like that of Leni Riefenstahl, strike a responsive chord all too easy to heed."

Were he to film them again, Russell would have made his earlier docudramas less laudatory. He told Gene D. Phillips: "My first biographical films on TV coincided with the textbook idea of what such a film should be: you were supposed to extol the great artists and their work, and I did this in my film about the composer Edward Elgar, for example. . . . Deification of the artist is wrong. He should be presented as a human being who, despite his faults, managed to create lasting works of art."

●

Russell had seemed so much more subdued in 1968, just before making *Women in Love*, when he directed *Song of Summer*, a BBC film about another Nietzsche enthusiast, the British composer Frederick Delius. Christopher Gable as Delius's meek assistant Eric Fenby was an extreme contrast to his overweening Strauss.

Song of Summer's very first image (cut out of the DVD release because of rights problems) is of Fenby playing the organ for a silent cinema showing a Laurel and Hardy movie—a job he likely considered grunt work. Perhaps to escape the grind, he turns Delius into an obsession. When he learns that Delius is blind and paralyzed, Fenby racks his brain thinking of ways to aid him. He finally writes to offer his services and arranges to visit him in his home outside of Paris, where he becomes the composer's amanuensis, copying down his final three compositions.

Fenby enters Delius's home, forewarned as he encounters a large portrait of Nietzsche on the wall. He finds that Delius (Max Adrian), the man who wrote such lovely music, is a temperamental codger and a petty Superman browbeating everyone around him. He barks orders to his servants and is at times cruel to his self-sacrificing wife Jelka (Maureen Pryor), who irritates Fenby with eccentricities of her own.

"In fact I did write a scenario years before on Delius, not including Fenby, but it was really a rather boring story," Russell claimed in the early 1970s. "Also I think a lot of his music, though it has moments of great beauty, is second-rate. But Fenby and Delius together is another story. It's a love affair and a death affair; it's one personality feeding on another and being destroyed for his trouble."

Delius greets Fenby cordially, but the atmosphere gets pricklier, at times forbidding, as the composer closes in on his newest victim with emotional and physical demands. Delius is petty, petulant, mercurial, and continually subject to spasms of pain. Walking is impossible, a bedpan is ever-present, and a mere pillow crease is like a needle sting.

Worse, Delius opines about everything from the plight of English music to the sham behind all religions—especially Christianity. When Fenby mentions some of the great symphonic masters, Delius retorts: "Beethoven, Bruckner, Mahler, and that lot with their long, driveling note spinnings—a complete waste of time." The composer also sounds unbearably patronizing when crowing about how he "got on very well with the Negroes" whose spirituals inspired him during a pilgrimage to Florida.

Throughout *Song of Summer*, Russell stresses personalities trapped in close quarters—a house full of anxiety as intense as the painting of Edvard Munch's *Scream* that adorns Fenby's guest room. Russell intensifies the claustrophobic atmosphere by using more than his usual number of close-ups. *The Dance of the Seven Veils* had been Russell's first chance to do a BBC production in color, so to complement what he saw as Strauss's cartoonish sensibility, he opted for vibrant, garish hues. But here, he uses the black and white to his advantage. Cinematographer Dick Bush bathes the indoor scenes in a stark monochrome, with the characters cramped in white rooms.

Russell was at one point going to film a sequence of the young Delius celebrating spring blossom time with a naked girl in the Lake District, but he instead shifted the narrative focus to Fenby, a recent Catholic convert, who soon discovers that Delius is a pagan pos-

Christopher Gable as the sensitive Eric Fenby in *Song of Summer*.

sessed. He bristles as Delius expectorates such Nietzschean notions as "English music will never be any good until they get rid of Jesus." The susceptible Fenby sweats, cries, and almost throws himself in front of a speeding train to end the pressure. Somehow he survives, but even years afterward he's damaged.

All the while, Russell reminds viewers that Delius's bouts of genius, and Fenby's struggle to record them, are hard work. But for Fenby, the hardness of his idol's personality dominates the plot, especially when a mysterious neighbor (Geraldine Sherman), and later Jelka herself, fills him in on the lecherous monster Delius used to be when he had control of his limbs: his orgies with Parisian strumpets, the subsequent abortions, and how Jelka finally won him as a husband when his ailing condition made it too late for any true romance. Fenby gets the final blow when he later finds out that Delius is blind and crippled from syphilis.

Russell adds some comic relief when the composer Percy Grainger (David Collings) drops by, and his famous, jaunty melody "Country Gardens" commands the soundtrack. Grainger throws tennis balls, pushes Delius's wheelchair at heartrending speeds, and tries making his invalid pal lighten up. But even this trickster faces Delius's dark demons when Russell flashes years back: Grainger, Jelka, and a Norseman have to lug Delius on a seven-hour hike up a Norway mountain, just so he could look at his final sunset before losing all sight.

This interlude shows how Delius's artistic whims drained all those around him. Russell's slow zoom on Delius's maniacal stare atop that Norwegian hill shows a Nietzsche-style Superman in all his inspired madness—and with three sacrificial victims dreading the task of taking him back down from the precipice. "If you ever get away from here," Grainger tells Fenby, "you'll never want to hear another note of Delius as long as you live."

Russell, aping his petulant subject, took the wind out of the cast's sails by making them do this scene early on. "If they're cold and walking through slush and mud," Russell boasted, "it humiliates them a little and shows them they're at the mercy of the elements, and of me." Carrying the onus of his crushed ideals from film to film, Russell makes *Song of Summer* more complicated and more engaging when he projects himself into Fenby. He even shows up in another choice cameo: this time as a priest making out with some floozy on a pew—much to Fenby's chagrin when he witnesses the event after seeking solace in the nearby church.

Even when his transcribing job with Delius is over, and he's back at home trying to enjoy a party among friends, Fenby can't get his mind off the ordeal and stands amid the revelry alone: a sweating wallflower. "To me this is a very frightening sequence," Russell reflects more than forty years after the film's broadcast. "I can identify with Fenby here. He feels just like I felt: every party I'd ever been to when I was his age, standing with a glass in your hand, hoping no one will notice you."

Russell based much of his script on Fenby's 1928 book *Delius as I Knew Him* and from additional tidbits he loosened from the author over wine. He was so faithful to both the text and the subsequent recollections that Fenby sobbed one day when he came to the set, moved at how Russell was so keen on exacerbating old sores.

"Shortly after it was shown," Russell later recalls of Fenby's reaction, "he had a nervous breakdown, one symptom of which was a complaint that made his skin come out in sores at the slightest touch. He couldn't put on any clothes and couldn't go out of the house for a year after seeing the film. I brought back all his feelings about Delius, and what working for him had done to his life."

When writing about the film for *Harper's* in early 1971, Richard Schickel called *Song of Summer* "the best dramatic television program I've ever seen." He pointed out how Russell's Delius invites disturbing questions about the conflict between art and love that Thomas Mann asked of his composer Adrian Leverkühn in *Doctor Faustus*: "What Mann states explicitly, Russell restates implicitly: genius, even more talent, often presents itself as preoccupation, requiring of the artist possessed by it constant worrying and nursing, the kind of endless care paradoxically analogous to what a parent must lavish on a retarded child. The artist may make an enormous contribution to the humane tradition, but only at the cost of his own humanity."

•

Dance of the Seven Veils aired on February 15, 1970, starting with a very British, understated BBC disclaimer: "It has been described as a harsh and at times violent caricature of the life of the composer. . . . This is a personal interpretation by Ken Russell of certain real and many imaginary events in the composer's life."

None of this mattered. Parliament still assembled to introduce a motion to condemn the BBC for showing it, with a twenty-Tory chorus shouting such epithets as "viciousness, savagery, and brutality." Other reactions were predictably fierce. "It was as if a man was being destroyed before the eyes of millions," James Thomas grumbled in the *Daily Express*. George Melly in the the *Observer Review* accused him of using Strauss "as an excuse for a baroque exercise in outrage, while at the same time faking a serious purpose." Peter Heyworth, in the same paper, called it "posthumous character assassination of the meanest and most unscrupulous sort."

Nietzsche, in book 3 of *Thus Spoke Zarathustra*, asks, "Who among you can laugh and be elevated at the same time?" Russell also wished his audience could have chuckled more and heckled less. "Those who were offended by it took the film much too literally," Russell explains in a 1970 interview with *Film Comment*. "It was meant to work on a deep symbolic level. For example, in order to get across the fact that Richard Strauss was uninterested in the Second World War because it didn't touch him personally, I presented a dream sequence in which Strauss is forced to watch his wife raped and his child murdered by the Nazis."

The BBC, afraid it had debased its reputation, staged a television panel discussion, giving vent to moralizers on an anti-Russell crusade. One of them was Mary Whitehouse, an outspoken bluenose who had already launched her Clean Up TV campaign back in 1964. "Mary Whitehouse wanted to sue me," Russell recalls to John C. Tibbetts. "She found she could only sue the land cable transmitting the program. Then Huw Wheldon made a speech defending the film and my right to say what I felt. That was a great moment."

An angry reader also responded to Phillipa Reid's account in *The Listener* about the tribulations of making the film: "According to Mr. Russell, who seems to take his role as a social critic very seriously, Richard Strauss 'was a very vulgar person, culturally and socially.' Such an insignificant pot to blacken so great a kettle." As for Reid, the movie seemed to offend her less than the snub Russell gave to a local music club's invitation to give a talk about it, especially since he sent his refusal on "a very long, very narrow sheet of paper completely covered by a lithograph of a naked black girl."

Forget the critics: the Strauss film's biggest casualty occurred when Russell lost his BBC job. The second setback was Strauss's outraged son, who imposed an embargo that forbade his father's music from ever accompanying future screenings. Unfortunately, Russell's first color television production was fated to show only one time. Years later, when he included snippets of it on the *South Bank Show*, he had to settle for *Johann* Strauss as the background score. As recently as September 2005, the film got withdrawn from a scheduled showing at the Rotterdam Philharmonic Orchestra's Gergiev Festival. This will not change until 2019, when the Strauss family's copyright protection expires. Fortunately, the Museum of the Moving Image in Astoria, New York, screened it in the fall of 2004 at a Russell retrospective (which this author attended), without incident and to an appreciative audience.

For a film rarely seen, *The Dance of the Seven Veils* has resonated through the years. Some, in Europe especially, caught glimpses of the film in bootleg form. Rainer Maria Fassbinder might have seen it, since the mark of Russell, especially this film, informs his delirious, solipsistic epilogue to the 1980 television series *Berlin Alexanderplatz* entitled "My Dream of Franz Biberkopf's Dream." The scenes of Biberkopf roaming like a lost soul in the afterlife are so Russell. As Teutonic angels in fiberglass blond wigs taunt him, Biberkopf watches as a rabbi holds a rosary and makes the sign of the cross; a grim reaper wields a cleaver and, to an aria from Wagner's *Tristan and Isolde*, hacks away at a pile of naked bodies in a slaughterhouse. Biberkopf's downfall climaxes with a crucifixion and an atom bomb exploding to the beat of Glenn Miller's "In the Mood."

"*The Dance of the Seven Veils* was something I badly wanted to do," Russell said while the controversy was still dying down, "and is a good example of the sort of film that could never be made outside the BBC, because the lawyers would be on it in two seconds. . . . The great thing about the BBC is that the quickness of the hand deceives the eye. Before anyone can complain, the film is out. But the price you pay with a really controversial film is that it's usually only shown once."

A BUNDLE OF TORTURED NERVES

"He is pigheaded, self-indulgent, arrogant, masochistic," the late Imogen Claire once said of Ken Russell to *Time* magazine. "But I like working with him more than anyone else." Claire was confident about taking such affectionate liberties when summarizing Russell's persona because he allowed her to play some of his more eccentric character parts, including her uncredited cameo debut in *The Music Lovers*.

In this film about Russell's romantic hero Tchaikovsky, Claire is a mysterious woman in white, likely a streetwalking courtesan, who appears just as the great composer tries to kill himself. Suffering a creative drought and regretting his loveless marriage, Tchaikovsky tries submerging himself in the Moskva River but ends up standing in the cold water only knee deep.

As the plaintive strains of his String Quartet no. 3 pervade the soundtrack, Claire strolls by with her leashed poodle, glaring back at him with a mocking grin. At this vulnerable moment, Claire's character becomes an ominous everywoman, reminding him of the mother he has lost, the wife he can't stand, and, since she's made up to look a bit like a female impersonator, the fey man he abandoned to pursue a phony "normal" life.

This was a typically arduous scene from Russell's tribute to the man whose Piano Concerto no. 1 in B-flat Minor once lifted him out of a mental breakdown. Russell's dream film about Nijinsky for United Artists never happened, but he finally got a chance to snatch the Tchaikovsky carrot that the studio had been dangling all along. He pitched the movie to the studio by appropriating a line from author Gerald Abraham's 1945 Tchaikovsky biography, which described the composer's fate as the "marriage of a homosexual to a nymphomaniac."

Tchaikovsky personified for Russell all of the beauty and horror of nine-teenth-century romanticism: the zeal for ideal love, the dolor of daily existence, and the inevitable obsession with death and self-immolation. "People call me self-indulgent," Russell said while defending *The Music Lovers'* lunatic approach, "but he was the most self-indulgent man who ever lived, insofar as all his problems and hang-ups are stated in his music. Some might say overstated but then they never experienced what he went through and wouldn't have the guts to put it down on paper even if they had. . . . His music, to me, has more pain in it than any music I know: self-inflicted pain, despair, suffering, precious little joy, and a kind of hysterical striving for love, a love so intense it could never exist."

Despite adoring his subject, Russell, the so-called pigheaded masochist with a penchant for deflating his own ideals, made no attempt to fete his idol with a stately and sterile Hollywood approach. Russell instead treated Tchaikovsky like a cruel headmaster. He subjected him to the cinematic equivalent of a caning and a hazing. There are no lovable characters, clear-cut morals, or signs of hope: instead, Russell lets his narrative implode with passion, violence, and darkness.

∎

Russell was aware that Dmitri Tiomkin had already made a return pilgrimage to the Soviet Union to score and act as executive producer for a Tchaikovsky film directed by Igor Talankin and released in 1969. Sanctioned with the Soviet imprimatur, this 153-minute exercise in tedium demonstrates the hazards of a censored history: a script full of stilted dialogue and pointless buggy rides. The actor playing Tchaikovsky registers zero charisma: a face condemned to lifeless portraiture, with never a hair out of place—even after he tries to drown himself.

Russell, of course, hated Talankin's stiff, respectable rendition. Years later, after his own version sparked controversy, Russell vented when traveling to the U.S.S.R. on a visit to the Tchaikovsky Museum in Klin. "I was curious to see the house in which Peter Ilyich spent the last unhappy years of his life," Russell recalls. "We saw Tchaikovsky's samovar, his antimacassars, and pictures of his mum and dad. We heard about the happy marriage and the medals he'd won but never as much as a breath of scandal which might tarnish such a highly polished ikon of the people . . . There were no pictures of pretty male bottoms to corrupt the young pioneers."

When Russell asked to see a picture of Tchaikovsky's lover Prince Alexei, the Intourist guide glared at him through spectacles. Russell re-creates the ensuing dialogue in his autobiography:

"Who?"

"Prince Alexei, Tchaikovksy's boyfriend."

"I know Sandy Wilson's *Boy Friend*. I never heard of this Prince Alexei."

"So you've never heard of the scandal surrounding Tchaikovsky's death?"

He shrugged indifferently. "How can scandal help us appreciate the work of a great artist?"

"*The Music Lovers* turned a lot of people onto Tchaikovsky," I replied. "If I hadn't told United Artists that it was a story about a homosexual who fell in love with a nymphomaniac it might never have been financed."

"And one of our greatest composers would still be resting peacefully in his grave," he said.

"One of your greatest composers quite admired it," I replied.

"Which composer?"

"Shostakovich. He saw it in England after the first performance of his Fourth Symphony. The one you banned for thirty years."

The guide's face darkened . . . "You hate Tchaikovsky," he spat back.

"No, I love him, but my love isn't blind."

"You telescope events and characters," he continued. "You turn his life into a frenzied carnival, all highs and lows, no moments of reflection and tranquility."

The Intourist guide was at least partly right about the scant "moments of reflection and tranquility." In *The Music Lovers* (initially called *The Lonely Heart*), moments of peace and harmless child's play are mere appetizers leading to the meatier horror. The point of the film is to show that Tchaikovsky's music—turbulent pianos, fluttering violins, and blaring trumpets—were not just hatched out of a vacuum; his art reflected a life fraught with insecurity and terror. And Tchaikovsky's homosexuality, far from being some unmentionable peccadillo, was the centerpiece in an internal and external war.

•

As with many of his subjects, Russell read bits of himself in Tchaikovsky: the flights of fancy, the temperament, and the striving for artistic integrity against people who never create and only conspire. *The Music Lovers* might seem a gross distortion of facts, but Russell and screenwriter Melvyn Bragg (who co-wrote

Debussy) were fairly faithful to their main source: *Beloved Friend*, the biography by Catherine Drinker Bowen and Barbara von Meck, wife of the grandson of Tchaikovsky's benefactress Nadejda von Meck.

Russell's alternately violet and violent directing mirrors the book's purple prose and fierce, romantic obsessions. Bowen's preface alone stirs the tempest: "If ever there was a living man, a man above all else human, a sinner, struggling, sweating, trembling in the ecstasy of too-sensitive nerves—forever worrying, forever repenting, filled with a furious remorse that required but one sleep to turn again to impulse and more trouble—that man was Peter Ilyich."

Published in 1937, at a time when Hollywood and the world suppressed such matters, Bowen's book got critically pilloried, mostly for a single sin: she put the composer's core conflict front and center. "Peter Ilyich was a homosexual," she writes. "This fact has hitherto been strangely ignored or covered up by his biographers; we exhume it, not to rattle the old bones of scandal but because it was in truth the very structure and architecture of the man's personality."

Judging from Bowen's sources, Tchaikovsky really was an artist driven by inner demons; he really did show slavish devotion to his mother, a future cholera victim; he had several male lovers but, as Bowen states, "recklessly denied his own nature." He whored for convention by marrying the man-crazy Nina Milyukova; he had a quasi-incestuous attachment to his sister; and his brother, who was also homosexual, tutored deaf and dumb kids, and did all he could to stir Peter Ilych to the spoils of a conducting career.

As in the film, Tchaikovsky jumped into a shallow river (presumably to induce pneumonia and not drown) and knowingly drank a glass of unboiled water during a cholera epidemic. He also really kept an obsessive correspondence with his benefactress Madame Nadejda von Meck, a jaded and moody widow. Desperate for Meck's approval, he feared she might find out about the erotic proclivities that he timorously referred to as "The."

The composer was, as Bowen describes, "a bundle of tortured nerves . . . flighty emotionally and liable to the wildest excitement over nothing." Russell agrees: "His music is absolutely hysterical because he had to hide the fact that he was homosexual; if he didn't, he'd be drummed out of nineteenth-century society. Well, this obviously comes out in his music, great music, but music of suffering, pain, and torment, and this very placid-looking gentleman who smiles out of his benign beard from these faded photographs is a mask for the torment . . . and it was obviously crashing around inside him."

Russell also re-creates what Bowen refers to as his "apoplectic symptoms." *The Music Lovers* beats to a neurotic rhythm, providing a cinematic counterpart to Tchaikovsky's many ailments: at least one nervous breakdown, troubled sleep, nocturnal trembling, what he called "heart cramps," intestinal spasms, dysentery, hallucinations, anxiety attacks, hypochondria, fevers, the urge to scream, the sensation of knives digging into his feet, and the feeling that his head would roll off at any moment. Russell lets his subject's sweeping musical furies mirror the inner storm—all conducted to perfection by Andre Previn with the London Symphony Orchestra.

Bowen chronicles Tchaikovsky's frantic letters, almost all of them to Meck, but since she depends on his correspondence with the woman spared all of Tchaikovsky's amorous details, readers must only imagine the life the composer led with his various lovers. Russell, taking a more exploratory approach, uses rollercoaster editing in the film's first scenes to show that Peter Ilych (Richard Chamberlain) and his boyfriend Anton Chiluvsky (Christopher Gable) had some exhilarating times together.

Most of the others who cavort around them at a street fair seem either miserable or courting danger: the dazzling and terrifying peasants breaking into dance, the Russian officers marching in lockstep, the gaggle of horny men pumping booze into a gypsy trollop. But Peter and Anton are oblivious to all of this. The rest of the world be damned: this opening sequence is one of precious few times the composer is noticeably happy. Russell's camera races with the frantic rhythms of *The Nutcracker*'s "Dance of the Clowns" as Peter and his mate plunge down an ice slide, romp about in puckish costumes, and scramble back home to conk out arm-in-arm on the master bed.

Tchaikovsky's family burdens him with worries from the start. His brother Modeste (Kenneth Colley) is especially fretful that Peter's relationship might be causing a scandal. Peter lugs this psychic baggage as he trudges over to the Moscow Conservatory to give a debut recital of his Piano Concerto no. 1 in B-flat Minor. The fact that Russell decides to complement the piece that has such a positive personal connection with "shampoo commercial" camp shows how, in his best films, he almost schizophrenically debunks the romantic Eden that a part of him still wishes he could attain.

Douglas Slocombe's cinematography looks so glossy and beautiful yet seethes with irony as Tchaikovsky plays the first movement while lapsing into a pastoral daydream. He imagines himself threshing through Elysian fields of wheat, relishing a glass of water (an augury of doom) that his loving sister Sasha (Sabine Maydelle) brings to him. Choreographer Terry Gilbert, whom Russell befriended years before when they performed together in a summer production of *Swan Lake* at an Eastbourne pier, has Tchaikovsky and kin improvise their own gawky little ballet by a lake that is, of course, embellished with swans.

As Russell told the *New York Times* in 1972, "*The Music Lovers* was not so much the story of Tchaikovsky as it was a black comedy about the decadence of romanticism . . . The core of the film is the destructive force of dreams, particularly on reality. The television adman's trick of passing off his dream as an attainable and desirable reality is to my mind the great tragedy of our age." But Russell and Slocombe film these sequences so superbly that beauty still seeps through the ironic filters.

Russell hasn't always been consistent with his "television adman's trick." Sometimes the irony is even less apparent. Years later, his *Vaughan Williams: A Symphonic Portrait*, which aired in April 1984 for England's *South Bank Show*, attempts to capture the composer's pastoral simplicity by having violinist Iona Brown take a slo-mo stroll through floral fields while playing a solo of "The Lark Ascending." Here is an instance when Russell indulges in eye candy that he sometimes calls ironic and other times lyrical.

Nina Milyukova (Glenda Jackson) is also present in the audience, not to hear Tchaikovsky but to follow her latest love interest—a beady-eyed Russian hussar (Ben Aris). As the concerto's second movement begins, Russell crosscuts Tchaikovsky's reverie with Nina's fantasies. She imagines speeding with her soldier in a carriage, gorging on champagne, and sneaking off into the woods for a quickie before snagging him at the altar.

Madame von Meck (Iza Teller) arrives late, but this is the performance that makes Tchaikovsky the focus of her empty life. She too feels emotional storms as Tchaikovsky elides into his third movement. Russell shifts back to the composer's thoughts: Chiluvsky and sister Sasha—two loves in his life—walk away and leave him stranded. His premonitions of solitude intensify as Russell zooms in on the ambiguous, if not slightly sinister, faces of Sasha, Chiluvsky, Meck, and Nina—each one a strain on the composer's lonely heart.

Tchaikovsky's instructor Nicholas Rubinstein, whom Max Adrian portrays with abrasive relish, is petulant and patronizing. When the concerto is over, Rubinstein mans the piano and pounds away in mockery before lashing out: "I really can't see why you bother to write it. Or perhaps one or two pages are worth saving, but the rest might just as easily be destroyed . . . It's not only trivial; it's bad, vulgar, women's stuff . . . I'm not altogether surprised, you know, a man who's as careless about his private behavior as you are is hardly likely to be much more scrupulous in his work. You're in danger of falling apart, my boy, and your music shows it."

His professor's effrontery is mild compared to what Peter experiences at one of Rubinstein's parties. He hears sweet operatic trills from another part of the house. The song, with the aid of a childhood flashback, is the same one his mother sang alongside him as he accompanied her on the piano. He ambles through a hallway full of reveling drunks to find the source of the aria, a young woman luxuriating in a bath. But she triggers memories of his mother disfigured from cholera, who languished in the hot water treatment that would kill her. Grabbing at the girl and screaming out "Mama," he requires several men to hold him down.

●

When casting the lead, Russell initially wanted Alan Bates, still enamored with his D. H. Lawrence impersonation. Bates was just as enthused at first, but he changed his mind. "His reason, I believe," Russell reflects, "was that he thought it might not be good for his image to play two sexually deviant parts in rapid succession."

Following his success with the television series *Dr. Kildare*, Richard Chamberlain was trying to reinvent himself. In 1967, Richard Lester chose him as the abusive husband in *Petulia*, telling the actor he saw the character as "a great looking, but empty Coke bottle." But Russell, when seeing Chamberlain in a British television production of Henry James's *Portrait of a Lady*, found him sensitive, pretty, and blessed with graceful hand gestures. Chamberlain played these attributes to his advantage, letting his all-American, prime-time television persona contrast with intimations of his own inner conflict.

Chamberlain is the ideal choice for Tchaikovsky. He's so photogenic that he's at times larger than life, but his mental and physical torture is all the more convincing when his surface beauty starts to crack. Stefan Kanfer, writing for *Time*, was being catty, but he, given Russell's predilections for Art Nouveau and symbolism, ultimately complimented Russell's choice by saying that "Chamberlain has the appearance and emotional range of an Aubrey Beardsley faun." Being homosexual, but decades from admitting it to a potentially hostile public, Chamberlain apparently transferred that inner anguish into his performance.

The Brits proved more open minded than the Yanks toward the ex-all-American. They liked him when he starred in *Portrait of a Lady* and when he played Hamlet at the Birmingham Repertory Company opposite another future Russell star, Gemma Jones, as Ophelia. Russell took in the actor's good notices but also recalls that Chamberlain had another saving grace: "When I learned at our first meeting that he could strum through the Grieg Piano Concerto, I knew we had found our man." And that really is Chamberlain playing, as the camera pans along with his fingers frantically striking up and down the keyboard to a Rafael Orozco recording, before Russell cuts to the actor's sweaty face.

Unfortunately, Chamberlain is relatively quiet in his 2003 autobiography about his best and most challenging role. When interviewed in the 1970s, however, he was astute about Russell's directing style: "I don't think Ken Russell is an actors' director, but he does create a fantastic atmosphere on the set as far as I am concerned. What he would do was, we would all be there with our preconceived ideas of how the scene was going to go; we'd run through the scene just prior to shooting but, instead of commenting on the interpretation, he'd say, 'That chair is *ridiculous!*' And the emphasis would suddenly be on an inanimate object that couldn't act, couldn't do anything. Seventy people would be running around in a blind panic because the chair wasn't right. And then of course in the confusion he would suddenly say, 'Right. Forget the bloody chair. Turn over camera. Action.'"

Glenda Jackson would also commend the director for the peculiar ways he handles his cast: "I like Russell. He's got all those warts and bumps. . . . He doesn't know anything about acting. He'll spend hours getting the set right or screaming abuse at people because a costume isn't absolutely correct in every fine detail, and then he'll leave you to play a scene entirely on your own. He can't do anything to help the bad actor."

Jackson's casting was remarkable, considering that she and Russell were not exactly on the best of speaking terms when they finished *Women in Love*. "I'd better not talk," Russell stated when shooting concluded. "I might say something both she and I would regret." Jackson was less demure, calling Russell "an utter physical coward" for putting his actors in peril while playing the voyeur.

As Nina, Jackson gets progressively frantic once her fantasy hussar finally visits her and leaves her bound and beaten at her bedpost. But she dusts herself off to pursue the next man, engaging Tchaikovsky in a letter-writing blitz. Russell pairs the real-life correspondence between Nina and Peter with the theme of Tchaikovsky's opera *Eugene Onegin*, based on Alexander Pushkin's verse novel about dashed romantic hopes. Peter is adrift at the piano in another of his callow and collapsible illusions, while Olga Bredska (Joanne Brown) sings the part from the opera when the heroine tells of exchanging letters with the man who will eventually reject her.

Tchaikovsky fancies too much of a coincidence and tries fusing art and life, making Onegin's situation his own. But his decision to marry Nina is a disaster from the start. Bowen's biography chronicles the remorse and psychopathic hatred that he ended up feeling for the woman he would call "The Reptile." Tchaikovsky's boyfriend is also distressed. The jilted Chiluvsky, whom Russell creates as a composite of Tchaikovsky's several lovers, and whose name is derived partly from the composer's real-life boyfriend Vladimir Shilovsky, dogs the newlyweds on their St. Petersburg honeymoon when they attend an outdoor production of *Swan Lake*.

Through clenched teeth, Chiluvsky summarizes to Nina the ballet's plot, projecting his woes by telling her about the prancing swain on the stage giving up his "true love" for some sham. Russell hints that Peter is already having his doubts. "Nina is watching the ballet with him," Russell later confirms, "and he has begun to think that she isn't the pure dreamlike creature he had in his mind when he proposed to her. To him she isn't the white swan but the black swan. And this is put into his mind by the evil genius who is his boyfriend Chiluvsky."

Gable had a difficult role: villainous at times but also sympathetic. Like Loerke in *Women in Love*, he is a fop, but he's also the only major character with a clear and consistent viewpoint. He tells Peter to "accept what you are; don't pretend!" But when he can't convince Peter that his marriage is a "charade," he yanks him off Meck's gravy train, shattering the dowager's silly fantasies by fabricating (at least through Russell's nonverbal allusion) a love story between Peter and his amanuensis, Alexei (Bruce Robinson).

Never too literal with biography, Russell fills in historical gaps with speculation as to why Meck suddenly withdrew her patronage, but he makes a somewhat educated guess. According to Bowen, Meck frowned on most conventions and considered herself "an atheist needing no God, a woman alone, needing no mate," but she also had a priggish Victorian streak that may have justified Tchaikovsky's mortal terror of her finding out about "The."

Chiluvsky is entirely right about the phony marriage. The infamous honeymoon carriage scene that follows relives—this time much more vividly—the moments that Glenda Jackson and Vladek Sheybal acted out in *Women in Love*. When the wedded woebegones leave St. Petersburg for Moscow, their Trans-Siberian Express becomes a Horror Express.

Tchaikovsky (Richard Chamberlain) shuns his true love, Count Chiluvsky (Christopher Gable), in *The Music Lovers*.

Russell wanted the inside of the train car to become Tchaikovsky's psychic prison, where he confronts Nina's nakedness. He also wanted some object to reflect Tchaikovsky's mental state, so he insisted that the car's ceiling lights waver back and forth as the train careens. To bolster the film's mood, he fills the soundtrack with selections from Tchaikovsky's *Manfred*, along with his *Pathetique* Symphony, which was, in Russell's words, "the most tortured music he wrote." On the set, however, Russell blasted through twelve-inch loudspeakers "a loop of the most barbaric fifteen-second section" of Shostakovich's "The Execution of Stepan Razin."

"It was so loud," Russell later stresses in an interview, "it became a solid entity. It even affected the men who were rocking the carriage. The cameraman was moving with it, the whole studio was possessed. And that comes off on the screen somehow."

Talking with Gordon Gow, Russell got more graphic, saying that Tchaikovsky "found himself locked in a sleeping compartment with Nina on a train hurtling through the snow at sixty miles an hour, rocking violently. It's like hell. . . . It's a little box six feet square. And he gets her drunk in it. . . . We show her taking off her things, and suddenly he's with a piece of meat. . . . She's a naked drunk. She passes out cold. And she just rocks about the floor, and he is trapped with this . . . piece of meat."

The sight of this "piece of meat" from the Royal Shakespeare Company terrified not only critics and viewers but also Jackson's husband Roy Hodges, who was still coming to terms with his wife's intellectual nudity from her earlier stage days. Jackson was forthcoming about the effect she sought and accomplished: "You see this horrible skeletal figure writhing around, and it's enough to put you off sex for the rest of your life."

In 1981, Jackson went into a sharper recollection of that scene for the *Daily Mail*: "They started rocking the coach to simulate the movement of the train. First a champagne bucket, glasses, a chicken, and knives and forks fell on me and I'm covered with broken glass and superficial cuts and Ken is there shouting, 'Wipe the blood off her, clean her up; it will never show.'" And in his book *The Post-Classical Predicament*, Joseph Horowitz sounds both ambivalent and stimulated: "The scene is debilitating for its intensity and funny for its extravagance. If we enjoy it, we feel guilty; if we don't, we are prudes."

●

Once Chiluvsky does his damage, Peter is exiled from Meck's maternal fold. He reinvents himself by becoming the money guzzler his brother Modeste wants him to be. As he slides into this bitter new phase, Tchaikovsky must also symbolically eliminate the psychic leeches that would otherwise distract him. This is when Russell kicks into his pre-rock-video mode, exploring Peter's angst with a nightmare fantasy—all fabricated on the Bray Studios backlot.

After Chiluvsky, Meck, Sasha, Nina, and others grab at him amid a wind-machine storm of flying confetti, Tchaikovsky turns the tables. With Modeste lighting the fuse, Peter subjects them all (with a bit more sadistic delay on Nina) to decapitations by cannon. All of this occurs to the pompous blasts of the *1812*

Overture—a commissioned piece Tchaikovsky admittedly composed "without warmth and without love"—while his sycophants catapult him to the top of a tower. The music blends beautifully with the tawdry rhythms of a can-can: Modeste scoops up fluttering bank notes, while Peter (with streamers still dangling from his arm) waves his conductor's baton before dissolving into his statue in the barren snow.

"Tchaikovsky hated the *1812 Overture* anyway," Russell contends in an effort to put the scene in context. "He thought it was a vulgar piece and he only did it for a commission. We show him being totally caught up in it and turned into stone by it."

•

"I felt sad about Nina," Glenda Jackson told the *New York Times*. "Nina was so much a victim of her lack of intelligence, her inability to control her own emotions. But she was unlikable, too, because she was a continual fantasist and—like all fantasists—dangerous and destructive. Fortunately, she was the weaker of the two fantasists. Tchaikovsky, after all, had a lifeline in his music. Nina had no lifeline."

Russell exudes mixed sympathies for his nymphomaniac. Nina's mother (Maureen Pryor), who comes to stay at the house and stir up more trouble, is an opportunist and a social climber who eventually acts as her daughter's pimp. She procures men off the street to impersonate such great Russian contemporaries as Nikolay Rimsky-Korsakov and Aleksandr Borodin. While Nina coddles the illusion that she is making her husband jealous, she also gets some thrills, gets pregnant, and leaves Mom to amass lots of spare change and gaudier feathered hats.

Tchaikovsky, now rich and jaded beyond his dreams, sends lots of money to Nina, but her mother hordes it, sending her daughter off to a filthy asylum. Russell's imagery goes from baroque to raunchy rococo as Nina writhes with her legs spread open over a grate, inviting the inmates below her to invade her privates. Nina really did end up in an asylum, but she was not committed until about three years after Tchaikovsky's death. Russell changes the chronology to depict their separate destinies in parallel time.

Tchaikovsky, meanwhile, has no dreams left; he is consigned to an opulent hell with only his badgering brother Modeste and a disillusioned Alexei as companions. Even Sasha is dead. Modeste at least gives him a title for his sixth and final symphony—"The Pathetic." To celebrate the occasion, Peter flouts his waiter's warning and drinks the fatal glass of unboiled water.

Russell ends the film with neither resolution nor peace. Nina, pacing the asylum yard, does not even have the delusion of her husband's love, requiring a straitjacket after she starts screaming, "He hated me! He hated me!" Peter Ilyich, his face now full of the pustules that covered his mother, also rants semi-coherently, "I tried to love her." The "her" is ambiguous: interchangeable with Sasha, Nina, Meck, and most likely his mother.

∎

The Music Lovers destroyed any stuffy decorum that Russell might have conveyed with *Women in Love*. And some critics got crotchety. Vincent Canby of the *New York Times* wrote as if he were an erection without a climax: "Never, perhaps, has one movie contained so many smashed champagne glasses, so many lyrical fantasies (with so many white swans), so many sordid confrontations, so many clothes torn off in twisted passion, so many references to the joys and terrors of artistic creation, even so much music—but all to such little ultimate effect."

Inveterate Russell hater Pauline Kael, whom *The New Yorker* continued to assign Russell reviews, wrote predictably about Russell not sticking to the biographical "facts," but she made one provocative point: "The film is homoerotic in style, and yet in dramatic content, it's bizarrely anti-homosexual." She also shares a quirky revelation: "Whose pornographic fantasy is it that all the women in the movie have yellowish teeth—threatening, irregular teeth—while the men have gleaming white ones?"

Roger Ebert was no fan. He had written the screenplay to Russ Meyer's *Beyond the Valley of the Dolls*, which was fraught with campy humor and large breasts but also included sneering depictions of lesbians, anti-"fag" remarks, and a hermaphrodite psycho. Despite all this, Ebert somehow felt comfortable using Russell's film as an excuse to moralize: "*The Music Lovers* is libelous not only to the composer but to his music." He at least noticed, albeit with the same outraged air, some of Russell's Freudian lures, describing them as "a grotesque jungle of candlesticks, potted plant stands, incense sticks, old champagne bottles, and gilt edges."

Stephen Farber of the *New York Times* was much keener to Russell's intent: "The film breaks down the conventional distance between spectator and material; it forces us to extremes. To understand *The Music Lovers*, one must be willing to experiment, to surrender to its voluptuousness; but responding does not mean abdicating intelligence. The film seduces us in order to involve us in the failures of romanticism."

When shooting finished, Chamberlain told Rex Reed that he "was determined to give up acting. I've never been so depressed, and it took me weeks and weeks to get over it. I love Ken and would do anything for him, but on a movie set he's so serious and demanding that he made Glenda Jackson and me do those scenes over and over, sometimes twenty times, until we couldn't move. It was no fun. That picture nearly put me in a loony bin. But I loved the film."

"Acting," Jackson later said about her *Music Lovers* moments, "always puts you in a life and death situation. But in that particular film everybody was living at the extremes of their lives." And despite scene after scene of mounting misery, an inner demon of hope propels Russell's narrative—the same one that inspired Tchaikovsky to create in the face of decay. As Bowen states, the great composer "loved life, not as your optimist loves it, unconsciously, taking it for granted—but rather with the furious and grateful joy of the pessimist who, expecting evil and eternal darkness, discovers every morning anew the sun."

Judging from Bowen's biography, Tchaikovsky was a failure as a lover, a husband, a social politician, and sometimes even as a friend, but amid all of the strife—and this is perhaps the only optimistic streak in his life as well as Russell's film—he kept at his art, even though his hand shook as he wrote the notes.

SACRILEGIOUS BITCH! THE DEVILS: PART ONE

In January 1970, on a return trip to London from Paris, the sensitive and sexually rebellious Derek Jarman met a young woman named Janet Deuters. Like Jarman, Deuters could rhapsodize for hours about theatrical sound, lighting, and other matters of stagecraft. The chat got livelier when Deuters revealed her friendship with Ken and Shirley Russell, enticing Jarman with a Russell project in preproduction: a movie all about sex, power, corruption, blasphemy, and demonic possession in plague-infested seventeenth-century France.

Jarman had a yen for the bizarre and already paid homage to the Italian Surrealist painter Giorgio de Chirico when designing the sets and costumes for a 1968 London production of *Don Giovanni* that John Gielgud directed. Deuters also sampled the outré when she played the wife of painter Ford Maddox Brown in Russell's *Dante's Inferno*. Now she played a provocateur, enticing Jarman with her descriptions of *The Devils* and Russell's planned cinematic pageantry of medieval apparel, outlandish theatrics, royal courts full of gender-bending libertines, convents rife with lunatics, and lots of gory crosses. Sensing Jarman would add new blood to this beast, Deuters promised to leave a good word with Russell the moment she got home.

Within twenty-four hours, Jarman got Russell's phone call and a visit the following day. At the time, Jarman lived in a former corset factory at London's Upper Ground district: a freezing warehouse littered with paintings and other arty bric-a-brac. Russell stood agog before one of Jarman's walls adorned with an array of cardinals' capes: one bedecked with garbage Jarman had dredged from a river; another embroidered in dollar bills. It was instant kismet: Russell christened Jarman the set designer for what would become postwar British cinema's greatest marvel and nightmare.

Russell had good reason to dramatize Aldous Huxley's *The Devils of Loudun*. The book is a lurid account of real-life events involving Sister Jeanne of the Angels, a hunchbacked and erotically frustrated Ursuline nun, who falls for Father Urbain Grandier, an oversexed Jesuit also fixated on guarding Loudun's independence. Sister Jeanne, sensing he has spurned her, triggers disaster by feigning demonic possession, accusing Grandier as her violator and evoking the power-crazed Cardinal Richelieu's forces to destroy both the priest and his prized city. And Russell couldn't resist when Huxley, amid the terror, describes Sister Jeanne and all the other players as "transforming the would-be sublime into the comic, the downright farcical."

Russell and Jarman were ideal collaborators for this combination Roman Catholic horror and clown show. Though about fourteen years his junior, Jarman shared many of Russell's obsessions: flamboyant period finery, gaudy jewelry, Surrealist painters, dead movie stars, and *The Wizard of Oz*, to name a few. Describing Jarman as "probably the last true bohemian," Russell appreciated this gentle renegade and fellow iconoclast, this unabashedly gay version of himself with whom he could relish history's dottier side.

"I thought at once," Russell told *Sight and Sound*, "this guy is for me! I talked to him, and he had an unstoppable flow of ideas. He was one of the most interesting people I ever met. He was very keen to do the film. We talked and talked for days on end. And even if I didn't always use his ideas, they invariably sparked off other ideas. I remember he wanted a dream sequence with Sister Jeanne burdened down with thousands of crucifixes and crawling through a desert of martyrs hanging from trees."

Like Russell, Jarman grew up detesting sports, loathed the piss-poor excuses for male bonding imposed in boys' schools, and sought refuge from the ruffians by embracing art and staging drag shows. Both also had eccentric females lording over their childhoods: Russell had his Mum and Aunt Moo; Jarman had his great-aunt Doris, who flouted convention and alienated her stodgy family by traipsing about in a state of heightened reality.

The two men also differed. Russell got his mind off the smell of his naval college peers by picturing himself in the South Seas, lying "on the beach with an exotic naked lady, drinking coconut juice, and making love." But Jarman survived his school days by waiting "in vain for a man to carry me off and initiate me—rescue me from suburban conformity." And unlike Russell, who held back vomit to the vibrations of masturbating bunkmates, Jarman was only nine when a classmate stole his heart. One night, he slipped into the boy's bed, but the headmaster's harpy wife walked in on the tryst and literally flung the mattress, along with Jarman's romantic dreams, to the floor.

•

Shortly before his death in 1963, Aldous Huxley wrote a letter to his son to share his thoughts on the prospects of turning *The Devils of Loudun* into a movie: "What on earth will they make out of it? I feel a great deal of curiosity—and apprehension." For many, Huxley's 1952 publication was disgusting, sensationalistic, blasphemous, and tailored to rile the Almighty. Anne Fremantle admitted in the *Saturday Review* that the book was well documented and organized, but she cringed at the descriptions of putrefaction, sexual sadism, and "Richelieu's halitosis": "Not since Swift has anyone so resented the fact of bathrooms; not since Donne, our decomposition."

Composer Ned Rorem proposed making it into an opera, but his plans vaporized. John Whiting got luckier, coming out in 1961 with *The Devils*, a Royal Shakespeare Company production that premiered at London's Aldwych Theatre to positive responses. Whiting tackled Huxley's daunting themes: church politics, holy hierarchies and their political corruption, the rights of states versus the rights of individuals, and, of course, sexual repression.

Whiting, like Huxley, implied that the seventeenth-century debacle was relevant to contemporary culture. Between 1623 and 1634, Loudun harbored a power grab between church and state that Russell also perceived as surviving into the modern world. As Richelieu fought to maintain a stranglehold over France and colluded with King Louis XIII to centralize his power, the cocksure Grandier posed a threat that was ripe for roasting, balls and all, at the stake.

Russell couldn't resist layering the story with his own devils, precisely his artistic convictions and erotic fetishes. Huxley, who combined historical biography with the imaginative language of fiction, already provided Russell with the template: "The good father who performs the exorcisms behaves exactly like the proprietor of a sideshow at a fair," Huxley writes. "These spouses of Christ have been turned into cabaret performers and circus freaks." Such passages allowed Russell creative latitude: "*The Devils* is a harsh film—but it's a harsh subject," he later reflected. "I wish the people who were horrified and appalled by it had read the book, because the bare facts are far more horrible than anything in the film."

Russell has sole screenwriting credit, but his graphic descriptions and curt, angry dialogue borrow from both Huxley and Whiting. The final result is just as Huxley intended: sadistic Vatican vaudeville routines that clash with alternately droll and puerile humor. Of all his work, *The Devils* shows Russell at his deftest in mixing horror with farce. A United Artists executive who took the time to read the script found its sacrilegious satire so potent that he decreed the movie industry's equivalent of a church excommunication: the studio dropped the project. But Warner Brothers soon took it on.

From the start, those working with Russell noticed how much he made *The Devils* his personal statement. A man of whim, he changed the scenario day by day, sometimes even hour by hour. Jarman was candid about this in his journal: "After lunch I had an interview with an intense young film student who is writing on Ken Russell and religion. He talks of Buber and French philosophies . . . impossible to imagine *The Devils* in this way? I don't even know how to tell him that many of the decisions were off the wall. Ken and I never discussed religion or the church."

Peter Maxwell Davies, who composed the score, also noted Russell's chameleon convictions in the 2002 documentary *Hell on Earth*: "He's got a mind which darts from one mood to another mood very quickly: from one opinion to another. I remember him saying one day this film was a political one; the next day it was a religious film; that next day it was about persecution pure and simple. He would have different attitudes at different times, and it changed him."

The Devils is delectably disorienting from the moment it flashes a disclaimer, the kind that Russell usually hates, which assures viewers that the movie is "based on historical fact. The principal characters lived and the major events depicted in the film actually took place." Russell uses it to his advantage by jumping right into a fantastic, ridiculous, and maddeningly beautiful scene.

King Louis XIII (Graham Armitage) stages a court masque fraught with female impersonators both on the stage and in the audience. In his tribute to Botticelli's *Birth of Venus* painting, the king emerges from a giant half shell amid an amateurish set design of shifting cardboard waves. The decor is flagrantly inelegant; the dancers' gyrations are deliberately comical. Russell also shows his flair for history when the king's court players perform—via David Munrow conducting the Early Music Consort

King Louis XIII (Graham Armitage) entertains Cardinal Richelieu in the opening of *The Devils*.

of London—"La Bourée," one of the several Dances from Terpsichore that the seventeenth-century German composer and theorist Michael Praetorius arranged for such royal revelries.

Though the masque is in his honor, Cardinal Richelieu (Christopher Logue) appears unimpressed. Reclining in his wheelchair like an effete matron and all dolled up in red satin finery, he makes the two stoic nuns flanking him seem masculine by comparison. Bored, jaded, and hopelessly holy, Richelieu fidgets and yawns as the king tosses coins to his pretty boy minions from a cardboard cornucopia. The cardinal and the king are essentially inverted mirror images: drag queen potentates, who preen and scheme for what Richelieu hopes will be "a new France, where church and state are one" and where Protestants are "driven from the land."

•

Jarman helped Russell contrast the desolate, alien worlds on both sides of Loudun's walls. Beyond, Huguenots are human chattel, and maggot-ridden corpses dangle from wheel racks. Within, the town resembles an infected hospital ward: white brick buildings contrast with scattered bonfires and piles of rotting plague victims. For this simultaneously medieval and futuristic cityscape, Russell and Jarman looked to Fritz Lang's *Metropolis*. "My source books are Ledoux, Boulée, and Piranesi's prison series," Jarman wrote in his journal. "All detail is sacrificed to scale as I want the sets as large as possible, and as forceful as the sets from an old silent."

When Warner Brothers took over, the studio imposed budgetary restrictions that nixed Jarman's plans for King Louis's gilded court and topiary garden. More and more of the grandiose Loudun sets, including the royal palace, got pared down. Jarman found that, once shooting started in August 1970, the penury inspired him. Pinewood Studio's garden proved green enough; the city walls, stripped down to a more frugal simplicity, became humongous edifices of white brick (painted beige to register white on camera). They offered a Loudun that was more abstract and timeless.

The two prickly personalities dwelling inside this medieval metropolis—Father Grandier (Oliver Reed) and Sister Jeanne (Vanessa Redgrave)—are mortal enemies drawn into each other's lives partly out of self-destructive desires. Their conflict is the prequel to Jerzy Kawalerowicz's *Mother Joan of the Angels*. The Polish film from 1961 was another of Russell's inspirations, as it followed Huxley's last four chapters, centering on events after Grandier's execution, when the demon Isacaaron invades Jeanne's body, and she becomes what Huxley describes as the "supernatural equivalent of a movie star." Kawalerowicz also focused on the ill-fated Father Jean-Joseph Surin (Mieczyslaw Voit), who attempts to purge Sister Jeanne of her devils and incurs his own satanic seizures.

Kawalerowicz's black and white film, though relatively restrained, included a terrifying Lucyna Winnicka as Sister Jeanne. But Russell shifts the focus from Surin to Grandier. He also makes Grandier an ambiguous character: someone whom viewers may alternately like and revile. At one angle, Grandier is a free spirit against the state, preoccupied with keeping both himself and his city "proud and erect"; at another, he is insensitive and vain—even his holy covenant seems narcissistic when he invokes his Lord to "pray for us all, especially me."

Casting Reed as Grandier was as faultless as his choice for Debussy and Rossetti. Reed had also been playing the cock of the walk off-screen for quite some time. Like Russell, he was at the apogee of his fame; he even went around calling himself "Mr. England." He might have beaten Russell in jujitsu while making *Women in Love*, but he almost always showed deference when the director cussed out his instructions. Russell's fury inspired him as he screamed most of his lines, whether through public pep talks to rally his people for Loudun's salvation or apocalyptic rants when he's finally dragged to the public square to face flames at the stake and the city's demise.

Not content to present a simple antihero, Russell forces viewers to think about Grandier's moral consistency. The priest's flaws are apparent early on. After he stands high on a church precipice, screeching for civic unity at a memorial service for the town's "late lamented governor" Sainte-Marthe, he struts with the funeral procession and alienates two key players in his destruction. The first is the effeminate Father Mignon (Murray Melvin), who takes umbrage when his boy attendants drop his train to hold up Grandier's; the second is the young Philippe Trincant (Georgina Hale), daughter to the town's leading magistrate and Grandier's recent concubine, who watches from the sidelines, waiting for a flirtation but getting Grandier's snooty indifference instead.

Grandier is such a lout in his opening scenes that his heroic journey never seems completely tenable. Naked with Philippe while teaching her Latin (as her dad requested), Grandier reacts to the unwelcome news of her pregnancy by telling her she "must learn to bear your cross with Christian fortitude, my child." He then hogs the foreground, combing his moustache and digressing into a monologue about the failures of the flesh. Philippe begs for help, but the priest shuns her. Huxley's book is more lucid about Grandier's capricious attitude, making it clear that Philippe's father, Magistrate Trincant (John Woodvine), is also Grandier's friend. On a quest for martyrdom by incurring the town's hatred, Grandier corrupts the daughter out of "a perverse desire to betray him."

Jarman's fondness for the aesthetics of alchemy come alive when Adam the surgeon (Brian Murphy) and Ibert the chemist (Max Adrian)—two charac-

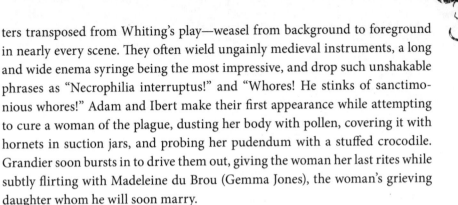

ters transposed from Whiting's play—weasel from background to foreground in nearly every scene. They often wield ungainly medieval instruments, a long and wide enema syringe being the most impressive, and drop such unshakable phrases as "Necrophilia interruptus!" and "Whores! He stinks of sanctimonious whores!" Adam and Ibert make their first appearance while attempting to cure a woman of the plague, dusting her body with pollen, covering it with hornets in suction jars, and probing her pudendum with a stuffed crocodile. Grandier soon bursts in to drive them out, giving the woman her last rites while subtly flirting with Madeleine du Brou (Gemma Jones), the woman's grieving daughter whom he will soon marry.

●

Though not a Method actor, Reed channeled whatever screen persona Russell gave him. He was a sport most of the time on the *Devils'* set but had his ranker moments. An anti-intellectual and dyslexic to boot, he found the script's sixteenth-century Latin intimidating. He confided to associate producer Roy Baird that he refused to memorize it and would tell Russell to "piss off." Smart enough to know when to stroke an unruly actor's ego, Russell relented a bit and allowed Reed to bark up snippets of dialogue from pieces of paper floating in holy water or discreetly scrawled on the bread he breaks when performing communion.

To make Grandier's atonement as authentic and grueling as possible, Reed had to shave his head. To this he readily complied, but got belligerent after finding out he also had to shave his eyebrows. Russell fought melodrama with more melodrama. He paced the set in circles that grew smaller and smaller as he flailed his arms in the air and shouted, "God! We might as well not make the film at all!"

Reed insisted they could still make the film, but that such a minor detail as shaved brows wasn't important. Russell shouted back: "Of course it's important. They shaved off all of Grandier's bodily hair and then stuck red hot pokers up his arse." Reed consented but under one condition: a Lloyd's of London underwriter had to make out a claim for half a million pounds against the chances that Reed's brows grew back askew and jeopardized his waning days as a sex symbol.

Russell had more grief in store when securing the role of Sister Jeanne. He had Glenda Jackson in mind, but after lying like a dog beneath the garlic-breathing Reed in one film and playing a head-shaved slut confined to a nuthouse in the next, she blurted an unequivocal no. "Ken wanted me to be in this film *The Devils*," she told the *New York Times* in 1971. "But I was worried about playing another neurotic, sex-starved lady, albeit a nun. Ken is a very complex man, and

I think he was personally hurt when I told him I didn't want to do the film. If it still stings him, I guess that's the way it has to be."

Jackson's refusal had nuances. She liked the original script, especially a final scene that came close to Huxley's conception when he writes, "After her death, which came in January 1665, the prioress's comedy was transformed by the surviving members of the community into the broadest of farces. The corpse was decapitated and Soeur Jeanne's head took its place, in a silver-gilt box with crystal windows, beside the sacred chemise."

Russell visualized this disembodied head on an altar in a glass casket—an addition Jackson thought stunning. She got miffed when he decided to take it out. "I had to admit that was true," Russell later acknowledged. "She'd loved the idea of her head in a casket and everyone worshipping her on their knees. And with all that gone she'd have just been back in the madhouse again."

Beneath his unflappable exterior, however, Russell seethed over Jackson's rebuff and managed to hide it—that is until Rex Reed liberated the inner bitch. "I'm glad she wasn't in it," Russell cussed back when Reed, several months after the film's release, reminded him of the incident during an interview. "She's not a very good actress; she's very cold and intellectual. No emotion. She says she doesn't want to play the same parts, yet she did Queen Elizabeth on TV like a boring schoolmistress, and followed it up with a movie playing the same part. Giving a ghastly performance, from what I hear."

Vanessa Redgrave wasn't Russell's first choice, but she ended up the supreme one. The part needed to contrast Sister Jeanne's twisted body and mind with a conventionally beautiful face that Jackson couldn't offer. Viewers needed to see Jeanne as she imagined herself: an erotic heroine from out of some tawdry romance novel, draped in a habit out of circumstance more than conviction. The film had to provide a reason why she would fancy herself worthy of seducing a playboy priest. And Russell gave Redgrave the role of her career, despite such tribulations as the exorcism scene, when she had to heave what she recalls as "endless mouthfuls of Heinz vegetable soup."

Like most of the main characters, whose bodies prove to be prisons more than temples, Jeanne's deformity warps everything and everyone around her. Jarman stresses this by having the Ursuline convent's archways and doorframes complement Jeanne's stoop. Jarman presents Jeanne's world as one of inverted beauty: she is, after all, closer in form to the gnarled Christ icons adorning her halls than her upright subordinate nuns who mock her desires yet appear just as sexually famished.

Even with Jeanne's defect exposed, Russell still tempts viewers to suspend disbelief by focusing on Redgrave's flawless hazel eyes and noble facial structure. Michelangelo Antonioni emphasized her photogenic back in *Blow Up*, but

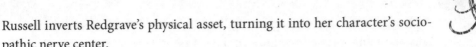

Russell inverts Redgrave's physical asset, turning it into her character's sociopathic nerve center.

While scolding one of her charges for peeking out the convent window to gawk at Grandier during Sainte-Marthe's procession, she fondles the skeleton key to her private chambers, hobbles to unlock the door, and peers through the barred windows to gawk at Loudun's lothario. She imagines herself as a gorgeous groupie with long red hair, greeting Grandier as he walks across water. She kneels to wipe his feet with her hair when he touches land, but when she looks up at him for guidance, she follows his glance to the spiny, reptilian monster surfacing through her crimson strands. She insists, "I'm beautiful," but her clamor for dignity is no match for Russell's cycloramic camera and the merciless gusts of his wind machine as the townsfolk and embittered sisters jeer at her hideous hump and her vain attempts to rise from the dirt.

As Grandier sputters bombastic pieties, browbeats what seems his exclusively female penitents, and jilts the strumpet he impregnates, he reaps more scorn. Meanwhile, Sister Jeanne's moist dreams about uniting with him physically, and therefore spiritually, intensify. Leading her nuns in reciting The Mysteries of the Crucifixion, she allows her mind to wander again, this time into the black and white miasma of a silent Cecil B. De Mille epic. She imagines the crucified Jesus morphing into Grandier and stepping down to embrace her. She kneels again, licks his stigmata, slips her tongue along his spear wound, and pulls him down for a lusty roll on the grounds of Calvary.

As Maxwell Davies's score and Stomu Yamashta's percussion approximate the hiss and rattle of rosary beads, Russell cuts constantly back to her at the convent as she pounds her rosary against her forehead, trying to block out the Biblical pornography to no avail. Instead, she inflicts her own stigmata by grinding the cross into her palm, while the devious Sister Agnes (Judith Paris) watches with horny glee as Jeanne runs out from the ceremony with blood on her habit.

Sister Jeanne can't quit Grandier, even after hearing rumors that he's married Madeleine du Brou in what one of his adversaries calls "a blasphemous nuptial mass."

Sister Jeanne of the Angels (Vanessa Redgrave).

After masturbating and flagellating herself with a spiked metal cat-o'-nine-tails, she's still obsessed and grows more delirious when learning that Grandier has turned down her invitation to be her convent's spiritual director. Taking the rejection badly, she starts spinning tales, insisting that Grandier is the phallic incubus that invaded her sanctuary, defiled her, and forced several of her sisters into a black mass. Now, all the townspeople who thought Grandier a pompous fraud, the women he'd betrayed, the men who secretly envied his priapic power, and the church doyens who wanted to wrest his secular authority have an excuse to take the wayward Jesuit down.

As the film's mayhem gets worse, Jarman shows off his attention to seventeenth-century period detail, which he derived from studying accounts and illustrations. He considered Cornelius Agrippa's occult philosophy and Robert Fludd's drawings—the aesthetics and philosophy of what he saw as a glorious prescientific era. Jarman also took suggestions from Dom Sylvester Houédard, the Benedictine historian well versed in such period niceties.

There's another pivotal scene where Jarman meticulously places hanging bladders and chemist jars inside of an apothecary's pharmacy that looks as if it's in the earth's bowels. Here is where the story's true devils fester, as the shifty lawyer Baron de Laubardemont (Dudley Sutton) plots with Ibert and Adam Trincant, the town magistrate, and Father Mignon after Sister Jeanne makes her accusations. All this leads up to the public exorcism, when they call upon a dodgy and ruthless witchfinder to drive out Sister Jeanne's demons with an enema.

●

Russell apparently adopted, with tongue in cheek, John Lennon's public image, circa 1968, of long hair and wire-rimmed glasses for the role of *The Devils'* most rancorous religious fanatic: Father Barré (Michael Gothard). In contrast to Lennon, who preached peace like an earthly messiah but eventually sang in "Imagine" about a happy world with "no religion," Barré was a true and terrorizing believer.

Huxley describes Father Barré as a zealot too caught up in his madness to be consciously deceitful, but Russell once again leaves open a window of doubt. Barré also appears to have more on his mind than saving souls, licking his lips while anticipating Sister Jeanne's recollection of the night Grandier and "six of his creatures" forced her and her sisters "to form an obscene altar."

As Huxley points out, exorcists of the time used enemas (or clysters) because they often perceived demons lurking in the lower intestine. Russell and Jarman also took a cue from Huxley's book when designing the convent's white tiles and reverberant acoustics. Huxley refers to Jeanne's exorcism as if "Barré had treated her to an experience that was the equivalent, more or less, of a rape in a public lavatory."

"I think I didn't have a problem finding a correct musical language for this very fevered atmosphere," Peter Maxwell Davies recalls. "I think it was part and parcel of the musical 1960s. I realized that with that marvelous set Derek created that this has got to sound as if it's taking place in a public toilet. And so it becomes louder than it is because it's echoing back at you, and it begins to have a resonance, which you want to get out of. There's a slight feeling that you don't want to stay there too long."

∎

Of all his films, *The Devils* has the least easily readable characters. Anyone coming to grips with both Huxley's book and Russell's treatment is liable to enter a love-hate relationship with both Grandier and the story's twisted sister. Like Russell, Huxley chooses anachronisms to lump Jeanne among "the comedians of the spiritual life." She has "the unobjective and therefore limitless and insane desire of the moth for the star, of the schoolgirl for the crooner, of the bored and frustrated housewife for Rudolph Valentino." Audiences might even empathize with her plight, especially after she realizes she has "wronged an innocent man" and tries to atone.

In *The Devils*, pariahs and villains sometimes welcome illicit sympathy. Russell can be especially partial to the erotic outcasts, the love-starved desperados whose manic outbursts betray an inner logic that the more "normal" characters lack. Through Sister Jeanne's eyes, Madeleine de Brou, whom Huxley calls "the town's most distinguished prude," is a "whore,"

"The face of a Virgin Martyr in a picture book." Sister Jeanne (Vanessa Redgrave) sizes up Madeleine du Brou (Gemma Jones).

"strumpet," "hypocrite," and "sacrilegious bitch." She's too good, too picture perfect—a feckless waif whose halfhearted excuse for reneging on her wishes to join the Ursuline convent—after secretly marrying Grandier—are all the more infuriating. Jeanne, now a lady-in-waiting who's waited for nothing, huddles briefly in the shadows of her incarceration before clawing with cathartic and righteous anger through the iron bars at this "face of a virgin martyr in a picture book."

Of all Russell's ambiguous characters, King Louis XIII gets the boldest strokes. As Huxley described him, the king "displayed a decided aversion for women, a decided, though probably platonic, inclination for men, and a decided repugnance for all kinds of physical deformity and disease." And Russell, always thinking through the gland, plays on the king's penchant for gender-bending boys. On the surface, Louis XIII is bitchy and frivolous, but deeper down he shows jaundiced wisdom, aware of the political chicanery around him and seeing right through both Grandier's and Richelieu's facades.

The king is also intriguing for the way Russell combines his character with two others in Huxley's book. One is Henri de Conde, whom Huxley describes as a royal prince and "a notorious sodomite, who combined the most sordid avarice with an exemplary piety." The other is an anonymous nobleman who visits the Ursuline convent at its orgiastic heights to corroborate Laubardemont's and Barré's claims of Grandier's possession but winds up debunking the whole affair. As all three men, the king shines a harsh lavender light on the proceedings, literally removing one mask to expose another.

The masked king brings a so-called sacred vial containing the blood of Christ, which is supposed to cure Jeanne of her demons, at least temporarily. Jeanne claims to be freed at the mere proximity of the holy relic, but when the king turns it upside down to show that it's empty, the mob erupts in hysterical laughter. Father Barré asks, "What sort of a trick have you played on us?" But the king has a comeback: "Oh, Reverend Sire, what sort of a trick are you playing on *us*?"

But even the venal, petty, and Machiavellian Baron ("Give me three lines of a man's handwriting, and I shall hang him") Laubardemont has three or four seconds of redemption. He might be Richelieu's foot soldier and able to blow a city apart with the mere nod of his head, but during Grandier's heresy trial, Russell closes in on his incredulous face as the priest (looking embarrassed himself) tries wooing his accusor with some holy spin, declaring his desire to find God "through the love of a

Sister Jeanne's exorcism.

woman." The moment is frightfully ambiguous, as viewers must ponder (if only briefly) whether they agree with the no-nonsense Laubardemont that Grandier is a fool for mixing religious devotion with domestic pleasure at such a dire hour.

◾

While Russell attempted to redeem Grandier by having him choose matrimony over loveless martyrdom (Whiting's play had him opt for the latter), *The Devils* portended signs of Russell's own troubled marriage. Those brave and creative souls who dare to blur an artist's life and work should enjoy the comparisons.

Trouble started when Shirley freaked out one day during one of the film's orchestrated frenzies and dashed from the soundstage. Until then, she was dedicated to the project, diligent in cultivating the Richelieu-era look and happy to take Jarman's advice that certain fashion-minded seventeenth-century French-women preferred an exacting shade of green lipstick.

But Shirley had stormed off her husband's sets during previous projects. "I do tend to walk out," she later told Gordon Gow of *Films and Filming*. "Regularly. Once on every film, I think. When we're filming there's a different sort of relationship between Ken and myself. There's a 'them' and 'us' feeling: 'them' being the production unit and 'us' being the wardrobe department. It's very strange. It's hysterical really. I often disappear for days and won't go near the place, and they have to try to coax me back."

Russell suspected the motives for her latest disappearances went deeper than costume. While on breaks between shooting, Shirley was taking driving lessons from Russell's chauffeur. Russell started wondering about what else transpired in his spacious 1947 Rolls Landaulette. "These lessons often extended well into the afternoon," he recalls in his autobiography, "as I discovered whenever I sent word for her to join us on the set to discuss one of her bizarre costumes and explain, for instance, which way round it should be worn. Shirley was never to be found and, although there was nothing unusual in this because as the director's wife she was a law unto herself, it nevertheless started me wondering if a little back-seat driving might not be involved."

Suspicions mounted, but the marital flare up didn't happen until about four films later, long after Shirley failed several driving tests.

◾

With his loud and often mismatched clothes, his passion for Mickey Mouse shirts or Donald Duck caps, and his increasingly tousled strands of long, gray hair, Russell commanded the set with a nobly neurotic personality. He became a reincarnation of Fritz Lang as he lashed out at incompetent minions and made untamed gyrations. Furtive behind-the-scenes footage from the documentary *Hell on Earth* shows Russell with eyes closed, caught in his own trance as he brandishes a tambourine and attempts to flood himself with the same furies afflicting his characters.

A major row ensued when Jarman had the temerity to remove some shutters from one of Loudun's houses without prior consultation. Jostled to discover them missing at shooting time, Russell railed. As Jarman recalled in his book *Dancing Ledge*, "He looked like the mad empress from some B movie—waving his cane, his long hair flowing, wearing a smock and enormous rings on every finger. He left the set shouting to the air, everyone looking at each other rather embarrassed."

While brooding and tramping round the set, Russell instigated communal anxiety. But even he and the crew didn't expect that hell would break loose in so many other ways. Problems with actors, particularly the extras, were ongoing. The husband of one of the nuns happened to be on the production team and leaked out stories to the press about orgies. Some of the extras reportedly ran out of the closed set bawling.

Russell allegedly plied the more inhibited orgy members with magnums of champagne at breakfast time to loosen them up. Several of the nuns who plea-sure themselves on Christ's effigy during a pivotal orgy scene resembled silky haired *Penthouse* models, but others had shaved heads and crosses carved on their foreheads—a look with a curious resemblance to that of Charles Manson's female acolytes during the highly publicized Tate–La Bianca murder trial. When several of Russell's extras balked at going bald, Ken softened them by promising to pay £150 per scalp.

Michael Gothard as the John Lennonish exorcist Father Barré.

"It was pretty gory," Rus-sell admitted to Rex Reed, "but they knew what they were getting into. I never force my actors to do anything they don't want to do, but English extras are the lowest form of animal, the dregs of the underworld, and they manhandled two of the girls a bit harshly, and the whole orgy scene got out of hand. Some of the electricians were running off the set from nausea. Then Actors Equity got into it, and there was a fracas in the papers. But actors love me."

∎

All along, Jarman was high on the movie's mood of alchemy and anarchy, but he did not take kindly to Russell consulting him on ways to assault English sensibilities and then ignoring his suggestions. To stress Louis XIII's decadence, Jarman suggested the king alternate between chomping on an al fresco dinner and shooting peacocks on his garden lawn. But Russell insisted that only real peacocks would work, a cruelty he avoided by turning the proceedings into a farce. Jarman, whose last words before his death in 1994 (at least according to his friend, the production designer Christopher Hobbs) were, "I want the world to be filled with white fluffy duckies," had to settle for Russell's alternative: a Huguenot prisoner forced to dress as a crow, flapping and flailing out of a giant cage until the king shoots him. Russell also wedges another of his lyrical anachronisms: "Bye Bye, Blackbird," the king giggles while offering Richelieu this latest piece of Protestant kill.

Another cinema of cruelty instance occurs when Grandier is under house arrest. Not bad enough that he has to listen to bloodthirsty Loudunites calling out for his execution, Grandier must now endure Laubardemont's censure: "You're going to be tortured," "You've lived by your senses, surely you can die by them," and "Hell will hold no surprises for you." Laubardemont's goons meanwhile wreck Grandier's belongings, mutilating his collection of nude statues with hammers and rifle butts. Off the screen, each hammer blow brought pain to poor Jarman, who had painstakingly recast the statues with Renaissance era accuracy.

Jarman also gasped as the thugs slashed a facsimile of Nicolas Poussin's oil painting, "The Triumph of Pan," that adorns Grandier's wall. "But when I built this room," Derek Jarman reflects, "I had no foreknowledge that Ken Russell was going to have it smashed to pieces in the scene in which Grandier is led to his death. I stood looking on with complete horror as this destruction was completed, carrying with it even the Poussin."

Some of Russell's apocalyptic effects presented logistic problems. The plague pit full of bodies that Grandier blesses had to consist of extras as well as mannequins, but Jarman recalls in his memoirs that the rich blood secured from a butcher drew hordes of wasps. "Ken, as usual, stormed around," Jarman writes, "the bodies shifting as a wasp flew too close even when the cameras were running. Nothing was right; the blood was a disaster. In the end he made me bring bottles of ketchup from the kitchens, which made everything worse as the wasps preferred it to the real thing."

Another instance of on-set carnage occurred for Loudun's climactic destruction. All of the buildings were properly detonated, and the assigned detonators only needed a hand signal to set off the charges. But Russell had a panic attack and yelled, "I'm not having this fucked up!" He stormed over to the camera to film it himself; unfortunately, the demonstrative Russell's raving gestures looked like explosion cues, and the charge went off before the cameras rolled. Ten days later, with rebuilt sets, Loudun had to be razed again, for real.

The film ends in a wasteland, with Jeanne douching herself of her devils, Laubardemont resigned that Loudun will finally die, Father Barré off to exorcise a nun possessed by devils in a three-legged dog, and Father Mignon locked away in a loony bin after realizing Grandier's innocence. And as a tattered Madeleine de Brou, freed but alone, exits Loudun's blitzkrieg, Russell fades the image to black and white; the desert beyond the city's shattered walls is still lined with corpses on wheels and scant vegetation—just as, if not more, desolate than the place she escapes.

Urbain Grandier (Oliver Reed).

SANCTIMONIOUS WHORES! THE DEVILS: PART TWO

"**T**his is not the age of manners," Ken Russell blurted to *Time* magazine in 1971. "This is the age of kicking people in the crotch and telling them something and getting a reaction. I want to shock people into awareness. I don't believe there's any virtue in understatement."

Russell's devilish agitprop was working. By now, the London *Observer* listed him among England's most influential figures—more important than even the former prime minister, Harold Wilson. Russell also set a record when *The Devils*, *The Music Lovers*, and soon *The Boy Friend* played at London's West End theaters simultaneously. And in 1971, America's National Board of Review gave Russell a best director award for both *The Devils* and *The Boy Friend*. Soon, he'd get another kind of accolade: a parody in *Monty Python's Flying Circus* when a man in a bird suit jumps into a bed of flowers with a Fleet Street banker, safari hunters, garishly attired genderbenders, and a couple of naked tarts for a sketch called "Ken Russell's Gardening Club (1958)."

The hubbub surrounding *The Devils* and its often-vilifying critical reception enhanced Russell's reputation. All this, even after the censors deleted the film's lollapalooza of all scenes: the "Rape of Christ," the inclusion of which in these pre-*Exorcist* days might have incited a Christian fatwa.

When British film historian and journalist Mark Kermode set out to find the long-lost footage, he sought the aid of an American archivist. But Warner's Burbank studios yielded nothing. The Holy Grail was, of course, back in England all along, and in 2002 Kermode discovered the missing pieces secreted away on a roll of film in some stray canister. *Devils* devotees finally had their prayers answered.

The missing scene transpires at the point in the film just after King Louis XIII (traveling incognito) tells the mob of maniacs in the Ursuline convent to

"Have fun," and his entourage of transvestites carries him off. Right after a nun gets sick of hearing Father Barré's tiresome rants and conks him over the head with a giant cross, the merrymaking starts. Priests ravage nuns, nuns ravage priests, and one priest bares his privates as naked sybarites swamp him. While Sister Catherine (Catherine Willmer) tears and burns pages from a Bible, Sister Agnes (Judith Paris) frantically strokes a giant candle between her thighs. Naked sisters then take down an enormous crucifix from the wall before shaking their cellulite over Christ's face and genitals.

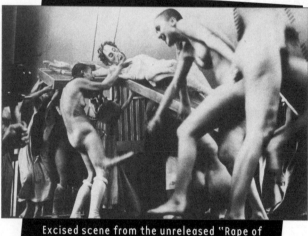

Excised scene from the unreleased "Rape of Christ" sequence.

Father Mignon (Murray Melvin) meanwhile scales a tall ladder for an overhead view of the orgy before pleasuring himself. Here, cameraman David Watkin, whose previous work included more sedate fare like *The Charge of the Light Brigade* and *Catch 22*, cannot resist the intoxicating osmosis as he and Russell bring the crucifixion orgy to a cinematic climax. With what is essentially a *jerk-off zoom*, the camera darts in and out of the orgy from Mignon's point of view and to the rhythm of his tugs. Amid all this, Russell makes repeated cuts to Grandier giving his quiet, solitary Communion before the Skiddaw mountains, unaware of the pandemonium that will swallow him upon his return.

"It was a harrowing story," Russell writes in his autobiography, *Altered States*, "graphically told, and left its mark on many of those involved. So did the music I used to create the atmosphere of religious hysteria it was necessary to whip up every day. And to that end I had four powerful loudspeakers placed around the set blasting out the grand finale of Prokofiev's cacophonous opera *The Fiery Angel*, in which an entire convent of nuns possessed of the devil get the screaming habdabs. Played at full volume through every take, this music of religious dementia possessed most of those who heard it in a similar manner."

For the "Rape of Christ," however, Russell returned to Stravinsky: "I found the most barbaric bit of *The Rite of Spring*, the music to which I had danced naked myself in my parents' house, and played it flat out. Without it the nuns were simply unable to cope; they were totally inhibited."

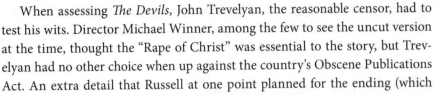

When assessing *The Devils*, John Trevelyan, the reasonable censor, had to test his wits. Director Michael Winner, among the few to see the uncut version at the time, thought the "Rape of Christ" was essential to the story, but Trevelyan had no other choice when up against the country's Obscene Publications Act. An extra detail that Russell at one point planned for the ending (which also showed up in Kermode's canister) had Sister Jeanne performing lewd acts on a bone from Grandier's charred remains: that alone would have put the original cut in legal peril.

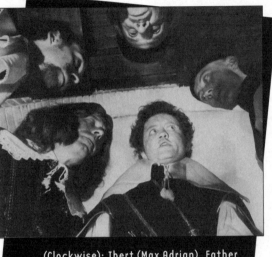

(Clockwise): Ibert (Max Adrian), Father Mignon (Murray Melvin), Baron de Laubardemont (Dudley Sutton), Magistrate Trincant (John Woodvine), and Adam (Brian Murphy) conspire to raise hell.

During a preview in a Mayfair theater, the British Board of Film Classification censors were already frantic, taking copious notes and whispering like geese ten minutes into the screening. In the end, the "Rape of Christ" was predictably sliced out. But more tribulation followed. After the film's London premiere in June 1971, the scathing critical reviews and the fact that at least seventeen local councils banned the film might be among several reasons why Trevelyan resigned from his post soon after.

Russell faced another British foe: the media-savvy Mary Whitehouse. Her knickers still twisting over the Strauss film, she continued to glare through horn-rimmed glasses at the heathen world, scolding in schoolmarm tones against all the indecent television fare that no one was forcing her to watch. She also commandeered England's National Viewers' and Listeners' Association to monitor any films that struck her and her cronies as blasphemous, morally spotty, and baleful to children. Her delicate sensibilities could shatter if the telly transmitted such epithets as "bloody" or any of those sadomasochistic *Tom and Jerry* cartoons.

In 1971, Whitehouse was a principal organizer of the Nationwide Festival of Light, a cadre of self-styled "holy" folks that included the former teen idol Cliff Richard and the conservative curmudgeon Malcolm Muggeridge. The organization encouraged churches to pressure authorities in small towns outside

London to keep *The Devils* out of local theaters. Outside of movie theaters that still showed it, Whitehouse and her zealots would sometimes stage sing-along prayer sessions, folk guitars and all.

While Trevelyan and Lord Harleck admired the version that finally became the British release cut, the U.S. was still breaking in its relatively new MPAA rating system and inevitably branded *The Devils* with an X, even after Warner Brothers cut additional gore and frontal nudity. In 1973, the studio wanted to cash in on the hubbub around *The Exorcist* and sliced more off for an R. Sadly, this would be the version, with a noisome pan-and-scan transfer and terrible sound, that the studio finally released on home video in 1981 and for which Great Britain would also have to settle.

In a 1972 interview with the *New York Times*, Russell mocked the scissor-snipes: "They said Mayor Daly of Chicago would get mad if we didn't cut certain things, but I could never see where *he* fitted in. Then a sales rep from Warner's said to me, 'Look here, Ken baby, I've made it with every broad from San Francisco to Timbuktu, but I'm telling you there were things you did in that movie that I wouldn't do to my own mother. We've got to start by cutting out all that pubic hair. Pubic hairs get you an automatic X.'"

•

As expected, wary critics retched. The *Observer Review*'s George Melly, another critic still smarting over *The Dance of the Seven Veils*, called *The Devils* "a hymn to sadomasochism." The *Evening Standard*'s Alexander Walker, who liked *Women in Love* but disliked just about everything Russell did since, threw another volley in an ongoing feud. In July 1971, he wrote: "Almost every serious question raised by the historical situation is thrown away by Russell in order to flaunt a taste for visual sensation that makes scene after scene look like the masturbatory fantasies of a Catholic boyhood."

Walker's remarks prompted a showdown on a late-night BBC news program. While Walker played the droll intellectual, Russell faced his adversary with a more pugnacious spirit. As Walker spouted his outrage, Russell accused him of citing scenes from the film that didn't exist. But Walker kept talking, while Russell waited to use his secret weapon—a rolled up edition of the *Evening Standard* that, as Walker later recalled, was rather thick that day.

"I don't make films for critics, I make them for the public," Russell retorted. But Walker, forearmed with anemic Stateside box office figures, replied, "The public isn't all that grateful, especially in America," whereupon Russell reddened, tensed his muscles, leaned over toward Walker, and shouted, "Well, go to America and write for the fucking Americans!" Russell then walked over and used his rolled-up paper to bop Walker on the head before storming off the set. He ruined Walker's immaculately combed coif, but the BBC switchboards clamored with viewers shocked less over the violence and more because "fucking" blared so audibly over the airwaves.

The Devils also made waves on the Continent, with Italy—Catholicism's cradle—giving it a mixed reception. In August 1971, Russell arrived in Venice for a press screening at the Lido Cinema Palace, but the Arean Theater, which was to screen its public release, pulled the film, fearing intervention from the police and bile from the Roman Catholic hierarchy. While the Vatican's newspaper, *L'Osservatore*, condemned the film's "perverted marriage of sex, violence, and blasphemy," Oliver Reed fumed Grandier-style at an afternoon press conference: "Why this hypocrisy? Why is it permissible to describe historic events in books and plays, though they must not be shown on the screen?" But many Italians who were not so subservient to papal whim and saw *The Devils* were by and large enthusiastic—enough to burn the doge of Venice's effigy after he attempted to slap the film with an embargo.

In the United States, the typical critics voiced their typical condemnation with typical nods to the status quo. "Even if the characters did exist and the behavior and times depicted are true," Ann Guarino griped in the *New York Daily News*, "to what purposes does one exploit a couple of rotten pages in history?—It's like opening up a can of worms." Charles Champlin, for the *Los Angeles Times*, declared it "a degenerate and despicable piece of art." *New York*'s apparently fatigued Judith Crist cried, "We can't recall in our relatively broad experience (four hundred movies a year for perhaps too many years) a fouler film." Louise Sweeney of the *Christian Science Monitor* at least had to placate a higher authority when she deemed it an "offensive mockery of Christianity."

Some critics were not above firing personal attacks. *Newsweek*'s Paul D. Zimmerman concluded that the movie demonstrated once and for all how "Russell has gone beyond extravagance to insanity." And the *New York Times*' Vincent Canby compared Russell to "a hobbyist determined to reproduce 'The Last Supper' in bottle tops." Smaller presses also sniffed: Dallas's *Iconoclast* said that it has "all the taste and restraint of a three-day gangbang," but the oddest and funniest came from the obscure Baltimore publication *Harry*, which called it "Goebbels in drag."

The *New York Times* also gave John Simon a seething forum: "Russell, who strikes me as something much worse than the mad artist—the mad anti-artist—will stop at no outrage in pursuit of effect for effect's sake. For him, the most aggressive blatancy is the exact equal of artistic impact. That there are people who consider the shock tactics of this bashibazouk consistent with artistry seems to me proof positive that our culture has reached the stage of paroxysm, after which, I suppose, there remains only rigor mortis."

●

Even if many now perceived him as Beelzebub reborn, Russell found advocates in several important places. Calling it "a delirious fresco," *Time* magazine's Jay Cocks considered *The Devils* "a movie so unsparingly vivid in its imagery, so totally successful in conveying an atmosphere of uncontrolled hysteria that Russell himself seems like a man possessed. . . . Russell lashes his actors into a histrionic verve that is reminiscent in equal parts of the Royal Shakespeare Company, the Living Theatre, and Bedlam." Jonathan Raban of the *New Statesman* called it Russell's best film and appreciated how "reality turns into joke, and joke into nightmare." The *New York Times'* Stephen Farber voiced a refreshing dissent from his colleagues when praising it as "a visionary work, a prophetic warning of the tenacity of ignorance and superstition." He qualified himself a bit by saying the film was "admittedly uneven, seriously flawed, but it is filled with the energy, passion, and imagination that make Ken Russell one of the most exciting and important filmmakers working today."

Far from being a negligible art-house novelty, *The Devils* was a major feature release that earned enough plaudits and scorn to assure its present-day status as a classic. Warner Brothers, with the aid of various reviews, pushed the film and—even after subjecting it to numerous cuts—did not shy away from using its scandal-friendly press clips as a box office draw. "Grisly, gutsy, masterpiece!" the *L.A. Free Press* chimed. "*The Devils* is a masterpiece as consumingly rich and as arrogantly original as the greatest works of art." And Bernard Drew of the Gannett News Syndicate teased the squeamish: "Some of you will hate this picture, some will love it, most of you are going to hate it and love it at the same time, as I did, but not one of you will be bored for an instant!"

●

For the cast and crew, the making of a lunatic masterpiece left torturous memories. "Oliver and Russell were undeniably disturbed by the experience of making *The Devils*," writes Oliver Reed's biographer Cliff Goodwin. "They could no longer hold a conversation or look each other in the eye. Sometimes they could not bear to be in the same room. There was an emptiness in the relationship which needed to 'lie fallow' until it recharged."

But Reed loved and defended *The Devils*, challenging Judith Crist to a televised debate, to which she didn't respond. Being ever the scamp, Reed tempered his praise with humor: "When I worked with Ken on *Women in Love*, he was starting to go crazy. But in the days when he made television movies about composers and writers, he was a sane, likable director. By the late 1960s, he was an insane, likable, film director."

Fellow renegade Derek Jarman, who would go on to collaborate on several other Russell projects, left *The Devils* feeling traumatized and depressed. But he also said he admired Russell precisely because "he would always take the adventurous path even at the expense of coherence." And by the time she came out with her autobiography in the mid-1990s, Vanessa Redgrave got over the aftertaste of Heinz vegetable soup being forced down her throat when she wrote, "I rank *The Devils* with *The Charge of the Light Brigade* as the two chief works of genius in the postwar British cinema."

Trevelyan might have played angel's advocate when censoring *The Devils*, but he did introduce Russell to the Reverend Gene D. Phillips, an American Jesuit involved with the Catholic Legion of Decency who also became one of Russell's unexpected allies. A mild mannered, somewhat willowy man, Phillips taught at Chicago's Loyola University, belonged to the Society of Jesus, and had an obvious love of the cinema. He contributed an essay about the cinema's treatment of gays for the 1975 book *Sexuality in the Movies*, came out with subsequent biographies of Russell and Francis Ford Coppola, and even incorporated *The Devils* into his curriculum.

But Phillips, who had seen the film back in 1971 with the "Rape of Christ" intact, split theological hairs when claiming it depicts but doesn't *commit* blasphemy. His rationale: that Russell juxtaposes the desecrated crucifix and the masturbating priest with Grandier giving a solemn Communion on a quaint, bucolic lakeside. Phillips saw this as Russell's attempt to show the Manichean duality between the sacred and the profane. It sounds righteous and academic but is about as convincing as the disclaimers that came with those road show exploitation movies of yore that promised to show girls giving birth, naked dancing teenagers, acrobatic circus freaks, and drug fiends shooting up—all strictly for "educational" purposes. *The Devils* offers much more—but not inspiration for "the Faith."

Phillips and Russell did, however, have a lucid motivation for eluding the "blasphemy" tag. Blasphemy incurred legal sanctions in England, and folks like Mary Whitehouse were itching for an excuse to take folks like Russell to court.

•

The Devils—in its most undesecrated version yet—appeared at England's National Film Theatre on November 2004, with the assistance of the film's original editor, Michael Bradsell, in a new, reconstructed print. In March 2005, this full version got screened again at the Brussels International Festival of Fantastic Film. Since then, a restored version has been showing up in bootleg form; with hope, and through the efforts of a petition traveling through the Internet, Warner Brothers might release a proper widescreen DVD, with audio commentaries, documentaries, and other extras.

"For all that, *The Devils* was the last nail in the coffin of my Catholic faith," Russell later confessed in his autobiography, "a faith that had sustained me for more than ten years and given my life purpose and direction. But my picture of God was hazing over: too much incense, too much stained glass, too much sci-fi in the sky. It was time to come down to earth. My Catholic missal was falling apart. I needed a new prayer book."

Still, Russell could not ignore those journalists out to bedevil him. Shortly after the film's release, Rex Reed joined Russell over what Reed called "a brandy and a sour English lunch that tasted like boiled socks." Reed tried ruining Russell's appetite as well: "You gave Catholics enough ammunition to gun you down for the rest of your life." Russell paused for extra breaths, rolled back his eyes, clutched at his steak knife, and spit back a mini-sermon:

> The church has always been appalling. I'm an ordinary, run-of-the-mill sinner who only pays lip service to the church, but I was trying to tell the truth about how it uses totally illiterate people to seduce everyone through terror. It has always been like that and it's like that now and the masses have always gone along with it. America is full of narrow-minded bigots who are terrified of any criticism of the church. They forced me to make twenty-three cuts before it could be released in America . . . Hypocrites! Some of my best scenes had to be cut. I had a great scene in which the nuns tore down the cross of Christ and stuffed his toes into their orifices. It was glorious stuff!

NAUGHTY, BAWDY BODIES

"**E**very blow must be a true one," Henri Gaudier hollers while pounding his mallet and chisel into a marble slab. "Every blow is a risk. You take your whole life in your hands. You can always tell a bad artist, like a bad doctor, by the fact he tries to surround his work with some sort of hocus-pocus. Sure, there's a mystery, but there's as much a mystery to the one who's doing it as to the one who's looking at it."

This fevered moment in *Savage Messiah*, in which Ken Russell finally pays homage to the man who inspired him during his direst days, summarizes Russell's paradoxical relationship to his own art. With the release of *The Devils* a year previous, Russell had already forged his hardest labor, his consummate masterpiece, his *Citizen Kane*. Now he started fearing that the bloom was off the Rosebud.

Gaudier blabbers on in the movie about the sacred creative act, but he doesn't really get to the other part about the creative act—when each blow of the mallet, swipe of the brush, or twist of the zoom lens leaves a draining afterbirth. It can come in the form of uncontrollable sycophants who distort the artist's meaning or steal his thunder, the artist getting sucked into his own media-generated hype, or worst of all, the artist ignored and left to founder in obscurity and poverty. Russell's post-*Devils* syndrome included all of these.

In a BBC documentary entitled *Russell's Progress*, Russell looked partly dazed as he skirted through an interview while escorted in the back seat of a Rolls Royce. He seemed a man choking in media smoke. And once saddled with that pretentious Frenchism "enfant terrible," he had to either perform a miracle by making a movie more shocking than *The Devils* or atone with something less intense.

At forty-four, Russell was still like a novelty-starved kid: constantly restless, wary of boredom, and terrified of potential disarray. Even as a recovering

Catholic, he still needed a sense of redemption. When *Films and Filming*'s Peter Buckley called him the "abominable showman," he was being affectionate, but there were too many out there ready to use the same expression with contempt. So, to exorcise his *Devils*, he got through his next two films by invoking the two people who meant so much to him: Gaudier, who embodied the ideal artist, and Dorothy Lamour, whose movies personified prefabricated Hollywood.

●

Russell opted for what initially appeared a lighthearted approach on his next picture: an adaptation of Sandy Wilson's musical *The Boy Friend*. He had several projects brewing. At one point, he planned to collaborate with Derek Jarman on a stage production for Covent Garden of Peter Maxwell Davies's opera *Taverner*, about the composer John Taverner's run-ins with the church. But the Wilson play, among England's favorite postwar productions, looked like the right cotton-candy antidote. Its story, set on the French Riviera, involves a finishing school where girls learn how to walk with poise and fall in love.

Sandy Wilson was no Aldous Huxley. Instead of penning damning prose about damned people, he wrote about youthful memories of cute songs that his older sister played on the gramophone at their Manchester home. Though they had to dance and sing on the sly when their strict Presbyterian father wasn't around, Wilson marveled as his sister did the Charleston to scratchy recordings of 1920s shows like *Show Boat* and *No, No, Nanette*. "Totally unaware of family troubles and financial difficulties," he recalls in his autobiography, "I simply absorbed the songs and dances of the day and grew up convinced they were what the 1920s were all about."

A friend, the actress Diana Maddox, later suggested he write a one-hour pastiche of favorite musical moments, which he unveiled in 1953 at the Players Theater. When it eventually moved to London's prestigious West End, the piece got longer. A year later, it was a Broadway hit, with Julie Andrews playing the lead part of Polly Browne, the doe-eyed ingénue who falls for Tony, the heartthrob and lad of noble birth posing as a messenger boy to evade his parents. Wilson, of course, closes his story with Polly and Tony walking off together on happy trails.

In his autobiography, Russell claims his decision to adapt Wilson's musical started as a bluff. He already knew Twiggy and her entrepreneur lover-guardian Justin de Villeneuve after giving them cameos in *The Devils*. Twiggy and de Villeneuve also knew Wilson, who claims the couple sought to buy *The Boy Friend*'s film rights, which MGM had already secured.

De Villeneuve invited Russell to hear some pop opera singer and to cavort at a press party afterwards. Russell was in an introspective temper that night when he retreated to a less populated corner of the room, glad when Twiggy joined him for some friendly conversation. But as usual, when Russell indulged in his hallucinogen of choice—champagne—he proved as flamboyantly verbal as he was visual. An obnoxious journalist overhearing him suddenly nosed in to ask impertinent questions, wondering if Twiggy and the director were planning something movie-ish. Russell blurted, "I'm going to make *The Boy Friend* with Twiggy."

What started as bubbly-induced braggadocio became media history by the next morning, when Russell got a call from an MGM-EMI attorney. Since MGM owned the movie option, the lawyer wanted to verify the buzz. Russell, fighting off a hangover, admitted he made the statement. But instead of sounding alarmed or litigious, the studio invited him to visit Metro London at nine o'clock the following morning.

Russell started filming in April 1971, having just made final edits on *The Devils*. And when he invited Rex Reed to attend *The Boy Friend*'s closed set, he was apparently unaware that the finicky critic had claimed *The Devils* "made me throw up." But he knew that Reed praised *The Music Lovers*; that was enough. During one of their lunches, Reed suggested that the director, by transposing Wilson's theatrical fluff to film, was going soft. But Russell retorted: "Don't be insulting. I haven't begun to shock people yet. I'm just doing therapy."

Russell's therapy became grief for others, especially when he started scaring Sandy Wilson. As production commenced, Wilson grew

Russell oversees Twiggy and Christopher Gable on the set of *The Boy Friend*.

increasingly fretful and helpless. He did not go to the set, but he soon felt queasy when noticing that the publicity stills made his blessed 1920s look more like the 1930s. He recounts his trauma of watching Russell being interviewed on television, especially when the show aired a clip from *The Boy Friend*: "Twiggy was apparently the unwilling victim of an open-air Roman orgy, the instigators of which were my old friends from Laurier's revues, Max Adrian and Moyra Fraser [an episode that was eventually excised from the film]. At the end of the programme I rang Joannie Rees [his agent], who was in a state of prostration."

Increasingly worried, Wilson wrote in his autobiography how he decided to tempt fate and endure some Russellscopic assaults:

> The only thing *I* could do was to take myself forthwith to see Mr. Russell's latest offerings, which I had hitherto resisted and which were both playing at the West End. I saw *The Music Lovers* in the afternoon and *The Devils* in the early evening and then staggered home, weak with shock and nausea, to find, to my relief, that *Lil' Abner* was showing on television. But my forebodings about the film of *The Boy Friend* were now increased a thousand-fold.

What started as therapy turned into another of Russell's delirious excursions. "The Sandy Wilson musical is mere grist for Russell's mill," a disapproving Pauline Kael sniped, "and his wheels never stop turning." From the start, Russell eschews Wilson's simplicity for flamboyance, turning the quaint into a grand, long, and overweening monstrosity of a musical that combines bits of Busby Berkeley, Fellini, *Monty Python's Flying Circus*, and some quirky British comedy reminiscent of *Carry On* films.

Russell changed the locale from a finishing school to a ratty old theater that, in turn, transformed into elaborate set designs as seen through the eyes of the players fantasizing about making the big time. Russell also showcased more of Twiggy's singing by interpolating two extra songs from *Singin' in the Rain*—"All I Do Is Dream of You" and "You Are My Lucky Star."

Russell also added a third narrative layer—a device he used six years before in *The Debussy Film*. "I heard an amateur dramatic society was putting on the show in Chingford, Essex," Russell recalls. "I decided it might be useful if I went along to see it. The cast got wind that I was there and played up to the hilt. I was sitting there in the audience watching the show, mentally visualizing how I was going to direct the film version, when the idea came to me." He presented the film as song and dance routines through the wishful fantasies of the various players, but a haughty Hollywood producer named De Thrill (Vladek Sheybal) has the most privileged viewpoint as he pays a surprise visit to the theater, looks down from the stage box, and conjures ideas of his own.

●

Jarman did not offer his designs this time, but Tony Walton, a set designer for films as diverse as François Truffaut's *Fahrenheit 451* and Richard Lester's *A Funny Thing Happened on the Way to the Forum*, presented a fantasy that leaned more toward the madcap movie musicals from the 1930s. "We shot then," Walton recalled, "at the EMI-MGM Elstree Studios, and I was like a child let loose in a candy store. I never dreamed I would have the opportunity to create such things as an Arabian Nights extravaganza, an airplane with dancers on the wings, a giant revolving gramophone turntable for another number, and even a complete Pixieland."

Peter Maxwell Davies trades the demonic clangor he provided *The Devils* for an olio of show tunes, making frequent transitions from scratchy gramophone noises to lush orchestral sweeps. When Polly (Twiggy) and Tony (Christopher Gable) duet on "I Could Be Happy with You," they go from lip-syncing with the gramophone to imagining themselves in a grand performance. But Russell yanks them back to peeling walls realism when the gramophone's scratchy shellac skips, and they are bit players again. Watching it all, De Thrill belches a condescending titter before projecting his own fantasy of Gable and Twiggy alternately tapping and waltzing atop a gigantic, spinning record. This also gave Russell and cinematographer David Watkin a chance to indulge in an overhead shot of human figures twisting on turntables into kaleidoscopic abstractions.

The turntable scene, Russell recalls, was nearly impossible to shoot. The Elstree studios were too low for the usual 35mm Panavision camera to capture the bird's eye view, so the crew had to import a 70mm camera from the States. He admits he was among those on their hands and knees keeping the dance floor shiny and spotless, despite the dust and dirt in the old, dilapidated Portsmouth theater that needed drastic refurbishing. In the meantime, MGM reps kept interrupting the drudgery with annoying phone calls, threatening to quash the entire production because they claimed Russell was going over budget and schedule.

Fans who love their Russell on the extreme might be initially disappointed at what seems only on the surface a feel-good movie, but they can regain heart when considering the exaggerated set designs, outlandish camera swoops, garish costumes, and overblown acting, replete with fluttering eyelids and catty dialogue delivered through clenched teeth. Those same fans might also take sadistic delight out of watching more conservative theater purists whimper over how Russell once again "distorted" his source. Even with the happy ending, never a Russell strong suit, the movie is still a bit bent. "There is really no difference between nuns with no clothes on and tap dancers in goggles," he would say. "It is all material."

Anyone fearing Russell had gone "soft" needs only the assurance of a nasty review. Writing for *Sight and Sound*, Jan Dawson (who had all of her anti-Russell prejudices already intact) proceeded to scoff at him for doing "wrong" what many Russell aficionados would find "right": "Time and again, it seems, he mistakes his distorting mirror for a window on the world. . . . In a uniquely perverse process, his source material is first trivialized, then—in its newly impoverished form—inflated to epic proportions."

From the film's opening title song, those of Dawson's tastes were sure to feel terrorized. Provincial would-be starlets take the hostilities they have toward one another out on their performances, clomping about the stage, trying to out-sing each other, and glaring into the camera with eyes so wide their socket moisture shines against the lights.

What seems like great acting was, according to Russell, an accurate reflection of real life intrigues among the movie's cast of stage hogs who conspired to grab the spot. Twiggy preferred sitting in the cold theater draped in an overcoat rather than put up with the other girls. Barbara Windsor, portraying the faux French wench, always managed to grab the punch line.

"A great deal of bitterness and jealousy also spilled over into life outside the theater," Russell recalls, "with hotel doors being kicked down in the middle of the night, punch-ups in bedrooms, and on one occasion the old dramatic overdose of sleeping pills. The film should have been called *The Devils Take a Holiday*."

Russell tries making some compromise with convention. Gable is the nice guy prototype that Dick Powell would have played in the Busby Berkeley backstage musicals. He's there to lend support for Twiggy the underdog, who is in turn a knock-off of Ruby Keeler. Especially when he dons the messenger boy costume, Gable looks like the perfect white-toothed heartthrob as seen through Polly's eyes.

All six feet and six inches of Tommy Tune assume the type of beanpole role that Hal LeRoy would have taken in numerous 1930s Vitaphone musical shorts. Tune's character also hoofs while nattering one heartrending tale after another, recounting his orphaned childhood, his dreams of stardom, and his unique ability to dance the "Double Trip Maxi Ford with a Knickerbockers Break."

Russell often enjoys inserting a scene or two in which the supposed pariah or villain has a sympathetic moment. In this case Maisie, the harridan of the troupe (played by Antonia Ellis, who would soon be a Nazi she-devil in *Mahler*), lends an ear and a tear as Tune goes into his hard-luck story. But she's soon back to being the most brazen of De Thrill's suitors.

"True to form," *Sight and Sound*'s Dawson writes, "Russell begins by filming not the work itself, but a ragged repertory production of it. This device provides a pretext for having most of the numbers sung out of tune and enables Russell, as *cinéaste*, to impose his caricatural vision by dwelling on the grotesque hyperboles of theatrical makeup." She adds: "Twiggy is spared the disfiguring effects of Russell's theatrical makeup, and her natural beauty (which has no need of the surrounding ugliness to set it off) is strong enough to survive even the director's practice of placing his camera dangerously near to his performers' larynxes."

Critics like Dawson, otherwise terrified of Russell's product, gave Twiggy raves for essentially being herself. Russell forbid her from putting on any actorly airs and got furious after finding out she was taking diction lessons on the sly. But viewers loved her dressed as Poor Pierrette, pining atop a glittery cardboard crescent moon for her Pierrot. She also stands out as "the Spirit of Ecstasy," a gilded human hood ornament atop a mammoth Rolls Royce at the close of "The Boy Friend" number.

But neither Twiggy nor Gable was the true star. That distinction belongs to Max Adrian as Mr. Max, the manic impresario. His over-the-top performance is reminiscent of Warner Baxter's apoplectic Julian Marsh in the 1933 film *42nd Street*, who supposedly recovers from a nervous breakdown but proceeds to direct Ruby Keeler, Ginger Rogers, and others with neurotic ferocity.

Perhaps more than any other Busby Berkeley choreographed backstage musical, *42nd Street* exposes the grit behind the glitter. "Two hundred people, two hundred jobs, two hundred thousand dollars, five weeks of grind and blood and sweat depend on you," Marsh tells Keeler's character when the weight of everyone's illusions falls on her shoulders. Russell, drawing parallels with Gaudier's marble and mallet, empathizes with Marsh's melodramatic demonstration of how much hard work, bruised egos, and shattered personalities go into putting on a pretty show.

Adrian's Max is, however, more comical than Baxter's Marsh, as he runs around backstage in a blue kimono adorned with butterflies, barks out orders like a diva, and looks as if he's about to have an aneurysm. He is already livid to discover that Rita Monroe, the show's prima donna, got her high heel stuck in a tram and broke her foot. He invokes Julian Marsh by urging Polly (drafted to be the understudy) with a memorable line: "You're going out there as a youngster; you've got to come back a star!"

Adrian, who had asthma and a bad heart, put so much fervor into the part that it is no surprise he collapsed on the set during the first day of rehearsals. Max's legs gave out, so Russell had to cast him as a convalescent during his duet with Georgina Hale on "It's Never Too Late to Fall in Love." But it all makes sense when Mr. Max presents his "latest cinematographic fantasy for the silver screen"—a home movie of nurses rolling geezers in synchronized wheelchairs.

Julie Andrews, who played Polly in the 1954 Broadway production, was slated to be Rita, the star with the broken foot (modeled on Bebe Daniels's role in *42nd Street*), who hobbles on crutches into Polly's dressing room to wish her grudging good luck. But Glenda Jackson arrived to take the part, apparently cooling off from her feud with Russell. "When I said no to *The Devils*," Jackson recalls in one of her biographies, "it produced the most bilious fury from him, so there was an exchange of heated letters, and I didn't hear from him for ages. Then he rang up and asked me to do a day for him on *The Boy Friend*. So I did." Still, Russell exacted some revenge by having her sit for about twelve hours with her leg in a plaster cast.

Though cut from its release print, *The Boy Friend*'s most outlandish sequence involves Russell's more elaborate reenactment of the Olympian dance to Ethelbert Nevin's "Narcissus" that he used in *Isadora*. He again has a group of young girls in Grecian robes prance around with floral wreaths in an Arcadian fantasy. But following a dissolve into another dream sequence, Twiggy imagines herself pirouetting along an idyllic, petal-strewn lake. Meanwhile, in another part of the forest, Mr. Max is a satyr, leading a bacchanalia that includes Hellenic flappers doing the Charleston.

Many prone to get overwhelmed by *The Boy Friend*'s length and frequent hallucinatory power are in for another jolt. Just as narrative decorum would ordinarily signal that it's time for the movie to wind down, BAM! Russell plows right into "The Riviera," the movie's big cardiac moment when manic tappers accompany delirious tracking shots along the soundstage. The sequence closes on the showgirls dressed as aviatrixes, flashing naughty poses on the wings of a biplane against a fake blizzard.

●

"The greatest thing to hit the screen since Monroe," Russell, with his gift for hyperbole, once called Twiggy. But reports also surfaced that Twiggy and Russell frayed one another's nerves from time to time; the possessive de Villeneuve contributed to the tension by quibbling over production details. At one point, Twiggy considered the whole experience a "nightmare," especially on the day Russell terrorized her by lunging onto the set dressed in a sailor's suit and gyrating into a manic dance. When asked what kind of childhood the director could have possibly had to merit such stormy antics, a seasoned Russell colleague rolled up his eyes and said, "He's having it now."

During his interview process, Rex Reed described a truculent Russell when he met him in the quiet, seaport town of Portsmouth during the shooting: "He was storming up and down the lazy cobblestone streets in knickers, boots, outsized tinted granny glasses, a black Dracula cape, and a stone crucifix, brandishing an evil cane with an ivory dog's head handle, and frightening the horses."

"Of course, when it was finished it looked such a jolly film," Shirley Russell recalled, "but it was really the one where everybody was miserable. I don't know why. There was something strange in the atmosphere. We had nervous breakdowns and near suicides among the company. Over one weekend, one girl nearly tore another's eyes out, somebody else kicked another person's door down, and one of the guys, a very nice person, was coming back to the location from London by train, and when the train halted at a siding, he just got out of it and wandered away into the middle of a field, and we had to go and fetch him. It had a peculiar effect on everyone, that film."

The critics, who should have been easier on this nuns-and-Nazis-free Russell, were generally not so charitable. According to *Halliwell's Film and Video Guide*, "The whole thing is an artistic disaster of some significance both to Russell's career and to the cinema of the early 1970s." Judith Crist carped again in *New York* magazine about "globs and globs of creamy campy overproduction."

On the British front, Russell sent a furious letter to the editors of the *Evening Standard*, insisting that Alexander Walker not be assigned to review *The Boy Friend*, noting that the critic's biases would taint his ability to make a fair assessment. The paper denied Russell's request but relished the good copy by printing both the letter and a rejoinder.

In his autobiography, however, Sandy Wilson, always craving too pretty a world, called Twiggy's performance "a tiny beam of pathos in a walpurgisnacht of self-indulgence." Years later, he reflected: "It wasn't painful. It was just astonishing. I have seen many Ken Russell films, and they are always outrageous and scandalous—the devil in the nude or something like that. Twiggy was the only sort of human being in it."

There are bright spots. Gene Siskel, writing for the *Chicago Tribune*, lauded it as a "mostly entertaining, always dazzling trip through Campsville." And John Coleman in the *New Statesman* wrote, "Russell has found the perfect objective correlative for his extravagant turn of image."

●

Vladek Sheybal, who had many tales of terror to recount about his own stage experiences, tried all he could to help Russell push the film into a darker direction, tickling the director's prurient ears with stories about a famous actress who literally gave knee-jerk reactions to oral-friendly Hollywood moguls.

Russell planned to stress the lesbian relationship between Maisie (Antonia Ellis) and Fay (Georgina Hale) but chickened out because he thought it to be "at odds with the fairy tale atmosphere of the plot." But a little later, he expressed regret for not including it, lamenting what he called "the phoney goody-goody quality of the artificial musical plot."

The Boy Friend's flighty dancers and the frills gave Russell hoofer fatigue. He was also disgusted by all of the cuts the studio insisted on making and instead focused on a project that would be shorter and more scaled back. If *The Devils* and *The Boy Friend* proved enervating, Russell needed a film with more of a cozy, simple mood, and with a minimum of greedy hands eviscerating his pie. It was time for his long-awaited tribute to Henri Gaudier.

"I'm sick of this reverential approach to artists," Russell barked to the *Los Angeles Times* in 1971, when discussing *Savage Messiah*. "They're human beings too, and I'm not afraid to look 'em in the eye." Russell is at his artistic best when he makes his artistic idols, no matter how much he loves them, stumble. But here, he denies viewers such pleasures. Gaudier once professed in his many fawning letters to Sophie Brzeska, "A fine and noble artist must also be a simple, good, and beautiful man," but one wonders why Russell felt compelled to take him at his word. Uncharacteristically reverential toward his subject, Russell committed the sin of letting sentiment eclipse his gift for irony.

Savage Messiah's premise—that the creative spirit must thrive against enemies and entropy—is endearing and irrefutable. The film also equates art's hard work with the toil of relationships—particularly the platonic May-December match between the struggling Henri (Scott Antony) and Sophie (Dorothy Tutin), a Polish woman of noble lineage and an aspiring novelist twice his age. Both are so highly strung, insecure, angry, and obnoxious that the drama at least stays fevered, even if the two characters end up being not all that sympathetic.

MGM, happy with its truncated version of *The Boy Friend*, agreed to pick up the *Savage Messiah* tab once Russell delivered the finished product. In the meantime, he took out a second mortgage on his home, practically drained his savings account, and also got financial backing from the Lee International Studios, a place that Russell describes as "a derelict biscuit factory on the banks of a stagnant canal." It would be the locale for several of his subsequent films. Russell also made *Savage Messiah* more of a family affair, with his daughter Victoria, along with his four sons Alex, James, Toby, and Xavier showing up as extras.

H. S. Ede's biography, from which Russell takes both the film's title and much of the information, is a scant narration interspersed with a deluge of letters Gaudier wrote to Sophie and several other associates. Ede's Gaudier is enamored by "the simple life of the fields," but exiled in his artist's garret, he admits that, despite his love of nature, the commercial corruption all around him is perversely inspiring.

Ede also provided what was essentially a Gaudier-approved version of Gaudier: the bohemian innocent who, despite a habit of lying and exploiting rich patrons, was steadfast in his goal to twit the "common bourgeois folk" and be the schoolbook model of the hungry artist who "always suffers, mostly because of the enslaved people who surround him, bleating like a lot of sheep."

Still, even Ede could not resist presenting an antihero whose physical weakness belies his metaphysical prowess. Instead of Antony's robust and somewhat athletic hooligan, Ede's Gaudier is thin, gaunt, and delicate, with sunken cheeks and eyes, susceptible to colds, headaches, and nosebleeds, neurotic, partly anemic, and prone to bouts of anger, tears, and depression.

Derek Jarman, who returned as Russell's set designer, visited Ede for his research and came away with a different impression of the artist: "I found Gaudier an equivocal character, and still do. He might have boasted that there were no artists except himself, Brancusi, Modigliani, 'we the moderns,'—but his life, cut short at twenty-three by a bullet in the trenches, hardly gave him time to prove it. He left a small body of stylistically uneven work, much of which decorated his biographer Ede's home at Kettles Yard in Cambridge. When I arrived there I felt like an intruder. Ede told me he saw Gaudier as the god Apollo in a golden sunset."

The limited budget also forced Russell to focus on the characters. This was not a blessing for Jarman because it meant less elaborate decor. But despite how some have referred to this as Russell's "quiet little film," *Savage Messiah* is full of jolting camera work and quick, loud (almost rapacious) dialogue. The screenplay, on which he collaborated with Christopher Logue, is all the more intrusive since Russell dispenses with a musical soundtrack for most scenes.

∙

Gaudier starts by fulminating with a variation on his simple and quaint notions of artistic purity while on top of a statue outside the Paris library where he and Sophie admit they're both lonely and become instant friends. But even his bloated ego gets pricked when he escorts Sophie to the Louvre, his "real mother," and gets the snub from the gallery personnel for refusing to tuck in his shirttail. The museum attendant (Peter Vaughan) expresses philistine wisdom when accusing Gaudier of having "an artistic tizzy." Outside the museum's doors, Gaudier mounts a giant Easter Island head (that Jarman molded out of polystyrene) to declare, "Art is alive: enjoy it, laugh at it, love it, or hate it, but don't worship it!"

Sophie is already reduced to being Gaudier's passive audience, but she sets the emotive tone when dragging him to her humble quarters to prepare soup. Her ensuing monologue being one of the film's high points, Russell nurtures every close-up while cutting intermittently to the slaughtered vegetables. Sophie lacerates cabbages, eviscerates potatoes, and castrates carrots as if they're old

Henri Gaudier (Scott Antony)
atop Derek Jarman's Easter
Island replica.

ghosts she's trying to excise. She rages about a horrid childhood when her mother called her stupid, how she got set up with "an old fish fop" and languished as a governess amid baby shit, how she got the reputation as "the biggest whore in the Latin quarter," and how she's just "a snaggletoothed old hag" not really worthy of a young man's love.

The scene's fury literally bled into real life. "The first time I did the vegetable scene," Dorothy Tutin remembered, "I cut my finger. I didn't stop—Ken hates to stop—and somewhere in the back of my mind as I saw the blood flowing was the thought 'Ken will like this.'"

Tutin was a relatively obscure actress at the time. Her first significant film part was as Cecily Cardew in Anthony Asquith's 1952 version of *The Importance of Being Earnest* and a year later as Polly Peachum in Peter Brook's *The Beggar's Opera*. She got a CBE in 1967 and in 2000 became a dame, a year before her death. But a harbinger of her destiny with Russell occurred back in 1961, when she played *The Devils*' Sister Jeanne in a Stratford-on-Avon Company Production of John Whiting's play.

Despite peer praise, she never tired of criticizing herself: "I find what I do abominable," she once admitted. "I pick away at myself because I am not as perfect as I would like to be." It was an insecurity that Russell probably milked when he got the most out of her performance, sometimes putting her in uncomfortable situations. One of them involved some very bulky bloomers that she hated wearing and that Russell, like Erich von Stroheim before him, insisted she keep on for period realism, even though no one would see them.

In *Savage Messiah*, Russell draws bold battle lines between artists and society, as well as true art and commercialism—black and white concepts that he executed with more impressive gray shades in previous films. In *Isadora*, Russell could temper the love for his subject with scenes of grand bathos. Viewers could empathize with the great dancer's desire to achieve her vision in the face of hostility but could also understand why her efforts were bound to turn into kitsch. Russell's Gaudier elicits hardly any of that tension—a naivete that made the more skeptical Jarman uncomfortable. Jarman also had disagreements over designs and was bewildered when Russell insisted, "The central image of our movie is the titanic struggle of the sculptor to release his genius from the intractable marble."

In the end, Jarman's aesthetic niceties showed up in two important moments that break the mood of artistic piety. When Henri and Sophie visit their new-found dilettante friend Angus Corky (Lindsay Kemp), the home's ornate paintings and fixtures offer a breather from Gaudier's dreary basement bungalow; it is also a contrast to the natural lighting, which Russell and the director of photography, Dick Bush, deploy in most of the story.

Here, Henri and Sophie meet the effete art dealer Lionel Shaw (John Justin), the crotchety publisher Thomas Buff (Ben Aris), a severe looking gender bender named Mavis Coldstream (Imogen Claire), as well as a crimson-haired communist and Elizabeth Siddal impersonator named Kate (aptly Judith Paris). These poseurs, like *Women in Love*'s Loerke and *The Devils*' Louis XIII, are harsh and repulsive aesthetes on the surface, but they pull some surprises with their whiffs of wisdom. Shaw appears to see through Gaudier's bluff and expresses a distinct dislike for Sophie after she eschews dinner table manners with her hysterical rendering of an ersatz Polish folk tune called "Two Fleas," which Tutin composed for the film to reinforce the early signs of her character's insanity.

Later, Jarman supplies another ironic twist with his design for a nightclub called the Vortex, where Shaw's cognoscenti congregate. Jarman modeled it somewhat on the Cave of the Golden Calf, a nightclub that Frida Uhl (the second wife to August Strindberg) inaugurated and that Wyndham Lewis helped decorate. Gaudier was, after all, a doyen of the Vorticist movement; inside these "unnatural" settings, he hogs the limelight as shamelessly as one of *The Boy Friend*'s stage whores.

When Thomas Buff yells out from the audience, "Shut up and grow up," Russell at least deflates some of Gaudier's gas at a point when he's most unbearable. This doesn't stop Gaudier from ranting that he is "the new genius of the planet Earth," grabbing at his privates while sputtering some song-and-dance routine about a "concrete Venus with the all-electric crotch."

When he and Sophie move to London for a life of penury, Gaudier plays the working-class hero but bewitches his fellow day laborers by carving a nude on the pavement with his riveter. Desperate, he must follow through with his boast one evening that he could have a bust ready for Lionel Shaw by the morning. So he sculpts in a fury through the night at a marble slab he'd stolen from a graveyard. Russell's camera moves around him, often at low angles, as Gaudier chisels away with the rhythms of a mad conductor birthing a masterpiece, which is in this case his famous 1913 female torso.

As Russell explains, "Gaudier's life was a good example to show that art which is simply exploiting to the full one's natural gifts is really bloody hard work, misery, momentary defeat and taking a lot of bloody stick—and giving it . . . if you really want to show the hard work behind a work of art, then a sculptor is your very best subject. I was very conscious of this in the sequence where Gaudier sculpts a statue all through the night. It's the heart, the core of the film, the most important scene to me."

After seeing a newspaper headline of the Rheims Cathedral in flames as a result of the German bombardment, Gaudier goes off to fight in the First World War. A grieving Sophie, missing out on paying Gaudier a last goodbye, will eventually slide into madness. Though Russell spares her the elaborate asylum scene he gave Nina Tchaikovsky in *The Music Lovers*, he leaves Gaudier's motives for going to the front a bit ambiguous: has the burning Rheims goaded Gaudier's patriotism, or has

Henri Gaudier (Scott Antony) cups his family jewels in a surrealistic nightclub scene with Gosh Boyle (Helen Mirren).

it made him so disillusioned that he charges toward the enemy with nihilistic rage? "I like the war," he writes in a letter from the trenches. "I'm in lots of action. Each night we go out and kill Germans. I have killed at least four myself. When the shells go off, it reminds me of thunder." Listening to Corky read this aloud, Thomas Buff, who previously told Gaudier to shut up and grow up, spits back again: "Whoever wrote that should be shot!" Gaudier finally took a battle bullet in June of 1915.

•

Savage Messiah closes where the high drama begins: a gallery. But this time, Gaudier's works are the disembodied commodities on display—and in the kind of museum that he anachronistically derided at the start of the film as "pure and air-conditioned for the American tourists." Russell seems to get ambiguous again: Is it art, or is it product? Is he venerating the work with lush lighting as if it were an idolater's graven image, or is he letting it revolve on a platform to suggest an analogy between high art on display and the hoopla involved in showing off a glossy showroom car?

Once released in the fall of 1972, *Savage Messiah*'s critical response was often no kinder than it had been toward Russell's more extreme movies. Art historian Robert Hughes wrote that Russell indulged in the "disembowelment of history." This time, Pauline Kael called Russell "a one-man marketplace, a compulsive Hollywoodizer . . . always turning something from the artists' lives into something else—a whopping irony, a phallic joke, a plushy big scene." John Simon abhorred it in the *New Leader* but wrote that Tutin "glowed like a jewel inside a pig's bladder."

Russell couldn't win either way. The *New York Times*' Vincent Canby, who'd been scathing to Russell in the past, didn't think the film was "compulsive" enough, and he even got facetious: "Although the performances are full of hysteria, *Savage Messiah* is so tame that it almost makes one long for the excesses of the earlier Russell films, which so overwhelmed the senses as to become anesthetically soothing, like loud rock."

There were, however, some distant voices of support. In *Cinema* magazine, Stephen Farber, who lauded *The Devils*, credited *Savage Messiah* for being "accessible and seductive." And Paul Zimmerman of *Newsweek* extolled Russell for "communicating the white-hot energies of the creative act." But even Russell later admitted, "The film of mine that was least successful was *Savage Messiah* which, although worthy, wasn't cinematic enough. I leant too heavily on the script; it could have been a radio play."

Though *The Boy Friend* and *Savage Messiah* seem to have contrary moods and themes, Russell, the irascible but secretly humble son of a shoe salesman, uses both films to address an infuriating inequity: artists without independent wealth risk making issues of subsistence drain their creative vision. Amid this clamor to survive, the best creative act needs a cudgel; creative statements have to be pounded out and screamed. The troupe of graceless tarts who bat their eyelids, stamp their heels, and try their klutzy best to make art grow from a dingy theater floor are, in the end, no less noble than the manic sculptor who burns the midnight oil to chisel out a neoclassical torso that another working class hero might regard as just a headstone with boobs.

16

THE COFFIN AND THE CODPIECE

"**D**ear Barbra S," Ken Russell began a letter to Barbra Streisand dated July 26, 1971. "I have sneaked away from *The Boy Friend* for an illicit weekend with Sarah Bernhardt. I think I have turned her from a monumental bore into quite an attractive proposition."

If all had gone according to plan, *The Legend of Sarah* would have been a Streisand coup and a Russell triumph. Russell's letter also included his film treatment: descriptions that promised lots of pomp, camp, and material more complex and disturbing than the simpler "therapy" of *The Boy Friend* and *Savage Messiah*.

The Bernhardt story was, in keeping with most biographies of the legendary nineteenth-century French actress, to have a heaping helping of morbid overtones. Russell had it begin with Bernhardt lying in a coffin, ready to be buried amid a "very Aubrey Beardsley" setting: an orchestra and chorus chimes in the background as Oscar Wilde, Europe's crowned heads, and even the pope assemble to see her off into the next world.

Count Robert de Montesquiou, a dandy and epicurean on whom Marcel Proust modeled his Baron de Charlus in *Remembrance of Things Past*, presides over Sarah's ersatz funeral. According to Bernhardt's biographer Cornelia Otis Skinner, Sarah staged this prank several times: someone, if not Montesquiou, really did serenade her fake corpse with a parody on a song more widely known as "On a Bicycle Built for Two."

> Montesquiou refers to the assembly as her lovers, and himself as the greatest of her lovers.
>
> He sings this song (to the tune of "Daisy, Daisy") as he mounts the dais and climbs into the bier and lies down beside the "corpse."

Sarah, Sarah
Give me your answer do
I'm half crazy
All for the love of you
It won't be a stylish marriage
I can't afford a carriage
But you'll look sweet
In a winding sheet
In a sepulcher built for two.

After this funereal frolic, Russell exposes the ruse:

> Sarah opens her eyes, smiles, and embraces her lover as the lid is lowered. The crowned heads of Europe and the pope then dance a shimmy around them as the scene dissolves to:
>
> Sarah in her dressing room making up for *La Dame aux Camelias*. Still youngish. She remains like this throughout the film. On the dressing table a bottle of gin. She has obviously had a few and is talking to herself. Her surroundings are bizarre; the place resembles a jungle as much as a room—ferns, palms, jeweled props, statues, paintings, the odd snake, a cheetah—hundreds of photographs and souvenirs. Over her mirror the famous photograph of her lying in the legendary coffin.

By the early 1970s, Sarah Bernhardt was a fading memory. Old press clippings, photographs, scratchy Victor recordings, a few creaky and rarely seen silent pictures, and reproductions by the Czech-French painter and poster designer Alphonse Mucha, which tonier college students put up on their dormatory walls, were meager reminders of the woman once dubbed "The Divine Sarah" and sometimes "The Magnificent Lunatic."

Still, Bernhardt was ready for a movie tribute as lavish as her life. The early 1970s was also a time when audiences flocked to repertory theaters to watch old movies, when the androgynous aesthetics of glam rock melded with an interest in Art Nouveau designs. Her morbid sense of humor and gaudy theatrics, along with her often gender-bending appearance and bisexual mystique, would probably also have appealed to fans of Alice Cooper and David Bowie.

In her time, she seemed to have been everywhere at once. Along with Montesquiou and Oscar Wilde, her coterie also included Emile Zola, Victor Hugo, Gustave Flaubert, and Gabriel D'Annunzio. Freud wrote of his head "reeling" when he saw her perform in 1885; D. H. Lawrence likened her to "a gazelle with a beautiful panther's fascination and fury."

"No actress in the theater ever had more written about her," Skinner claims, "more gossip true or false told about her, more ecstatic praise or viscious censure showered upon her." Whether soaring over Paris in a hot-air balloon or entertaining San Quentin convicts on one of her many trips to America, Bernhardt was a life essentially waiting for Russell's part history, part comic-book approach.

"She was young and irresponsible," Skinner continues, "and at times her behavior was that of someone slightly demented . . . She could take a warmly sympathetic, even intimate, interest in a friend one day, and a week later greet the same person with the cold detachment of someone being introduced for the first time. Her temper was as volatile as ever. It was nothing for her to hurl a hairbrush at a maid and, next moment, by way of atonement to hand her a piece of jewelry."

Like the sickly courtesan Marguerite Gauthier from Alexandre Dumas's *The Lady of the Camellias*, whose part she'd play on the stage again and again, Bernhardt was preoccupied with death since at least her teens, when she obtained the rosewood, white-satin lined coffin where she'd sometimes sleep. Though she lived to be seventy-nine, she imagined herself dying young. A sickly child, she incessantly coughed and once in a while spewed blood. She liked such Gothic mementos as bats and skulls and even hung out with corpses in the Paris morgue.

Streisand shared Russell's desire to revive the woman who used to play dead. "Yeah, I think it's inevitable I'll play Sarah," she told *Look* magazine in December 1969 (shortly after she appeared in *Hello, Dolly!* and as she prepared for *The Owl and the Pussycat*), "but there's nothing in the works yet. I can wear my hair in the frizziest look, and you know Bernhardt once acted Hamlet, not Ophelia, and so will I."

Physically the star of *On a Clear Day You Can See Forever* bore a fairly strong resemblance to Bernhardt. And if the project worked out, the public could have enjoyed seeing Streisand take on a role that was more outrageous than her usual output and with a director who would guarantee a performance from her that was more garish and melodramatic than anything she had done or ever will do.

Russell's treatment traces Bernhardt's days as the daughter of a Jewish courtesan brought up as a Catholic and sent to a convent school, her stint with the Comédie-Française, her sensational tours of London, New York, and across America. He addresses the highlights from her acting career and expressionistic style, stressing how she yearned to play the title role in Oscar Wilde's *Salome* before England's Lord Chamberlain banned it. She was Joan of Arc, Cleopatra, and Hamlet. And in one of her bolder moments, she played Napoleon's sickly and melancholic son who longed to recapture his father's lost empire in *The Eaglet*, a play that Edmond Rostand wrote just for her and that premiered in March 1900.

But Russell centers on her most famous role as Dumas's consumptive, which both Alla Nazimova and Greta Garbo would make famous in films entitled *Camille*:

> As she gets ready for her greatest part—Marguerite Gauthier—she continues talking to herself and we realize that all the main events in her life were connected with this play which she revived twenty-two times. The remainder of the film concerns these events—but interspersed between each "Camelia" episode comes a section concerned with other aspects of her life and art.

Playing on the art and life connections, Russell addresses how her Gauthier role "parallels her own predicament almost exactly with the character of the drama," particularly her sad love affairs. She loved the Belgian Prince de Ligne, who failed to marry her because his uncle, obeying the king's orders, intervened and talked (possibly bribed) her, a commoner, out of a romance that threatened royal proprieties.

Russell also deals with Bernhardt's love for Jacques Damala, a so-called diplomatic Apollo whom Russell refers to as "a Greek gigolo." Damala was supposedly so handsome that he drove some women to divorce and at least one to suicide. And he hypnotizes Sarah with his oleaginous accent and hand kissing, eventually conning her into letting him play Armand to her Camille.

By the time he gets to Sarah dressing as a man and leading "an idyllic existence" with another of her lovers, the painter Gustave Doré, Russell makes the story more comical and at times surrealistic. Sarah highlights her trip to the United States with a visit to Thomas Edison at his Menlo Park home in a "macabre midnight meeting." When the inventor "records her voice—films her—a grotesque Sarah flickers across the screen."

Russell outlines other exploits as Bernhardt travels across the American boonies on a train named after her:

> Sarah playing "Camelias" before cowboys in the Wild West—in a tent which is blown away by a hurricane.

> Sarah on the "Bernhardt Special" (train) with lovers—attacked by bandits.

> Sarah practicing with pistols to protect herself from indignant "Mothers of the Sons of America" who wished to save their country from this French courtesan.

Bernhardt looks back on a subsequent tour of the States, when she agreed to star in a 1911 film version of *The Lady of the Camellias*. Her Armand is Lou Tellegen, another conceited ham with Grecian beauty. She in her late sixties and he in his early thirties, this next tryst was destined to be another emotional train wreck. But she would also star in her most remembered film, playing Queen Elizabeth I, with Tellegen as the Earl of Essex. So overtaken by her own performance, she supposedly proclaimed, "I am immortal! I am film!"

After she supposedly pleads with Emile Zola to write a story about the persecution of Alfred Dreyfus, and as the Great War is waged, Bernhardt is in her seventies and finally has her right leg amputated following a bad fall on her knee that never healed after thirty-odd years. Russell planned to include a reference to the cable she got from P. T. Barnum, who offered $10,000 to include her severed limb as one of his attractions. But even having to hobble with a wooden leg and plagued with continual bouts of uremia, she summons the strength to entertain troops.

Russell also probes another scandalous chapter in her life: Marie Colombier, an actress she had hired for her troupe, who gets resentful when Berhardt doesn't help her absolve her debts. She starts serializing stories in the French press about the thirty-six-year-old star's exploits during the American trip—which would culminate in a book entitled, *The Memoirs of Sarah Barnum*. "Sarah Barnum," Russell writes, "a libellous gallery of scandalous events concocted by a jealous actress in her troupe—Marie Colombier—whom she horsewhipped. (They were possibly true after all.)"

This all sounds so over the top, so characteristic of a prima donna's indulgence—both Bernhardt's and Russell's—but it's all recorded in various Sarah Bernhardt biographies that had surfaced through the decades. In his treatment's final section, entitled "La Morte aux Camelias," Russell prepares for Sarah the type of swan song he savored in *Isadora*:

> We have now reached the point where we have covered the major events in her life and a number of her dramatic portrayals. The time has now come to reveal that this has been a drunken old woman remembering her past.
>
> A call boy knocks at the door of her room which is now far less exotic than when it was first seen. In fact it is dirty and tatty.
>
> "Five minutes please."
>
> Sarah goes to walk out of the room and falls over. The boy rushes forward to lift her. As she struggles up we see she is not a strikingly exotic woman but an appalling old crone of seventy-two—("I thought for a minute I had both legs," she says—),

hair dyed, face thick with makeup like cracked plaster. Lipstick smeared haphazardly over her face.

This is Russell's moment for bawdy burlesque as vaudeville's specter hovers. As the boy lifts her toward the stage, she encounters tawdry showgirls and a red-nosed comedian telling off-color jokes. But she is about to experience one last moment of distinction, reciting her immortal lines as Dumas's doomed heroine:

> Refusing help, she drags herself—half hopping—half crawling onto the stage to play for the 10,000th time her greatest role—an eighteen-year-old innocent girl on the threshold of life and hope.

Russell stressed how much he wanted to depict "a life episodically remembered through an alcoholic haze." He wanted "to combine the truth of her life with elements of 'what might have been'"—a narrative style merging fact with impression conjured through whimsical brainstorms:

> The initial idea came to me in a flash (as they say). I'm convinced it's the only way you could make it. Hope you agree and that I hear from you soon.
> Yours, Ken R.

Streisand apparently didn't give Russell an opportune response. *The Legend of Sarah* never even went to the funding phase. More time passed; both ended up distracted with other projects. Fans of Russell, Streisand, or Bernhardt could at least imagine Streisand's response as (or if) she perused Russell's outline: a gleam of genuine interest, a grimace of disgust, or a distracted smile as she got ready for *What's Up, Doc?*

Russell wouldn't encounter the future *Yentl* until the early 1980s, when he entertained the idea of having her play the lead in another woebegone project: his film version of *Evita*. For several years, Sarah Bernhardt was in cinematic limbo, but in 1976 a *Reader's Digest* production called *The Incredible Sarah* came out, directed by Richard Fleischer and starring, in the title role . . . Glenda Jackson.

●

A couple of years later, Russell got closer to realizing another of his "what might have been" movies. This time he had funding from the Italian company PEA

(Produzioni Europee Associati) that brought such fruit-to-nuts histories as Fellini's *Satyricon* and Pasolini's *Il Decameron*. Russell's film was to be about another French rogue: François Rabelais, specifically Rabelais's *Gargantua and Pantagruel*—the story of two giants that, judging by available descriptions of Russell's plans, was likely unfilmable. But with quixotic illusions that the moneymen temporarily fed, Russell and an Italian crew scouted the Umbrian plain for locations.

With *Gargantua*, Russell would have returned to the violent vaudeville he displayed in *The Devils*. The sixteenth-century French satirist, scholar, and lapsed monk earned the term "Rabelaisian" for writing that is loaded with bawdy, grotesque, phallocentric, and scatological satire about art, law, philosophy, and especially religion—concepts that also had a snug fit to Russell's worldview.

Around the spring of 1973, Russell embarked on filming the story that Rabelais began around 1532 with *Pantagruel*, about the exploits of Gargantua's equally endowed son. It was so successful that Rabelais wrote the follow-up narrative *Gargantua*, stuck this new story into the beginning of the first tale, and published the mammoth tome *Gargantua and Pantagruel*—a work of such girth, mirth, and mad vulgarity that he had to evade church authorities by hiding under the anagram "Alcofribas Nasier." While the tales offered facetious anecdotes about religious leaders and lawless lawyers, Rabelais also contrasted the barnyard humor of anuses and phalluses with discussions on astronomy, medicine, music, theology, war, and of course, the clergy.

Russell appreciated Rabelais's chronic analogies between religious hypocrisy and the body's untidy functions. Aldous Huxley, who likely had Rabelais in mind when plumbing intestinal pits in *The Devils of Loudun*, was also a fan: "Mass for mass, there is probably more dung and offal piled up in Rabelais's work than in Swift's. But how pleasant is the dung through which Gargantua wades, how almost delectable the offal! The muck is transfigured by love; for Rabelais loved the bowels which Swift so malignantly hated." George Orwell thought otherwise: "So far from being 'healthy' as is always alleged, he is an exceptionally perverse, morbid writer, a case for psychoanalysis."

Rabelais's depictions were so graphic that the *Gargantua and Pantagruel* volumes were condemned as obscene and subject to censorship from the Sorbonne—the University of Paris's theological faculty. Roman Catholic authorities were especially livid over the lewd satires on the papacy. But Protestants also hated him: Calvin cited Rabelais as an offender among "curs who assume the attitudes of comedy in order to enjoy greater freedom to vomit their blasphemies."

At the moment of his birth, the enormous Gargantua emerges from his mother's left ear to shout, "Give me drink, drink, drink!" With a premature taste for booze and "phlegmatic of bum," the boy could dress in the best of blue satin and white worsted and still soil the finery. His codpiece embroidered in gold and adorned with precious gems was a sartorial marvel, especially for his nurses, whom he'd feel up and who would fondle him back. "One would call it my little spigot," Rabelais wrote of the nurses' zeal, "another my ninepin, another my coral branch, another my stopper, my cork, my gimlet, my ramrod, my awl, my pendant . . . my erector, my little red sausage, my little rogue of a prick!"

"Testiculotitillation," a term Rabelais apparently invented (according to James Le Clerq's *Gargantua and Pantagruel* translation), is also Russell's pipeline from the crotch to the intellect. He even intended to subtitle the movie, "The Man with the Biggest Prick in the World." But even with the phallic ceremonies intact, Russell's version was to culminate in one of the most significant parts of Rabelais's story: the building of an abbey in the make-believe province of Thélème.

This Abbey of Thélème would flout convent conventions: no walls, no clocks, coed quarters, and only handsome monks and pretty nuns with cheery dispositions allowed. Thélème also thrived by the motto inscribed at the entrance, "Do What Thou Wilt." Rabelais conceived the phrase under the assumption that people, left to their true natures, would do no evil and that pleasure, without church shackles, is a political act.

Rabelais later inspired Aleister Crowley, with his Hermetic Order of the Golden Dawn, to go into the Sicilian village of Cefalu sometime in the 1920s and build an actual Abbey of Thelema. But Crowley's version of "Do What Thou Wilt" may have been at variance with his predecessor. Crowley, who gained notoriety as "The Great Beast," staged wild parties and other iniquitous rites to tease out lots of sensational British press—stories of drugs, orgies, human sacrifices, and bestiality. These tales would later inspire Russell to dream up another of his never-made projects: a film based on Crowley's exploits.

Derek Jarman, whom Russell again chose as a partner in crime to design *Gargantua*, shared his zeal in his memoirs:

> The Russell designs included an altar with Coke bottle candelabra. There is a detail of the king's porn palace, a window made with pink marble legs and those ruched theatre curtains like a cancan dress. The notes also have precise descriptions of style, e.g., Pompadour Gimcrack. There's an avenue of monumental hammers-and-sickles, a swimming pool with a Warhol soup can lilo, a gold raft with a sail in the shape of a silver fish. The Abbey of Thelema is a ziggurat with a double spiral staircase built like Hadrian's tomb—with woods, and surmounted by a two hundred foot ornamental

urn sprouting a tropical garden . . . On and on, page after page. My favourites were some carriages in the form of sailing boats—sails painted with hearts, clubs, diamonds, and spades.

Though he saturated his retelling of Rabelais with embellishments from twentieth-century pop culture, Russell transposed the tale the way the author might have done had he thrived in an era of movie cameras and special effects. Like Rabelais, he intended to lampoon both organized religion and secular politics: how both become yokes to drive the masses, repress the spirit, and cramp artistic style. In the end, the churches of the East and West turn out to be miserable failures. The story devolves as religious zealots go about trying to slaughter a flower power cult, while Catholics and Protestants—personified as Popinjay and Lutherape—duel it out to the bloody end with crucifixes instead of phalluses. A red rain soon falls to halt the carnage, but instead of portending the apocalypse, it turns out to be Pantagruel spitting down his precious wine, turning the warring factions into intoxicated pussycats who forego hostility for a bacchic love-in.

Warner Brothers also planned to back the film with the help of producer Alberto Grimaldi, but Gargantua's wine and piss party evaporated when funding also dried up. Russell did, however, preserve some of the spirit and spunk behind Rabelais's themes in his subsequent features, particularly *Mahler*, *Tommy*, and *Lisztomania*.

MAHLER SIEG HEIL!

"**M**y film," Ken Russell once explained about *Mahler*, "is simply about some of the things I feel when I think of Mahler's life and listen to his music." This helps explain why the narrative is more discursive than most other Russell films. It flows like a dream through Mahler's imagination, shifting from past to present and every so often wandering into images that could only exist in a future beyond the composer's death in 1911. (Russell anachronistically refers to German Expressionist silent movies, Third Reich processions, twentieth-century American comedians, and a scene from an early 1970s film by Luchino Visconti.)

Russell's flair for rich imagery and surreal excursions thrives best with strong story lines, so to harness *Mahler*'s reveries, he splits the narration. The story's shell—Mahler's 1911 train ride from Paris back to Vienna following a stressful engagement in New York—goes from A to B. But by veering, often asymmetrically, into Mahler's remembrances and nightmares, Russell plays against a straight timeline. The film's mood swings from the cozy humanism of his BBC work to the excessive burlesque he would master in *Tommy* and *Lisztomania*. In the process, Russell presents Mahler the genius and the demigod, the family man and the doomed consumptive, as well as the noble conductor and a precursor to the vaudeville comic. This is what makes *Mahler* so alternately inspiring and nerve-racking.

The music and images stress this somewhat schizophrenic effect. For the soundtrack, Russell secured the services of the distinguished Bernard Haitink, who was at the time acting as principal conductor of the London Philharmonic. Dick Bush was again his cinematographer and did exactly what the film dictates—an unsettling shift between warm, humanistic drama and edgy surrealism. He contrasts the Lake District's beautiful, almost too-perfect, blue skies with the murky nighttime woodlands, where worms abound.

Trying to elucidate the movie's mad method, Russell claims he structured it to approximate the rondo, a musical form with a recurring refrain and variations: in this case it's Love overshadowed by Death, particularly the death of innocence, trust, and—worst of all—creative aspiration. "The life span of a man is measured in years," Russell explains, "but the screen time of a film about him must be measured in minutes. Given this fact and the nature of the medium, so far as I am concerned, the impressionistic technique works the best. When every second counts, it is often necessary to say two things at once; which is why I frequently introduce symbolism into scenes of reality."

Interested more in impressionistic history than literal truths, Russell at one point uses Mahler to vent his own grudge against literal-minded critics. The composer encounters an annoying journalist named Siegfried Krenek (Kenneth Colley), who asks Mahler whether bad health or bad press nixed his New York conducting plans. Mahler replies, "I was tired of skyscrapers and sarsaparilla." But when he tries qualifying himself by saying he wanted to find "a place near Vienna, where I can breathe again," Krenek assumes he is referring to his congested lungs. "Why is everyone so literal these days?" an exasperated Mahler retorts. "I was speaking metaphorically."

Russell inserted this scene because he uttered a similar comeback to Gordon Gow during a 1970 interview for *Films and Filming*. Apparently Gow, thinking too literally, interrupted the chat to make sure that Russell wasn't referring to an actual slaughterhouse slab when describing Tchaikovsky's sex-starved wife Nina Milyukova in *The Music Lovers* as "a piece of meat." Russell speaks metaphorically throughout the story.

One of Russell's strongest metaphors is nature, both its majestic and hideous sides. This is a big reason why he got drawn to Mahler; he shares some of the composer's inspirations and contradictions, especially about the delights and horrors of the untamed world. Mahler and Russell could talk a good game about god's creatures, but they could also dread them.

Mahler intended his Third Symphony, which opens Russell's film, as a pantheistic celebration of life's forces, with such titles as "What the Animals in the Forest Tell Me," "What the Flowers in the Meadow Tell Me," and "What the Cuckoo Tells Me." But his spooky violins can also connote swarms of insects or nests of reptiles, just as fiery horns can suggest a mammal stampede. Mahler might have enjoyed the company of kittens when shutting himself up in his composer's hut, but as his wife Alma Mahler recalls in her memoirs, "His love of animals was theoretical only."

Nature sometimes attacked Mahler: chirping birds interrupted him while he tried composing songs about chirping birds, an eagle startled him when it crashed through the window of his summer cottage, and his faltering heart nearly gave out when a crow darted from under his sofa. Even the lethal strep-tococci in his throat joined the hordes of flora and fauna teeming to ruin him. In his alternately lyrical and horrific adaptation, Russell too captures much of this war with the organisms.

Russell ignites this connection between Mahler's imminent death and the forces of nature that enchant and destroy in the film's opening montage. The composer's quiet little lakeside hut bursts into blazes, Mahler screams from behind the window of a coffin that is also engulfed in flames, an angel of death stretches out her arms to greet him on the other side, and Mahler's two small daughters appear more

Mahler's apocalyptic opening.
(Photo by and courtesy of Leonard Pollack)

as apparitions from the next world, staring into the camera.

The camera soon skulks along craggy rocks to a boulder carved with Mahler's death mask. A figure stretches out of its white gauzy chrysalis, finally breaking free as it crawls over to the stone face, writhing in erotic contortions while kissing its mouth.

Suddenly Russell shifts to Mahler and wife Alma on a train. "I had plenty of tunes until you killed them all," Alma (Georgina Hale) snaps back after Mahler (Robert Powell) describes the dream he just had of being a worshipped hunk of stone—all to the section of his Third Symphony that he calls "What the Rocks Tell Me." When he tells Alma that he also envisioned "a living creature struggling to be born," she replies, "At last, you've noticed."

While delving into another tale of a brilliant and doomed composer, Russell also returns to the story of an egomaniacal artist and the woman who sacrifices her art and ego for him. Alma, however, doesn't stoop without resisting. "It's terrible to destroy something that's alive and nobody notices," she continues, lamenting that she has become his "shadow." Another nightmare follows, this time possibly from Alma's perspective, as Mahler descends a staircase, surrounded by adoring hordes. In a top hat and mourner's suit, along with a black stocking over her face, she follows him—not only as his subordinate but also as one of several memento mori that vex Mahler throughout the film.

Viewers cannot help but root for Alma as she contemplates whether to continue being the shadow woman or to leave Mahler and abscond with the handsome and insolent soldier Max (Richard Morant). Russell creates Max as a composite of Alma's many real-life lovers that included the architect Walter Gropius and the artist Oskar Kokoschka. Max boards the train to claim her, but he also digs at Mahler's mortality fear, asking how his Tenth Symphony is coming along while reminding him that Beethoven and several other great composers barely lived past their ninth.

Mahler knows this and, in another dream shift, conjures the worst-case scenario. To the dolorous soundtrack of "Trauermarsch" from his Fifth Symphony, Russell returns to the image—in homage to Carl Theodor Dreyer's *Vampyr*—of Mahler screaming from behind his coffin window. Mahler's nightmare has another specter to watch over the proceedings: a bust of Beethoven, whose stony stare looks scarier with what appear to be touches of eyeliner.

Russell's dream of Mahler's dream—wild, campy, and anachronistic—is faithful to the gloomy thoughts Mahler entertained while composing the piece. Mahler included phrases from the popular kids' song "Frère Jacques" in his First Symphony as parody, inspired to write the work after seeing a German fairy tale illustration of forest animals lugging a dead hunter off to his tomb. Russell, of course, embellishes the vision. Alma joins Max and several other pallbearers in S.S. uniforms. They goosestep while toting the coffin from the graveyard to the crematorium, while a lachrymose version of the tune counterpoints the death march. Soon, Alma performs a bawdy cancan atop Mahler's coffin before the Nazis roll Mahler into the flames. Once the cremated Mahler returns with only his knowing eyes intact among his ashes, Alma dances more: first with feathers and then in a strip tease as she flirts with the S.S. men before gyrating obscenely in front of an Egon Schiele–inspired portrait of her late husband. She finally rides naked on a gramophone's humongous horn while Russell's camera slowly enters its abyss.

During shooting, particularly for this dream sequence, Hale had the hardest time trying to convey a sympathetic character. She knew that anyone aware of Mahler's life was also keen to the fact that Alma had a jolly time after the composer's death, with three more husbands and a chance to aggrandize herself in an autobiography.

Alma Mahler (Georgina Hale) joins S.S. men to celebrate Mahler's legacy.

Mahler dreams of "a living creature struggling to be born." *(Photo by and courtesy of Leonard Pollack)*

When Russell demanded that she act the whore and mount the gargantuan megaphone, she got so nervous she started breaking out in red hives. Her efforts in the part paid off when she received a 1974 BAFTA (British Academy of Film and Television Arts) for "Most Promising Newcomer to Leading Film Roles."

•

"Where music is," Mahler once claimed, "the demon must be." Faced with the job of depicting that demon, Russell had to contend with finagling finances, haggling over locations, and scrambling to get approval from the composer's daughter. Anna (Glucki) Mahler, who held certain rights to her father's legacy, initially turned Russell's project down, noting what she saw as his unflattering treatment of Tchaikovsky in *The Music Lovers*. The Nazified Richard Strauss couldn't have helped matters either.

Still quaking over the debacle he got into with the Strauss family, Russell was determined to win Anna over. He assured her that he would portray her father's lust to create despite Mahler's adversaries, his neuroses, and mounting physical weaknesses. Anna agreed to take a second look at *The Music Lovers*, gleaned sympathetic nuances she missed the first time, and gave the project her blessing.

But Anna Mahler, who was by then a distinguished sculptor, might also have been relieved that, despite the film's flamboyance and hysteria, Russell's script was relatively kind to Gustav. He could come across in the movie as curt, sarcastic, and paranoid, but Russell's Mahler is relatively mild-mannered and even magnanimous—more exasperated than exasperating.

Some biographers were less restrained. Mahler's pal Walter Bruno wrote of "The impression of a demoniac nature." Harold C. Schonberg, in *The Great Conductors*, describes a man not only demonic but "neurotic, demanding, selfish, noble, emotionally undisciplined, sarcastic, unpleasant, and a genius. His actions throughout his life strongly suggest those of a manic-depressive. Periods of gloom and silence alternated with periods of violence and vehemence."

Born in an indigent village, somewhere between Prague and Vienna, Mahler once described himself as "thrice homeless, as a native of Bohemia in Austria, as an Austrian among Germans, and as a Jew throughout the world. Everywhere an intruder, never welcomed." He was a disaffected youth who had to fend off hooligans, subliterates, and a troubled family. The neglected and sometimes abused mother, the distant and sometimes abusive father, and Mahler's desperation to escape his family-imposed fate are also themes congenial to Russell's history. Mahler was, however, probably a bit more morose than Russell. As a teenager, he had a flair for dark melodrama and once wrote to a student pal asking, "What way out is there but self-annihilation?"

Mahler had another quirk that Russell must have found especially appealing: a penchant for mixing what prevailing standards dictate as the highest with lowest of tastes. He infused his symphonies with a mishmash of styles that included Czech folk tunes, Jewish lullabies, wedding marches, and funeral dirges. "No one was more subject than he to brusque switches of mood for no apparent reason," biographer Jonathan Carr notes. "No composer leaped more abruptly from the major to the minor mode, even within the same phrase, or more often undercut a noble chord with a banality."

Carr also mentions a youthful epiphany that inspired Mahler to merge the tragic with the trite. One day, sickened by having to witness Mom and Dad fighting again, young Gustav fled the family house of horrors. On the street he encountered a hurdy-gurdy man playing some tinny rendition of the popular Austro-German folk tune, "Ach, du Lieber Augustin" ("O My Darling Augustine"). The music cheered him up, likely in a droll way, and made the contrast between life's pain and parody too beautifully ludicrous not to inspire future compositions. The situation also evokes Russell's affinity for loony calliope ditties that show up in *Dante's Inferno* and several others of his earlier movies.

This hurdy-gurdy anecdote has an extra layer, since Mahler supposedly related it to Sigmund Freud during their four-hour stroll together in the Dutch town of Leyden. Freud's biographer Ernest Jones unearthed a letter in which Freud recalls Mahler telling him about the incident. Jones, in turn, speculated that Mahler suddenly realized "why his music had always been prevented from achieving the highest rank through the noblest passages, those inspired by the most profound emotions, being spoilt by the intrusion of some commonplace melody."

Like some of the other artists Russell admires, Mahler appreciated the beauty of exaggeration and vulgarity whenever the muse demanded. Critic Alex Ross could easily be describing Russell when assessing Mahler's "swooning intensity of emotion: not only the famous grandeurs and sufferings, but also the intermediate states of waltz-time languor, kitsch-drenched sweetness and sadness, medieval revelation, military rancor, dissonant delirium, adagio lament."

When Mahler escapes from dreary conversation to let his mind wander, he enters a collision course with Russell's idiosyncrasies. Especially in this film, Russell encourages the train of thought to derail into a netherworld of interpretation, where the line between analysis and projection is arbitrary—if not pointless.

The most curious example occurs when Mahler gazes out his train window to a version of himself from Luchino Visconti's 1971 film *Death in Venice*—adorned with black hair dye and rouge while flirting with a young boy who seductively whirls around lampposts in a sailor's suit. Russell plays the "Adagietto" from Mahler's Fifth Symphony as the sad, romantic background to this reverie—the same piece that Visconti used to dramatize the tragedy of a frustrated older man pining for his Lolito.

Other than the fact that Visconti used Mahler's music throughout *Death in Venice*, Russell has deeper reasons for this cross-reference. Thomas Mann, who was Mahler's contemporary, also wanted to convey the final days of a dying artist when writing the novella on which Visconti based his foray. While visiting Venice to work on the story, Mann (who met Mahler previously in Munich) came across the composer's obituary in May 1911: the coincidences between Mahler and his protagonist Gustav von Aschenbach—who both die at about the same age—proved too uncanny for him to ignore. Mann changed Aschenbach's facial features to resemble those of Mahler. He now saw Aschenbach and Mahler as tragic figures impelled to create while at death's door.

Mann's Aschenbach is about fifty, disillusioned with his writing career, and desperate for a fresh ideal of beauty. He escapes to Venice and there falls in love with Tadzio, a Polish lad who lingers and leers along the Lido beachfront. Mann's *Death in Venice* implies mirroring: the author saw himself and Mahler in the fading Aschenbach who, even as cholera ate away at him, took the time to marvel at Tadzio's Grecian beauty.

The Visconti connection gets more open-ended when Russell puts another of his eerie zooms on Mahler's expression as he watches the nonverbal exchanges between the older man and the adolescent strumpet. Apart from a bit of a smirk, the composer doesn't seem at all annoyed or shocked. Though not as enigmatic as Garbo at the conclusion of *Queen Christina*, Powell's Mahler registers a mystified expression as he watches this alternate version of himself who is also dying.

When Visconti made *Death in Venice*, he was also in a midlife crisis and projected himself into his troubled aging character. Like Russell, Visconti reconfigured real persons to conform to his private thoughts, but Visconti, by fusing Mahler and Aschenbach into one man, was in many respects even more brazen than Russell. This scene might also suggest that Russell is siding with Mahler, at least on matters of aesthetics. In contrast to Aschenbach, who rhapsodized over Grecian and classical linearity, Mahler was more akin to Russell when he fed his soul on craggy, asymmetrical, and often grotesque art. The love object's gender was not the problem (Mann initially planned to base his novella on Goethe's infatuation with a young girl at Marienbad); Aschenbach's piss-elegant standards of beauty conspired with the cholera to kill him as he followed a chimera that was all too beautiful, aloof, and unattainable.

●

From Visconti, Russell switches to an Isaac Babel story, when delving back into Mahler's disturbing childhood. It starts when the composer cringes at a "brass bloody band" that blares from a reception committee outside one of the train's stations. Mahler refuses to greet his fans and runs into the lavatory to clear his head. But Russell wanders with him as the narrative drifts back to Mahler's frequently miserable boyhood next door to a military barracks. Here, the routine clatter of drums and stomping boots likely prompted his lifelong phobia of military marches.

Russell opens by tracking along a brick wall lined with barbed wire; off-camera sounds of Prussian marching orders paired with dreary brick buildings suggest, if only for a moment, a concentration camp. But these are the humble Bohemian quarters where his dad, Bernhard Mahler (Lee Montague), a spirits and wine distiller, and family dwell. As young Gustav (Gary Rich) discovers his father in a next-door warehouse getting carnal with a local slut, Russell hammers home the phallic brutality by having the boy witness all this through a busted window, his tortured face offset against the foreground silhouette of a pitchfork prong.

Mahler's dad gets nasty and thrashes his son about the head when he learns of the boy's slacking school performance. Bernhard Mahler's brusque table manners don't do much to redeem him either. The Mahlers' supper scenes are rife with Yiddish caricatures as they speak with their mouths full, speculating with stereotypical moneylender gestures about the hourly wages of Franz Liszt and Felix Mendelssohn.

Some of the family interludes are byproducts of an earlier Russell project from 1972, when he planned to adapt an Isaac Babel piece for a BBC arts show. The project never materialized, but he supplied Mahler's childhood with bits from Babel's short story "The Awakening." Babel writes of a boy in the Odessa district and his tyrannical violin teacher named Mr. Zagursky, who processes one child prodigy after another. Russell's version of Zagursky is the benign taskmaster Sladky (Otto Diamant), who taunts his piano students with regimented scale exercises and keeps all the crowns he earns under a bust of Richard Wagner.

Russell borrows some of Babel's dialogue, with some alterations, when Mahler's grandfather (Arnold Yarrow) promises to arrange Gustav's lessons with Sladky, but Gustav's Uncle Arnold (Benny Lee) scoffs at the Sladky Academy, calling it "a factory of Jewish dwarfs with laced collars and shiny patent leather shoes." A horrified Hollis Alpert later cried in an article for the *Saturday Review* that the scenes "might have been written by Dr. Goebbels."

Russell adapts another part of "The Awakening" when Gustav meets a significant bucolic buddy. Babel's story is also about a little Jewish boy with hydrophobia who almost drowns, but a character named Nikitich saves him, teaches him and other children about sandcastles and songs, and later pokes his walking stick out at various trees, bushes, and birds, telling the boy, "A man who does not exist in nature the way a stone or an animal exists in it will not write a single worthwhile line in all his life."

In *Mahler*, Nikitich shows up as Old Nick (Ronald Pickup). He glides into the film playing "Ach, du Lieber Augustin" on his concertina, the same tune the real-life Mahler remembers from the hurdy-gurdy man. But Nick also has a yen for "Frère Jacques," which he plays over and again as he incites Gustav's curiosity, teaching Mahler the secrets of nature he would later transpose to his symphonies.

●

Russell encountered a few preproduction snags in this, his first of several Goodtimes Enterprises endeavors. David Puttnam, who ran the company along with Sanford Lieberson, planned to shoot the film in Bavaria. The German backers, however, abandoned the production. Stripped down to smaller change, Puttnam was still committed to the project and simply shifted the crew up to Russell's beloved region of Keswick—a change that gave Russell more opportunities to milk the ambiance of the Cumberland Lake District and its Skiddaw Mountains and simulate Mahler's summer residence at Maiernigg.

Scenes of young Gustav swimming and cavorting with the birds, the lakes, the trees, and the horses also had a behind-the-scenes story that is almost as abusive as the Mahler family fracas. When the somewhat undernourished-looking Gary Rich auditioned for the part of young Gustav, he admitted he wasn't the greatest at the piano but boasted of being athletic. Russell already had problems casting the young Tchaikovsky in *The Music Lovers* and now had apprehensions. He called Rich's mom regularly to make sure he labored at his piano lessons and would be at least able to pretend he's playing the scales.

When the time came to film young Gustav plunging into Keswick's cold Derwentwater Lake to impress the gutter-rat schoolmates who taunt him with anti-Semitic barbs, Russell felt he could at least count on Rich's athleticism to get through the simulated drowning scene. The script required Rich to swim out too far, so that Nick and the boys would then save him.

So there was Russell with the camera crew, waiting to get this potentially dangerous part of the plot out of the way. Rich stripped himself down to his underwear, ready to take the plunge. Suddenly, he squeaked out his confession: he couldn't swim. Russell reacted with surprising composure and even mustered up paternal instincts by assuring the boy he would be safe. Rich was now under the impression that he only had to go in the water for a brief dip. But as Russell barked his orders on an offshore boat through a bullhorn, Rich found out the long shots weren't enough. Russell also needed him to almost drown in close-up.

Russell told Rich to bundle up, sit snugly in a boat he was assigned to stay in between takes, and wait for further instructions. When his boat reached the one carrying Russell and his crew, Rich reached out for Russell to help him on board. Russell suddenly and conveniently lost his balance, a commotion that made the boy fall back into the chilly lake. Without missing a beat, Russell zoomed on Rich's contorted face struggling to stay afloat.

"Gary managed to swim half a dozen strong strokes before giving up the ghost," Russell bemuses. "It was the most convincing drowning scene I have ever seen on the screen. The little bugger couldn't ride a horse either—so we tied him to the saddle and whipped the stallion into a gallop—only kidding! HONEST!"

Russell's sadistic streak couldn't have traumatized the young actor too much, since he was sporting enough to appear in the director's next film. "I watched him play," Russell recalls after putting Rich through a keyboard rehearsal, "and thought if I ever made a film of Frankenstein's monster as a young piano prodigy, I need look no further than Gary." He followed through in *Tommy*, with Rich as a Frankenstein monster rock star.

●

Russell and Mahler share another peccadillo: they converted to Catholicism. For Russell, the choice was based on aesthetics and not Vatican canon, but the film portrays Mahler's decision as purely mercenary. After visiting his fellow composer Hugo Wolf, now confined to an asylum and fancying he's the Emperor

Franz Josef of Austria, Mahler gleans wisdom in Wolf's madness. Wolf, think-ing Mahler has come for a royal dispensation to take a post as court conduc-tor at the Vienna State Opera, tells him to remove his drawers. Saddened, the raving "emperor" informs Mahler that, since Wagner's wife, the anti-Semitic Cosima, "rules the world of music," a Jew has no chance of getting the job, short of reattaching his foreskin.

Mahler looks back to the moments when he made the decision to symbol-ically reattach his foreskin in exchange for "the keys to the kingdom of the Vienna State Opera." And for the following scene, Russell might have intended a spiteful jab not only at Alexander Walker but more specifically to art critic Robert Hughes, whose review of *Savage Messiah* in *Time* stated that Russell's "appetite for excess verges on petulance" and that "to judge from his publicity, Russell believes that his erratic mediation between Vasari and Groucho Marx tells some truth about the creative process of his hero."

Sometimes negative critics can unintentionally inspire artists to make big-ger and better transgressions. This was the case when Russell at least indirectly flipped Hughes the bird by incorporating Groucho Marx and his zany brothers into one of Mahler's most vital scenes, when Gustav lies about in a room with his sister and two of his brothers, arguing over artistic integrity, money, and the best way to dig the family out of its fiscal rut.

Brother Otto (Peter Eyre) is Chico, pecking away at the piano what he calls "simple tunes for simple minds"; the effeminate Alois (Michael Southgate) is Harpo, applying eyeliner and a blond curly wig while crowing about his plans to seek what his folks perceive as a dishonorable showbiz career in America. Gus-tav, in a straw hat and flicking a cigar, is the wisecracking Groucho, announcing he's going to perform the ultimate sell-out: become a Roman Catholic. Justine reacts by dropping her tureen of stuffed cabbage and cries, "Oi!" But the foppish Alois looks vindicated by the news as he honks Harpo's trademark taxi horn and winks into the camera.

The Robert Hugheses of the world would call this Groucho Marxism "taste-less" posturing, but in spirit, Russell's pairing of Mahler with America's vaude-ville scamps is historically astute. The Mahlers were three Jewish brothers wanting to go into show business. Gustav, like a Yiddish comic of the vaudeville circuit, is an uprooted Jew reinventing himself to entertain a vaster audience. Gustav's brother Alois takes the deracination a step further, primping up for the New World, where acts like the Marx Brothers would bind their Yiddish theater roots with mass entertainment. The result: the early twentieth-century variety show and its blend of the "high" and the "low."

∎

Russell jumps from vaudeville to its gaudy child, the cinema, in the notorious section that makes a comic-book parody out of Mahler's 1897 conversion to Catholicism. In Ken Russell's hands, the composer's compromise is so horrific and humiliating that only satire does it justice. As Russell told BBC 4 in a 2005 interview: "I think it really echoes his music, you see. There's a lot of parody in it . . . particularly in the Ninth Symphony, where one of the movements is called 'Burlesque.' That is the movement I use for his conversion to Catholicism, because that was a burlesque."

The scene, precisely titled "The Convert, Starring Cosima Wagner with Gustav Mahler," begins when Mahler, looking a bit like Charlie Chaplin's "little tramp" dressed as a rabbi, schleps with a huge, steel Star of David up through the fields of Valhalla. Cosima Wagner (Antonia Ellis) meanwhile stands above him on a high altar, a Nietzschean superwoman, dressed as a combination Nazi Stormtrooper and Hell's Angels biker. While Mahler awaits her ritual commands, she robotically goosesteps and makes compulsive "Sieg Heil" salutes. This is Russell revisiting his childhood themes of warlord Huns and the flickering ghosts of German Expressionism, especially since the courtship between Mahler and Cosima evokes Fritz Lang's borderline slapstick in *Die Nibelungen* when Brunhild challenges Siegfried (in the guise of King Gunther) to feats of derring-do.

First: there is the "Baptism of Fire," as Mahler jumps to Cosima's cracking whip through flaming hoops emblazoned with crosses. Second: the "Intercession of the Sacred Heart" pits Mahler in a simulated crucifixion—a target for Cosima's dagger throws. Third: Cosima watches defiantly as Mahler forges the Star of David into Nothung, Siegfried's enchanted sword. Fourth: as Siegfried, Mahler

Mahler (Robert Powell) courts Cosima Wagner (Antonia Ellis).
(Photo by and courtesy of Leonard Pollack)

merges Roman Catholicism with Norse myths. He takes on the challenge, with some whimpering, to slay the dragon of the old gods. But Mahler's Siegfried looks more like a craven Stan Laurel as he frowns, scratches his head, and hobbles into the fire-breather's cave.

Russell drags in more allusions to American vaudeville as well as the birth of the sound film as Mahler runs out of the cave. With a soot-covered face, he pleads on bended knee like an Al Jolson minstrel, begging to be released, but Cosima won't hear of it. He soon reemerges triumphant, carrying a pig's severed head as his victory symbol before reaping his reward by committing the ultimate kosher crime: he feasts on the pig's snout and washes it down with a stein full of milk.

A silent movie title card announces, "Along Came the Talkies," and Cosima sings praises for her new Siegfried (who looks more like a frail Isaac Babel than an Aryan Ubermensch) to the beat of Wagner's "The Ride of the Valkyries." Mahler and Cosima, now Valhalla newlyweds, crest atop the hilt of a mammoth version of Nothung before being baptized in a golden shower of coins.

Mahler (Robert Powell) and Cosima Wagner (Antonia Ellis) celebrate a different *Sound of Music*.
(Photo by and courtesy of Leonard Pollack)

Since he chose to use various excerpts from Wagner's work to tell his story, Russell wanted one poignant bit of Mahler's "Adagio" from his unfinished Tenth Symphony as an augury of doom. It appears in the very first frame when Mahler's hut catches fire, later when he finds his brother Otto dead on the floor after a suicide, and during one of Mahler's near heart attacks on the train.

Another omen shows up during Mahler's trip: an African princess (Elaine Delmar). She agrees to Mahler's request to exchange compartments but puts him off when letting him know she'd read all about his dark obsessions in the *New York Times*, insisting despite his protests to the contrary that his Ninth Symphony is about "death the pitiless enemy, death the joker, even death the lover." Russell's eerie, deliberate zoom on her taunting expression and slowly closing eyes stands out as one of the film's most enigmatic and haunting moments.

Russell acted the martinet with regard to Mahler's failing health, having him take vigorous swims in the lake outside his hut and inserting a shot of him jogging just as a doctor warns him about overexertion. He also portrays the guilt Mahler felt over the death of his elder daughter Maria ("Putzi"), who perished before she reached her fifth year from scarlet fever—three summers after he composed the *Kindertotenlieder*, his five "Songs on the Death of Children."

Soon, however, Russell includes a segment from the *Kindertotenlieder*, when his two little daughters frolic in a forest during an approaching storm. Once they are safe at home and tucked away in bed, one of them jumps out from the middle of the night in a cold sweat crying for "Mommy." The next image is of a baby-sized coffin on Mahler's piano, while Anna von Mildenburg (Dana Gillespie), the movie's sinister soprano who appears in the film's opening, returns to hold out her forbidding arms—a mistress of doom who, like Janey Morris in *Dante's Inferno*, stands at the prow of a boat sailing toward the void.

In *Mahler*, Russell also does what he doesn't do well, providing some moments of almost Hallmark-card sentimentalism. When Alma decides to leave Max at his terminal stop and to ride on with Mahler, the composer is aglow with gratitude. Mahler's petty power games, his fears of cuckoldry, and his sound suspicion that Alma will carouse from man to man once he is dead all seem to pass like a low-grade fever. He finally opens up to his wife and confesses that she was "the one bright positive spark" behind the otherwise morose Sixth Symphony. "As long as my music lasts," he tells her, "our love will last."

Mahler's marital ceasefire still doesn't fend off vultures lurking around the bend. The kindhearted doctor on the train (Andrew Faulds) chides Mahler for having heart problems around the time he started writing his "morbid songs," but pronounces a favorable diagnosis. But Dr. Roth (George Coulouris in a short but memorable role) is on the Vienna platform, desperate to warn Mahler that his days are numbered. "You can go home, doctor," Mahler tells him. "We're going to live forever!" Russell literally suspends the Mahlers' happiness in a freeze frame before they get the grim news.

Gustav's reconciliatory words to Alma could be an honest attempt to end the story on an up beat, but Russell could also be satirizing all of those spoon-fed movies that always have to conclude on a ducky note. "The ending of the film out-Hollywoods Hollywood," Russell once said of its final frames.

Russell, here as in other films, adds his autobiographical voice as one more veil in his narrative dance. Years later, in his television autobiography, *Portrait of an Enfant Terrible*, he would include the opening scene of Mahler's burning hut to comment on his own domestic discord: "All of the films I shot in the Lake District, and there were many, reflected some aspect of my life there. Most of the time life was fun—sometimes destructive, as when my marriage went up in flames, and I was estranged from my children for a while."

Mahler did win Russell some acclaim with the 1974 Best Technical Achievement Award at Cannes. Some critics scoffed, and one got ugly even before production began. When he initially expressed his interest to subject Mahler to the Russellscopic touch, Russell had to contend with his ongoing adversary Alexander Walker, who got so livid at the prospect that he, in his review of *The Music Lovers*, threatened to pursue the director with an elephant gun if he dared. Russell, otherwise unfazed by snooty critics, detected Walker was dead serious this time around and carried a big stick just in case the potential assassin got gamy when he faced him on the BBC's *Film Night* show in February 1971.

Some critics saw the finished product and disapproved, but for those who love Russell's films precisely for their autobiographical indulgences, these were unintended compliments. "His *Mahler*," John Coleman opined in the *New Statesman*, "this latest in his kaleidoscopic, deeply empathetic films about composers and their hang-ups, seems to me the largest aberration to date: almost a dare. How far, he might be asking, can I impose a private vision on the public imagination?" "They are dreams," the *New York Times'* Richard Eder wrote specifically of *Mahler* but also of most Russell biopics, "and as such depict the dreamer much more clearly than they do the figures that appear in them. As far as the audience is concerned, it is almost as if Tchaikovsky, Liszt, and Mahler had taken turns making films about Mr. Russell."

A SADOMASOCHISTIC SESAME STREET

Years after *Tommy* the album and the movie became part of pop culture lore, Pete Townshend responded to an interviewer in a fitful mood: "'See me, feel me, touch me'? Where did that come from? It came from that little four-and-a-half-year-old boy in a fucking unlocked bedroom in a house with a madwoman. That's where it came from." This apparently long-repressed (and possibly disfigured) nightmare of child abuse was also the film's secret fuel, the impetus that brought Townshend's story international attention and established Ken Russell as one of pop music video's progenitors.

From his BBC days onward, Russell wanted to make a clatter through the clutter and grab the viewers' ever-decreasing attention spans. He was an iconoclast waiting for rock music to seek him out. And since *Tommy*, no one has surpassed him at pairing aggressive electrical guitars, thumping bass lines, and frenetic percussion with screeching voices, contorting bodies, and gnashing teeth: images sometimes as grotesque as a Francis Bacon painting. With *Tommy*, he also got immersed in a fantasy dominated by primary colors and cartoonish characters—a sadomasochistic variation on the heavy-handed image and message style associated with *Sesame Street*.

Young Tommy's "amazing journey."

The rock opera's original story is about little Tommy Walker, who gets traumatized after seeing his dad kill his wife's lover. The event is so unbearable that he loses his hearing, speech, and sight. While enduring Dad's mental maltreatment, he's also physically abused by his cruel cousin and lecherous uncle. He then escapes into a fantasy world by developing a knack for pinball, becomes a world celebrity, regains his senses, turns into a messianic cult figure, gets pegged as a fraud, incurs the wrath of his psychotic followers, and leaves behind the slain bodies of his parents to attain an inexplicable redemption. How could Russell resist?

•

Tommy's backstory, even years before Townshend relived his newly recalled sexual trauma, helps explain why Russell took on the project. When the Who released *Tommy* in 1969, Townshend lived in a psychic blur. He was saturated with hallucinogens and disillusioned over the rock star demagoguery that brought none of the transcendence he'd anticipated. But he at least made his mark on an era of rock history that championed such concept albums: themed works rife with heady lyrics often printed on the sleeves and intricate studio embellishments that encouraged thoughtful listening instead of raucous dancing.

Putting the album together, Townshend looked to other influences. Christopher "Kit" Lambert, the son of composer and conductor Constant Lambert, collaborated with his partner Christopher Stamp (brother to actor Terence Stamp) to make the Who a star attraction. Like Russell, Lambert had theatrical ambitions and loved flamboyance. He came up with the idea of giving *Tommy* an overture and insisted that the marriage of rock and opera was a given.

Townshend had little trouble convincing his fellow prima donnas to go operatic. Singer Roger Daltrey may have been diminutive, but his knack for prancing about on stage was equal to his fondness for swinging his fists. Drummer and calculated loony Keith Moon indulged in antics that got crazier, more contrived, and more annoying as the 1970s progressed. Playing *Tommy*'s dirty old kiddy diddler Uncle Ernie was the next logical step. Only bassist John Entwistle carried himself with comportment on the stage and before the press. But he too, desperate to get the group out of its creative and financial rut, was willing to try something new.

The story of an abused boy also reflected the grudge Townshend still carried from his days as a middle-class art-school student, when he was grist for the bullies but had no fighting instincts. The cruel cousin Kevin, who makes Tommy submit to nasty games when the parents are away, is Townshend's version of the everyday hooligans who made his own youth miserable. Townshend also based his "Sally Simpson" vignette—when an avid girl fan gets mutilated while rushing to reach the messianic Tommy on the stage—on witnessing Jim Morrison throw a fan a sucker punch just as a woman in the audience fell on her face while trying to touch the Lizard King.

In 1969, the subject of child abuse, laced with drugs and religious anarchy, was so alarming to some that at least one critic tagged the album and the group with that most self-righteous of one-word negations: "sick." But *Tommy* made its impact. The band incorporated it into its live shows at Woodstock and the following Isle of Wight festival. Then, *Tommy* ascended to the London Coliseum and New York's Met. Leonard Bernstein, keen on pressing the counterculture pulse, praised it; the Who even regaled the royal family with a performance.

Flattery through adaptation was inevitable: an easy-listening instrumental called "Overture from Tommy" by the Assembled Multitude arrived in 1970, a soft pop medley of "Pinball Wizard"/"See Me, Feel Me" by the New Seekers hit the charts in 1973, and there was even a *Tommy*-themed Canadian ballet. The masses were happy, but cranky rock purists, in their foolhardy quests for "authenticity," sniffed. All of this, of course, made the Who avatars of arena rock, or as Entwistle bristled in 1970, "snob rock." The Who's managers approached Russell as early as 1970 about a filmed version. Meanwhile, the crafty and aggressive Robert Stigwood, who already explored messianic rock when producing the movie version of *Jesus Christ Superstar*, came along to procure interest and funding. All the while, Stamp and Stigwood kept Russell at the top of their shortlist.

The most significant event occurred in 1972, when the London Symphony Orchestra performed a more classically inclined adaptation with massed strings. This got Russell listening. He tried taking in the Who's original album, but he played one side and thought it "rubbish!—I couldn't make head nor tail of the story." As always, his ears were trained for such Romantic composers as Elgar and Tchaikovsky, so he got immersed in the London Symphony version after catching a performance: "I heard it. I saw immense possibilities in it. I wasn't into rock as such, but I recognized this was something very special."

●

In some respects, Russell and Townshend were kindred spirits. Both were insecure about their output and sensitive about negative critics. They both married their art-school sweethearts and had tempers that could ignite and subside in five minutes. They could be sullen, sarcastic, and depressive but also amiable, inspired, and inspiring when the time arrived to at last create something. Both also had bouts with religious yearning—or at least the theatrics of religion. Russell provided the Catholic camp; Townshend had the Parsi platitudes, thanks to the spiritual advice he got from the Indian yogi Meher Baba, whom he credited on the *Tommy* album as an "avatar."

After Baba fell to his death from a seizure in January 1969, Townshend tried communing with the avatar's oversoul. But by the mid-1970s, he ended up, like many others, wallowing in spiritual darkness. This is when Russell arrived to recharge Townshend's flagging muse and transform *Tommy* into a hyperactive hippodrome that, once emblazoned on the screen, even its author could barely recognize.

The collaboration wasn't smooth. After Townshend started showing what Russell recalls as "a lorryload of scripts," they started exchanging ideas and sifting out the chaff. "I talked to Pete Townshend for six months," Russell told the *New York Times* in 1974, while *Tommy* was still in production, "and still neither of us ever said outright to each other what it is about." Russell found that *Tommy*'s plot had many loose ends. It lacked sufficient background about Tommy's dad, Captain Walker, and the story's time span—stretching through the two world wars—was too vast to digest. Russell helped Townshend bridge gaps in the narrative by having him write new lyrics and several new songs.

Drinking themselves silly, Russell and Townshend fiddled about with the script, working out the themes of corruption, pain, and redemption. When the alcohol loosened tongues and the personal demons spewed out, Russell had the advantage over Townshend in matters of childhood recall. He could mentally relive moment-by-moment every horror: the movie monster, the man in the cinema with the slithery hand, Dad and the reptiles, getting locked in a garage with a gorilla, and of course, the German bombs.

But Townshend, like a UFO abductee erasing memories of an alien probe, had supposedly repressed Tommy's inner demon for twenty or so more years. Even Russell, the consummate rude awakener, couldn't shock Townshend into reliving the primal scene. Not until around 1991, when he brought it to Broadway, could Townshend really see, feel, and touch the creature he had created.

Until then, Townshend was plagued by what he calls "two black years." "I was a very, very clear-cut post-war victim of two people who were married in the war too long," he recalled to *Uncut* magazine in 2004. "So, I went to stay with my grandmother, who happened to be off her fucking head . . . I can't remember particularly clearly, but I know it was very, very unpleasant. I got involved with weird shit which involved some erotic and sexual stuff; that's all I know." This was the same "madwoman" who, on a fateful day when she told him to turn down his amplifier, inspired the adolescent Townshend's first guitar-smashing tantrum.

Oddly, the two child abuse songs "Cousin Kevin" and "Fiddle About" come from Entwistle's pen. Perhaps Townshend outsourced them to dodge a mental minefield. And Russell enjoyed filming the Cousin Kevin (Paul Nicholas) moments that occur as Tommy's mother Nora Walker (Ann-Margret) is too bemused by her reflection in the mirror to realize she is allowing a psychopath to babysit her son. Kevin grimaces into the camera as he ties Tommy to a chair, almost drowns him in a bathtub, lines his toilet seat with nails, drags him by the hair down a sickly yellow hallway, blasts him with a fire hose (that Daltrey claims, perhaps joking, Russell wielded off camera), and finally scorches Tommy's rump with a steam iron. When Uncle Ernie (Keith Moon) later arrives and Tommy's bedclothes come off, the screen eventually goes as black as Townshend's recollection.

Russell also tampered with the Captain Walker character. The album had him kill his wife's paramour and become the story's heavy. But Russell reasoned that the impressionable Tommy would be more shocked seeing his father murdered instead.

This change has drawbacks: the facile heroism and conventional bond between father and son worked against the film's ironic and sporadically sinister tone. Had Tommy Walker's nemesis been his actual father, the movie would have been even edgier. Captain Walker (Robert Powell) could have started out as the nice, storybook dad who ends up disfigured in the war both physically and psychically. (Years later, when taking *Tommy* to Broadway, Townsend went back to his original script.) Another of Russell's motives for the change, however, was to put more of the focus on the lover and wicked stepdad Frank Hobbes, precisely because he suspected Oliver Reed would make the role one of the funniest and most menacing performances of his career.

∎

Adding Reed to the cast also reinforced themes of abuse, sexual mischief, and the reliable phallicism relevant to the circus off as well as on the screen. Since *The Devils*, Oliver Reed—the self-proclaimed "Mr. England"—had drunk heavily, had extramarital flings, and become a legendary flasher. At the slightest provocation, he'd whip out what he called, "My snake of desire, my wand of lust, my mighty mallet." "In years to come," writes Reed's biographer Cliff Goodwin, "Oliver would take little persuading to produce his penis—in bars, private parties, on planes, on film sets, and still more press conferences."

Reed indulged in other types of unmannerly swordsmanship. When he played Athos in Richard Lester's *The Three Musketeers*, he brandished a rapier on the set, injuring himself and a stuntman. His costars were also in peril. He fought with Raquel Welch and kept Richard Chamberlain in continual dread. Off the set, he raged on. While shooting the Lester film in Spain, the cast and crew took weekend refuge in Madrid, where they stayed in a five-star Hilton. An inebriated Reed staggered into the lobby one evening, stripped, and dove into a giant fish tank. By the time the police finally arrived, the press had feasted on another international scandal.

Reed would go on to frighten bar patrons with his hammered histrionics; he'd smash glasses, throw over tables, and taunt more cops who'd have to drag him off to a temporary cell. Still, he wasn't fully sated until he again taunted the longhaired, bearded, and often sandal-clad Russell—whom he still called Jesus. Reed consulted with Russell while working on his own film script: a period piece involving the murder of Sir Thomas Beckett. He phoned Russell about possibly directing it, but Russell had his own plans.

The moment Reed greeted him at his baronial country mansion in Surrey, Russell again confronted the *maso* side to his sadomasochism. Reed, in his Athos costume and with rapier in hand, thrust the sword into the air and flashed the same primal teeth he'd bared when giving Jesus a jujitsu flip a few years before. Smelling Russell's fear, he dropped the rapier and grabbed a more intimidating six-foot broadsword. He threw it, and Russell—much to the surprise of both—caught it. "Imagine you are standing on the altar steps, Jesus," Reed barked, "and I'm coming at you, coming to spill your guts and rub your sanctimonious nose in them. It's you or me, trying to split each other in two."

Russell tried humoring him with banter about Beckett, but Reed, deaf to reason, interrupted: "Now get up on the altar steps. Prepare to meet thy maker, heretic." He then called Russell's bluff by hurling himself at him but accidentally gashed his own chest. Reed told the story his way in his autobiography, fingering Russell as the aggressor: "I soon realized I was fighting for my life, screaming for him to stop."

The exact details of this Broome Hall incident remain a semi-mystery, but Russell's visit was well worth the trip to hell. Reed proved ideal for the part of Frank Hobbes, the blustering boob who woos Nora Walker and proceeds to make Tommy despondent. But Russell didn't have to endure a swordfight to know this; he had only to see Reed as Bill Sykes, the nasty piece of work in *Oliver!* who manhandles Charles Dickens's threadbare orphan with the same fiendish glee.

●

Russell's best films are violently cathartic, and *Tommy*'s most brilliant moments occur when Reed and all of the other major players display facial and bodily paroxysms that, while not curing the characters, offer some vicarious release for viewers. A great example is the Christmas scene, when young Tommy (Barry Winch) sits in his usual catatonic state. He is inside a toy car, indifferent to the brats and their parents dancing around him. Reed's most terrifying moment in the whole film could arguably be when he glares from behind an expressionless Santa Claus mask, screaming so loudly into Tommy's dead eardrum that the child blinks—all this just before Russell plies his malevolent jerk-off zoom to match the "Christmas" song's refrain, "How can he be saved?"

Reed continues scowling and howling into the camera, pacing in what seems a black magic circle as he cusses at Nora for giving birth to such a hapless cipher. With Nicky Hopkins providing such audio touches as tinkling bells, this Yuletide moment turns into one of raw anger. Reed is the Hammer werewolf all over again. Ann-Margret, when asked to characterize Reed's singing in such rabid moments, called it "a husky growl that comes right up from his stomach."

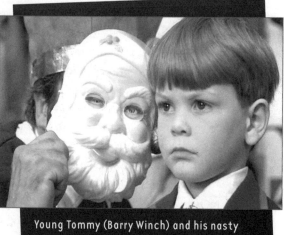

Young Tommy (Barry Winch) and his nasty stepdad (Oliver Reed) at home for the holidays. John Entwistle also called Ken Russell "a psychopathic Father Christmas."

Tina Turner, as the Acid Queen, is nearly as scary. Her lips quiver and her eyes get locked in an amphetamine daze after she attempts to "cure" Tommy, who is by now a teenager. She places him in a space-age iron maiden lined with hallucinogenic syringes. When the acid takes effect, Tommy imagines himself as his father; then, he reverts back to his life in the womb, when his mom fainted in a munitions foundry after hearing his dad was missing in action. Inevitably, Tommy's acid experience makes him fancy himself a Christ figure: the iron maiden is his crucifix, and the V. E. Day poppies nailed to his body draw blood.

Russell also uses the acid scene to display his own fear of reptiles, as Tommy morphs into a skeleton laced with writhing snakes. While shooting this sequence, the camera operator was so frightened that Russell bravely took over. He would joke about it years later on a DVD audio commentary: "I shot it up a ladder with cycle clips on my trousers in case I was invaded; but I got away scot-free. But the terrifying thing was, when we counted the snakes after the shooting, one was missing and is probably still lurking in the woodwork—ready to strangle and kill!"

Nora (Ann-Margret) in Tommy's acid fantasy.

Childhood war memories also helped Russell focus the film's distempered energy. While he, eighteen years Townshend's senior, had spent part of the war in a cinema-induced haze, his memories of the overhead Luftwaffe were still vivid. Townshend, on the other hand, was post–V. E. Day, one of the "angry young men" who felt ostracized by his elders as well as his peers. He at least fit a convenient sociological niche: the disaffected U.K. youth—not unlike the teddy boys and girls Russell photographed next to London's bomb ruins two decades before. "I wanted to write this thing about how spirituality had come from street anger," Townshend said in his *Uncut* interview, "that had come from suppressed teenage disaffection that had come from post-war denial."

Russell's autobiographical contribution in this regard starts right at the film's beginning, with the sun descending behind Captain Walker's silhouette atop a Lake District mountain. Captain and Nora Walker are the postcard-perfect couple, alternately lolling on the floral hillside and embracing under the Lodore Falls. But an alarm sounds to abort this spell of bucolic bliss, and Captain Walker gets called back to duty. Russell pays tribute to the film *Brief Encounter* as Nora bids a tearful farewell; the captain rides away on a steamy train before boarding his Wellington bomber.

With the movie shifting the story's first part to his familiar World War II era, Russell even has Tommy born on V. E. Day; the flags and crowds celebrate the armistice outside the window of the hospital where Nora delivers him. The film's locations at Portsmouth and Russell's hometown of Southampton already suffered Nazi assaults. Now, Russell was back to impose more, albeit simulated, carnage. He shouted, "Higher, higher!" during an early scene involving a bomb attack. "For God's sake, throw some petrol on it, someone!" Years later, Townshend marveled at "the Britishness" of Russell's vision: "So, you open up with this scene of three sexy chorus girls with gas masks on walking across rubble, and you see this teddy bear in the rubble. What you know is that this is something Ken has seen."

As he stood on the set, likely incensed by thoughts of those Nazi attacks, Russell played the commandant dandy. The sight of Russell hollering out orders with his silvery mane, shaggy beard, pop art T-shirts, tartan trousers, and cherry red face inspired John Entwistle to describe him as "a psychopathic Father Christmas." Some, like Ann-Margret, called him "Cuddly Bear."

Either way, Russell had to prove to Columbia that its $3 million-plus budget was worth the while. And sometimes, even Russell had to defer to a higher authority. A case in point occurred when he was filming the scene involving disabled Marilyn Monroe worshippers. The shooting took place in an actual church belonging to a Portsmouth army barracks. The commandant arrived, saw what was happening, called it blasphemy, and ordered them to stop. But Stigwood called the War Office to smooth matters over. The "Temple of Marilyn Monroe" sequence evolved from a previous Russell script. While filming *Savage Messiah*, Russell and Derek Jarman worked on *The Angels*—a grand and subversive production that got MGM's interest. Referring to it as "a sort of Russell *48 1/2*" (per Fellini's *8 1/2* and Russell's age at the time), Russell again probed the often-invisible tether between the sacred and the profane.

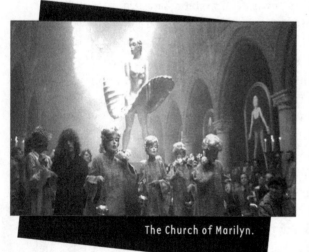
The Church of Marilyn.

The Angels' central theme was hollow idolatry. A pop star named Poppy Day becomes a deified commodity and gets even more god-like after fans learn of her disappearance in a plane crash. They resurrect her into what Russell describes as "a giant sized statue . . . with cripples praying for a cure as they line up to touch her golden calf." The story twists when Poppy reemerges as a survivor who'd been lost in a jungle. When her rescuers arrive by helicopter to enshrine her, the fans suspect the entire event is a hoax and turn into a disillusioned mob that eventually stones Poppy to death.

PHALLIC FRENZY

Eventually, MGM pulled away from *The Angels*, but Russell salvaged bits of the script and marveled at how much his themes corresponded with Townshend's. *Tommy* also allowed Russell to return to the contradictory theme in his early *Lourdes* film: the suspicion that behind every miracle lurks a scammer.

Poppy Day became *Tommy*'s giant, plaster replica, frozen in Monroe's infamous wind-blown dress pose from *The Seven Year Itch*. As phalanxes of paraplegics and other cripples flock to touch her healing toes, an apparently stoned Eric Clapton leads a procession that features censer-waving acolytes in rubber Marilyn masks. Arthur Brown officiates the Holy Communion, screaming out the lyrics to Sonny Boy Williamson's "Eyesight to the Blind," while the congregants ingest godhead in the form of pills and swigs from a bottle of Johnny Walker Red. But when Tommy finally takes his turn to touch the healing harlot, he topples the false idol, the statue crumbles, and he's still in darkness.

●

Russell also interpolated material into *Tommy* from another aborted script. *Music, Music, Music* was to be about a fictional composer named John Fairfax, who forsakes his grand religious rock opera *Jesus on Venus* to write television commercials. But after selling out to Mammon, he suffers what Russell describes in his autobiography as "a crackup with all the products associated with his jingles, including baked beans, detergent, and chocolate, all erupting through the TV screen and engulfing him in goo."

Russell, continually griping about having to lower himself by doing ads for Britain's commercial television in the 1960s, also seems to be looking darkly back on his ads for baked beans, chocolates, and detergents. He was particularly annoyed at having to provide the illusion of flowing soapsuds by reversing the action of the camera as the suds went down a drain.

These moments from *Music, Music, Music* inspired the messy scene in which Ann-Margret's guilt-ridden Nora, luxuriating in a fluffy white bedroom with a fluffy white marabou covering her body, cusses at her now-famous Pinball Wizard son who glares at her from the television. To accompany this, Townshend wrote "Champagne," which Nora sings while hitting her bejeweled fingers against her remote in an attempt to block Tommy out. Not even the alluring commercials for "Rex Baked Beans" and "Black Beauty Chocolates" can calm her down: she fumes when her son's saintly mug keeps invading her airwaves. So, she throws a champagne bottle through the tube, and all the suds, beans, and chocolate spew out at her like projectile vomit from the screen. "I was the guinea pig," Ann-Margret recalled to a *New York Times* interviewer. "No one had tried this first, and they came with such speed, such momentum, that it just knocked me back."

Soon Russell has her groveling among the foam and fudge, whipping up an orgasmic rage as she straddles a sausage shaped and (now chocolate lubed) pillow. Ann-Margret's husband, the producer Roger Smith, happened to walk onto the set while all of this transpired. He looked aghast and speculated then and there that his wife's career as a glamour queen had come to an end.

"I'm totally de-glamorized," she admitted. "There are only a couple of times throughout the movie when I can look nice. The rest of the time it's how *bad* I can look, with dark shadow on my cheeks to hollow them, and black rings around my eyes." Worse, Russell had her thrashing so violently during her soap-suds rapture that the jagged glass from the broken television ended up cutting her. Neither she nor Russell knew what was happening until they noticed the suds turning pink.

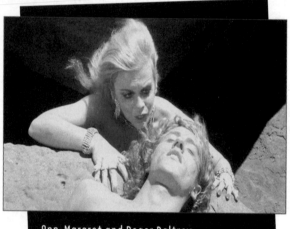

Ann-Margret and Roger Daltrey.

As Nora Walker, Ann-Margret jumps into spasmodic dances one moment, sings stridently the next, and sometimes contorts her face so tightly that it resembles a fist. In this process of morphing her from a glitzy and safe Hollywood vixen into another of his maniacal harridans, Ken Russell should have canonized her Saint Ann-Margret. Though the story is about her used and abused child, she gets roughed up just as much. Russell also makes her bathe in a wintry cold mountain stream, have her false fingernails yanked off, age from twenty to forty-five, and even at one point forsake makeup. She finally gets killed in a bloody mob riot after one of Tommy's cynical disciples smashes a bottle over her head.

●

Tommy also had its production snags. Townshend was worried about the casting, particularly with Ann-Margret ("too glamorous") and Reed ("can't sing"). For Reed's singing, Russell and the sound crew had to literally cut and paste words and phrases together from tape since he could barely croon a note. Daltrey was also not Townshend's first choice for Tommy; he did not even necessarily see the band having that major a role in the film. He initially considered Tiny Tim for the Pinball Wizard and Lou Reed for the Acid Queen. The role of the doctor who tries to cure Tommy was to go to Christopher Lee, but Robert Stigwood thought of Jack Nicholson and talked the actor into taking the role for a one-day shoot.

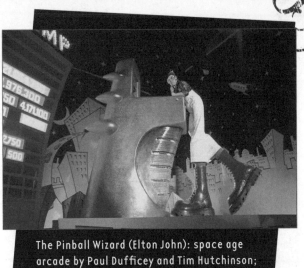

The Pinball Wizard (Elton John): space age arcade by Paul Dufficey and Tim Hutchinson; skyscraper boots by Shirley Russell.

For Russell, Keith Moon posed behavioral problems. When Moon and Reed got together, they would go on what Townshend diplomatically calls "drinking competitions." But the barroom lunacy seeped onto the set. During the burlesque sequence when Nora meets Frank at Bernie's Holiday Camp, Russell's plans to film at an actual resort got squelched when Reed exposed his snake of desire at one of its social functions; the proprietor—far from charmed—booted the whole crew out.

Daltrey was brash enough to do many of his own stunts and came away with his share of cuts, wounds, and burns. Even Russell, whose concern for a good take could overshadow worries about possible injuries, wanted to cancel a scene when the Black Angels, a Newcastle motorcycle gang, got into a skirmish with a rival pack. But the Angels promised they would merely play football while the camera rolled, not specifying that the ball would be a gang member's head.

The flaming pavilion on the Southsea pier that shows up at the film's end was an actual fire that ignited when some of the arc lights overheated. As the flames spread, the firefighters and townspeople scrambled to staunch the disaster. When Russell griped, "We will probably have to find another set," representatives from papers like the *New York Times* were around to overhear. Russell figured he'd be accused of deserting a disaster had he and the crew left it, but that he'd also be accused of gloating had he stayed. He chose to gloat and included it in his ultimate battle scene.

Tommy's ending is not so satisfying. One moment Tommy Walker is part of an exploitation racket; the next he is achieving some kind of spiritual nirvana from out of nowhere after watching his mother get murdered. Russell seems more interested in portraying his holy Lake District as the soul's cleansing place, as Tommy swims toward the Lodore Falls where his parents conceived him. But the untrammeled nature is nowhere near as arresting as the artifice. The cool blue chlorinated pool, where Tommy has his literally eye-opening epiphany, looks more transcendent than the mountain's rocky stream.

The closing shot banned in South Africa.

Russell's zest to capture the transcendental beauty of Skiddaw, however, had even less miraculous results for the South Africans. Their censors snipped out the final image of Tommy standing atop the mountain to welcome the sunrise, thinking it too pagan. The excision, of course, destroyed the story's circular pattern, since the film opens with Captain Walker watching the sun fall.

"Your senses will never be the same," read the ads as *Tommy* premiered at New York's Ziegfeld Theater on March 18, 1975. It assailed viewers in brash, loud, and glorious five-channel Quintophonic Sound. The London premiere soon followed at Leicester Square. By then, Russell's cinematic tale of tribulation, redemption, and the evils of mass advertising precipitated an unprecedented promotional campaign with badges, mirrors, patches, posters, stickers, T-shirts, and, of course, an original soundtrack album.

Some critics were kinder than usual. The *New York Times*' Vincent Canby, a Russell nonbeliever, admitted this time that his funhouse style worked. He spotted the director's tribute to old vaudeville and concluded by stating, "It's all fairly excessive and far from subtle, but in this case good taste would have been wildly inappropriate and a fearful drag."

As expected, Russell's version of *Tommy* divided audiences: they were enthusiastic, stunned, or appalled. Many fans of the Who likely saw Russell's idiosyncratic layers bewildering, while all the fuddy-duddies hoping the director would go back to his more subdued BBC fare finally threw up their hands for good. Even Townshend was initially stymied: "The result was a much more literal film than I expected. It's an exaggeration in some ways, almost burlesque at times."

While promoting *Tommy*, Russell wore outlandish clothes; glared through red, Rabelaisian eyes; and shook up interviewers with his joyous rage. He had a choice encounter on *Russell Harty Plus*, a London Weekend Television talk show. Clad in a silver-studded denim jacket, he wagged his finger at Harty, at his beloved England, and especially at its newly reelected Prime Minister Harold Wilson: "This country's in a weird, feeble, grotesque state, and it's about time it got out of it. And the reason it could get out of it is rock music. And I think that Townshend, the Who, Roger Daltrey, Entwistle, Moon could rise this country out of its decadent, ambient state more than Wilson and those crappy people could ever hope to ACHIEVE!"

On that same show, Russell also lauded (and embarrassed) Townshend by calling him the new Shakespeare. "Well, Ken's a bombastic sort," Townshend later reflected. "I really shouldn't speak for Ken any more than I should . . . but, making the *Tommy* film, both of us, me certainly, were on the brink of alcoholism. Ken and I would be up till two in the morning talking about the next day's shooting, and he used to get up at five! So I think by the time he was on the Russell Harty show and said that comment, he probably hadn't slept for six months and was living on champagne, I don't know."

Years later, Russell would remember *Tommy* as being one of his best times as a director. But shortly after it opened, Russell confessed to journalist Kathleen Carroll: "In the making of this film . . . there was a lot of suffering. Three assistant directors cracked under the pressure, but they survived. *Tommy* really was very tough and upsetting." In March 1975, Russell told the *New York Post*, "That's one of the things I like about film, it's sort of an odyssey, you get a lot of people on a ship, and you go off on a Grecian adventure, meet the cyclops and the sirens and the hydra with the head full of snakes and cross the Styx and some people die along the way."

There are some imperfections: crowd extras stare into the camera, Tommy's eyes change from childhood brown to adolescent blue, Cousin Kevin slides a scalding steam iron across Tommy's bottom with the cord unplugged, too many 1970s hippies look too droopy, and the climax isn't as engaging as the gorgeously photographed madness leading up to it. Even so, *Tommy* triumphs because of its angry and stirring story, its demented and joyous vigor, its brave refusal to look graceful or fashionable, even while showcasing so many pop stars. Russell also spends all 111 minutes committed to capturing a moment's passion, regardless of any technical gaffes that now and then seem intentional. All of these traits make *Tommy* a paradox: a film that feels artificial and primal at the same time.

ORPHEUS EXTENDING

Franz Liszt, composer, conductor, piano virtuoso, genius, poseur, and sex hound, dies but manages to get to heaven. There, with a seven-lady chamber ensemble, he plucks a celestial melody on a harp, his famous nocturne "Liebestraum no. 3," or "Dream of Love." But an off-screen voice, so primly British that it could only be the Almighty, breaks the mood to announce that Liszt's former pal turned parasite, Richard Wagner, has emerged from Hell's bowels to inflict an apocalypse.

Liszt and his acolytes must now hop into a pipe organ–propelled rocket ship to slay the beast back on Earth, where Wagner has morphed into a hybrid of Frankenstein's monster and a rock 'n' roll Hitler. Now razing Berlin, he has already obliterated almost the entire world with his electric guitar/machine gun. But cosmic crusader Liszt soon reduces the Teutonic prince of darkness to skeletal rubble by zapping rainbow-colored rays and restoring peace to whatever's left of the planet.

The above description, enough for at least a single screen epic, is merely one of several climaxes in *Lisztomania*—the film that established once and for all Ken Russell's refusal to pay any more token favors to biographical "realism." *Lisztomania* contains many relevant facts about Liszt—his music, the people who had affected his life, his marital problems, his womanizing, his recourse to religion, and of course, his strained relationship with Wagner—but it goes further into the deep end than even the swastika-adorned portrait of Strauss from five years before.

Released in 1975, shortly after *Tommy*, *Lisztomania* continues Russell's harder, more satirical edge, with more lavish sets, more crazed acting, more frenetic plot pacing, and a premise that is simultaneously silly and fantastic.

When the German poet Heinrich Heine coined the term "Lisztomania" in 1841, he saw the intense and almost dangerous effect that Liszt exerted over his audiences. Hormonally agitated ladies—supposedly even nuns—screamed and fainted in his presence. Concert fans clawed at one another to grab one of the many gloves that he'd coquettishly remove and fling to the stage floor. He'd then charge them up with rhapsodic arpeggios and other theatrical flourishes.

If the romantic Heine imagined a future when such charismatic composers could magnify their grandeur through vast, intimidating sound systems and electronic screens, he might have pictured Russell's version of Liszt: a combination rhinestone Elvis and cockney Liberace. Heine might even have envisioned Russell as the Svengali of Lisztomaniacs, bellowing for more cycloramic camera movements, more wind machine gusts, and more hyperbolic, high-strung dialogue.

Russell chose *Lisztomania* over another biopic he'd planned called *The Gershwin Dream*. He probably figured that the gentleman who composed *Rhapsody in Blue* couldn't hold a candelabrum to the cad who wrote the *Hungarian Rhapsodies*. Russell also saw Liszt as Romanticism's baby and the precursor to the modern pop star.

Like other great names that caught Russell's eye, Liszt fought internal wars. He was torn between love for his music and his prurient desires, his guilt about leading a cushy lifestyle and sitting idly during the 1849 Hungarian rebellion against the House of Hapsburg, his desperation for the kind of commercial success that would also belie his artistic integrity, and most important, the queasy fact that Wagner was eclipsing him as Europe's symphonic superstar.

In theory, the link between a sexy nineteenth-century Hungarian composer and a mid-1970s rocker seemed easy. Both Russell and Roger Daltrey (keen for another title role) wanted to rekindle *Tommy*'s spark. But when he took his script to Goodtimes Enterprises producer David Puttnam and the golden calves at Warner Brothers, Russell entered a creative quandary. He thought he could once again shock audiences with a free hand, but he started getting dictates.

Puttnam, with more of an ear for pop than classical, rejected several of Russell's initial ideas as too arty and didn't want to play up the twisted Liszt-Wagner bond. Russell also claims that Puttnam and his colleagues were responsible for casting Ringo Starr as Pope Pius IX and for inserting a barely intelligible square dance number in the opening scene. But they also tried humoring Russell with perks. Besides being the first movie encoded with a Dolby Stereo optical track,

Lisztomania also offered Russell the challenge to put together an outlandish narrative that, as Warner Bros. publicity would later promise, "out-Tommys *Tommy*."

Even with the compromises, Russell took a quixotic dare that most of today's directors—so dependent on advertisers, publicists, and focus groups—would be too timid to consider. Instead of dumbing down his script, he proved all too kind in assuming that audiences weaned on arena rock and disco would welcome a movie about a long-dead European composer and a plot full of heady subtexts. If viewers sat and watched it stoned, they could chuckle at the outlandish sets, costumes, and histrionics, but *Lisztomania* also offered a cornucopia of artistic and historical themes: references to musical and literary luminaries of the time, allusions to other movies, and a comic strip excursion that ends by linking Wagner's notions of German superiority to the rise of the Third Reich.

But for all of its controversy and eventual neglect, *Lisztomania* is proof that even when Russell placates pop sensibilities to draw in bigger crowds, he still ends up with idiosyncratic results, requiring more footnotes than most of today's art-house independents. No matter how insane it looks the first or second time around, the film gets better for those who have the patience to pay it repeated visits. *Lisztomania*, for this reason, represents a cinematic netherworld that *Film Quarterly*'s Ross Care describes as "sadly dangling, a brilliant, unique, and intensely personal film in search of an audience which perhaps doesn't even exist."

"My film isn't biography," Russell once explained to a public still smarting from *Lisztomania*'s surrealistic assault. "It comes from things I feel when I listen to the music of Wagner and Liszt, and when I think about their lives." He was also thinking of Liszt as a superhero. But instead of giving him muscles of steel, Russell gave him a pelvic Popsicle—a phallic reminder of Liszt's carnal and creative energy that literally grows to obscene dimensions and gets him into lots of trouble. This is apparent from the very first scene, when Liszt kisses both of the Countess Marie d'Agoult's (Fiona Lewis) nipples to a metronome's beat. As the countess ratchets up the rhythm, and Liszt starts smacking in silent movie time, the foppish Count d'Agoult (John Justin) barges in to initiate a duel with steel swords.

Liszt pops out of bed with only a sheet around his loins, scampering about the room to save his tender spot from his assailant's rapier. Even as Liszt swings from a chandelier and totters on a ledge, the count still stabs at Liszt's testicles and singes them with a candle. Meanwhile, the countess, gloating at the two stooges skirmishing over her, already finds a substitute as she munches on a banana.

Russell claims he was caught off guard when he heard Rick Wakeman's barely decipherable square dance tune (not listed in the credits) blare over this swashbuckling spoof. But the lyrics are at least lucid during a nicely photographed silhouette when the count's "sword supplied by Bendy toys" goes limp. Limp or not, he manages to subdue the rogue, nail both him and the countess inside a piano, and place it on the tracks of an oncoming train. Pow! Bang! Crash! It's all just one of Liszt's slapstick reveries as the rude flashes of cameras jolt him back into the present: he's now miles away from the countess, fending off sycophants at a preconcert press fete in Paris.

Russell's party scene—crammed with nineteenth-century musical and literary luminaries—is among *Lisztomania*'s highlights. Wagner (Paul Nicholas) barges into the café swinging his fists and dressed as a sailor punk with "Nietzsche" inscribed on his cap's brim. He nags Liszt to perform selections from his opera *Rienzi*, but the other leading lights flitting in and out of range steal Wagner's thunder.

A snarky Liszt snaps, "Piss off, Brahms!" and even calls him "a right wanker" when the famed composer bugs him with questions. A genuflecting Frédéric Chopin (Kenneth Colley) coughs tubercular blood onto the leg of a *tres* butch Madame George Sand (Imogen Claire), who soon treats Lola Montes (Anulka Dziubinska) to a Sapphic smooch. A corpulent Gioacchino Rossini (Ken Parry) tries keeping his wig intact while wolfing down a chicken leg and a vanilla ice cream cone, urging a sickly Hector Berlioz (Murray Melvin) to "Eat!" Never shy with ethnic caricature, Russell also has Felix Mendelssohn (Otto Diamant) respond to Wagner's accusation that he is "the Yid who only makes music on a cash register." "Music, schmusic!" he tells the cantankerous kraut. "It's a living, dear boy."

When Liszt leaves the celebrities behind and takes to the stage at a concert for the Beethoven Memorial Fund, hordes of bonnet-clad girls fly into predictable hysterics. Historically, Liszt was among the first of the great composers to attract such mass crowds. And to reinforce this notion of Liszt as the original pop idol, Russell and set designer Phillip Harrison decorate the stage with allusions to Liberace: Liszt's gaudy jacket, the tinsel-curtain backdrop, the candelabra perched on the piano, and also the way Liszt hits his fingers against the keyboard with flinging arms.

Wagner sits among the teenagers, but he's not prepared for Liszt's object lesson on how art must often submit to the dictates of commerce. Liszt starts playing selections from Wagner's *Rienzi* but soon intersperses them with sneaky strains of "Chopsticks"—the tune the girls are bawling to hear. As the "*Rienzi/Chopsticks Fantasia*" gets more feverish and an enraged Wagner storms out of the auditorium, Russell pops up in a cameo as the orchestra conductor, alerting Liszt that a past paramour with a baby carriage has come onto the stage to demand child support. Russell also has some self-referential fun. In the theater boxes are two older dames: a "Millionairess" (Iza Teller), presumably Madame von Meck from *The Music Lovers*, and a "Most Promising Actress" (Georgina Hale), presumably Alma from *Mahler*. But the most important figure is Princess Carolyne Sayn-Wittgenstein (Sara Kestelman) of Russia—the shrew who'll lure Liszt into a Faustian pact.

●

When Liszt sneaks out from his domestic drudgery once Marie d'Agoult becomes his wife, he visits the Princess Wittgenstein at St. Petersburg. This is where Russell takes the tale into surrealistic pornography as he plays on Rabelais's scatological obsessions as well as Aubrey Beardsley's humongous genitalia drawings for *Lysistrata*. Oliver Reed (who snuck a blink-and-you-miss-him cameo in *Mahler* as a train conductor) pops up as the princess's servant, escorting Liszt to the royal ass-chamber. Fresh air sickens the princess, so she has buttocks sculptures jutting out from the walls to douse Liszt with special gases. Trying to plug up the fumigation holes with his clothes, he ends up naked except for his sword and belt—defenseless and diminished enough to don one of the princess's dresses to keep from catching cold.

Set designer Harrison, who would work on Russell's *Valentino* and go on to design movies ranging from Herbert Ross's Hollywood nostalgia in *Pennies from Heaven* (1981) to Mark A. Z. Dippé's satanic gore in *Spawn* (1997), also shares Russell's fancy for pop anachronism. He adorns Sayn-Wittgenstein's palace with hallowed images of Bill Haley, Elvis Presley, and (for continuity with *Tommy*) Pete Townshend—all done up to resemble Russian Orthodox icons.

"Music, like sex, should be approached in a religious spirit as one of the holiest things in life," the princess dictates to Liszt as she stands among her phallic columns. Liszt then gets symbolically sucked into a demonic bargain as the princess turns into a giant and pulls him into her mammoth vagina. No sooner does he enter this porthole in time than he finds himself standing on a pedestal, with Marie d'Agoult, George Sand, Lola Montes, and other ex-girlfriends clawing at him before burrowing under his dress.

The princess meanwhile becomes a Mother Mephistopheles with bat wings, smirking as Liszt screams to her for help and throwing him a lyre instead of a bone. But even when he sounds so angelic, strumming and singing his "Orpheus Song," the clawing coven around him drowns his melody by trilling out a chorus of compressed echoes reminiscent of early 1960s pop tunes.

The princess smirks even as she watches Liszt's penis suddenly extend twelve feet into the air. One moment the girls are riding it like Rockettes at a Radio City show; the next they're like Gargantua's nurses, wrapping it with Maypole ribbons

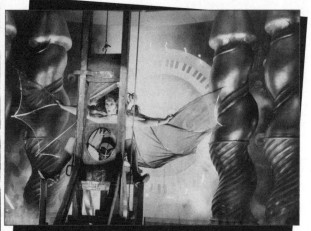

Princess Carolyn Sayn-Wittgenstein (Sara Kestelman) waits for Liszt's end of her bargain.

and doing Busby Berkeley scissor-kicks beneath it as his "Liebestraum" takes on a striptease beat. But Liszt's laughter during this song and dance number becomes an agonized cry as his gigantic joystick rides toward a specially fashioned guillotine. As an embodiment of the vagina dentata, the princess sings out her demand for his soul to the tune of Liszt's "Dante's Symphony."

Once he awakens from this new nightmare, finding the only appendage he hurt was his thumb against the piano, Liszt's fantasy castration has figurative meaning: he is now essentially Wittgenstein's pet. And she proves to be an officious businesswoman who presents him with a contract that transfers custody of his children to legal guardians, setting him free from the alienated Marie d'Agoult, who has already published a scandalous book about him. He consents to Wittgenstein's wishes but loses his boyish locks, starts to age, and gets progressively grim the more power she wields.

Staring down from his royal heights at the war ravaging his country, a rueful Liszt sings out strains from his "Funerailles." Marie d'Agoult and two of his children fall to bomb shrapnel, a burning baby carriage topples in the street, and a pile of dismembered soldiers remind him that he has sold out his people for luxury.

But Wittgenstein also starts losing power. After staging an ostentatious wedding ceremony, in which she fine-tunes the bishops' attire, she gets spurned. The pope (Ringo Starr) refuses to annul her present marriage, and Liszt seems relieved. Knowing her rendezvous with Liszt, at least in this world, is over, she bids him farewell with an anachronism: "We'll say a few Hail Marys and drink a few *Bloody* Marys together."

Despite her appearance as a comic book villainess, Russell's version of Princess Carolyne has some historical accuracy. She really smoked strong cigars, exuded a masculine bearing, failed to win Liszt's hand when the pope refused to grant her a dispensation, and retaliated against the papacy by writing a twenty-four-volume tome entitled *The Interior Causes of the Exterior Weakness of the Church*. But contrary to Russell's version of events, she remained Liszt's soul mate through most of his life.

"Mine is a highly susceptible, intense, voracious sensuality," Richard Wagner once crowed about himself, "which must somehow or another be indulged if my mind is to accomplish the agonizing labor of calling a nonexistent world into being." It was only a matter of time before the man who uttered this would get the portrayal he deserved: the mythical Nietzschean Superman in cartoonish colors. With such an obviously inflammable personality at his disposal, Russell set out to infuriate more critics and music purists than ever before by making Wagner *Lisztomania*'s übervillain.

History loves megalomaniacs, so Russell dedicates the weightier part of *Lisztomania* to Wagner and his pan-Germanic ideas, particularly the ideology behind the four-opera opus *Ring of the Nibelungen*: Nordic gods and goddesses, Aryan heroes and earth mothers, mortals and beasts who simmer in a cauldron of Norsk legend. Russell's story intensifies when he fuses boyhood memories of the lords of the Luftwaffe bombing his town and Fritz Lang's *Siegfried* flickering against the walls of his garage.

History records Liszt and Wagner as occasional friends and champions of one another's work; they would at times even ingratiate themselves to one another in public. Tensions mounted when Wagner got a bit larcenous with some of Liszt's melodies and stole Liszt's daughter Cosima, impregnating her with his master race mandate. Russell has always regarded such Teutonic ideals with rage, ridicule, and queasy fascination. And this is the point in the story at which his preference for parable over the official "truth" wins out.

Converting from Communism to German Nationalism, Wagner still seeks out Liszt's musical inspiration—a juncture that Russell dramatizes with another nightmare. An eerie soundtrack swells as Wagner stands in front of a red moon eclipsing the sun. He sprouts fangs to declare, "I shall write music that will fire the imagination of the German people and bring to light a man of iron to forge the shattered fragments of this country into a nation of steel."

Richard Wagner (Paul Nicholas) lunches on Liszt.

Liszt, knocked out after Wagner spikes his wine, lies slumped over his piano, pounding out a zombified funeral march as the Teutonic prince of darkness gnaws into his neck—a moment as darkly erotic as any vampire film. Liszt emerges from what is apparently another bad dream, but Wagner has already run off to resurrect the spirit of Siegfried, leaving Liszt with his "latest pamphlet": a *Superman* comic book.

Liszt, temporarily free from Wagner and finally rid of the princess, takes holy orders and becomes a Franciscan abbé, but he can't stop womanizing. Pope Ringo pops into Liszt's boudoir like a funhouse goblin and atones for his dull performance by wearing vestments that—thanks to Shirley's gift for detail and to Ken's fetishes—bear the embroidered faces of Joan Crawford and Judy Garland. But his holiness is not impressed to discover Liszt in bed with Olga Janina (Nell Campbell), the real-life Cossack who loved the aging composer so much that she threatened to shoot him if he left her and then turn her revolver on herself. But the pope gets down to business: Liszt's daughter Cosima has abandoned her husband Hans von Bülow (Andrew Reilly), who was once Liszt's prized pupil, to run off with Wagner, the "Antichrist." In order to atone for his past sins, Liszt must now become Wagner's exorcist.

∎

With its shrill satire and dialogue shot out in staccato sarcasm, *Lisztomania* (like *Valentino* soon to follow) calls to mind how an R-rated version of the 1960s television show *Batman* might look. In 1965, executive producer William Dozier and television writer Lorenzo Semple Jr. sent Bob Kane's creation over the top with garish sets, exaggerated acting, and relentless irony. The result was heresy to many Kane aficionados who could not appreciate or apprehend that the show was what Dozier called "joking against the characters."

When the story switches to Liszt's quest to find Wagner in a spooky Bavarian village, Russell begins with a tribute to both 1930s Universal horror films and Hammer knockoffs from the late '50s and early '60s. Liszt approaches village Jews to ask the way to Wagner's castle, but they all react by shrieking and scuttling away in the manner expected of movieland Transylvanians. When he finally goes to knock on Wagner's door, he encounters a cuckolded Bülow, reduced to a half-mad servant still lucid enough to warn Liszt that Wagner's music has become "an evil drug masquerading as a universal cure."

Liszt, gaping through a balcony window, witnesses Wagner's reenactment of the *Ring* cycle's opening, when Alberich, the dwarf among the Nibelungen, dwells in the earth's entrails to take the beautiful Rhinemaidens up on their dare to forsake all love in return for the Rhinegold. Fritz Lang's *Die Nibelungen* made him into a hideous, feeble troll unfit for love, but Russell turns Alberich into a rapacious giant with a diamond Star of David engraved in his forehead and the strength to lift the Rhinemaidens over his head before ravishing them. To Rick Wakeman's heavily synthesized version of Wagner's "Magic Fire Music," Russell records the orgy with dizzying camera spins, while Wagner's teenaged crusaders, with red capes and *W*s emblazoned on their chests, try keeping a candlelight vigil as they gape and quake at Alberich tainting their ancient blood.

When Cosima joins Wagner for a ritual consecration of the "übermensch," Russell turns the occasion into a Nazi rally rock concert. Liszt looks on in horror as Wagner lifts another of his tunes to sing of how "the flowering youth of Germany was raped by the beast." Wagner dons a blond Siegfried wig while singing his praises of "Teutonic godhead," while his followers chime along in the same way that Liszt's fans hummed to his "Chopsticks" performance. And when Wagner and Cosima finish the number with gauche choreography, they call to mind the memorable scene in *Batman*'s premiere episode, when Adam West's superhero does the "Batusi" with Jill St. John.

•

"They say that music is the gay science," Wagner tells Liszt while showing off the laboratory gadgets that will charge life into the "Man of Iron." This "gay science" is a glib reference to the title of Nietzsche's aphoristic work, in which he tells his reader "to live dangerously! Build your cities under Vesuvius! Send your ships into uncharted seas! Live at war with your peers and yourselves! Be robbers and conquerors, as long as you cannot be rulers and owners." Wagner takes this as a call to manufacture what he calls "Thor": a synthetic Siegfried slumped on a gurney, a gangly corpse in a plastic Halloween mask.

As Wagner powers his electrical generator with rotating shellac records that blare fierce German marches, a primitive IBM computer belches out variations on surnames ending in "Stein." All this is supposed to

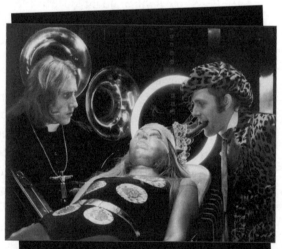

Richard Wagner (Paul Nicholas) creates the "Man of Iron" (Rick Wakeman) as Liszt (Roger Daltrey) tries to save the world.

program the monster to know his enemies. But when Thor kicks into life, he is none other than Rick Wakeman, stepping out from the shadows as soundtrack maestro. He yells "Stein!" But he's not interested in pursuing any Goldsteins, Silversteins, or Rubensteins; he's just thirsty. Wagner is confused but quick enough to hand him a stein full of beer.

To Wagner's chagrin and Liszt's delight, the new Siegfried can do nothing but spastically pace, giggle, guzzle more beer, and literally piss on the flames of German glory. Liszt says he "looks like a character out of a comic," making a wry commentary on all of the characters, including himself. But Wagner turns out to be a difficult devil to save. He's immune to the Bloody Mary mixed with holy water that Liszt concocts. A superhero battle ensues as Liszt plays his "Dance of Death" on a flame-throwing piano, igniting a cacophony of shattering glass, flying doors, and electrical fires. As Wagner's Teutonic sword transforms into one of Russell's dreaded snakes, his castle walls crumble over him. With his dying breath, Wagner orders Cosima to prepare for his resurrection and incarcerate her father.

Lisztomania comes close to true horror whenever Cosima shows up—the one whose mother calls her a "wicked child" from the start and who, in real life, became an ideologue reputedly more anti-Semitic than her husband. Veronica Quilligan, who would be in such lighter fare as *Robin and Marian* and *Candleshoe*, is thoroughly convincing in this darker role. But instead of

Richard Wagner reborn as the überman.

the leather-clad dominatrix in *Mahler*, she is here a perpetual teenybopper who inwardly warps.

Cosima starts out as a sympathetic victim of her father's neglect, but after she starts playing around with a Liszt voodoo doll, she evokes the psychopathic "Little Rhoda" from *The Bad Seed*. To avenge Wagner's death, she starts sticking her dad's likeness with long hairpins. "How does it feel to be neglected?" she says over his agonized screams, "The greatest musical failure of the nineteenth-century!"

Soon Cosima resurrects the FrankenWagner, who rises from his tomb to kill off hordes of Jewish pawnbrokers as well as many of his followers. While leading a gang of Wagner's caped crusaders to pelt the streets with explosives, Cosima takes the time to look up at her dad peering helplessly through Wagner's swastika stained-glass window. She impales her doll's heart to exact her final vengeance.

●

Liszt awakens from what seems another nightmare. But now he's in a pearly white heaven, plucking his "Dream of Love" with a redeemed Cosima and six of his dream lovers—a lady for each color of the rainbow—at his side. It's an over-wrought tableau that recalls Birkin and Ursula embracing among the flowers in *Women in Love* or Tchaikovsky's all-too-perfect summer picnic in *The Music Lovers*. Liszt's afterlife is all sweetness, light, and virtue, but Russell appears to be alternately deriding and lauding this morality play. Look closely for the phallic columns holding up their celestial pedestal.

Russell is very adept at capturing, even in comic book form, the tribulations and terrors wrought by *Die Nibelungen*. But a pithy comment that film historian Paul M. Jensen once made about Fritz Lang easily applies to Russell as well. Jensen asserts that Lang could not portray the romance between the two principal characters in the 1922 film *Dr. Mabuse, The Gambler* "without having them slip into absurd exaggeration; he cannot depict happiness successfully."

Though *Lisztomania* closes with such a saintly gauze, Russell is a more engaging sentimentalist earlier on, when Liszt realizes his relationship with Marie d'Agoult has gone rank. He pores through old photo albums to daydream about nicer times when they shared a humble Swiss chalet.

Just as Russell's Mahler magically envisioned a scene from Luchino Visconti's *Death in Venice*, so does his Liszt imagine he's Charlie Chaplin's tramp from *The Gold Rush*. As Daltrey sings lyrics he composed to "Dream of Love" over the soundtrack, Liszt and Marie make light of their poverty, jumping and dancing in silent speed despite the addition of three hungry offspring. Marie knits one heart-shaped blanket or pillow after another; even the split in the derriere of Liszt's pants has a Valentine patch. But the smiles sag as a creatively and financially drained Liszt slumps at his piano, and the threadbare family soon exits the chalet into a snowy landscape. The choreography is splendid, the Chaplin send up is hilarious, and Liszt's glycerin tears when the story flashes back to the present are nearly as shiny as his jewelry.

Once again, Russell triumphs by committing what convention calls an aesthetic no-no: he makes an art out of working at cross-purposes. He tries redeeming his romantic subjects at the same time as he lampoons them.

■

After *Lisztomania*'s release, and in the wake of the even more alienating *Valentino*, critic Michael Dempsey (a previous Russell sympathizer) was exasperated to see Russell's films get what Lewis Carroll would call "curiouser and curiouser." He could not forgive Russell for being on the verge of becoming what he called "a ringmaster of hyperthyroid camp circuses." In his frustration, he also sensed Russell's own weariness, fancying that the studio pressures to make bankable product were eroding the director's psyche. "Maybe I was just tired of making composer biographies," Russell admitted to John C. Tibbetts years later. "I know I needed to give it a rest for a while."

The usual critics took the usual umbrage. *Newsweek* whined about "a freaked out charade," and Richard Eder in the *New York Times* sniffed at the "post-Beatles rococo." "For Mr. Russell," Eder continued, "the shortest line between two points is a pretzel, preferably painted gold and doped." The reliably negative Pauline Kael derided what she called Russell's "sacrilegious-mischief comics" and accused him of "disappearing in a giant crotch."

But others, such as *Film Quarterly*'s Ross Care, applauded: "Ken Russell is an intuitive symbolist and fantasist, a total filmmaker who orchestrates his subjects in much the same manner that a composer might transcribe a musical composition from one interpretive medium into another (as, for example, Liszt himself did with certain works by Wagner and Berlioz and other composers of the period)." And as mentioned in this book's introduction, the *Catholic Film Newsletter*'s Michael Gallagher surprised viewers with his endorsement, declaring that if Rubens can be sensual, Russell can continue being excessive.

Despite Puttnam's meddling and any superficial likeness to such lighter fare as *The Rocky Horror Picture Show* (released the same year), *Lisztomania* survives as one of Russell's most visually dynamic, comically raucous, and intellectually charged efforts. Franz Liszt is credited with saying, "Truly great men are those who combine contrary qualities within themselves." So Russell, stooping so low yet going over so many heads, is more faithful to his subject than Liszt was to any of his lovers.

20

VALENTINO AND HIS DOUBLE

"**W**hat do you think I've got there?" Rudolf Nureyev shouted as a few more inches of garden hose grazed the inside of his pants. "A cunt?"

According to Ken Russell, Nureyev shot this mouthful on the set of *Valentino* as the crew prepared for a grisly prison scene. The setup involved Valentino and his domineering girlfriend Natacha Rambova getting hitched in Mexico, even though he's still technically married to his first wife. Once they're back in the States, the cops nab the newlyweds on bigamy charges and lock them in the tank.

Natacha's rich daddy, the cosmetics giant Richard Hudnut, posts his daughter's bail, but poor Rudy has to stay in the hoosegow full of derelicts until the banks open the following morning. It is here that Russell's film shifts from frenetic camp to outright horror. The handheld camera pulls back through Valentino's viewpoint, and the prison bars are in full view as Rambova departs: this is Russell's warning that something grisly is about to happen.

Valentino (Rudolf Nureyev) teaches the tango to Vaslav Nijinsky (Anthony Dowell).

Valentino now contends with prostitutes, jealous thugs, and the snarling guard—all daring him to drop his drawers and expose "the eighth great wonder of the world." To make matters worse, the guard slips a diuretic into Valentino's coffee while denying him toilet privileges.

Hell breaks loose: Rudy slips in a pile of vomit; a whore itches for the sheik to give her a shake, while another taunts Rudy to "stick it through the bars"; and a snaggletoothed sex fiend aptly named Willie (Dudley Sutton) plays with himself, edging closer to Rudy's face until he climaxes. The impatient guard shoves his nightstick into the star's pelvis and laughs hysterically as Rudy now stands in a puddle of his own urine. Rudy can only mutter Italian prayers while climbing toward the cell's ceiling, but his caterwauling tormentors make sure he suffers a martyr's humiliation.

Just about everybody involved with *Valentino*—from its producers to its actors—hated the jail scene's vileness and violence. For this very reason, Russell insisted that it stay. It had to be gruesome in order to expose the rift between Valentino's hype as a sex idol and the anti-Valentino backlash that fermented outside Hollywood's protective bubble.

By inducing the Great Lover's bladder convulsion, Russell made a brave move. He risked a backlash from uptight Hollywood historians and necromantic hags who refuse to acknowledge that their suave and supernatural "sheik of Araby" would have tolerated such an indignity or even deigned to take a leak. It's also a provocative allegory for the film's ultimate story: Valentino as a good-natured and asexual, if not bisexual, dreamer who gets caught up with women who ruin him and a Hollywood dream factory that reduces him to a pretty tailor's dummy destined to get kicked around.

But Nureyev wasn't interested in such subtexts. For him, the scene was important for one reason: to remind viewers that he toted a trouser snake and not a worm. "More hose!" he squawked to the prop man.

"It was *Women in Love* all over again," Russell thought as he compared Nureyev's pocket rocket jitters to Alan Bates and Oliver Reed almost soiling their undies over having to wrestle in the nude. "Anyway," Russell continues, "the prop man was all poised to turn on his remote-controlled tap, and I was about to tell the first to roll camera. "

They tried discreetly keeping the hose in Nureyev's sweater while shoving additional inches. "The prop man looked at me for guidance," Russell continued. "I nodded three times. The hosepipe grew another three inches and appeared to develop a curl."

"I knelt down to straighten [the hosepipe] out," Russell goes on, "and jumped when it gave a wiggle. The hair rose on my neck as I realized I was handling the real thing. We should be making a monster film, I thought, as I coughed and begged pardon—'The Man with Two Dicks.'"

∎

The events leading to *Valentino*'s prison nightmare are riddled with whimsy, serendipity, and eerie synchronicity. Nureyev had already annoyed Russell after helping to nix the director's plans for his never-made Nijinsky movie. After watching *Isadora*, he had full warning of Russell's less than reverent approach. Still, the king of international ballet tempted fate by portraying Valentino as a good natured sap, a simple waif of a man who dreamt of lording over an orange grove but fell prey to Tinseltown's psychic leeches, a not-so-Great Lover (whose first wife locked him out of the hotel suite on their wedding night) with a legendary "eighth great wonder" that was, in essence, a well-endowed phantom limb.

From the start, producers Robert Chartoff and Irwin Winkler, as well the film's screenwriters Mardek Martin and Russell himself, scrambled for a star. "We didn't know where to look," Chartoff explains. "We went through the list of leading men from A to Z, and we found many who had marvelous qualities but no one who would ignite the spark of enthusiasm. . . . We even speculated on what Valentino would be doing if he were alive today. He might well be working in an Italian restaurant in London, rather than in the dance halls of New York, and we thought of checking out the trattorias. We were desperate."

Nureyev was initially slated to play, in this, his big movie debut, the part of Nijinsky, but agreed to swap roles. But his prior bookings forced the production to get postponed for a year, giving Russell more time than usual to rework the script and wedge in more thematic parallels between Valentino and the man who would play him. Pairing the modern dancer with the 1920s icon yielded provocative results. Both men evoke a more elegant, less sweaty, and more androgynous type of male beauty. There are some, including Nureyev, who believe Valentino was asexual.

Russell has waffled on this issue, agreeing sometimes with Nureyev but also speculating that Valentino was homosexual. He toys with the gay Valentino ideal a little bit in the film but ultimately chickens out. Only years later was Russell more forthright about the matter when writing a favorable review in London's *Sunday Times* for David Bret's 1998 book *Valentino: A Dream of Desire*, a biography positing that Valentino was a man's man in the best sense: "From the moment Rudolph Valentino exposed himself in the church at the age of twelve, a legend was born. And it is this legend that David Bret follows from the cradle to the grave, exposing in the process the greatest closet queen of all time."

Russell makes some allusions to his protagonist's possible communion with the homosexual muse early on, when Valentino and Vaslav Nijinsky (Anthony Dowell) dance a handsome tango together to some Argentine song crackling out of a king-size gramophone horn. It's an indelible scene that Russell recalls fondly, especially since he claims he was the one who informed Chartoff and

Winkler that Valentino really did teach Nijinsky the dance step that he also helped popularize in the 1921 film *The Four Horsemen of the Apocalypse*.

As Shirley started on about three hundred costumes, and Phillip Harrison planned the sets that varied from an opulent funeral parlor to silent movie re-enactments, Russell helped to fine tune the research. It was a meticulous job evident in the period decor—a look that also reflected the 1970s craze for both Art Deco and Art Nouveau. As with every Russell endeavor, the music was paramount. The score takes some anachronistic dips with variations on the *Grand Canyon Suite*, which Ferde Grofé did not finish until about five years after Valentino's demise, but it somehow fits Russell's theme of Americana gone haywire.

●

Nureyev's penis anxiety and general paranoia over the hose begs for some Freud-by-numbers speculation. Perhaps it goes back to his childhood, which began in March 1938 when he was born on the Trans-Siberian Express—the same train on which Russell portrayed Tchaikovsky's ghastly honeymoon. His mother and her other children traveled through the winding Ural mountains en route to her husband, an officer in the Red Army during a flashpoint of Stalin's reign. From that moment, Nureyev may have been the product of Tatar Muslims, but he was ordained to be a rootless wanderer and cosmopolitan loner. In his own words, he "had no real sense of 'belonging'; no real country or house to call my own."

Rougher boys smelled blood and tortured him. "When threatened or pro-voked," his biographer Diane Solway writes, "he would fling himself to the ground and cry until his tormentors left him alone." The family politics of his postwar boyhood suggest those of *Tommy*'s meek messiah (at least the way Pete Townshend originally conceived him). In 1946, the maternal sanctity Nureyev enjoyed with his mom and sisters ended when Dad returned from the war. And life with Father was dismal.

To the eight-year-old Rudolf, this prodigal dad was a gray-coated, hulking interloper who stank of authority, showed little to no affection, and insisted on subjecting him to dull hunting and fishing excursions. Once, while he and Dad were in a steam room, Rudolf got an erection. The decorated army major responded like a Stalinist, dragging the boy home and beating him silly. While schoolboys twitted him for preferring pirouettes on the soccer field to kicking the ball, Rudolf's father also continued thrashing him every time he discovered the boy was taking dance classes on the sly.

After he defected from the Soviet Union in 1961, the French authorities granted Nureyev asylum. Not long afterward, he leapt from stage to stage and country to country with Margot Fonteyn, also finding time to traipse in camera range with the likes of Princess Margaret and Jacqueline Kennedy. By the 1970s, most in the know understood that his photogenic presence with pretty gals was all show. He was an imperious guy, but he also elicits sympathy when Solway writes, "'Me and my women,' Nureyev would sigh with a note of derision, 'but where are the men?'"

Amid all of the glamour, pampering, and countless press-friendly female sidekicks, Nureyev felt the sexual hypocrisy draining his soul. He was perhaps relieved to let Russell cast him as a sexual enigma, even though his primly Catholic pal Loretta Young tried dissuading him. He also fancied he was destined for the role, claiming Vittorio de Sica suggested he play it years before.

•

No amount of hosepipe, however, could match Nureyev's swelling ego. After a standing ovation at New York's Metropolitan Opera House for his farewell performance in Tchaikovsky's *The Sleeping Beauty*, he arrived in the Spanish resort town of Almeria (where many of the outdoor scenes were shot) in no mood to take orders. He got into his first tizzy when Russell told him to trim his silky mane into a close-cropped 1920s-style gentleman's cut.

Nureyev was now thirty-eight, unsure of his future in a profession where being thirtysomething is considered close to elderly. Though he studied several of Valentino's silent movies and made every effort to duplicate his dance steps and gestures, he felt himself coming up short, primarily because switching his heavy Russian accent to a heavy Italian accent and speaking it all in English yielded verbal goulash.

"They sounded as unalike as a mandolin and a balalaika," Russell would reflect. But he also admits that the language problem had a perverse asset: "Who knows what would have happened if Valentino had survived till the talkies? Maybe his premature death was a blessing in disguise, for on the evidence of an old gramophone record he certainly had a very pronounced accent."

Casting Nureyev as Valentino was another of Russell's quixotic bouts with "the truth." Sure, they had the same first name, both were immigrants who made good in the new world, both danced like slinky felines and revered Nijinsky. But the dark and exotic Valentino is absent here. Nureyev's hair is brown and his skin almost chalky white. Anyone watching Russell's final product is likely to conclude that Nureyev's performance is intended to alienate: this is supposed to be Valentino, but it really isn't Valentino. It works better as the story of a famous dancer impersonating a silent actor who was also a dancer: theater of cruelty crossbred with the theater of the absurd.

During the production, while brooding over whether he'd made a mistake, Russell could always blame Shirley, who was among Nureyev's ardent cheerleaders during the casting decision period. As he thought of their crumbling marriage, Russell probably surmised that she was exacting some kind of pre-divorce revenge by forcing him into a psychological tango with his star. But even Shirley must have felt some regret when she took great pains to design a period jacket for Nureyev, only to have the raging Russian tear off its many buttons before hurling them at her—and this was just his *first* costume fitting.

Such offscreen fracases were necessary for Russell to create another of his neurotic masterpieces. With Nureyev around, the movie was bound to reflect an atmosphere of tension and spite. He tried to dominate every social situation, upstaged Russell as a gourmand by practically inhaling caviar and vodka while talking incessantly at dinners, and showed contempt for his costar Michelle Phillips by assailing her with the "C" word again and again. Russell, who could also be a pill, met his match: the world's greatest dancer playing the world's greatest lover became the world's greatest ass-pain.

Leonard Pollack, who was a special stills photographer for the film, provides some insights into how Russell's temperament, and his relationships with his wife and other work mates, likely added to *Valentino*'s fierce style: "Shirley or I would arrive on the set, and Ken would confront us in a violent, agitated tone over some issue that neither of us had a clue about. After his fit, Ken would immediately go to take nine or ten. And the reason he did this was to throw everyone off guard—especially the actors—to get something new and fresh that wasn't rehearsed."

●

Russell had too many other bugs whizzing inside his head to coddle Nureyev's increasingly monocratic ego. His mother was tottering on the brink of madness, his soon-to-be ex-wife was growing more distant by the hour, and he had to get the film—which accrued a bigger budget than anything he'd done before—into the producer's hot hands on time. Still, nothing could convince Nureyev that size didn't matter.

"It's going to look as if you've got water on the knee," Russell shouted back to him, "and it's a well-known fact that Rudy was known all over Hollywood as Wee Willie Winkie."

Nureyev might have been defensive about his family jewels on the set because he knew that Russell planned to portray his character as a whipping boy. Russell essentially had him play a variation on the title role of *Petrouchka*, the puppet Nureyev brought to life in his 1963 show with the Royal Ballet. Like the puppet,

Nureyev's Valentino is misbegotten and passive, thriving in a spiritual wasteland, scurrying like a human pinball from one manipulator to the next. Russell even had plans to use a *Petrouchka* reference: Valentino would watch a production of the ballet from a theater box while gangsters pummeled the hell out of him.

"As a man," Nureyev observed of Valentino, "he seems to have been completely confused. He was in a predicament. He found himself in a situation with which neither he nor anybody else could cope. That's how success works. Everybody becomes jealous and possessive and demanding, and when they don't get what they ask for, they start to tear you to pieces."

•

Valentino is officially based on the Brad Steiger and Chaw Mank biography, *Valentino: An Intimate Exposé of the Sheik*, but its tone is also similar to that of Irving Shulman's *Valentino*—an enjoyable book that many Valentino devotees revile but that anticipates Russell's satirical voice. Shulman's style, like Russell's dialogue, shoots out flowery volleys and crass quips the way that Ben Hecht's novels and screenplays lampooned potentates and pretenders of the stage and screen. And like Shulman's account, the film centers on the personalities who assemble to see Valentino lying in state at Campbell's Funeral Parlor.

As with *Isadora*, Russell approximates the *Citizen Kane*–style narrative, as the dead protagonist's life unfolds from the perspectives of the women who did their best to either help or hurt him. Beginning with a scratchy old shellac version of "There's a New Star in Heaven Tonight" and silent footage of fans clawing through police barricades to see and feel the body, the true seers of Valentino's destiny, three of Hollywood's biggest moguls, look over the coffin. Paramount's Jesse Lasky (Huntz Hall), MGM's Richard Rowland (Alfred Marks), and United Artists' Joseph Schenck (David De Keyser) haggle over last minute distribution deals and how to turn the star's untimely death into a box office boost.

Various biographies corroborate the image of Valentino as a cipher of sorts: a dressmaker's dummy in the flesh who mourned his mother's absence and depended on domineering women for financial and emotional sustenance. Much of this story unfolds right away, as an obnoxious reporter at the funeral parlor corners Valentino's former girlfriend Bianca de Saulles (June Bolton). She brings us back to the time she got Valentino in trouble with her bigoted gangster husband Jack de Saulles (Robin Brent Clarke).

De Saulles sees Bianca and Valentino dancing at Maxim's tearoom where, for a fee, handsome men trip the light fantastic with lonely old ladies. "No more tea-time hops with dagos," de Saulles sputters to Bianca as he stomps onto the dance floor. "Waltzing with wops is one thing, but he's a pansy!" Instead of defending her employee, Maxim's owner, the buxom and ruthless Billie Streeter (Linda Thorson), fires Rudy on the spot. She's already been annoyed with him for giving Nijinsky and Bianca private lessons, but she and the gangster are also immersed in their own affair. An unusually crafty Valentino manages to photograph them in the act for evidence to help Bianca get a divorce. But after de Saulles and several of his goons try busting up their plans, barging into Rudy's home and punching his face, Bianca eventually shoots the bastard. Valentino, to avoid getting implicated in the murder, leaves New York.

Valentino becomes a creature of poise when June Mathis (Felicity Kendal) takes control of the narrative. The actor's benefactor, she recalls to another nosy reporter the first time she saw him at the famed 1920s L.A. nightspot Baron Long's. The baron (Anton Diffring), an officious German infuriated with his drunken star dancer Marjorie Tain (Leland Palmer), warns both Tain and Valentino, her Mediterranean dancing partner, that he's close to firing them. He's especially worried about a rough Hollywood crowd scheduled to arrive that evening, led by an obstreperous hog modeled on Fatty Arbuckle.

Armed with a joy-buzzer, Mr. Fatty (William Hootkins) terrorizes the club the moment he enters, calling the baron a "Bavarian bum" and bullying the starlets with whom he holds court. He saves his real bile for the besotted Miss Tain as she gets tangled in a beaded curtain before her entry, staggers onto the stage, falls into Valentino's arms, and makes the house roar when breaking a heel. Fatty, imbibing steins full of brew, inundates the room with catcalls: "Hey sister, you dance like my ass chews gum!" "46 skiddoo! And that means both of you!"

All the while, Mathis is watching the fiasco from a balcony, impressed when Valentino grabs Fatty's best girl (Carol Kane) to help him finish the act. In between Russell's cruel close-ups of Fatty's sweaty, quivering, and enraged expression, Valentino spins the starlet around the dance floor before carrying her away to her home, leaving the bloated boor whimpering away with his joy-buzzer still in hand.

Kane is just another bubble headed Hollywood sycophant who lucks into a luxurious mansion and seems content as another of Valentino's platonic companions. Russell uses the scene for a higher purpose, implying Valentino is about to submit to being another Tinseltown commodity. Claiming it's her maid's day off, Kane's character serves up an elegant tureen loaded with French fries. Had the ketchup bottle's label been turned toward the camera, the scene could have been a product placement for Heinz. The junk food lunch—a "mutton dressed as lamb" metaphor—dominates the foreground to distract from any potential humanism in their heart-to-heart discussion about what it takes to succeed in movie land. As Kane advises, "All you need in movies is to look sincere. Let me tell you, brother, looking sincere in this town is a lot of hard work."

Now smitten with Valentino, Mathis is back at her studio, showing producer Richard Rowland clips of Valentino in some comedy shorts. But Rowland dismisses him as a "schmuck," assuming Americans want the homegrown smarm of the cocaine addict Wallace Reid. Mathis barely convinces him that the public, bored with the boy next door, hungers for a Latin lover.

"Whoever heard of a dago playing a dago?" he later asks Alla Nazimova (Leslie Caron) just before she swoons over sepiatone rushes from *The Four Horsemen of the Apocalypse*. Watching Valentino as the gaucho wield his whip and do his feline dance, she knows she's found the Armand who'll play opposite her Marguerite in a version of *Camille*. Rambova (Michelle Phillips), who enters the story as Nazimova's girlfriend, is less impressed with the gaucho and makes a crack about his "married virgin" reputation.

"Every day is Halloween in Tinsel Town," Mathis tells the reporter as the story flashes back to the funeral parlor. Nazimova now enters, flanked by servant girls in purple veils and trailing a cape embroidered with white camellias—a tribute to an Aubrey Beardsley drawing for Oscar Wilde's play *Salome*.

Valentino and Alla Nazimova (Leslie Caron) in *Camille*.

When Nazimova takes over the story, Russell combines her character with that of Pola Negri, the screen virago notorious for her theatrical fainting spell at Valentino's funeral. Nazimova drapes her blanket of camellias over the coffin and, with her eye on every camera in the room, drops to the floor. Some of the cameras aren't ready, so she has to get up and faint again to make sure she graces the *New York Post*'s front page. As the reporters wait to hear her side of the story, she time travels to her first encounter with her Armand on the *Four Horsemen* set.

"Which one is Italian boy whose name wafts like garlic on every breath in town?" When Caron's Nazimova uttered this line, Nureyev recalls that people on the set laughed uncontrollably, especially since Caron (noted for more regal and serious roles) plays Nazimova as a mannered buffoon with a terrible Russian accent.

But Caron's over-the-top performance is dead on. She, like Rambova, is among the art harpies that Russell loves to satirize: characters like Gosh Boyle in *Savage Messiah* and Princess Wittgenstein in *Lisztomania*, who will trod over anyone to fulfill their aesthetic demands. She and Rambova drive their Rolls Royce convertible into the studio lot in the middle of a shoot, knocking over the actual horsemen as they charge across the makeshift desert. The horseman representing Death snaps back at her: "You can take your art, lady, and stuff it up your ass!"

Once he becomes a pampered pet for his new substitute mothers, Valentino undergoes a transformation. He starts out as the amateur actor dressed as a World War I soldier and becomes a neurasthenic leading man in Ray C. Smallwood's *Camille*, the 1921 film about the consumptive courtesan that Russell lampoons with overwrought kissing in front of a globe full of fake snow.

Some critics thought Phillips was out of character, but her dress and her manner seem to accurately reflect what a woman of her time, with her looks and in her position, would do and say. "I read Valentino's autobiography," Phillips told *Interview* magazine as the film was wrapping up. "It's called *My Personal Diary* and it's rare. So I knew a lot about Natacha through his eyes, which was important, and I also was very fortunate in the fact that I found her sister, who is still alive."

While a feminine cabal helps shape Valentino's destiny, another enterprising woman edged into the movie from behind the camera. Vivian Jolly, an American twenty-five years Russell's junior, started hanging around the set. She'd previously sashayed into Russell's life as an errand girl on the set of *Savage Messiah*. Since then, she'd gone back to New England, become a film studies major at Boston University, and returned to London under the pretext of making a documentary about the making of *Valentino*.

Shirley was wise to the Vivian-and-Russell mating call but kept the bile inside, at least for a little while. But when she discovered the young gatecrasher sitting in Ken's director's chair, she opened her fury for the entire crew to see. She demanded that Vivian get banned from the set or else she would quit and leave Russell to tinker with the costume fittings himself. Russell had no other choice but to submit.

∎

While most of *Valentino*'s shooting took place at EMI's Elstree Studios in Borehamwhood, Russell needed a facsimile of a Hollywood studio lot. But the crew could not afford to rent a real one in L.A.; that is when they flew over to Spain for a simulation of a simulation. There, the local peasants dressed as gaucho extras, horse droppings shriveled under the heartless heat, burning tires simulated battlefield flames, Michelle Phillips complained about having to wear full lingerie, and Russell sweated while waiting for the tardy actor hired to play director Rex Ingram. When the actor finally arrived, Russell recalls that he was overdressed for the part: in sheepskin chaps with a ten-gallon cowboy hat and obviously drunk. Russell, who never cared for Westerns anyway, burst the guy's bubble: "They're shooting *Return of the Magnificent Seven* over the hill. Keep walking."

Then, Russell pretended to be patient and gave the staggering cowpoke a chance. He tried helping him over to a wooden ladder leading to an elevated platform, where Ingram would sit and shout directions over a megaphone. The souse also suffered from vertigo, so Russell tried lowering the platform to let him ascend the ladder with baby steps. The actor then started asking all sorts of niggling questions about how to apply his "motivation" for the part, despite the fact that his essential lines were "Action!" and "Cut!" Perplexed over the accent he was supposed to affect (Ingram was apparently born in Kentucky but cultured at Princeton), he got even more confused and nervous, and wound up sliding down the ladder on his own vomit.

As assistants escorted the mess of a Tom Mix off the set, Russell noticed the light was running out but couldn't find another Ingram. Inevitably, the auteur ended up playing the auteur. Russell, though nowhere near the real life Ingram's slim and dashing figure, gave a splendid performance as the dictator in jodh-purs and laced boots, wailing to the crew from a deck chair and bopping his assistant across the head for failing to recognize Nazimova as "the uncrowned Queen of Metro."

Ken Russell as Rex Ingram.
(Photo by and courtesy of Leonard Pollack)

Russell's Ingram impersonation got him into a bit of trouble when the spurned actor sobered up and vowed to retaliate. He also got grief from Actors' Equity for usurping an actor's job. Dreading the thought of reshooting with an Equity member or excising the scene altogether, he did some sleuthing and discovered that, from his days in the chorus of *Annie Get Your Gun*, he had been an Equity member since 1950, had never resigned, and therefore had every right to steal his own scene.

Valentino intensifies when the ballsy Rambova dominates the story. With Rudy lying beside her in the California desert on the set of *The Sheik*, Rambova consults with Meselope, an ancient Egyptian whose bones she continually examines to predict her and her boy toy's fate. But Lasky—a character so cunning that he's almost lovable—comes galumphing along with director George Melford (Don Fellows) to squelch Rambova's bluster, reminding Rudy to save his energy for "the big rape scene" scheduled in the morning.

Russell splashes more sepiatone with a bawdy reenactment of *The Sheik*'s erotic assault. Jennie Linden (Alan Bates's butter-faced frau in *Women in Love*) returns with a cheekier role: the silent star Agnes Ayres who cowers on her divan yet catches a quick glimpse at her assailant's equipment before surrendering. But the narration gets a bit fuzzy with a switch back to Mathis's viewpoint (or perhaps Rambova's idea of what Mathis and other gullible gals might fantasize about). She's sitting in a cinema with a crowd of other dazzled matinee fans, imagining herself as the chalky-white damsel riding away on with the sheik on his white stallion.

Mathis's dream of a macho marvel is no match for the androgynous dress-up photo shoot that Nazimova organizes in her Garden of Alla. To the tune of Chris Ellis's twee vocal rendition of "The Sheik of Araby," Russell honors Nureyev's fondness for Nijinsky by letting him portray the lovely satyr from the ballet *Afternoon of the Faun*, based on the Debussy work that Nijinsky choreographed and performed back in 1912. Russell could have played that moment out more, considering how Nijinsky astounded Paris audiences by suggesting masturbation with a scarf. But, as with the rest of the movie, Valentino glides through the performance with sexless aplomb—even if Nazimova gets jealous when she catches him and Rambova kissing, freezes the moment in a photo, and sells it to the press to stir up a love-nest scandal.

A Faun and his nymphs (Michelle Phillips, Rudolf Nureyev, and Leslie Caron).

When Rudy and Natacha run away from the media hubbub to get illegally hitched in Mexico, Russell sets up the events leading to the enthralling prison scene. An ill omen appears: Mathis hears about Rudy's incarceration while she's watching rushes from *Blood and Sand* as Valentino's matador gets pronged in the bullring. She tries getting bail money from Lasky, but he is more focused on the scandal's free publicity to fork over the necessary $10,000: "The more the press knocks the boy, the bigger the box office."

Huntz Hall, once the wisecracking Dead End Kid and later the bumbling Satch in the Bowery Boys series, was once in a production with the real Nazimova when he was just three years old. Here, he is wonderful as the steely-eyed but practical mogul, relaxing in his mansion, examining actor photos while a caged, and apparently insane, albino gorilla jumps and snorts in front of him.

Once he survives his horrific prison night, Valentino is more at Rambova's whims than ever before. He consents to her luxurious demands for full script approval and a job as artistic advisor on all of his future projects. Lasky, who hears Valentino's new ultimatum while on the set of some wacky Western, snaps back his own: "If you so much as take a pratfall in a Mexican two-reeler, I'm gonna slap an injunction on your little Italian ass!"

The movie's tempo starts to skid a bit when George Ullman (Seymour Cassel) enters the scene, invading Valentino and

The notorious, almost censored, prison scene.

Rambova's private beachcombing hideaway to lure them (despite Lasky's injunction) back into show business. They go on a tour to promote a beauty substance, doing interpretive dances while a giant "Mineralava" bottle, looking more like a Good Humor ice cream truck, spins along with them on the ballroom floor. Lasky comes out from the wings to witness the thunderous applause and connives a deal with Ullman to bring the stars back to Famous Players–Lasky, even if it means submitting to Rambova's ridiculous terms.

The illusion behind Valentino's legend gets more lucid when director Sidney Olcott (John Justin) vies with Rambova on directing Rudy's love scene for

PHALLIC FRENZY

Monsieur Beaucaire. Valentino is all done up like the "painted pansy": a powdered wig, powdered face, and a heart-shaped beauty mark on his left cheek. Rambova and Olcott dictate his every romantic move with costar Lorna Sinclair (Penelope Milford). This also gives Russell time to make another *Citizen Kane* homage, evoking Welles's hilarious moment when the camera moves up to register the stagehands' disapproval of Susan Alexander's terrible singing. Russell too sets his camera on the stagehands as they toss a pink powder puff down into Rudy's lap.

When no one on the set fesses up to this harebrained, homo-baiting act, Valentino and Rambova storm off the set. But Valentino's old-world compulsion to maintain appearances forces him back, where he can at least project a show of "honor" by pretending to have sex with his costar in his bungalow. Lorna, though, is off in her own world, riding him as if he were a coin-operated hobbyhorse. As she bounces away in her sheik fantasy, Rudy just lies beneath her with a bemused smile, looking at his watch and sporting what is presumably a limp linguine. But looks being everything, they return to the set to redo the love scene. Everyone around presupposes that "nature" took its course, as strains of Tchaikovsky's *Romeo and Juliet* seep into the soundtrack.

∙

All along, Russell has kept *Valentino* at a sinuous pace: the story lithely slides through gab and snappy patter; then it suddenly strikes with moments that are relentlessly macabre, such as Rambova's séance, when she consults both Meselope's bones and a crystal ball for the next career move.

A whirlwind of music and rage follows as an adoring mob chants outside Valentino's window. A hysterical woman leads the throng, screaming out variations on one of Valentino's published poems:

"YOU—are the spirit that moves the universe!"

"YOU—are the power of all religion!" The séance table shakes, the mob gets louder. Valentino jumps up to gaze through the curtains at the apocalyptic cult he's inspired.

"YOU—are my vision of heaven!"

"YOU—are the food of Love!"

Rambova shrieks and scurries when Valentino scatters her idol's remains. She's whipped up into such a jealous rage over Rudy's adulation that she vows to turn his worshippers' heaven into hell. Even when he tries appeasing her with the motions of lovemaking, she only wants to "shock them with the truth."

"YOU—are the dream that intoxicates."

"YOU—are my friend, my love!"

The face of the woman leading the Rudy coven takes on a psychopathic luster, dissolving into Rudy's as he lies in state. Second to the prison scene, Rambova's séance is *Valentino*'s most powerful and disturbing sequence. The handheld camera, the sweaty faces, and the shrill dialogue help, but perhaps the most potent force is Stanley Black's mood music. It creeps into the scene and reaches a spooky crescendo, adding to the dark incantation of what is essentially a variation on a black mass.

Before her big exit, Rambova weeps crocodile tears: "The winds of destiny tore us apart," she whimpers while putting her hand over the corpse's rouged face. The reporters snap shots of her kissing Nazimova, "Here Comes the Bride" blares out, and they walk away like Aubrey Beardsley–blessed newlyweds.

Valentino's loveless marriage seems benevolent compared to what was going on between the two stars off screen. Nureyev worked much better beside Miss Piggy during an appearance on *The Muppet Show* (shortly after *Valentino*'s release) than he did with the ex-Mama from the Mamas and the Papas. Russell, good at depicting marital malaise and currently embroiled in his own, was likely amused to watch his leading actors seethe at each other. Phillips later described this provocative role as "the most miserable working experience of my life." She recalls the love scenes being the most grueling, claiming, "He hated the fact that he had to kiss me."

∎

"I only want to be accurate up to a point," Russell told the *New York Times*' Janet Maslin not long after *Valentino*'s premiere in the fall of 1977. "I can be as inaccurate as I want to—it makes no difference to me. I'm writing a novel. My films are novels, based on a person's life, and a novel has a point of view. I'm not interested in making documentaries."

Oddly, while some might lunge at Russell for his so-called inaccuracies, *Valentino* sticks to many of the facts. Russell is also best when he twists them. The tempo starts falling short, however, when he gets to Valentino's ringside fight. Up to this point, Russell presents Valentino as the male version of a hapless heroine in a seduction novel: guileless enough to allow greedy guys and gelding gals to cajole, exploit, and ultimately reject him. Now the story gets more predictable as Valentino resorts to primitive "honor" codes imported from Castellaneta, the Southern Italian village where he was born.

Ullman and Valentino are on the town in Chicago, when some sharp-talking hooker (Nureyev's voice coach Marcella Markham) leads them to a speakeasy. There, they just happen to catch a nasty "Pink Powder Puff" production number based on a *Chicago Tribune* article that impugned Valentino's "masculinity."

Pink Powder Puff Revue.

H. L. Mencken, who dined with Valentino about a week before the actor died from peritonitis in August 1926, claims a scandal brewed when a journalist entered a swanky hotel men's room to find a coin-operated machine dispensing pink talcum powder. He saw this as a symbol of the American male's creeping effeminacy and somehow put the onus on Valentino's brilliantine head. The sensitive gentleman who played Armand so convincingly in *Camille* felt the stirring of ethnic blood and wanted to save face by challenging his accuser to a duel or a fistfight.

Mencken, urging against both, felt pity for the desperate young man. "In brief," he concluded in a piece for Baltimore's *Evening Sun*, "Valentino's agony was the agony of a man of relatively civilized feelings thrown into a situation of intolerable vulgarity, destructible alike to his peace and to his dignity. . . . It was not that trifling Chicago episode that was riding him; it was the whole grotesque futility of his life."

According to Valentino lore, the Great Lover, under the tutelage of his pal Jack Dempsey, once flexed his muscles and engaged in a one-round sparring match with a *New York Evening Journal* sportswriter on the roof of the Ambassador Hotel. But it seemed more a press-friendly event. He never really fought the bloody battle Russell puts him through. In Russell's version, Valentino holds a press conference to announce his desire to fight the man who disgraced his "honor," but a disgusting drunk named Rory O'Neil (Peter Vaughan), also an ex-heavyweight champion from the navy, takes the challenge on behalf of the actual offending journalist who's too old to even walk.

America now seems to hate the foreign fop who suffers the double whammy of being an Italian and a "fairy." The crowds cheer for O'Neil, while Valentino gets relegated to what the referee calls "the pink corner." The real Valentino made sure the press recorded him as the victor with nary a scratch; Russell makes sure he gets knocked around, punched, and bloodied. But the sheik surprises everybody by hurling a sucker punch that leaves O'Neil down for the count.

Russell could have taken a bolder step and questioned the customs that would demand such goofy machismo, yet he at least goes part way. Valentino might

win the fight, but he finally looks like an idiot succumbing to idiotic norms. Not content to win, he has to take the evil-tempered mick up on another dare to see who can out-guzzle the other in a whiskey competition. The two mugs stack up their glasses and get soused to the point of coma, but Valentino wins again—only after he burps in O'Neil's face. And like a Russell hero, Valentino staggers back home to a pyrrhic victory. Alone in his mansion, he struggles to grab one of the oranges he's kept on a table to remind him of his agricultural dream. His pelvis then attacks him, and heaven's new star finally shines.

Russell planned a plot twist at the film's funeral parlor opening that the producers unfortunately truncated. According to the original script, Frankie Campbell, the mincing funeral director whom Lindsay Kemp plays so well, had much more screen time. As Lasky, Schenck, and Rowland kibitz over Valentino's laid-out body about box office grosses and how many days it takes for a corpse to decompose, Campbell comes along to brush the moguls aside, open the casket lid, and examine his handiwork. He doesn't like the way Valentino's hands fold against his chest:

> *He takes the scissors from his assistant, brushes the sweating Lasky aside and bends over the corpse. As the three men watch in horror, Campbell deftly slices off Valentino's left thumb. He covers the resulting cavity with the right hand and smiles with satisfaction. He turns to the gaping, dumb-mouthed studio heads.*
>
> CAMPBELL
> But wax will last forever.
> *He closes the lid, tosses the thumb to Lasky. Then he steers the numb and passive executives by the elbows to symmetrical positions about the coffin—giving them "marks."*

CAMPBELL
(while he's doing it)

That's right, gentlemen—wax. I too have a business to promote; I too am interested in the long run. You may be hot shit in California, but you're in my picture now!

If this part remained intact, *Valentino* would have been even more ironic. Viewers could smirk as they watched the overacting characters faint, share stories, and shed glycerin tears over a wax dummy, unaware that the real body is on a stone-cold slab in a secluded vault—an image that survives in the release print's closing credits.

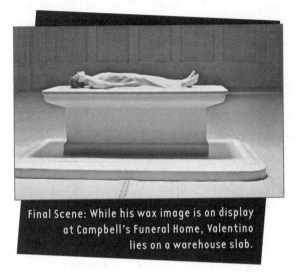

Final Scene: While his wax image is on display at Campbell's Funeral Home, Valentino lies on a warehouse slab.

∎

"I was casting doubts on his manhood," Russell recalls, with tongue thrusting in cheek, of Nureyev's prison-scene snit. "Discreetly, I asked him which side he dressed and on receiving his curt reply instructed the prop man to pay out more hosepipe. He did so and, kneeling at Rudy's feet, I negotiated it as delicately as possible down to the right leg of his knickerbockers—from the outside, of course. Acting the spaniel, I looked up for approval. But the master did not throw me a bone . . . we reached a compromise, and the tube was hauled up a couple of inches. We tried a dry run. The crew nearly wet themselves. It looked as if Rudy was wrestling with a snake halfway down his trouser leg. Eventually I persuaded him it would look more convincing if he clutched his bladder, and we got it in the can."

After all the hemming and hawing with Nureyev and the wet clothes, Russell finally captured the cathartic prison melee that spits out the movie's message about fleeting fame and fragile sexuality. The scene was also potent for having Bill McKinney as the guard—the same actor who played the hillbilly rapist in *Deliverance*.

The prison scene survived, but Russell fought hard to keep it. He recalls in his autobiography all the lunches he had with *Valentino*'s backers—those grueling sessions of lox, pickles, sauerkraut, and endless cups of Tab—when he had to insist that forcing the piss out of Valentino was vital to the story. The backers kept insisting otherwise as they tried placating him with damper deli dishes. Close to hurling from a belly full of smoked salmon and sour cream, Russell instead tossed his paper plate into the trash, aborted the conversation, and eventually got his way.

The film's gala premiere was just as lavish and decadent as the movie's set designs. Princess Margaret came to the London version; New York held it at the Iranian Embassy, with the likes of Andy Warhol, Diana Vreeland, and Halston adding a Studio 54–era flavor. *Variety*'s year-end report of top grossing films for 1977 listed *Valentino* at number ninety-eight.

But by now, *The New Yorker* seemed to be publishing Pauline Kael's anti-Russell tirades for their campy hysteria. "*Valentino* is a five-million-dollar graffito that will circulate around the world. What Senator Joseph McCarthy did to people's reputations is nothing compared with what Ken Russell does, and if his victims aren't around to lose their livelihoods, neither are they around to defend themselves."

For a film so disliked by critics, ill remembered by its actors, and sporadically disowned by its director, *Valentino*, even in those closing moments when it slips, has an allure and a power. It is the last of the great Russell features that defined his 1970s career, his tightest and most staccato script since *The Devils*. *Valentino* is an ill-tempered, rude, often violent gaze into shallow glamour and the dark soul behind what nostalgic flibbertigibbets call "Classic Hollywood."

As *New York Times* critic Janet Maslin wrote, "When Rudolf Nureyev, who plays Valentino with a fierce sense of style, is abused or insulted, he looks magnificent. The screenplay represents Valentino as a fairly meek character, but as played by Mr. Nureyev, he seems positively to thrive upon affronts to his dignity."

The star likely didn't take Maslin's appraisal as a compliment. "You know I did one film that I regret having done," Nureyev told director James Toback when discussing the prospects of doing another movie several years later, "and I detested the director." Russell recalls having supper with his new girlfriend Vivian after the movie wrapped. She pointed out all the new white hairs he'd sprouted after his tiffs with Nureyev. "I can't wait to get his dongle on film," he told her. "Do you think he'd feel insulted if I shot it on eight-millimeter?"

WAITING FOR DRACULA

21

"**U**nbankable" was a word Ken Russell started hearing too often after *Valentino*'s lackluster critical responses and box office grosses. Like a dictator now forced to play the damsel in waiting, he anticipated a lucrative call from his Hollywood agent, Robert Littman. In the meantime, nothing was happening, yet everything was happening. His wife Shirley finally left him, his Mum was in a mad house, and his hopes for an epic career were, from what he could gather, dashed.

Russell had had two consecutive commercial flops, along with a reputation for being abrasive and abusive. And no matter how lousy the actors, how bad the distribution, or how unfair the critics, the director usually bears the brunt of a bomb. So if *Valentino* was to be the criterion for future success, he had lots of atonement ahead. A three-year limbo ensued.

To make do with what Caitlin Thomas once called "leftover life to kill," Russell sought refuge in his usual pastimes: cooking dinners, listening to his vast record collection, and tending to the pets. "Unbankable"? Why the hell should he care? Maybe he and his girlfriend Vivian could be like Valentino and Natacha when they tried dodging Jesse Lasky by being like Robinson Crusoe, living on love, past laurels, and at least the illusion that "pure art" still existed. He had his Lake District farmhouse, where he could feed the neighbor's sheep, dabble in painting, play Scrabble; he could also tend to a new daughter named Molly and take walks with a Staffordshire bull terrier that he called "Poopass."

•

From *Mahler* to *Valentino*, Russell dropped hints of his troubling domestic situation into his plots. But when it finally happened, his divorce from Shirley in

1979 was devastating. As their wedding anniversary neared, Shirley brought Ken a ribbon-adorned envelope on a tray. Inside were the remnants of love letters Vivian had written to him (and that he thought he'd smartly stashed away in his record album jackets). Russell left the house the following day and joined Vivian in a studio apartment.

Three years after she died in 2002, Shirley's ghost still plagued him. During an interview with the *Times* (London) he said, "I was unfaithful, but I didn't really hide it and we got over it. I didn't know that Shirley was having an affair for a few years. When I found out, it blew my mind; she had always been so moral and censorious. I walked out on our twenty-first anniversary and asked my driver to take me to a car showroom, where I bought an Alfa Romeo Spider."

With Vivian in her late twenties and he in his early fifties, Russell felt twinges of a second boyhood. Visiting New York, Russell and Vivian felt bored and drained while trudging up the Guggenheim Museum's inclined aisles. Russell eyed one of the courtesy wheelchairs, plopped into it, and feeling like Henri Gaudier in *Savage Messiah*, shocked the crowd by taking a makeshift roller-coaster ride down the spiral ramp.

But when those momentary highs ended, Russell felt he was on a different kind of downward spiral. He wandered in that existential Siberia that the movie industry calls "between pictures." But with Russell, the situation worsened when he was between wives. He would marry three more times; whenever another wife vanished from his life, he'd dream up vitriolic visual metaphors for subsequent movies.

By 1978, his spiritual guides were also withering. Catholicism was now only good for its theatrics, invocations to Henri Gaudier-Brzeska lost their potency, and even the Lake District seemed at times more a faded postcard than Coleridge's paradise. But he did not give up on his Eden. There, he and Vivian baptized their new baby, Molly, on what he calls "an icy torrent beneath a Maxfield Parrish sky on the snow-clad slopes of Skiddaw."

●

Russell was soon again at Skiddaw's feet, this time as a prodigal son returning to British television. The occasion was a Granada TV production called *Clouds of Glory*, which Russell and cowriter Melvyn Bragg planned as a series of hour-long tributes to the great Lake Poets. Shirley remained to design the costumes, but the two films in the series would be the last of their collaborations.

The first installment, *William and Dorothy*, deals with William Wordsworth's complex and nearly incestuous relationship with his sister. Russell plays it out with relative restraint as he assembles a couple of members from his *Valentino* troupe. Felicity Kendal is Wordsworth's sister Dorothy, a sickly and slightly mad character, who languishes on her death bed while recalling with her brother all of their platonic memories—good and bad. Again, Russell lets Kendal practically spit out her lines with the same mixture of panic and blandness that she exuded as June Mathis.

William Hootkins also returns, trading in his blobby boob parody of Fatty Arbuckle for the statelier role of Reverend Dewey, an ardent Wordsworth fan, who takes a sabbatical and travels three thousand miles to enjoy the Lake District that Wordsworth's poems celebrate. He gushes while walking with Wordsworth along the Cumberland countryside and gazing at the shores that inspired such poems as "I Wandered Lonely as a Cloud."

David Warner, famous as the maniac in *Morgan* and later as one of the heavies in *Titanic*, is the troubled Wordsworth. He sports an appropriately melancholy face throughout as he shares with both Dorothy and the reverend his misgivings about his work and life.

What should be pastoral calm becomes a clamor as Wordsworth tramps upon the rocks, thrashes the ground with his walking stick, glares into the camera, and shouts out the words to his poem "Louisa," all about an idyllic time with a girl who "hath smiles to earth unknown."

Russell contrasts Wordsworth's melancholia with images of the Lake District's birds and flowers—slick and vibrant lap dissolves that a television commercial could easily deploy to sell soda pop or even cigarettes. He gets back into form, however, when Wordsworth goes to France at the height of the Reign of Terror. He sees peasants terrorize the countryside, assaulting one another in a mock-up royal procession that features a man dolled up as a raggedy Marie Antoinette. "The Revolution has gone mad," he cries to Dorothy upon his return. "How can they use that guillotine?"

The visceral connections between Wordsworth's sister Dorothy and Russell's cousin Marion are irresistible. Like Wordsworth, who idealized Dorothy as a blood relative with whom he might fall in love, Russell retained his psychic ties to the girl from his childhood whose adventurous spirit yanked her to the other side.

"Isolation can encourage morbid thoughts," Wordsworth tells Dorothy when she frets about how he kills off Lucy, a figure in the poem "She Dwelt Among the Untrodden Ways," whom Dorothy fears her brother created to augur her own death. When she finally expires, Wordsworth is gutted: he lost his true love, the critics have scorned him, and most of the public has ignored him.

But just as Russell craved for someone to save him from depressing times, Wordsworth reaches out for redemption and finds the Reverend Dewey. Accepting his role as inspiring angel, Dewey literally screams out lines from Wordworth's "Ode: Intimations of Immortality."

•

William and Dorothy has a relatively sweeter temper, but Russell vents his post-divorce angst on the second *Clouds of Glory* installment: *The Rime of the Ancient Mariner*. Russell is his best when he directs as if the camera were attached to his nervous system. This power rebounds when he renders Samuel Taylor Coleridge a biological casualty, vexed by opium addiction, insomnia, constipation, and the urge to murder his wife.

Russell structures the story on Coleridge's poem about the troubled seafarer who braves storms until an albatross, a white bird of good omen, swoops by to guide him and his crew to kinder currents. But the mariner kills the bird and, realizing he'd done "a hellish thing," feels the albatross's vengeance as he encounters "death-fires" upon the waters.

Soon, the parched and frightened sailors hang the dead bird around the mariner's neck in an attempt to palliate the gods. But the sailors eventually perish, leaving the mariner to face his fate: "Alone, alone, all, all alone, / Alone on a wide wide sea! / And never a saint took pity on / My soul in agony."

Russell turns the mariner's albatross into his wife Sara Coleridge (Kika Markham), whom he portrays as a battle-ax just waiting to get bumped off. As Mrs. Coleridge keeps nagging about the money and the baby, Russell ties her in with Coleridge's poem: "slimy things did crawl with legs / Upon the slimy sea."

But in another of those cathartic scenes when the most horrid violence offers guilty pleasure, Coleridge rids himself of his pecking hen once and for all by thrusting his crossbow in her chest. As he haplessly rows his boat, the image of Sara's impaled body, resembling a figurehead on a ship's prow, drifts in and out of the narrative.

Even without this shocking plot twist, Russell courts controversy with the movie's subtitle: "The Strange Story of Samuel Coleridge, Poet and Drug Addict." Laudanum, the opium-based substance that ruined Elizabeth Siddal and that allayed Dorothy Wordsworth's pain during her last days, returns to vex England's literary giant.

David Hemmings plays the famed poet who, from the very first scenes, is in a drug-induced rage. He rummages madly through his belongings, flailing through the woods, and at last looking ecstatic when an equally frenetic woman holds up a green bottle of the opiate he craves. But he must sail away to calmer waters to enjoy his fix because the lady who gave it to him, presumably Mrs. Coleridge, won't stop yelling at him.

Coleridge screams a lot, calls his Lake District poet compatriot Robert Southey (Ben Aris) a "pious fraud" for having introduced him to the shrew, and cavorts with the poet Robert Lovell (Murray Melvin) who recites some dirty doggerel about being with "Miss Sara / On the banks of the Susquehanna / Sharing my banana." Thomas De Quincey (Ronald Letham), author of *Confessions of an English Opium-Eater*, also makes an ominous appearance, letting Coleridge cringe at his feet for another fix.

In parts, *The Rime of the Ancient Mariner* is Russell at his frantic best. Though he pays respects to the poem's dull closing homily about finding salvation in the homeland and the church, the bluenoses at PBS's *Masterpiece Theater* refused to give it an American airing. The show's host, Alistair Cooke, reportedly found it too disgusting. Russell was to make a third part called *King of the Crocodiles*, all about Robert Southey, but Granada reneged.

■

Russell, still waiting for a buzz from the Robert Littman hotline, tried some diversions, among them a couple of silly interviews. A London publishing house lured him with the idea of writing a nonfiction book about life in the "swinging sixties." After driving six hours from his home and waiting in a lobby he likened to "an aircraft lounge—business class," Russell noticed a fashionably attired female executive strolling through the lobby to scout her target. She darted straight for some dashing dandy who seemed in his mid-thirties. Embarrassed, she got the receptionist to point out the real man: "Forgive me for not recognizing you, Mr. Russell. I was expecting an *enfant terrible*."

In a tired and apparently meek mood, Russell tried shrugging off her gaffe: "You're as young as you feel." They shared awkward moments in an elevator ride to her cigarette butt–littered office before sitting down to talk shop. The saucy interviewer, too young to have truly experienced the 1960s, attempted to wring out from Russell tales of wild parties, drugs, and horny rock celebrities.

But Russell, whose only admitted substance abuse (other than his absorption in music) was snuff and sundry booze, struggled to be as polite as possible in the face of one stupid question after another. He might have appeared to the world as an autocrat who brandished a whip on his set, smeared his actors with fake blood, tossed his cast into simulated orgies with a masturbating priest, and—perhaps most satanically of all—inspired the rock video, but Russell didn't come across as the diplomat of decadence the publishers had expected.

Russell felt more removed from London's "scene" than ever before. Still, he tried accommodating the interviewer one more time by recounting a trip he and Twiggy took to view the camera obscura at Brighton's Royal Pavilion. Twiggy had a yen for chocolate, put some money in the slot machine, and got her fingers stuck when reaching for the candy bar. They both tugged and tugged until finally an attendant retrieved her hand with the gentle force of a screwdriver. That was it: no drugs, sex, or rock 'n' roll—plus the incident occurred in the 1970s, not the '60s.

The interviewer grew more restless. Russell tried again to verbally stimulate her: "As for parties, we usually had an end-of-picture party where we all linked hands and sang 'Auld Lang Syne,' but apart from that the only party I can remember attending in the '60s was a garden party at Buckingham Palace, where I met Princess Margaret."

Not able to drudge any dirt about the princess, the young exec now gave Russell darting glances, suspecting he was toying with her: "But you were the enfant terrible of British films. You were the wild man of the BBC. You gave wild parties and had a terrible reputation. You can't deny it."

Russell made only one admission: he did have a terrible reputation. This, of course, wasn't enough. He was too mild-mannered, too tolerant of her insolent inquiries, too straitlaced to have made so many twisted movies. Realizing she had no prey, she tried capping the situation with a quip: "Perhaps you've just mellowed with age." She then got up and went onto the next journalistic conquest, wishing him the best of luck in the 1980s. Russell was inconsolable: "Whatever happened to the 1970s? I wondered, as I went down in the lift, aging with every floor."

•

Besides his marriage ending and his remaining youth sucked dry, Russell's Mum, whose sanity had frayed through the years, was now committed to a state institution and submitting to shock treatments. During *Valentino's* post-production stage, Russell went back to England to see how she was surviving.

Dad, so far removed from his previous incarnation as the snake-wielding sadist of Ken's childhood, drove him to the sanitarium one Sunday morning. When he encountered her, she seemed a shadow person: "She was thin and gaunt. Her blonde hair, usually a frizzy halo, was now cropped and straight. She sat there in the visitors' room, in her pale blue smock, as noble as an aged Joan of Arc—until Dad produced a bag of toffees and she dissolved into a giggling schoolgirl."

Dismayed at her failing memory, Dad was especially troubled when she looked at Ken and muttered, "Would the gentleman care for a sweetie?" Russell knew he'd reached an impasse: Mum, Dad, and Aunt Moo were still breathing, but his old history was turning its back on him. Just as his movies falter when he resorts to sentimentalism, so did his manner when he confronted this stark reminder of mortality. He sat, tried to smile, and watched her chew her candy.

Matters only got worse on a subsequent visit, when she got transferred to Fareham, an asylum Russell claims she often threatened to send him to during his boyhood whenever he got naughty. It wasn't the quaintly off-kilter mental hospital he depicted in *Elgar* or the fortress of filth where he thrust Tchaikovsky's wife in *The Music Lovers*. It was instead an overly sanitized institution with a seemingly endless corridor. Ambling toward her room, he flashed back to happier childhood memories of creamed teas, exotic cafes, and endless cinemas.

But there was Mum, the woman who once fed his cinemania, now mumbling nonsense to herself while waiting for her ticket to the hereafter: "I noticed with an involuntary shudder that her feet were bare on the cold stone floor. She seemed neither to know nor care and stared straight through me with no sign of recognition."

But the stench of disinfectant and the sight of stiff-lipped attendants lording over senile ladies proved worse than any nuthouse delirium he might have scripted. He needed an excuse to get out of there—another interview: this time on a local Southampton television talk show.

To brace himself, he hopped into the Bassett Hotel bar and gulped down at least four Scotches. From there he took a bus to the wrong studio; then, he arrived at the bar where he was scheduled to meet the interviewer and producer of a program called *Viewpoint*. There, he chucked down a pint of ale before going to the makeup room.

Once he sat in the studio and felt the mike digging through the inside of his shirt, Russell heeded the flashing red light. But he got blindsided by the first question: "Mr. Russell, you have the reputation of being something of a martinet on the studio floor. Is this simply malicious gossip or is there a modicum of truth to it?"

Perhaps unconsciously imitating his ailing mother, Russell sat there a bit dazed and mumbled some kind of answer. Suddenly, the red light shut off; he felt someone remove his mike and heard the host thanking him for coming to the show. A chunk vanished from his memory, so he wound up meeting the producer in a restaurant around the corner from the studio, hoping to find out exactly what had happened. As they munched on roasted pigeon and downed champagne, Russell learned that he had entered a parallel world unfit for airtime.

"Apparently, on being asked if I was a martinet in the studio," Russell recalls in his autobiography, "I'd leaned forward, examined the interviewer's makeup, and asked why he'd been made up to resemble a Chinaman, saying that I would have promptly fired the makeup person if they ever produced work as bad as that for me, unless, of course, it was a Chinaman they were making up. I'd also have fired the lighting cameraman for accentuating the bags under the interviewer's eyes, but I'd have fired them both without shouting or fuss. They'd just collect their two weeks' wages and go."

Delirious or not, Russell essentially answered the interviewer's question. The news of his sudden drift into on-air madness unhinged him so much that he got to the toilet just in time to barf up all the booze and roasted pigeon. Tactfully leaving the restaurant and staggering down another seemingly endless corridor to his hotel room, he plopped on the bed. The bleating of his bladder, however, shook him from his near-coma.

Groping for a light switch in the pitch-black room, he grabbed a door handle instead. "It was the largest bathroom I'd ever seen," he recalls, "over two hundred feet long, only there was no bath or loo or bidet. Click! The door closed behind me. I was standing in the hotel corridor—stark bollock naked!"

As Mother Nature started kicking down his door, Russell scrambled to no avail for a potted palm behind which he could void. Amid this air-conditioned hell, he dragged his bloated birthday suit further down the corridor, fearing a woman's scream, a fist in his face, or an arrest: "I never felt more alone, alone, abandoned, unreal, lost in a dream of Jean-Paul Sartre." He thought of relieving himself in an ice machine, but a sand-filled ashtray proved even better.

About a pound lighter, he still had to heave himself into a nearby elevator that transported him to the reception lobby. Doddering through the foyer, and holding his hands over his privates, he triggered a timely memory: "It was an image that had long haunted and disturbed me, that picture of condemned Jews walking to the gas chamber. I had often wondered why they didn't stride out, heads held high, arms swinging. Now I knew."

Those familiar with a notorious 1974 film by Liliana Cavani might appreciate some naughty irony: the naked Ken Russell—imagining he's a Nazi death camp inmate—sought solace from the night porter. Russell tried explaining the situation to the man in uniform, but like a commandant with petty power, the night porter got a wee bit sadistic as he dangled his passkey. He called Russell a "silly old fart," teased him by asking whether he was cupping his hands over the "crown jewels," but finally escorted his victim back to his plush incarceration.

After what seemed a humiliating eternity, Russell encountered a miracle: "I stepped into the room, stone-cold sober, and noticed an envelope on the floor that I must have overlooked before. I opened it. Inside was a telephone message: 'Development Deal—*Dracula*.' I gave a long sigh and crossed myself."

●

It was 1979: Frank Langella, a hit with the Broadway production of *Dracula*, now appeared in the big screen version. That same year, Germany's Werner Herzog released what is essentially a scene-by-scene remake of F. W. Murnau's *Nosferatu*. In the middle of this vampire vogue, some trade magazines started buzzing about a new, flamboyant Ken Russell adaptation of Bram Stoker's novel.

The film was to open with Jonathan Harker seeking out Castle Dracula to give the count the deed to Carfax Manor, but he encounters bizarre warnings when entering the town of Bistritz. Russell included a Rabelaisian carnival procession with "masked mummers operating giant, articulated bats and a float of the sinister figure of a medieval prince, belching fire and smoke from its mouth and ears. The town band is playing a funeral dirge."

Harker urges the reluctant coachman to drive to the castle, but by the time he witnesses a girl getting slaughtered in some pagan ritual, the coachman morphs into a werewolf. Impaled bodies litter the landscape, and howling wolves pursue Harker's carriage as he fights off the werewolf to drive off alone. When he finally encounters Dracula, he notices that the count resembles some fire-breathing figure he saw in the medieval parade. Russell then burlesques the horror with discount store props: the coachman pops up to peel off a werewolf mask, the slaughtered peasant girl, whole again, teases Harker with a rubber bat.

Marinating in another of the obsessions he'd already toyed with in *Valentino*, Russell specified that the walls of the count's drawing room be adorned with Aubrey Beardsley's drawings for Oscar Wilde's play *Salome*. Russell's Dracula likes to "dabble a little in . . . acupuncture," but he also aspires to be a great patron of the arts. He regrets that Beardsley died so young, and that he did not help him when he might have had the chance.

Russell planned to restructure Stoker's story less as a tale about the literal loss of blood and more about the psychic vampires that prey on other people's creative efforts. His Count Dracula loves the arts so much that he seeks to immortalize them, not by doling out money but by bringing the artists back to life as vampire comrades. Before making her immortal, Dracula pontificates to Mina about the theology of aesthetics:

> What is the love of God? Little by little he reveals to you the wonders of the earth, like a parent offering a child a glittering box of sweets, then just as you reach out eagerly, he snatches them away. Those whom he loves, die as quickly as May flies while we, whom he hates, live on and on . . . How jealously God guards His immortality. Shakespeare, Michelangelo, Tchaikovsky: as soon as they challenged him with their vision of heaven, he cut them down— until we started to fight him. Now some of our greatest artists are

Nosferatu. But if it were known, they would be persecuted for sorcery, demonology, persecuted for creating eternal beauty. So, once in a lifetime, they change their identity, even their style.

"What use to me is your soul," the count continues. "God is welcome to it." His seduction is so smooth that Mina latches onto him as if he were a matinee idol: "As Dracula kisses, bites, then draws blood from her neck, Mina imagines she is bedecked in a silver wedding dress rising in her lover's arms to the stars."

Russell claims that Mick Fleetwood was eager to play such a hambone lead. Even with his intermittent fear of flying, Russell was so overjoyed at this prospect that he traveled by jet to see a Fleetwood Mac concert in Washington, D.C, thinking that perhaps the group might also be right for a *Dracula* soundtrack. He was relieved when the concert got called off and he had the chance to talk about business, marveling at how the gaunt and pale Fleetwood looked as though he'd have to do very little acting.

According to Russell, Mick offered to take the Method to new depths by draining a pint of blood from his body each day throughout the shooting. But soon after Fleetwood left the hotel room, Russell's producer rang to tell him that, with Langella's upcoming film as well as a couple of other vampire movies in the making, the Russell version faced an eternal grave.

The death of the *Dracula* project augured a new direction in Ken Russell's career—a circuitous route of false starts, a couple of Hollywood semi-blockbusters, and—in an effort to be "bankable"—some artistic compromises. Once Littman finally called with something tangible, a movie about hallucinogens and mysticism, Russell was in for the trip of a lifetime.

FAUST FREAKS

"**S**ome of the most neurotic, miserable, poorly married men I've met in my life are among the most fascinating and interesting people I know," Paddy Chayefsky once proclaimed, "as are confirmed

bachelors, homosexuals, lechers of the worst sort who suffer the tortures of the damned. I enjoy these people more than others."

Shunning shallow notions of "the norm," Chayefsky believed people should harness their neuroses for creative purposes. "Hysteria is addictive," his son Dan once said of his dad, "and he felt it worked for him." One would think that he and Ken Russell would have had a beautiful friendship.

Chayefsky and Russell both liked to eat, gab, throw their weight, and fuel their work on anger, frustration, and tortured love. Both also had nightmares: Russell's involved being covered in gray matter; Chayefsky's were about being crushed or smothered. They were passionate and at times bellicose about their craft, yelling at producers, photographers, actors, and anyone else who interfered. They also had a mutual fascination with Edgar Allan Poe. Chayefsky especially marveled at stories about the great and troubled author channeling his fury in both his work and in sarcastic retorts to the critics who did him dirt. Paddy and Kenny: a new variation on Poe's "William Wilson," a tale of doppelgangers quaking in each other's shadows.

They also had some aesthetic affinities. Russell could have conceivably directed Chayefsky's stage production of *The Passion of Josef D*. The play about Stalin elicited boos and hisses when Leon Trotsky pranced about as an arrogant fop in a white Afro wig, claiming in falsetto his hog's share of credit for the Bolshevik Revolution. Shattered Trotskyites invaded the Ethel Barrymore Theater, purchasing tickets just to jeer. Even those tethered to the mainstream balked: Howard Taubman of the *New York Times* accused Chayefsky of distorting facts and rewriting history. Chayefsky seemed a man after Russell's heart.

Yet their working relationship culminated in Russell declaring that Chayefsky "resembled an overweight Trotsky, dressed as Chairman Mao, talked democracy, and practiced fascism."

•

By the late 1970s, Chayefsky was a Hollywood titan. In the '50s, he'd gilded the "Golden Age of Television"; as a screenwriter, he'd earned three Academy Awards for creating a lovable Italian sap in *Marty*, exposing institutional corruption in *The Hospital*, and screaming—through his anchorman and alter ego Howard Beale—against corporate greed in *Network*. His forte was brisk dialogue that at least some considered "naturalistic." Drama for him was a means to tackle large and preachy themes.

Accustomed to prestige, success, and having his way, Chayefsky elicited the nickname "Prince Paddy." And like a royal pain, he pissed others off as he arbitrated over casting, acting, editing, scoring, and directing. He even bragged about how he "meddled from one end of the business to the other." When *The Hospital* was ready for public screenings, he would check out movie theaters to make sure the sound was working properly and the projector lenses were clean.

When the timing was right, Prince Paddy could be the poster boy for comportment, but if the conversation veered into such quicksand topics as his box office failures, he could erupt into what his biographer Shaun Considine describes in a firsthand account as "hot verbal lava." His fists would tighten, his eyes would glare, and his body would tremble before he expelled epithets like "asshole" at anyone who dared challenge his wisdom or utter what he'd interpret as an offensive compliment. "Paddy could make an argument out of an egg-salad sandwich," his longtime pal, the playwright Herb Gardner, once joked.

There were two Chayefskys. The familiar Prince Paddy was what his son Dan described as "almost hyper, turned on, a nightclub act, a pinball machine, like Robin Williams or Liza Minnelli." And then there was Sidney Aaron (his given name), the bookish and beleaguered Jew among gentile ruffians. His biographer describes Sidney as "morose, very withdrawn, unable to share his thoughts with anyone." At a humble five feet, six inches tall, Sidney was a flunky with his fists, but he survived by cultivating an incendiary vocabulary to ward off the mostly Irish and Italian bullies on his Tibbett Avenue neighborhood in the Bronx.

Drafted into World War II, Sidney was lousy at firing a gun, hated getting his head shaved, and resented having to obey some hayseed sergeant. He also perceived anti-Semitism in the hallowed armed forces. All of this duress inspired him to get brasher. He even adopted what would become his professional name as the result of a ruse to get out of kitchen duty. When he lied and said he had to go to Catholic mass that day because he was half Irish, the gullible officer dubbed him with the shamrock soubriquet "Paddy." He soon ate pork, swore a lot, and defied the Torah's sanctions against self-aggrandizement. The diffident Sidney changed, almost in lycanthropic fashion, into the ill-mannered Paddy.

Paddy became Rumpelstiltskin with a Napoleon complex—a thimble of a man bloated with ironic wit and boundless spite that belied his size. Chayefsky would later admit that this Jekyll-Hyde schism was one of the inspirations for his *Altered States*, a script that not only explores the effects of mind-altering drugs and isolation tanks but also addresses the split between the human and the beast.

So when the time came for Rumpelstiltskin to meet the "psychopathic Father Christmas," Russell must have arrived as the gentile from hell. With red skin and an even redder nose, he resembled not only a besotted Santa but also an oversized leprechaun; the succulent aroma of roast pork might as well have emanated from his pores.

For years, Russell's politics with screenwriters had been shaky. He begrudgingly allowed Larry Kramer to get screen credit on *Women in Love*, but in many future films he managed to emblazon his name either exclusively or right alongside (if not above) the initial screenwriter. Now he had to deal with a man all puffed up after the *Boston American* called him "a current somewhat god of writers," *Newsweek* hailed him as "a more amenable Von Stroheim, a pocket Zola," and Belgium's *La Libre Belgique* slavered all over him as "the most intelligent writer Hollywood has been known to attract." Paddy was also armed with contracts that gave him supreme sway over direction, script changes, camera angles, and set designs.

Paddy's plays, with slice-of-life dialogue that he once likened to people being wiretapped, were meat for Method actors who also blossomed during television's golden age. In the 1950s, scenery chewers like James Dean, Rod Steiger, and John Cassavetes would give eyeteeth to flutter across the stage and sputter his relevant homilies. But Russell, who was not a fan of Method acting and would rather concentrate on a misplaced chair than squander good lighting time over "motivation," was all the more leery at having to consult with Chayefsky over every script nuance.

●

Chayefsky was immersed in writing the *Altered States* screenplay long before Russell entered the drama. In his research, he questioned doctors at Columbia

University about genetics and made anthropology inquiries at the American Museum of Natural History. To make the script more erudite, he also spoke with several scientists at the Harvard Medical School, Duke University, the City University of New York, and the Maimonides Medical Center in Brooklyn on matters of endocrinology and psychophysiology. After absorbing Aldous Huxley's *The Doors of Perception* and Dr. John Lilly's mystical literature, he proceeded to California's Stockton State College; there, he dropped into an isolation tank.

Altered States is about Dr. Edward Jessup, a disillusioned scientist who wants to probe his inner being. But like Urbain Grandier, he is so caught up in his megalomania that he does all the talking while his swooning female counterpart pretends to have a mind but ultimately submits. The story becomes more about Jessup's repressed hostilities toward Emily, the woman he eventually marries.

During sex, Jessup concentrates less on Emily and more on visions of "God, Jesus, crucifixions." Chayefsky wanted to make Jessup so self-absorbed that, failing as a husband and dad, he separates from his family. When he floats in tanks and gets in touch with his inner demon, Jessup was to fall from grace and eventually die—an ending much different from the happy pabulum of his final version.

As he assembled his eighty-seven-page treatment, Paddy envisioned surrealistic interludes redolent with Catholicism. Jessup sees Christ on a handkerchief before journeying into his brain to find a "swollen, obviously aroused vagina, into which his whole body was plunging with trembling anticipation." The Catholic excesses get more Darwinian as Jessup combines the isolation tank with hallucinogenic drugs. This results in a psychochemical reaction that makes him mutate into something simian.

Altered States came tailored for high-octane cinema, but Daniel Melnick, an executive at Columbia Pictures, thought Chayefsky should novelize the screenplay first; that way, producer David Begelman would see a literary endeavor and get impressed enough to advance a million dollars for a film-in-progress.

During the summer of 1977, as Russell did last-minute languishing for *Valentino*, Chayefsky typed away. As he wrote, he projected himself into his protagonist, making Jessup an earnest if self-indulgent soul who searches for divine knowledge but keeps courting a darker demon. He was now struggling with whether to have Jessup croak or to let love conquer all. The process got so enervating that Paddy suffered a heart attack before he could finish the last chapter.

●

Once he left the hospital and submitted to a Type-A personality test, Chayefsky got a doctor's warning: stop harboring so many self-destructive thoughts and avoid alcohol, caffeine, and fat. His diet got blander, but he continued to obsess over his story's ending. One version had Jessup and Emily as mortal enemies. As in the film, she would call Jessup "a Faust freak," but Emily also had more bite and wasn't the fawning shadow woman she became in the later drafts. The heart attack apparently softened Chayefsky as he opted to save Jessup from his Frankenstein destiny through a woman's love. The finished novel, which Harper & Row published, bore the dedication: "For my wife, Susan. For my son, Dan."

Despite the novel's lackluster sales, Chayefsky was determined. But choosing a director proved harder than planned. The first choice was *Network*'s Sidney Lumet, but he quit after haggling over money. Next in line was Arthur Penn, Paddy's chum since their army days. Both Paddy and Penn agreed to cast a then unknown named William Hurt for the golden-haired goy the story required.

Hurt, engrossed in the mythology of the Method, burst into tears after reading the script, touched by Jessup's search for truth and love. "I never had a friend as great as Emily," he wailed, "who could get me across a river that wide." Blair Brown, through persistence and repeated auditions, got the part of Jessup's maternal martyr. Columbia Pictures then brought in John Dykstra, who handled special effects for *Star Wars*. The effects underwent constant permutations as they thought of ways to make Jessup's transformation from a man into a beast convincing. They put Hurt in a body cast; Brown got wrapped in latex, so that makeup man Dick Smith could make her flesh appear as if it were burning. But when Penn went against the author's specifications by making Jessup's lab look like a futuristic planetarium instead of a humble basement, Paddy fired his pal and the search continued.

●

Russell's agent Robert Littman had a droll and sometimes taunting sense of humor. He could enliven a conversation by impersonating Dino De Laurentiis with a faux Italian accent, or he could get a journalist all hopped up with some juicy Hollywood gossip while demanding every word stay "off the record." And he had a knack for twitting Russell's brittle ego. Littman dropped the other shoe by informing Russell that, for *Altered States*, he got chosen as director number twenty-seven on a list that included Woody Allen, Ingmar Bergman, Bernardo Bertolucci, John Boorman, Brian De Palma, Francis Ford Coppola, Richard Donner, Bryan Forbes, Arthur Hiller, Richard Lester, George Lucas, Roman Polanski, Sydney Pollack, Nicolas Roeg, John Schlesinger, Martin Scorsese, Steven Spielberg, François Truffaut, Orson Welles, Michael Winner, Franco Zeffirelli, and Fred Zinneman.

Paddy's agent and *Altered States*' producer Howard Gottfried came up with the idea of hiring the man whom *Time* magazine called "the cinema's dilly

Dali." "I thought he would be worth considering," Gottfried remembers. "Ken has tremendous visual talent. Of course, in hindsight, if I knew he was going to be such a putz, such a miserable son of a bitch, I would never have recommended him."

Columbia was enthused because the studio was still basking in the afterglow of Russell's blockbuster *Tommy*. Chayefsky, who had yet to see a Russell film, sat through some screenings. Those around him who knew better spared him Gustav Mahler practically performing fellatio on a pig's snout or Richard Wagner as a Franken-Nazi. Instead, Chayefsky marveled at *Tommy*'s cavalcade of cripples adoring the giant Marilyn Monroe statue and at Ann-Margret getting pelted with suds, beans, and chocolate. What really sold him was *Savage Messiah* and its dialogue rattling like machine gun fire.

On the evening of the day that he initially met Paddy in New York, Russell hugged him and accepted his script. But knowing he was about to make unprecedented compromises, he went back to his swank penthouse suite at the Sherry-Netherland Hotel, placed a call to England, and whimpered to Vivian about taking on, for the first time, a movie just for the cash. Despite Vivian's encouragement, he feared for the worst.

●

"The day after he was hired to direct *Altered States*," Chayefsky biographer Shaun Considine writes, "Russell learned that the courtship phase of his induction was over. He was now on the production payroll, so he was moved out of the penthouse to a cheaper room at the back of the hotel, with no view of the park. The hasty script meetings, held in Chayefsky's musty office on Seventh Avenue, were equally cheap and cheerless, he complained."

Since Russell regards food and drink as part of life's sacred rites, he got testy when Paddy started imposing his post-coronary restrictions—or what Russell called a "parsimonious dictatorship in culinary matters." Luncheons and committee meetings nurtured on dull, de-fatted staples, mostly pressed turkey sandwiches and decaffeinated Sanka, were too much to bear. Living by Rabelais's precept that "truth lurks hidden in wine," Russell preferred to pig out on sirloin and imbibe Chateauneuf du Pape '75. There were also sensibility clashes: once in L.A., Paddy was content to stay at the relatively modest Beverly Hills Hotel, but Russell was adamant about living in a private Beverly Hills bungalow.

For a little while, Russell abided the limp lettuce lunches and what he increasingly regarded as a silly script. He declares in his autobiography that Paddy "was quite put out and quite unable to discuss the burning question of the moment—

whether the banana used by Dr. Jessup in a lecture on male aggression should be green or yellow." Russell vented his aggression in other ways. He started demolishing Arthur Penn's set and replaced Joe Alves, the original production designer, with a British compatriot named Richard McDonald (sometimes Mac-Donald). Dykstra was another casualty. Russell wanted a new look and took on Bran Ferren, a future R&D honcho for Walt Disney Imagineering, who gave Russell what were considered, in pre-CGI days, "state-of-the-art" illusions.

Paddy resisted the Russell-Ferren approach. He particularly hated the way they presented the story's isolation tank sequences: "In a scene our hero is supposed to be in complete sensory deprivation," he complained to *Saturday Review*. "Russell had him in an upright bronze boiler, dog-paddling around, and the whole thing is lit up like a Halloween scare. Meanwhile, there's all this narration about total silence, total deprivation, total darkness."

Here, Chayefsky uncharitably describes one of the movie's few successes. From the moment Jessup's goggled face pops up in its glass bubble, to the opening titles snaking horizontally across the screen, the mood gets progressively more alien as the camera pulls back in a slow establishing shot. Jessup is framed in a round window reminiscent of an antiquated television set, and the basement where the tank is housed looks truly malefic. Soon Russell supplies a favorite visual motif: iron bars. They appear (like the alchemist's dungeon in *The Devils*) as floor gratings that let in an eerie light from beneath. Jessup's colleague Arthur Rosenberg (Bob Balaban) is at the controls, dictating the stages of Jessup's immersion in his journal; all the while, John Corigliano's creeping score helps create an alternate world even before the hallucinations begin.

•

For Prince Paddy, the mere thought of a director demanding equal say in the production was unbearable. Russell as well was not always comfy with his script-writers. Characterizing his newfound adversary, Russell compared Chayefsky to the simian monster Jessup was to become: "The monkey on my back was always there and wouldn't let go," Russell gripes. Recounting a time when he and Paddy visited the Bronx Zoo's Primate House for research, Russell claimed, "I once saw Paddy, who had rather long arms and a pronounced stoop, give a pretty fair imitation of a chimpanzee on becoming agitated over a remark I made concerning his dialogue."

This was also a war of cinematic tastes. "He keeps the actors moving all the time," Paddy complained. "You can't concentrate on what they're saying." "He sees things in terms of scenes, on a stage, almost flat," Russell retorted. "I'm a great believer in the choreography of the camera, like it's one of the actors." Russell also complained, "One problem with Paddy was that I don't shoot scenes as he was used to having them shot . . . I try to avoid the covering shot, long shot, close-up technique. Instead, I try for long, fluid sequences."

Russell accused Paddy of loading his script "with scientific mumbo jumbo which the actors spat at each other across a long table watched over by Paddy and myself at either end. Paddy wanted everyone word perfect, and we sat there day after day until they were, and then he asked them to overlap their dialogue so that what had been barely comprehensible before degenerated into incomprehensible babble reminiscent of the Bronx Zoo."

Ever crafty, Russell toyed with Paddy's script by telling the actors to mouth their dialogue while eating; that way, they could spew off their social science slobber as if in a domestic brawl. The script's pedantic speeches were also rife with Americanisms that Russell, no matter how long he hung out with the sandwich-and-Sanka crowd in the studio commissary, could never quite master.

•

Jessup's lines, which clog up most of the screenplay, are at times the most problematic. Hurt's downbeat and sultry voice could potentially trigger catalepsy with the wrong material. Imagine having to direct Hurt saying, "What dignifies the Yogic practices is that the belief system itself is not truly religious. There is no Buddhist God *per se*. It is the Self, the individual Mind, that contains immortality and ultimate truth."

A choice scene occurs when Jessup and Emily meet at a party. Flustered over Paddy's words, Russell seems intent on inflicting a symbolic heart attack through caloric voodoo. Emily, a physical anthropologist, tries flirting with Jessup, coyly nibbling on a carrot stick while asking him about his line of work. Jessup, on the other hand, globs on the mayo, piles on the ham and Swiss, and munches away while giving Emily a cholesterol-coated answer: "Toxic metabolite stuff. We're more or less replicating Heath's and Friedhof's strategies, trying to find maverick substances specific to schizophrenia. I think we're chasing our tails. What do you do?"

Other arduous moments involve a scene in an Italian restaurant, when Jessup is about to go to Mexico to try out some authentic Amanita Muscaria. In a farewell dinner surrounded by hanging slabs of cheese and non-kosher salamis, Hurt staggers right along with cinematographer Jordan Cronenweth, around the vino-laden dinner table, toting his own bottle while raising his deadpan voice among the cross talk to declare, "Memory *is* energy, it doesn't disappear, it's still in there, there's a physiological pathway to our earlier consciousness; it has to be, and I'm telling you it's in the goddamned limbic system."

This was essentially dialogue impossible to film without implying some kind of satire to give it context. But when Russell tried spicing up the scenes by having the actors jump around or by staging some kind of background frenzy to counterpoint the jargon, Paddy grew livid. "You're only the writer," Russell would fire back each time Paddy lodged a complaint.

A game of intrigue followed as Russell got word that Paddy was sneaking into lavatories to consult with the actors behind his back. Hurt and Brown, terrified that the production would get called off and they'd lose their first big roles, cried together one day, terrified by Russell's thunder as Paddy stormed off the set. "He was grilling the actors behind my back when they were supposed to be taking cues from me," Russell complained to *People* magazine. "I went home and got sloshed and called him everything under the sun. It must have made his beard turn blue."

Hurt was also developing a son's fixation on Russell. Leery about Russell's choleric reputation, Hurt felt more comfortable after noticing Russell was wearing Betty Boop socks. Russell recalls that Hurt "must have spent more time with me during the filming of *Altered States* than with his girlfriend. In fact, I remember him shouting to me across Santa Monica Boulevard at the top of his voice one warm autumn evening, 'I love you.' And his girlfriend was at his side at the time, holding his overcoat. I think if his bed had been a little bit bigger I'd have been invited to join them . . . The trouble with Bill is he can't stop talking. In the end his eternal nattering, usually about himself, became so unbearable that Viv and I would only take him out to dinner if he remained silent throughout the meal. If he spoke he paid the bill. He never got further than the fish course before having to get out his cheque book."

∎

During initial consultations with Chayefsky, Russell mixed sweet and sour sauce into his sarcasm: "You can't improve on perfection, Paddy. Why don't we rehearse the scene where Jessup fucks Emily on the kitchen floor? I'd appreciate your input on the grunts." Paddy bit back: "I'm only concerned with matters of dialogue right now, Kenny. In matters of barking dogs, grunting ape-men, and moaning lovers you have carte blanche."

Howard Gottfried's version of the story paints Russell as a duplicitous, manipulative ogre: "He would make real lousy remarks. Just anything to get Paddy upset. He was really looking to dislodge Paddy from any position of authority, that was obvious. He more than baited Paddy. He wanted to debase him, to irritate him." Inevitably, principal filming started out with Paddy and Kenny no longer talking.

FAUST FREAKS

Chayefsky held sway by monitoring every word of dialogue through a headset. The tension also drove him into a depression, but Russell appeared invigorated by it all and at times exacerbated the situation: "I can't possibly direct this movie with all your incessant talk going on," he hissed at Gottfried in reference to the on-set consultations with Paddy. "I'm out here in California trying to make a movie," Paddy typed in a letter to his friend, the playwright Owa, "which has been a horror from the beginning . . . We started shooting the fucker last Friday, and the director not only has turned out to be a monster, but a monster with not enough talent to make it worthwhile. Man, I'm tired of battling, I truly am."

At dinners, Paddy's frantic mannerisms elicited more chuckles than sympathy as he ranted to his friends about the rocky Russell horror show. Russell was also showing some emotional wear and tear. One evening at his rented abode, he tried relieving his tensions with a dip in the pool, but he overheard Vivian (who had since flown over from England) and Littman gabbing away in the patio about how he was sabotaging the project and had to be put in line. Russell emerged from the chlorine, shrieked at both of them, and then ran to the phone to subject Paddy to another tongue-lashing.

Vivian and Littman panicked but couldn't wrest Russell's hand from the receiver—even when Vivian poured a bottle of Pimms No. 1 over his head. The sound of Paddy's voice at the other end of the receiver made him more furious: "Why don't you take your turkey sandwiches and your script and your Sanka and stuff it up your ass and get on the next fucking plane back to New York and let me get on with the fucking film."

●

Russell's nightmares worsened when Columbia, nervous about the Paddy-Russell feud and the cost of the demolished sets, bailed out and left the bid open for Warner Bros. According to Russell, Warners' president Ted Ashley, who censored all those pubic hairs from *The Devils*, said he would only take on the film if Russell were fired. But it was too late. Russell recalls, "I'm sure that Paddy would have been happy to let me go if Howard [Gottfried], always the realist, hadn't convinced him that to introduce a new director at this stage with only two weeks to go would have spelt disaster."

Russell knew Paddy was in a tight spot and turned the tables, insisting to Gottfried that Chayefsky be barred from the set. And Russell got his way: Paddy went back to New York, stipulating that he see the daily rushes via Air Express to make sure not a word of his dialogue got sullied. Grabbing at his contract as if it were his lifeline, he watched the rushes with friends and went into tirades: "Look! Look! What do you think of that shit?" It got to a point that, even three thousand miles away, Russell still worked his mojo. "They're destroying my script," Paddy would cry. "They're wrecking my beautiful story."

A rancorous regent in exile, Paddy redirected Russell's bellicosity to Gottfried, screaming at him for being so easy on the limey lout. As a result, Paddy started flouting his doctor's orders, ingesting heaping helpings of salami and other fatty delights. He tried arranging a trip back to L.A. to monitor Russell's progress, but the Warner Bros. executives told him to stay home. But this insult came with a face-saving consolation: Paddy could still collect his share of the royalties but did not have to put his name on the screenplay. The credits would instead read—Sidney Aaron.

Though he formally distanced himself, Chayefsky could not help tempting fate by sneaking in a few more rushes. He recoiled at one particular scene— the penultimate moments when Jessup becomes a blue-eyed half-ape. Paddy had a diminutive Nigerian soccer player in mind for the part, but Russell, still attuned to the grandeur of Isadora Duncan and Nijinsky, hired Miguel Godreau, a Mexican ballet dancer whose primitive pirouettes would turn whatever serious science fiction was left in the story into another Russell farce. "Up to that moment, the scene is completely realistic," Paddy subsequently remarked. "The janitor hears something in the lab and creeps in to check. Then a ballet dancer suddenly jumps out of the tank doing a *grand jeté*. You're into *Planet of the Apes!*"

●

The Russell-Chayefsky clash was also apparent in the contrasting way each responded to the isolation tank. For Paddy, who truly believed in his character's desire for redemption, the submersion into water and the sound of his amplified heartbeat were "a warm return to your mother's womb." Russell attempted a similar experience but ended up "entombed in a blackness that not even Paddy could have dreamed of . . . Instead of becoming carefree, I fell victim to every anxiety, every neurosis, every evil thought left behind by all those nutters who'd peed in the dark before me, as I was peeing now."

Russell underwent his tank trauma in "a house full of bad vibes," where a man who resembled the Incredible Hulk and called Russell "Mr. Twilight Zone" escorted him to meet a creature called "Maw." "The inside smelt of dogshit," Russell recalls, "and when I met Maw I thought I'd met the Yeti." As they walked him down a murky hall and into a back room, Russell encountered "a sinister black casket that would not have been out of place in a Dracula movie, and neither would my strange companions, come to that." When Maw told him to "Strip off now," Russell denuded down to his socks before the Hulk picked him up and dipped him into a vat that resembled the gray goo from previous nightmares.

Claustrophobic, frightened of the dark, terrified of nature's slimier elements, and feeling his sirloin-engorged gut displacing more water than he'd expected, Russell suddenly remembered Edgar Allan Poe's story "The Premature Burial"; he too now feared being interred alive. He pounded on the isolation coffin's lid to no response; he pounded again until finally the Hulk and his Maw brought Falstaff back into open air. He was a fleshy mass that laughed and trembled as they draped him in a bathrobe.

This was not the first time Russell got psychedelicized while trying to get a grip on Dr. Jessup's mind. A few days earlier, he and Vivian had brought little Molly to relax by the kidney-shaped poolside at Shelley Winters's Coldwater Canyon estate, where they were staying. Driving a Ford Thunderbird at the time, Russell had opened his glove compartment to discover what he describes as "a transparent packet with a rainbow logo containing dehydrated mushrooms."

With the niceties of Sunday brunch over, and the Mexican maid Lily tending a napping Molly, he and Vivian decided to take the trip:

> Nibbling and giggling, we waited impatiently for something to happen—either for us to grow large or small or to jump in the pool and start a caucus-race. Actually something far more sinister occurred. The extensive garden, which until now had seemed akin to a tropical paradise, began to assume a disturbing malevolence. The plants and trees . . . took on a positively threatening air, more animalistic than botanic. The waving palm leaves were savage claws ready to tear our flesh. Wherever we looked there was no escape. Around the pool, down the slopes from Charlton Heston's garden and up the hill from a starlet's pad, the carnivorous jungle was on the march, stirred on by a stiff breeze from Malibu. We were surrounded by cruel, green talons, the bared fangs of vicious razor-sharp leaves and snaking tendrils lashing at our bare bodies.

All the horror Russell encountered was worth at least some of the pain. *Altered States*, despite its warty script, lackluster acting, derivative story, and dim ending, grabs the cinematic gonads whenever Jessup hallucinates. When Jessup encounters his own smiling face submerged in an aquarium, Russell adds autobiographical décor by sticking in a couple of eels. Soon, Jessup sees his cancer-plagued father crying out from a hospital bed, tearing a cheap cloth replica of the Shroud of Turin off his face and turning away when his son offers a lily-white copy of the Holy Bible. Jessup also envisions the fires of damnation, a

Dr. Jessup (William Hurt) hallucinates among the congers.

slaughtered lamb, and a crucified messiah with the head of a seven-eyed goat. All of this makes a brilliant segue into the close-up of a schizophrenic patient (Deborah Baltzell) grimacing into the camera through a sickly blue video screen, her face adorned with electrodes.

Shortly after the movie's release, Russell related another mind fugue to the *Soho News*:

One script detail that the film's producers insisted on keeping concerns Jessup's experience in Mexico, when a drug used in Indian ceremonies is said to induce a common experience in all users. . . . I was trying to think of ways to get this idea across. I was sitting in my garden in Los Angeles, thinking for hours, and I found myself gazing at an umbrella. And that's actually how I made the connection between the mushroom and the tree of knowledge. . . . We had a man, a woman, and a tree painted on the wall of a cave. The mushroom, the rocks shaped like mushrooms, the atomic mushroom cloud.

Though he falls into the cliché of the dopey gringo demurring to the "all-wise" native, Jessup's resulting scene, when he tastes the ancient Toltec porridge, is noisy, oppressive, and scintillating. When the magic mushroom stew takes effect, he's immediately pelted with flares, knocked to the ground, and exposed to a cavalcade of primordial and biblical assaults.

Again, Russell sneaks in his private phallic mythos: Jessup looks at a cut on his hand and finds the wound has turned into a lizard, a boa constrictor tries choking him as he imagines mass crucifixions. Corigliano's score approximates Peter Maxwell Davies's music for *The Devils* as Jessup's dream becomes the red-tinted, solarized footage from a silent movie: bodies impaled on crosses, hordes of sinners diving into hell's flames, and Russell's ever-taunting lizard lording over the fiery abyss. In a bid to tie in mystical visions with a troubled marriage, Jessup sees a komodo dragon turn into his wife, before both he and Emily erode in a sandstorm.

Pauline Kael, whose chronic dislike for Russell and his films made her less than trustworthy, was this time more on target when she bemoaned *Altered States'* "dismal, tired, humanistic ending." To Russell's credit, he too had problems with it but had no other choice.

Throughout, particularly during the carnal interludes, Emily perceives Jessup as "an unmitigated madman": "Even sex is a mystical experience for you. You

Dr. Jessup (William Hurt) encounters an evolutionary forebear during his Mexican trip.

carry on like a flagellant, which can be very nice, but I sometimes wonder if it's me that's being made love to. I feel like I'm being harpooned by some raging monk in the act of receiving god."

After ninety-something minutes of being bombarded with domestic screeching matches and intense visuals, viewers are supposed to buy into a Band-Aid epilogue as the Jessups reconcile and the doctor forsakes demonic science for "family values."

•

Before *Altered States* was unleashed on the general public, Warners held previews. Among the first was at a shopping center in suburban San Diego for a sneering audience of what Russell calls "overweight women in slacks with beehive hairdos." But a group of mostly UCLA students in Westwood gaped before a 70 mm screen with six-track stereo and loved it. Russell states: "Many of the kids went back time and again for the hallucinations alone—sitting in the foyer between trips, getting high, while a lookout was bribed to stay in the auditorium, enduring the dialogue until it was time to poke his head around the door and shout 'next hallucination!'"

The film got an official release in December 1980. *Time* magazine classed it among its top ten movies of the year, while the Oscars nominated it for best sound and score. *Time*'s Richard Corliss lauded Chayefsky's characters like a linguist: "His characters are endlessly reflective and articulate, spitting out litanies of adjectives, geysers of abstract nouns, chemical chains of relative clauses." It did well financially, but this was the first time no variation on "Ken Russell's Film of . . ." appeared on the credits over the title.

"Its strangeness, which borders cheerfully on the ridiculous, is its most enjoyable feature," the often-sympathetic Janet Maslin wrote in the *New York Times*. "The direction, without being mocking or campy, treats outlandish material so matter-of-factly that it often has a facetious ring." *Variety* also expressed some enthusiasm: "Russell has downplayed much of Chayefsky's heady philosophy by having the actors, especially Hurt, rattle off their jargon-laden speeches at breakneck speed."

Paddy Chayefsky celebrated his fifty-eighth and final birthday with two cakes: one bore the candied squiggle of "Paddy Chayefsky," the other "Sidney Aaron." Following his *Altered States* trauma, he faced other demons. Another adversary, a medical research assistant, pounced from out of nowhere, slapped a lawsuit, and claimed he should have gotten a "coauthor" script credit. But with attacks of pleurisy and other ailments, he was ready for a glimpse into a cosmos that needed no superlatives.

Chayefsky died on August 1, 1981. His last words, scrawled on a pad, were to his wife: "I tried. I really tried."

OPERATIC PUNKS

On April 18, 1982, Derek Jarman wrote the following in his journal: "Ken is deeply disillusioned with the cinema, the end of a love affair. Whenever the subject comes up there is a sadness, tales of betrayal and hopes dashed. Making *Altered States* was a nightmare. He had no support, only petty opposition from the film company."

As Ken Russell tried clearing *Altered States* from his mind, he and Derek Jarman were collaborating again, this time with their sights on opera. It all started when Russell, waiting by the phone as forlorn as ever for more work, finally got another call from Robert Littman with a new kind of offer. But Russell felt a twinge of nausea when hearing that the project was Igor Stravinsky's *The Rake's Progress*.

A lover of "classical" music but not shy about expressing his dislike of other "highbrow" pastimes, Russell declared that (excluding Pete Townshend's *Tommy*) opera for him was akin to a magnum of chloroform. It was, in fact, Stravinsky's *Rake* that started him yawning. "When they first asked me to do *The Rake*," he told *Time* magazine, "my heart sank because I had this memory of the most boring evening of my life." Some of the works of Verdi, Donizetti, and that übermensch Wagner also made him sleepy, but he claims that "it was finally Stravinsky's *Rake* that had got me swearing I'd never enter an opera house again, even if you paid me."

Yet many critics, particularly his more reserved English compatriots, have hurled the term "operatic" to describe Russell's stylistic excesses. And though they usually intend this as a patronizing epithet, even Russell aficionados can appreciate his operatic affinities. Russell's invitation to Florence to put some life into the *Rake* at the 45th Maggio Musicale Festival seemed a panacea for desperate times.

"Florence: Every evening Ken and I find a different restaurant to eat in," Jarman continues. "We establish a routine. At about eight we have a drink at the bar on the Piazza Signora. He crosses the square with his white hair and sailor suit. You can spot him a mile off; he has a great physical presence. We have one strong common bond: a love-hate relationship with our art which sparks off ideas."

In Italy, opera is not always relegated to the lofty status that it has in England or the States; it's regarded more as a carnival for everyday folks to enjoy. And Russell, with his fluid and often-manic camera gyrations, seems ideal for some of opera's grander moments: the fracas of shouting, wild gestures, and even fights that might ensue offstage if a production grates against audience expectations.

■

Russell and Jarman had made an aborted attempt at opera back in 1972, shortly after working on *The Devils*. The Royal Opera House was to commission a production of Peter Maxwell Davies's *Taverner*, which is about the sixteenth-century composer John Taverner and his run-ins with England's church canon. Jarman had in mind what he described as a "modern opera in a style which belongs to the 1970s."

Plans involved a cyclorama depicting travelers in the Gobi Desert. Taverner himself was to be dressed in Reformation wear, his wife decked out in 1930s attire, and the orchestra conductor in a bishop's miter. The opera house roof was supposed to be littered with dead oxen. There was even a William Castle–style gimmick, with theater seats wired to detect and amplify audience whispers. The most merciless feature was a lowered doorway that would have forced audiences to enter the theater crawling. But the plans to turn Covent Garden into a sado-masochistic circus ended over creative differences.

Now it was March 1982, and Russell prepared his *Rake* with a novel approach. He thought of W. H. Auden and his cowriter Chester Kallmann, meditating over their intentions when they penned the libretto. The opera, which had its Venice premiere in 1951 and a New York debut in 1953, had received mixed reviews, especially from pesky purists who objected to its deliberate anachronisms. Already Russell sensed friendly territory, aware that both Auden and Stravinsky considered the opera's story of soul-trafficking and moral corruption a timeless tale.

■

Russell and Jarman retell the story of the poor eighteenth-century rogue Tom Rakewell, his love Anne Trulove, and the ungodly forces that separate them.

Rakewell runs into some money from a departed uncle, just as a Mephistophelean figure named Nick Shadow arrives to guide him down a dark road. As Rakewell makes his picaresque journey through London society's greed and debauchery, he still entertains guilty memories of his Trulove, even once he becomes a brothel regular. Trulove, meanwhile, combs the city's mean streets to track down her beau.

Rakewell becomes effete and cynical, succumbing to Shadow's devious plan to have him marry Baba the Turk, a bearded lady who represents the antithesis of true romance. Poor Trulove is devastated, but the jealous bearded Baba constantly jolts hubby out of his ennui by accusing him of wanting Trulove all along. Not content to leave Rakewell in domestic agony, Shadow also plots to decimate his finances, having him invest in some kind of preposterous machine that promises to eliminate poverty. Thinking such a philanthropic project might win Trulove back, Rakewell falls for the scheme and lands in the financial shithouse, watching as his worldly possessions get auctioned.

When the time comes for Rakewell to honor his Faustian pact and forfeit his soul, Shadow teases him with a last chance at redemption: a card game. But when he wins, Rakewell still ends up in Bedlam—mad as a March hare as he fancies himself a mythical Adonis to Trulove's Venus. Russell's *Rake* leaves behind a queasy moral about how easily the devil can set up a lounge chair inside an idle mind. For an extra kicker, Nick falls to his doom—not into a grave, as the original libretto specifies, but by stumbling onto the London Underground's third rail.

Russell was also not the first to plug Stravinsky's *Rake* into a futuristic time machine. Back in 1967, Sarah Caldwell did a production in Boston that turned Rakewell into a hipster for the psychedelic age as he shimmied in discotheques and mounted motorcycles. Ten years later, the Glyndebourne Festival Opera's version included set designs by David Hockney. So Russell was following a contemporary tradition by adding new anachronisms.

In Russell's *Rake*, the strident politics reflect England's so-called Winter of Discontent, as "Iron Lady" Thatcher ruled over a vast malaise of unemployment while pining for the days of the empire. Anne Trulove bears an uncanny resemblance to Princess Di. Nick Shadow, in his long, black leather coat and post-punk accoutrements, embodies both a pimp and a drug dealer. Even the 1982 Falklands War has metaphors with a chorus garbed in army camouflage.

Russell also adds his personal quirks: a huge David Hockney painting here, a plastic blow-up doll in black knickers there. When Shadow extracts Rakewell's payment while on the London Underground's platform, the subway's customary wall advertisements are now the same Hogarth paintings that inspired Stravinsky's opera. Jarman, who helplessly watched Russell destroy his *Devils* sets, managed to save him from spattering the paintings with graffiti.

Jarman by now had established his own erudite cult following as a director. In 1976, *Sebastiane* saluted the saint in homoerotic laurels; in 1977, *Jubilee* took an alternately whimsical and violent look at the punk scene; and in 1979, *The Tempest* made a radical stab at Shakespeare, an effort compromised when Jarman couldn't get the legendary and ailing comic actor Terry Thomas to play Prospero.

More politically minded than Russell, Jarman's journal shows he was intent on reflecting England's topical woes:

> There are more than enough scandalous moments in *The Rake* to keep the journalists happy and the myth of an aging *enfant terrible* afloat. These are also weak spots, as they allow copy to be sold sensationally at the expense of a truly original mind . . . The Rake wears a T-shirt depicting Mrs. Thatcher as a vampire holding a skull—"Alas, poor England, I knew her well."

At the Teatro Comunale to celebrate Stravinsky's centenary, Russell and Jarman joined Riccardo Chailly, the *Rake*'s conductor, who from time to time during the production consulted with Russell on musical matters. The occasion approximated Babel as performers from Sweden to Chile and Bulgaria got corralled into mouthing the production in English, with which few were conversant. But for all the irritation, Russell was the happiest since his early BBC days; he felt he could once again get creative and clumsy—all for the joy of experiment.

The opera proceeded at the Teatro della Pergola, with Cecelia Gasdia stealing the show as Anne Trulove. She made an astounding impression on the director, particularly when hitting a resounding high E in the last refrain of "I'll Go to Him." For Russell, this alone was an experience worth all the previous headaches—a moment he claims "transported" him.

Russell, always ready to slide pop culture trinkets into his stories, adorns Rakewell in Elvis-style gold lamé and has him wield a Sony Walkman. Forget the ill-fitting costumes, badly painted scenery, clownish makeup, ratty wigs, missed cues, and constant backstage dissonance: the Italian audience by and large loved what it saw. "Modern London is perfectly at home in the Pergola Theatre," Jarman would boast when the opera got decent reviews. "My operatic punks and new romantics have a flamboyance which mirrors the eighteenth century." He was so "flushed with the opera's success" that he put some of its energy into his revision of what would become his 1986 film *Caravaggio*.

Topical politics materialized again. Russell and Jarman rankled the stagehands, who were all set to abandon the production when a symbol for the

Solidarity movement became part of the set design. This was the height of the Reagan-Thatcher Cold War, with Communist loyalists despising the Polish labor organizer Lech Walesa—the man whose efforts fired the first volley in toppling the Soviet Union. Anti-Solidarity stagehands threatened a massive walkout.

Russell also contended with morality wars when he announced his plans for casting the inflatable sex doll. The Italians balked, claiming such things didn't exist in Italy. But Russell managed to smuggle one in from London; still Jarman ended up having to sew knickers over the offending parts. Some of the crew were also outraged when Russell specified that the angels tote huge shafts.

"There is certainly nothing boring about this *Rake*," *Time*'s Michael Walsh writes. "For all its flashy images, the production captures the opera's cautionary moral spirit . . . Mainly this was a Ken Russell show—and probably the curtain raiser for a new career."

•

A year after talk of the *Rake* makeover, Russell felt brazen enough to tackle Giacomo Puccini. It was a timely move. *Madama Butterfly*'s 1904 story, about the U.S. Navy lieutenant who betrays a Japanese geisha, would soon become a Broadway smash with *M. Butterfly*. Of course, he thought the story needed an anachronistic facelift. "I wanted to get across Puccini's message—the *real* clash between East and West," Russell told the *New York Times*. "I mean, I feel the piece was prophetic. Why, for example, should Puccini have chosen to set it in Nagasaki? He could have chosen hundreds of other places in Japan. Well, when I saw that, the rest just fell into place. I worked back from the bomb and ended up in a brothel."

The music is the same, and the Italian is intact, but the story gets updated to World War II on the eve of the Pearl Harbor attack. Richard McDonald, who designed the sets for *Altered States*, fashioned the two-tiered apartment house, where much of the drama takes place. The protagonist Cio-Cio San (Catherine Lamy) becomes a hooker with a pimp, scouting Nagasaki's red-light district for lonely yet hard-nosed Americans like Lieutenant Pinkerton (Robert McCauley).

Russell also wanted the story to illustrate the basis for *Butterfly*'s frequent daydreams. He went back to the source and restored Puccini's references to opium smoking: "Basically, though, I'm treating the opera like an opium dream, and when Pinkerton and Butterfly sing their Act I love duet, it's not that Pinkerton really loves her, it's just that he's smoked some opium and he's caught up in an opium dream of love."

But Cio-Cio San, enamored with the American dream as it's portrayed in gussied picture magazines, flirts with tragedy. She tries being the ideal American housewife, donning an apron emblazoned with the stars and stripes, serving up huge breakfast portions of cornflakes and Coca-Cola, and placing an opium pipe next to Pinkerton's morning coffee.

Because Russell's version stressed the opera's send-up of both East and West, there was no time for cross-cultural sensitivity. To combine his love for bawdy romance with slapstick, Russell assented to his actor McCauley's suggestion that, as the mighty Caucasian, he should exert his military prerogative by lifting Cio-Cio San like a piece of Oriental luggage. He would haul her into the bedroom and, with a full frontal assault, plop over her as they launch into a duet. The routine brought humorous results, but at least one diva from Korea objected to the symbolic imperialism. Russell caricatured her complaint: "Me no lie alongy top side Prinkerton. Me fry home, Kolea, chop, chop!"

For the wedding feast, Russell staged a rowdy party full of inebriated sailors, prostitutes, and pimps all chugging beer and Coca-Cola. The climactic calamity, when Cio-Cio San commits hara-kiri, sizzles with sardonic camp. Her son, the Americanized byproduct of her interracial romp, wears a Mickey Mouse mask as he approaches her dead body. And McDonald spares no modesty in climaxing with a world in which America and Japan become, much as they do in the film *Blade Runner*, a symbiotic dystopia. Huge, lighted signs for Cassio, Nissan, Sanyo, Sony, and Toyota reflect the days of Japan's capitalism from the early 1980s, when Tokyo mastered the auto assembly line, Americans gobbled sushi, and a popular song's expression "Turning Japanese" was also slang for the gleeful, upturned expression round-eyed guys bare when pleasuring themselves.

Russell's *Madama Butterfly* enjoyed performances from the Continent to the Spoleto Festival in Charleston, South Carolina. Gian Carlo Menotti, the production's art director, might have had doubts at first about Russell outraging the conservatives but ended up in tears, pronouncing the final results as "something extraordinary."

Others, however, with their predictable purviews wrote their predictable pans. After catching a performance when John Matheson led the Charleston Spoleto Festival Orchestra, John Simon lamented in *New York* magazine over the way he saw Russell make "mincemeat of history, social, and psychological credibility." He wailed over Cio-Cio San's American junk food breakfast: "There is also a gigantic ketchup bottle. And no sense whatever. In the end, a feebly simulated atom bomb blew everything to smithereens. Then came a nightscape of an American town, with neon signs of Japanese products overwhelming a lonely Coca-Cola sign. First, apparently, the U.S. raped Japan; then Japan raped back. Russell should be forcibly restrained."

If Puccini can get embellished with an American shrine replete with soft drink icons and Abraham Lincoln needlepoints, then surely Gioacchino Rossini could also partake in Russell's pie-fight approach to the "classics." Thus, in the spring of 1984, Russell staged *The Italian Woman in Algiers* for the Geneva Opera in Switzerland. In *Lisztomania*, he had portrayed the Italian composer as a corpulent buffoon. Perhaps with these comic memories, Russell decided to base Rossini's work on *Lost in a Harem*—a Hollywood opus dating from 1944 and starring Bud Abbott and Lou Costello.

That same year, Russell had already slouched back toward the Movieland Mammon, shocking and stroking viewers across America with his second Hollywood feature, *Crimes of Passion*. But he still had time for Puccini with a scandalous *La Bohéme* for Italy's Macerata Festival. Here, Puccini's character Mimi is transformed from a Paris naïf who sells flowers into a druggie. In Act 4, set in what was present-day 1984, she succumbs to a heroin overdose; her friends come to pay their respects clad in leather jackets, some strumming on electric guitars.

One scene required artificial snow, so Russell and his team ran about to stores, buying up supplies of the canned Christmas tree variety. He sprayed almost every prop he could find with Yuletide whiteness. However, many of the Italians saw red. The Milan newspaper *Il Giornale* declared Russell an "undesirable, to be accompanied politely but firmly to the border." The article then compared Russell's transmogrified version to "inviting a Ugandan or a Norwegian to make pizzas in Naples."

Russell was having such a good time with these experiments that he shrugged off any enemies he might have made along the way. "I admire opera singers," he declared in 1983, "because they're doing such a stylized thing. They're trying to be realistic while doing a stylized work of art, which is so bizarre! Operatic acting goes against credulity, but it transcends reality and goes to a super-reality—a surrealism, a super-consciousness. And that's what excites me about opera."

∎

In 1985, Russell complemented the demigods and monsters in his upcoming feature *Gothic* with a production of Charles Gounod's *Faust*. Staged at the Vienna State Opera with Erich Binder conducting the Wiener Staatsoper Orchestra and Choir, Russell's treatment seemed relatively tame. It still has some of Russell's trademark touches: devils, damnation, redemption, and the choreography of raving nuns. There is also some gasp-inducing satire and sacrilege: Mephistopheles sings beside a giant Golden Calf that has slot machine reels for eyes; he later urinates into a font of holy water.

The opera opens with Faust (Francisco Araiza) alone in his study, immersed in his books and feeling futile. Russell gives a nod to Fritz Lang's *Metropolis* and James Whale's *Frankenstein* as Faust gets a coffin delivered to him, has a dead woman's body placed on a table, and then reanimates her with an electrical apparatus that descends from his laboratory ceiling. Recharged, she writhes like the chrysalis that opens *Mahler* but soon dies again, leaving Faust even more depressed, suicidal, and vulnerable enough for Mephistopheles' temptation to sell his soul in exchange for renewed youth.

Russell adds a detail to instigate more conflict into the story's romance. In the first two acts, Marguerite (Gabriela Beňačková), whom Mephistopheles (Ruggero Raimondi) conjures to tempt Faust, is a nun. Here, she gets skittish toward Faust's initial flirtations out of religious duty as well as girlish pride. The opera comes full circle as Marguerite, dishonored and condemned, faces the guillotine. The blade descends on her neck, her soul ascends to heaven, and her headless corpse rises from her coffin, pointing the condemnatory finger at Faust as Mephistopheles whisks him to the underworld.

●

By this time, Russell was also celebrating his love for surrealistic settings in the music video, a form he came into relatively late, considering he was its progenitor. One of his first was his 1985 promo for Elton John's hit "Nikita," where he continued his surrealistic visions of the glasnost era. Though the Russians usually consider Nikita a boy's name, Russell had to consider mainstream MTV tastes and made Elton's love object a girl, albeit a very androgynous Soviet soldier. While Elton sits in a swanky red convertible taking snapshots of her, the boyish Bolshevik stands on the Russian border, glancing back with steely eyes that read, "Nyet!"

But "Nikita" was one of Russell's less inspiring contributions to MTV aesthetics. His treatment of Elton's 1985 hit "Cry to Heaven" had more operatic pizzazz, and used his baby son Rupert, who was just learning to walk. "I saw an allegory of the troubles in Northern Ireland and how the innocent are always the victims," he recounts. "Accordingly, I showed how a toddler . . . attracted by flashing lights, colorful machines, noise and clamor, runs onto a busy building site thinking it's all a game and wanting to join in. His black beret lying in the gutter says it all. That too was censored by the BBC. When the record companies saw what was happening, they dropped me like a hot condom."

But Russell had better luck and seems to have been more inspired when exploring a pop video with a distinctively gothic look. And it was also based on an opera of sorts: Andrew Lloyd Webber's *The Phantom of the Opera*.

In 1984, Webber, along with producer Cameron Mackintosh, started hammering out a musical interpretation of Gaston Leroux's famous novel about the deformed and masked man who haunts the Paris opera house. He was about to marry singer Sarah Brightman, who was all set to play the heroine Christine. Staging preliminary vignettes at his estate at Sydmonton, Webber went through various lyricists and focused more and more on turning his operatic musical into a serious gothic romance.

By July 1986, they had Act 2 ready but still needed to get the entire production prepared before its scheduled West End premiere in October. Webber wanted the music to stress rock 'n' roll roots and agreed that a pop single would be the best promotional vehicle. Steve Harley, famous for his 1970s glam band Cockney Rebel and the original Phantom choice before Michael Crawford came along, joined Brightman in a duet on the main theme, "The Phantom of the Opera," which songwriter and producer Mike Batt set to an electro-pop beat and heavy metal guitars.

The record was a U.K. success. But Webber needed a video promo to really get audiences enthused about the upcoming musical. He put aside previous casting disputes he had with Russell over an *Evita* movie and got him to pile on garishly gothic settings, raging actors, and carefully placed snakes.

Brightman's eyes are wild and wide; her soprano hits frantic highs as she sneaks from her dressing room into the opera house's catacombs. As she rides a boat with a skull on its prow through a dry ice canal, the Phantom, draped in a vibrant red cape and in a mask gilded with golden curls, draws her into his lair by waving his arms and shaking his fist like a spastic silent movie star.

Soon Brightman, clad as Queen Cleopatra from the Near East, trills and thrusts out her arms in postures reminiscent of both Zita Johann as the Egyptian Princess whom Boris Karloff tries to sacrifice in Karl Freund's *The Mummy* (1932) and Dorothy Comingore as Susan Alexander during her screeching stage crescendo in *Citizen Kane*. Brightman turns into a caterwauling siren on the final notes, helpless as the Phantom—in an eerie

Sarah Brightman duets with Steve Harley from Russell's 1986 pop promo video for Andrew Lloyd Webber's *The Phantom of the Opera*.

silhouette—cuts down the chandelier that drops onto her starry-eyed boyfriend in the audience.

Russell did a couple of other less notable *Phantom* videos—one of Brightman walking along a graveyard while singing "Wishing You Were Somehow Here Again," and another duet, this time with Brightman and Cliff Richard on "All I Ask of You." But the Brightman-Harley duet, which took only a week to shoot, packs in the gist of the musical's message and story in just over four minutes.

Taking his operatic fervor from video to celluloid, Russell accepted the invitation to contribute a segment to the 1987 anthology film *Aria*—ten cinematic interpretations from notables including Robert Altman, Jean-Luc Godard, Derek Jarman, Franc Roddam, Nicolas Roeg, and Julian Temple. Much of the impetus came from producer Don Boyd, who wanted each director to avoid sticking to the traditional characters and just let the music inspire new stories. Boyd gave each fifty thousand British pounds, handed out copies of the RCA music catalog, and left the rest to the creators' whims.

Still troubled over the death of a friend, who had helped him with *Madama Butterfly,* in a car crash, Russell used the tragedy to illustrate Puccini's "Nessun Dorma" ("None Shall Sleep") from *Turandot.* In this nine-minute excursion, a female crash victim (Linzi Drew) languishes between two worlds: one, a dream in which ancient priests adorn her with diamonds and paint her body; another, where paramedics try reviving her while a sinister surgeon glares from behind his mask.

Dying goddess (Linzi Drew) from Russell's "Nessun Dorma" segment in *Aria.*

Meanwhile, a handsome, blond Prince Charming (Andreas Wisniewski) alternates between being her boyfriend and a paramedic as he tries bringing her back to consciousness with a kiss.

On "Nessun Dorma," Russell's visual influences are more Kenneth Anger than ever before, with the focus on mystical jewelry and cultic ritual reminiscent of such Anger works as *Invocation of My Demon Brother. Aria* got a mixed critical reception, but some admitted that Russell's was the best of the lot, including *Time*'s Richard Corliss: "Emotionally, it takes preposterous risks and pulls them off."

•

Mephistopheles reemerged in 1989 with a production of Arrigo Boito's *Il Mefistofele*, an olio of traditional Italian opera with a Wagner thrust. This time, Russell recast Faust as an old hippie with a yen for smoking pot. It is another story of good and evil, only now the serpent tempting Adam and Eve takes the form of a vacuum cleaner hose. As he did with the otherworldly pinball championship in *Tommy*, costume designer and scenarist Paul Dufficey transforms Russell's whims into the third dimension. He fashions a stage where a television set appears throughout as an inaudible chorus. There is also another of Russell's obligatory crucifixions, along with Nazis that toss nuns into flames to fuel Mephistopheles's rocket ship.

In writings and in conversations, Russell could extol the virtues of fine champagne, cascades of Chianti, lager and limes, caviar and cakes, creamed teas, and ribbons of fettuccine Alfredo. He was, therefore, in his element when turning Marguerite's prison into a modern Italian kitchen. The prisoner becomes a modern housewife who irons away to daytime television, dreaming of an escape from connubial servitude.

Russell boasts in his autobiography of his previous operas causing "a scandal in Vienna, fistfights in Spoleto, and riots in Macerata." Now, the Italian authorities devised more fail-safe plans when the Grand Opera of Genoa hired armed riot squads to stand at the theater entrance to fend off any potential maniacs. But some of the testier moments occurred in the early phases of the production, when an irate conductor stormed out of rehearsals, offended at the thought of conducting "Faust and Helen singing their love duet over a bowl of pasta."

Russell recalls another harrowing time with this reinterpretation: "And when Marguerite's mother was found cut up in cling film in the refrigerator and her drowned baby seen going round and round in the washing machine, it was time for tear gas. I was lucky to leave the theater uninjured, but needed a police motorcycle escort to take me to the reception afterwards. From then on, until the heat was off, I was accompanied everywhere in public by two plainclothes men from Rome."

Despite Russell's fondness for swastikas and his fixation on Donald Duck and Mickey Mouse, Genoa basked in the attention that their Fellini of the north was giving them. Russell received a medal, a painting, and plates of homemade macaroni from a gracious tenor. "Record shops gave me records," he recalls, "people bought me drinks in cafes, and in the streets passers-by either stopped me for my autograph or spat on me."

Russell was forthright with the *New York Times* in 1983 when asked if opera was his calling:

> For five years I bumbled around being a dancer, but I wasn't any good at it. Then I bumbled around for only one year, thank God, at trying to be an actor. I bumbled around being a photographer, but I used that to become a cinematographer. Then I bumbled around for twenty years making films. I feel I'm still serving my apprenticeship . . . You see, I feel that I'm not a totally free agent—that my life was planned out—that I was meant to do all the things I've done, to antagonize people, to make some people happy and others unhappy. It's fate! Besides, after all those miserable years making films, it's time for a bit of fun, and directing opera is a lot of fun. It's what I've always wanted to do, but didn't know it!

THE DECO DILDO

In the early 1980s, Barry Sandler gained fame as the screenwriter for *Making Love*, a tale of romance between two men that, for Hollywood, was world shattering. Along with his lover at the time, A. Scott Berg, Sandler constructed the story from personal frustrations, nauseated by the abysmal homosexual roles—usually suicides or psychopaths—that the studios previously conjured.

"Are we going to threaten people? Frighten people? We wanted to get attractive people who had decent jobs," Sandler reflects from his office at the University of Central Florida, where he now teaches film studies. "I felt bad growing up with all these negative images, with gays as the butts of jokes and movies like *Advise and Consent*, which presented an ugly vision of gay people. I was just turning thirty, reevaluating my career; I had to write a movie that gay people could look at with a positive image."

Making Love's three main characters were physically attractive, had charm and discretionary income, lived in the lofty parts of L.A., and rarely had a hair out of place. There's even a happy ending. The two gay men Zach (Michael Ontkean) and Bart (Harry Hamlin) separate, but Zach finds a live-in boyfriend; his alienated wife Claire (Kate Jackson) ends up a good sport, with an enlightened attitude and a new man as well. There's also a likable, zany old lady friend (Wendy Hiller) who reads Rupert Brooke poems aloud .

Other than an ominous scene when Harry Hamlin's character goes into his refrigerator to swallow (what appears to be) an antibiotic before a night on the town, *Making Love* exuded a mood of libidinous innocence. Its plot crested on the then-prevalent assumption that with money, material success, and sexual preferences out in the open, gay people too could partake in America's cuddly suburban dream. In short, Sandler wanted to play nice with the mainstream.

Making Love did reasonably well at the box office when it premiered in the winter of 1982 and eluded the violent backlash so many hand-wringers advising him against making it had predicted. Still, Sandler found that much of the world wasn't playing nice in return. He recalls the groans that straight audiences made during test market screenings. Matters got worse.

Before the film's release, the national news already sounded out health alarms, and ultra-conservative god-pods proclaimed through satellite networks that the "gay plague" was the Almighty's retribution. *Making Love* arrived in theaters just at the cusp between a hopeful world and this new nightmare world. So, no more nice guy! Sandler opted for some "fuck you" therapy and wrote the screenplay for *Crimes of Passion*.

●

Ken Russell, meanwhile, was in an utter funk. He'd just walked out from a deal to direct Andrew Lloyd Webber's *Evita* because he didn't like the star that producer Robert Stigwood insisted on using. On his way back to England from L.A., he sat pouting on the plane but tried amusing himself by perusing some scripts that agent Robert Littman had handed to him a few hours before. By the time he debarked at Heathrow, he knew that *Crimes of Passion* was also essential therapy.

For Russell, Sandler's story of Joanna Crane (Kathleen Turner), an emotionally scarred and frigid sportswear designer by day who leads a double life as a $50 hooker named China Blue by night, was just a lacy lure. The meat of the movie was the Reverend Peter Shayne (Anthony Perkins): a dirty, sweaty, sexually obsessed Bible thumper who pursues China Blue with warnings about the wages of sin yet clamors for her carnal communion. He also has the foulest mouth in town and looks especially menacing when wielding a sex toy that resembles a hybrid of vibrator, shark, and missile.

For Russell, *Crimes of Passion* didn't cover new ground—nothing could out-devil *The Devils*—but it allowed him to ply his obsessions against a new social backdrop: the Reagan-Thatcher years and the rise of televangelists like Jerry Falwell and Jimmy Swaggart.

To counterbalance the Reverend and the Whore, Sandler's script also has a third party: an Everyman named Bobby Grady (John Laughlin). This all-around nice guy and former varsity football champ is also in a rut. He has *Making Love*'s suburban dream house, but the paradise on the installment plan he hoped would be his electronic surveillance business cannot pay the bills. Worse, his wife doesn't stop nagging him.

Grady starts moonlighting as a private detective, working for Joanna Crane's boss to see if she's been selling company patents to a competitor. But when Grady

THE DECO DILDO

gets mixed up with Crane and her China Blue alter ego, the Reverend Shayne isn't far behind. From there, the story bumps between these three desperate souls: their "normal" and "deviant" paths collide and, at least with the movie's original ending, converge in a kind of purgatory.

•

Russell relished this dark-side-of-paradise approach. When he took on Sandler's script, he might have also retained William Blake's notorious aphorism about John Milton writing the epic poem *Paradise Lost* not to justify God's ways but "because he was a true poet and of the devil's party without knowing it." For Blake, God proved a bore full of stilted sermons, whereas the devil—Lucifer, the light-giver—offered true salvation with unfettered and sumptuous verbiage.

For Russell and Sandler, the Reverend Shayne embodies both extremes. He pretends to speak for Jehovah, but his thoughts are so twisted that they imply a paradoxical path to wisdom. His lines are the movie's funniest, filthiest, and most foresighted. He pleads on a street corner: "How long Lord? Shalt thou be angry forever? Shall they jealously burn like fire? Shall we keep on fucking and pissing in each other's faces?" He speaks into China Blue's soul: "Behold this wicked woman; she falls, she mends, she crawls, she bends; she sucks it, fucks it, picks it up, and licks it; you can whip her, beat her, maul her, mistreat her; anything you want, as long as you don't touch her."

Anthony Perkins brought some of his own demons—or at least some inventive pluck—into the picture. In his early fifties, he allayed a midlife crisis with a bit of a comeback, reprising his Norman Bates role in the 1983 film *Psycho II*. Still, he was desperate to restore his reputation for intelligent acting, even if this meant out-nutting the nuts he'd already played. Perkins loved the Reverend Shayne. Each day at the close of shooting, he kept Shayne's sweaty clothes and Nikes on; he slept in them to bask in his character's fetor of faith.

In Sandler's initial plans, Shayne was to be a psychiatrist. But Perkins had just finished playing the psychiatrist Dr. Dysart in the Broadway production of *Equus* and felt more challenged portraying a preacher of the "Moral Majority" ilk. Russell knew the role was the actor's calling and allowed him to add quirks. Perkins got the idea to sniff real amyl nitrate as Shayne ogles a beat-up naked dancer in a peepshow. He also designed the elaborate shrine to China Blue that includes a picture of Christ in a blond wig and other paraphernalia indistinguishable from Russell's lapsed Catholic phantasms.

•

Despite the story's lurid and depressing outlook, *Crimes of Passion* was one of Russell's happier directing experiences. After the Chayefsky debacle, he was relieved to work with a screenwriter he did not have to continually confront, someone he could even like. Perkins and most of the cast also got through the production relatively bruise free. The ambiance on the set was mostly sanguine; the principal actors also agreed to take less than their usual salaries.

First impressions might suggest that Russell chose Turner for his star trollop because of her sultry presence in *Body Heat*. But her comedic talents alongside Steve Martin in *The Man with Two Brains* did the trick for him. Watching China Blue change her accent from that of a Brooklyn sharpie to a Southern bimbo, or sitting on a gynecologist's chair pretending she is "Miss Liberty" while a john worships her, no one can say that Turner wasn't willing to take chances and milk laughs.

Turner had her limits, however. In a scene when a john climaxes, she has to simulate the look of spunk mixing with her blood-red lipstick. Russell gave her a choice: banana or lemon flavored yogurt; she chose the lemon. But according to Russell, "I remember when I said, 'You need to give a good, hearty swallow: would you like mussels or winkles?' she slapped my face."

Sandler commends Turner for taking such a dirty part: "And here Turner was in *Romancing the Stone*, this total sweetheart, and she does this 180-degree turn. She believed in the film enough and was willing to waive a clause in her contract that said she could go no further than an R rating."

Russell has a more jaundiced view, claiming that once Turner garnered so much success during her *Romancing the Stone* promotional tour, she started getting the shivers over what stains China Blue might leave on her resume. He remembers having to sweet-talk her constantly over the phone: "Anyway, that's what I firmly believed until I heard a rumor that she had already signed a contract, and the production company threatened to sue the pants off her if she reneged on the deal."

Turner also told Russell that she had qualms about what she read as the script's anti-American slant. "But I talked her out of that one with an extremely passionate pro-American speech,"

China Blue (Kathleen Turner) with "Superman."

Russell discloses, "which gave me no trouble at all as I meant every word of it. For, believe it or not, but for the heavenly intervention of Hollywood, I would never have had a feature film career. No, I've precious little to thank the Brit film industry for. However, in the event, I lied. *Crimes of Passion* is an extremely anti-American film."

Any disagreements between director and actors were, considering Russell's past politics, mere verbal bagatelles. And when Turner and Perkins unite on the screen, their rapid fire, harlot versus holier-than-thou brawls are obviously Russell's favorite moments. Russell, who doesn't like to over-rehearse, was tickled to see the actors expectorate Sandler's simultaneously raunchy and witty lines.

> Shayne: Do you recognize me, child?
> China Blue: Sorry, I never forget a face, especially when I've sat on it.

> Shayne: Save your soul, whore.
> China Blue: Save your money, shit-head.

> China Blue: I make a great Joan of Arc, can't you tell?
> Shayne: I imagine you do spend a good deal of time on your knees, my child.

> China Blue: I'm healthy as a horse; I'm fit as a fiddle and ready for cock.
> Shayne: Whores and metaphors don't mix.

> Shayne: You're the head of your class, or is it the class of your head.
> China Blue: Oh, a man of words: he makes up in diction what he lacks in dick.

But amid their badinage, one unadorned exchange resonates more than any other:

> China Blue: Who are you? You're not a reverend. Who are you?
> Shayne: I'm you!

■

Russell's longtime cinematographer Dick Bush does a commendable job probing *Crimes of Passion*'s troubled interiors. He drenches China Blue's cum-stained flophouse, appropriately called Paradise Isle, in purple excess: floral wallpaper against neon lights flashing outside the window. China trammels the pavements, sashaying in a silky blue dress that Russell and a costume consultant chose from a Sears Roebuck catalog. In contrast, when China changes into Joanna, Bush complements her tastefully sterile mansion, which Shayne later refers to as "Paradise Lost," with a chilly blue light. The photography is especially jarring in a scene when Joanna lies under icy-colored sheets during another sleepless night.

When the story makes repeated shifts to Grady's suburban Hades, Bush opts for an overly lit setting but with colors that are mellow and wholesome. The film starts out with Grady (John Laughlin) in a therapy session, at the suggestion of his pal Donny Hopper (Bruce Davison). He initially insists there's nothing wrong with him or his marriage. But when a cynical woman insists he's probably "a lousy lay," she ignites a tirade: "I'm not the one who complains how tired I am every night. Getting her to make love is like asking her to run the Boston Marathon, and then those times that we actually do go through with it, I don't know whether to embrace her or embalm her!"

A few seconds with Grady's wife Amy (Annie Potts) explain his frustration. In its final form, the movie portrays her as a wet blanket who can only badger and brood. Husband and wife engage in 1980s-style talk of hot tubs, Cuisinarts, and video recorders that cost $1,000. But Amy recoils at one of their backyard barbecues when Bobby tries to impress his Bud-guzzling buddies by performing "the Old H.P."—a pantomime of a human penis that Sandler remembers as a ritual from his frat house college days.

To the swelling movement of Strauss's "Also Spoke Zarathustra," Grady, with medicine balls attached to his feet and topped with a shower cap, slowly pushes his muscular body upward until, at Strauss's crescendo, he's fully upright and spewing milk. His wife is so disgusted that Grady has only to look at her otherwise enigmatic facial expression when they're in bed later that evening to know she doesn't love him anymore.

Bobby Grady (John Laughlin) as a human penis at a backyard barbecue.

Sandler wanted to round out Amy's character more by adding a scene in which she confides with a friend about how she wants to reach out to her husband and face her own problems. Russell, more interested in keeping the plot's pace, insisted on deleting it. Much of this was also a result of Russell's personal tastes.

"Ken had an aversion to shooting the scenes with Grady and Amy," Sandler remembers. "He had the passion with China Blue and Shayne. He shined when he did those scenes; they were his favorite. He adored Tony. Those were the money scenes. He didn't feel comfortable with the American idiom. He didn't have a great fondness for American suburban life. Those scenes went, but that deleted scene gives Amy more sympathy; she's more conflicted, she feels guiltier, she's torn and doesn't know what to do."

●

The musically canny Russell contrasts hell in the suburbs with hell in the whorehouse through Rick Wakeman's synth rock variations on Antonín Dvořák's "New World Symphony." This was intended partly as a pun on New World, the company that released the film (and gave Russell subsequent headaches), and also a reference to the story's deflation of the middle class American dream. A wistful little melody accompanies Amy's pouts, a steamy saxophone stalks China as she strolls down her red-light district, and a little piccolo whistles for the skin flute variations.

Except for the narrative's frequent trips into Grady's suburbs, *Crimes of Passion*'s style has the rollercoaster velocity of a music video. And to remind the world that MTV derived much of its high-octane, music-image fusion from him, Russell slipped his own rock video—a movie within a movie—about the banalities of married life.

Russell already filmed an erotic mixture of music and image on a tribute to Gustav Holst's *The Planets* a year earlier. Along with Eugene Ormandy and the Philadelphia Orchestra, this fifty-minute non-verbal experiment he did for London Weekend Television provides often bold, funny, and graphic interpretations. Mars (Bringer of War) is Hitler; Venus (Bringer of Peace) shows up as a visual pun with an attractive and naked beach bather. Russell could only go so far, however. He had to answer to Holst's daughter Imogen: "I couldn't show fingers playing the piano, or concentration camps for Mars or sex for Venus." Still, Julian Barnes sniffed in the *London Observer*: "The only obvious thing Russell spared us in his 'Planets' was a visual joke about looking up at Uranus."

Back in England, Russell shot the *Crimes of Passion* video vignette with his daughters: Victoria as the bride and Molly the bridesmaid. The groom is some young man who happened to be Victoria's sweetheart at the time. And Rick Wakeman also flashes in as a black-cloaked wedding photographer. For this surrealistic excursion into connubial follies, Russell employs loud guitars and

Maggie Bell screaming out the lyrics to Wakeman's song, "It's a Lovely Life," another rocked-out variation on Dvořák's "New World Symphony."

The handsome yuppie newlyweds in the video celebrate their suburban dream. But when their silver set falls into their chlorinated pool, they dive in—wedding clothes and all—to retrieve the precious spoons and forks. The little bridesmaid meanwhile cries about the doves that also fell over and drowned in their gilded cage. The wet newlyweds, shivering on chaise lounges, morph into skeletons that, like the Gradys, are transfixed by the tube.

Victoria Russell as a barren bride in the *Crimes of Passion* music video segment.

•

As life with the wife seems more and more like a day of the dead, Grady's growing infatuation with Joanna Crane poses other problems when he tries to crack her icy exterior. But when he assures her they can reach that beautiful commingling they had in their first encounter, he seems to forget that those moments of bliss had a price tag: he was paying China Blue to impersonate an airline stewardess for "Flight 69 non-stop service to Paradise." Russell, eager to evade an X rating, avoids male frontal nudity. Instead, he and Sandler suggest the contours and heft of Grady's groin guppy by focusing on his feet. China slowly unravels his athletic socks before sucking on his big toe—a moment that Russell hails on his DVD commentary as "quite erotic." It's a cinematic benchmark (movies usually portray gals as podosexual recipients) that the foot-friendly Russell would have gotten around to sooner. But Sandler says, "I'm pretty sure I came up with it."

However, for the scene when Grady sleeps with the real Joanna for the first time, Sandler wanted the sex to go unfulfilled, figuring Joanna would still be too frigid and scared. But Russell, wanting again to move the story along, stuck in a happier alternative: a slo-mo interlude of their bodies caressing and faces smiling under glossy sheets to Wakeman's sickly variation on smooth jazz. It's Russell's "shampoo commercial" syndrome, but this time around the irony seems absent. Instead of existential angst, Russell captures what could pass as a television ad for a Barbara Cartland novel.

THE DECO DILDO

While Sandler and Russell enjoyed a relatively skid-free relationship, they had disagreements. Sandler's original script had Shayne reflecting on his days as a shoe salesman. But Russell didn't want too much of a distracting back story. When they got around to their sneak preview in San Francisco in the summer of 1984, Russell snipped out a humanizing section when a cancer victim's wife hires China Blue to give her husband what she cannot. As China enters his bedroom, she tries various sexy scenarios, but he looks through her as if already glimpsing the white light. At this juncture, she removes her wig and stops pretending. Russell thought it was too sentimental, but he agreed to put it back in with the official theatrical release.

There was also at least one time when Sandler was at the receiving end of a Russell prank. In a creative fit, Perkins, maybe remembering Sydney Greenstreet's menacing role as Count Fosco in *The Woman in White*, thought that the Reverend Shayne would look scarier with a monkey on his shoulder. Perkins approached Russell with the idea; he liked it immediately, but Sandler didn't: "I thought it would turn Shayne into a total buffoon. They saw how heated up I got; and the more heated up I got, the more they teased me. The next day Ken talked to the prop guy; they brought a trained monkey on the set and had Tony walk around with it on his shoulder, just as I'd feared."

There is one object that crops up in the film that would have upstaged Perkins's monkey, anyway. The film's bouncy moods between comedy and melancholia veer more into actual horror when China Blue looks into Reverend Shayne's leather bag to discover an array of "devil's playthings": "a tit pacifier," "a foam rubber pretty kitty," "an auto-suck," and "a beat-me eat-me licorice whip." But when she retrieves Shayne's silver dildo with its Art Deco contours, she asks, "Is this a cruise missile or a Pershing?" Shayne just calls it "Superman" and, in another fantasy, demonstrates its power by plunging it into an inflatable sex doll he imagines is the naked dancer he'd been ogling.

According to Sandler: "In the script that 'Pershing missile' dildo was actually a miniature statue of Superman that Shayne used as a murder weapon (or threatened to use), which Ken loved—for the irony. But the legal department of the studio told us Warner Bros. and DC Comics would not allow us to use it, and would sue us if we did (gee, I wonder why). Ken and I discussed alternatives, and we came up with the idea of a metal dildo (I'm pretty sure it was Ken's idea, sounds like it would be), and I integrated it into the script and dialogue."

Joanna's new stainless steel suitor threatens her through the rest of the film as the reverend prepares for the final reckoning. Since she dwells in a terribly tasteful home gilded in high-toned pornography, Joanna can only expect to die for art as Shayne breaks into her sanctuary and ties her—Crucifixion fashion—over her drafting table. To sanction his ritual, he swings over to her alabaster piano to yell some lines from the Ted Koehler–Richard Arlen favorite, "Get Happy." Then, as Wakeman's score goes ominous, Shayne approaches Joanna with his Pershing plunger, his vibrating conger, his pocket rocket with the razor's edge.

∎

One of the most wrenching and essential scenes— excised from the theatrical release—occurs when China Blue meets up with a man (Randall Brady) who is either rough trade or a real cop. After she handcuffs him to her bedpost, she rides on top of him as Russell's jerk-off zoom intercuts close-ups of her stiletto heels grinding into his bleeding legs with almost subliminal photos of police cracking down on

The Reverend Shayne (Anthony Perkins) as his China Blue alter ego in Russell's salute to *Psycho*.

1960s rioters. She gnashes his nightstick against his hot and hunky torso as he screams in agonized ecstasy. But this is merely a tease to the filet mignon moment, when she fulfills his ultimate desire by thrusting the truncheon in and out of what Russell likes to call the arse.

These moments are grisly, potentially arousing, and important for establishing an extreme juncture when Joanne realizes she's gone too far and should seriously think about putting her hooker costume in moth balls, especially after the spent cop spits in her face as she unshackles him. But such scenes put *Crimes of Passion* in postproduction duress. Once again, Russell watched his work getting sliced and diced and could do little about it. Sandler recalls the conservative backlash vividly: "*Crimes* was at the height of the Reagan era; the election year; we had the Meese Commission on pornography, which also made New World scared and anxious to cut. It made major stories in the *L.A. Times*. Every time we made a cut, there would be a story. Word had gotten out about how we had to cut the film to avoid an X rating; Ken was demoralized by it. Ken would do a little cutting, and it would still come back with an X."

THE DECO DILDO

During *Crimes of Passion*'s San Francisco sneak preview, Russell and Sandler squirmed at the boos and the hisses. Most of the protests were over the ending. As originally conceived, Grady heroically barges into a screaming Joanna's home. What he thinks he sees is the Reverend Shayne jumping out from the shadows to plunge his Deco Dildo into China Blue's back. But on a second look, the Reverend and the Whore have exchanged clothes. With a nod to Perkins' *Psycho* climax, the reverend's wig falls off, he falls into Joanna's arms, looks up at her, and says, "Thank you, China Blue." The camera flashes on all three characters, especially Grady's utterly perplexed expression, and ends right there.

Concerned about marketing, Russell and Sandler caved into viewer requests. Those (this author included) who caught the screening got to fill out an exit questionnaire. Unfortunately, the majority wanted an ending that explains what happens to the two male and female principals: a witless Frank Capra closure. So, Russell agreed with the New World brass to end where the film begins. Grady is back in therapy, now crowing about how he left his wife but found paradise with Joanna. They still have their problems, but they'd talked matters out, went home, and "fucked our brains out."

With this flaccid coda, viewers are only allowed to imagine their sloppy sessions between the prison bars. Joanna just killed a man, and by the way the murder is staged, it doesn't look like self-defense. Worse, with the reverend now out of the picture as the darkly moral compass, the story has no reason to continue. Like the confectionary ending in *Altered States* (over which Russell had no control) this also leaves discerning viewers with a sense of being ripped off.

Crimes of Passion is a great example of when any kind of focus group, or just a bunch of sample question cards, can falsify a movie that sets out to expose lies. Perhaps one day, Russell and Sandler will decide to release a copy closer to the sneak preview version—one that's not afraid to raise questions without resorting to patchwork answers. Because of all the changes both self-inflicted and imposed, including various versions on the video release, this is the Russell film with the least definitive version.

Compromises and all, *Crimes of Passion* was still strong enough to let most viewers know it wasn't meant to be a "feel good" film. And it had some sympathetic critics. David Edelstein, writing for the *Village Voice*, appreciated the "pent-up aggression against the opposite sex" that China Blue and Reverend Shayne show toward one another. Rex Reed wrote, "It's not a great film and sometimes even a mess. But I haven't been able to shake it off. As a frank and scalding exposé of the dark side of human nature, *Crimes of Passion* is unlike anything I've experienced."

•

Following problems with the MPAA, New World Pictures had a personnel shakeup. The company's new blood got iffy about the film's controversy. But Russell had dealt with bureaucrats and prudes before; he wasn't about to let such matters spoil his upbeat mood. Right after shooting, he and Vivian finally wed. The Reverend Shayne was now Minister Perkins, able to officiate after sending an application and a $10 bill to the Universal Life Church for some sort of diploma. On board the *Queen Mary*, which was still parked in Long Beach, Ken and Vivian stood before Perkins as he read passages from Thomas Hardy and William Wordsworth. The wedding reception also doubled as a cast and crew closing party, with a shellac Vaughan Williams record crackling in the background.

But all was not a happy marriage. Russell accepted a lower director's fee than usual, precisely because he invested in a share of the video market, which he predicted would be salable. "New World read my contract one way and I read it another," Russell remembers. "So I ended up with next to nothing—till I sued them. But by the time legal costs had been deducted and my agent had taken his cut it wasn't worth the aggro."

Through the years, as viewers watched it in repertory screenings, on video, and on cable television, *Crimes of Passion* elicited a bit of a cult. As recently as the summer of 2005, it inspired a troupe to do a stage version of the screenplay for Scotland's Edinburgh Festival Fringe.

Some walk away from this coarse, impish, and brutal movie aroused; others swear they'll never have sex again. The squeamish, however, cannot say they weren't warned from the start. The same anonymous woman at the film's opening therapy session, who accuses Bobby Grady of being a bedroom dud, reveals her own thwarted desires: "I'd rather get fucked by a vibrator than your cock any day. It's honest, loving, and I don't have to make breakfast for it in the morning."

PROMETHEUS UNGAGGED

A s the director who filmed Richard Chamberlain's fine features
blistering from cholera in *The Music
Lovers* and Oliver Reed's mug broil-
ing to a crisp in *The Devils*, Russell

> "Is there no escape from this madhouse?"
>
> —Dr. John William Polidori in *Gothic*

conveyed the face of horror as well as, if not better than, some of the cinema's
most renowned gore grinders. But there is one moment in Russell's work that
is perhaps among the most nightmarish of all—and in a project where viewers
would least expect it: his April 2, 1988, *South Bank Show* presentation, *Ken Russell's ABC of British Music.*

In what is otherwise an informative, giddy, and opinionated survey of British songwriters, conductors, and performers, Russell enters unsightly territory
as he sits in the box seat of a makeshift opera house. He pretends to watch a production of Benjamin Britten's *Death in Venice* but apparently doesn't approve
of the show and uses it instead as a salvo against both Britten and the British
critics. Without warning, makeup, or CGI effects, Russell shape-shifts into one
of those ogre-ish conservatives he usually derides.

Looking straight into the camera, he pontificates: "Benjamin Britten's operas
are held in high critical esteem here too, but are not so highly thought of abroad,
where audiences are less enthusiastic about child abuse, gay May queens, and
aging pederasts." But being a trickster, he offers subtle assurance that he hasn't
really been cloned into that high priestess of prudery, Mary Whitehouse. With
Freudian finesse, he seems to soften his homo-hostile barb by savoring a cham-
pagne-dipped French fry.

With his previous mock-up of Visconti's *Death in Venice* in *Mahler*, Russell
already seemed conflicted about Mann's tale of an older man with a yen for

a teenage boy. Perhaps it triggered memories of his movie-house molester or the unsalted sea captain who made him feel like a teenage tart. So Russell gets seasick about intergenerational trysts, but why the snit over "gay May queens"? Several of the gay actors, costume designers, set designers, and screenwriters he's worked with would likely shrug their shoulders at this question and attest to his gay-friendliness.

Raymond Murray, in his book *Images in the Dark*, goes further: "Despite being 'straight,' Ken Russell has more gay sensibility evident in his movies than most gay filmmakers, even if the images are not always 'politically correct' . . . Russell is also known for consistently working with gay writers, actors and set designers. With so much gayness running through his cinematic veins, it is no surprise that many think of him as being gay." Judging by the disturbing way he often depicts male-female relations, Russell is not "homophobic": he's just phobic.

Russell also has fun with appearing sexually ambiguous, writing anecdotes about how various people, undeterred by his wives and kids, either assume he's gay or a "latent homosexual." The stodgy bluenose perched on that phony opera box is not the same man who once chided the film *Yanks*—and particularly its director John Schlesinger—for not yanking its main soldier character out of the closet: "There's not a limp wrist in sight nor a single hard-on in the shower room. The entire male cast is heterosexual to a man, yet, according to some statistics, one GI in ten on active service was gay. All we get is a series of conventional love affairs. It would have been so much more exciting to see Richard Gere larking about on the moors with a member of the Home Guard."

█

Russell's next two features—*Gothic* and *Salome's Last Dance*—make *Death in Venice* (which has neither outright sex nor child abuse) radiate lily-white purity. They also prove to be the two best films from Russell's later period as they pursue verboten themes with an aptly overwrought style. *Gothic* in particular alludes not only to pederasty but also abortion, adultery, blasphemy, incest, self-mutilation, vampirism, and at least one attempted murder. It would also include a man-to-man kiss—tongue and all—between the immortal poets Lord George Gordon Byron and Percy Bysshe Shelley!

Using Stephen Volk's screenplay, Russell fashions *Gothic* with lots of fantasy but enough factual background. It relives a true account of a night that occurred not long after Byron met Percy Bysshe Shelley in Switzerland. In June 1816, Percy (Julian Sands), Mary Wollstonecraft Godwin (Natasha Richardson), and her half-sister Claire Clairmont (Miriam Cyr) meet at a place that Byron

(Gabriel Byrne) rented called the Villa Deodati. There, Dr. John William Polidori (Timothy Spall), Byron's biographer, personal physician, and (at least here) lover, also resides. Together, they brave a vicious thunderstorm by reading ghost stories about haunted hallways, specter-riddled chambers, and creaky stairs.

Variety called *Gothic* "The thinking man's *Nightmare on Elm Street*." Vincent Canby of the *New York Times* said, "It's as ghoulishly funny and frenzied as a carnival ride through 'The Marquis de Sade's Tunnel of Love.'" In a *New York Times* interview, Julian Sands, who puts in a powerful performance as Percy Shelley, and who previously wooed audiences as the romantic idealist George Emerson in the Merchant-Ivory production *A Room with a View*, also had amusement park rides in mind: "With James Ivory you are on a carousel, but with Ken Russell you are on a rollercoaster."

●

Gothic's pace is hysterical from beginning to end. The opening credits alone summarize the mixture of circus and horror that Russell jumbles so well. Thomas Dolby's melodramatic main theme literally thunders across the soundtrack to a black screen. A skull in the distance grows larger as it nears the camera. One or two critics accused Russell of borrowing from John Carpenter's jack-o-lantern opening in *Halloween*. But Russell seems to have ventured farther back in film history. Just as his Byron will uncover an ancient skull from Newstead Abbey, Russell might just as well have imagined himself unearthing the remains of Wini Shaw from Forest Lawn to re-create a skeletal version of her famous moment in *Gold Diggers of 1935*, when her face slithers out of the darkness toward the camera to sing "Lullaby of Broadway." Busby Berkeley's Hollywood backstage musical starts with a lightweight song and ends in horror when a fascistic-looking mob of hoofers pursues Shaw to the edge of a skyscraper window before she plummets to the concrete. Russell reverses the mood: any resemblance to conventional horror in the credits shifts gears to dark farce.

Nosy nineteenth-century tourists flock across the lake to view Byron's premises, vying for a telescopic peek at the man the salacious tour guide describes (quoting Lady Caroline Lamb) as "Mad, bad, and dangerous to know." From here on, Russell's disorienting style warns anyone expecting a stately literary tale to move on and catch a *Masterpiece Theater* rerun.

Dolby's score of blaring horns and spasmodic strings gets louder and more aggressive as Percy, Mary, and Claire dock at the Lake Leman shore. Like the Beatles in *A Hard Day's Night*, Shelley eludes his screaming fans with slapstick panache, scaling a wall, scurrying through the gardens, and hassling the peacocks on the estate grounds. Mary is already off to a rough start when she slips in mud even before getting to Byron's front door. When he greets them, Byron does nothing to comfort the weary travelers. He instead stands in front of his mammoth portrait to declare, "Then let us live and love, so that people will say the Devil as well as God is an Englishman."

A bit of Byron and Shelley backstory helps the plot along. Byron's life and work has incited speculations about bisexual debauchery. He married Annabella Milbanke in 1915, arguably more out of social propriety than passion, but he was also enamored with his half-sister Augusta Leigh. Tormented with rage, cruel impulses, a habit of sleeping with pistols, and a phobia of watching women eat, Byron was bound to assent to a separation from Milbanke a year later. And "On This Day I Complete My Thirty-Sixth Year," his last poem (written three months before his death), sparked sensation many years later when scholars finally owned up to the fact that it was about his unrequited love for a fifteen-year-old Greek lad.

Like Byron, Shelley delighted in flouting English proprieties. He was also a proud atheist who echoed William Blake's subversive notion that the Satan of Milton's *Paradise Lost* was God's moral better. But he acknowledged that Milton's Devil got too vengeful and grew ugly and cruel as a result. Shelley decided to give Satan a severe makeover: he turned him into the adorable and sexy hero of his 1820 lyrical drama *Prometheus Unbound*. In its preface, Shelley writes, "Prometheus is, as it were, the type of the highest perfection of moral and intellectual nature, impelled by the purest and the truest motives to the best and noblest ends."

Shelley's hubris went unchecked beforehand when, already married to someone else, he took the naive seventeen-year-old Mary off to Geneva to break bread with the man who drank vinegar to keep a chalky complexion and, like Shelley, thrived on the taste and tingle of laudanum: the same liquid opiate that rattled the brains of Russell's other protagonists Elizabeth Siddal and Dorothy Wordsworth.

Byron picks from his library *Fantasmagoriana*, a French translation of German horror tales published around 1812. Mary, Percy, Polidori, and Claire all project their

Percy and Mary Shelley (Julian Sands and Natasha Richardson).

private demons as they read aloud parts of a tale about a monster that Mary Shelley describes in her *Frankenstein* introduction as a "gigantic, shadowy form, clothed like the ghost in *Hamlet*, in complete armor." Shelley sees himself standing by a lake beneath a mangled body dangling from a tree, Polidori imagines the knight riding through the mist as an augury of doom, Mary sees it as an ogre edging closer to her sleeping child William, and Claire (the sybarite of the bunch) can only think of the fiercely endowed knight impaling her.

But *Fantasmagoriana* isn't enough. In the shadow of Horace Walpole's *The Castle of Otranto* and Matthew Gregory Lewis's *The Monk*, the five misfits try to better their predecessors with a ghost-story competition. As the blustering frat boys of flowery Romantic verse, Byron and Shelley think they have the edge. But history proves the meeker Mary Godwin and John Polidori as bigger influences on popular culture. Mary published *Frankenstein* in 1818, while Polidori came out a year later with his short story "The Vampyre," about an ashen yet handsome aristocrat named Lord Ruthven (supposedly based on Byron) who'd inspire Bram Stoker's *Dracula*. *Gothic* is essentially about a night when two previously unknown personalities nurtured the stuff of classic horror films.

●

"I rarely have dreams of death," Ken Russell writes in his autobiography, "but when I do they are usually very gothic affairs lit by flickering candles and steeped in ritual. Generally I am the victim, moving slowly in chains through the shadows towards the scaffold and the inevitable moment of execution, either by axe or noose. It is always night, and I always escape through an exploding maelstrom of fire."

As it seems, Russell tries making peace with his own ghosts by flooding *Gothic* with "old dark house"–style clichés, where faces appear at windows, shadows graze the walls, and ectoplasm floats. With the garish lighting and the hokey props, Russell also pays homage to Hammer Studios.

And of course, he also nods to James Whale, whose 1935 film *Bride of Frankenstein* starts with the same thunderstruck evening that makes up *Gothic*'s entire story. Whale's Douglas Walton plays a much mellower Shelley, Gavin Gordon chomps the scenery with his r-rolling Byron, and Elsa Lanchester is a droll and somewhat twitchy Mary. Whale, like Russell, loaded his film with relentless black humor, Catholic parodies, and a careening camera that barely lets viewers catch their breath. Though she doesn't play Mary, Miriam Cyr's more-than-passing resemblance to Elsa Lanchester is another Whale reminder.

Russell presents their Deodati night as if conducting a trip through a carnival ride, playing the fears for ballyhoo as the apparitions pop out like mechanical monsters in a Spook-a-Rama. Claire sees rats. Byron pines for his half sister Augusta, whose plaster mask he places on his girl servant's face for the illusion that she's still alive. Polidori fears an irate Jehovah swooping down to punish their blasphemy. Shelley sees breasts with eyes and feels stalked by a creature he describes as "trapped like a dream in human form." He is also the first to encounter an incandescent spunk that seeps from Deodati's ceilings. Mary, whose nightmares will be most important of all, sees snakes, horned dwarfs, and dead fetuses.

Mary gets lots of narrative time, even though she comes across through much of the film as humorless, whiny, and somewhat icy. Percy, by contrast, is exuberant and frantic, the most talkative of the group as he sips more laudanum and belches metaphysical rants. He eventually makes his way to a rooftop, naked and under the thundering skies, to proclaim lightning as "the fundamental force of the universe." His muscular back and clenched buttocks are alluring; his performance is what tight-assed critics might call "too over the top."

"I think these portraits are rooted in reality," Sands told the *New York Times* in 1987. "If people think otherwise, it's because of the later Victorian whitewash of them. These were not simply beautiful Romantic poets. They were subversive, anarchic hedonists pursuing a particular line of amorality. The film portrays Lord Byron as demonic and Shelley as on the verge of madness, but the film is an expressionistic piece, and that's not an unreasonable expression of their realities."

Claire (Miriam Cyr) and Byron (Gabriel Byrne).

Shelley and Byron are appropriately larger than life. They were, after all, among the progenitors of modern celebrity culture by helping to create their own legends. Byron savors his abysmal reputation and brags that he has "no virtues." He treats Percy with fraternal respect but also manipulates him in the manner of a suave suitor. He slobbers Claire with kisses but also regards her as a mindless slut, kicking her with his club foot when she calls it a cloven hoof. After he finds out she might be carrying his child, Byron starts making love to her, but his face emerges from her privates with bloody lips. Did he give her a vampire bite or induce a miscarriage? Russell prefers to tease audiences with unanswered questions, although in real life Claire eventually brought a Byron child into the world that didn't live long.

●

Byron sees in Mary a self-righteous spoiler, keeping him from courting her future husband. Russell, who is much more probing and ambiguous about his characters than many critics give him credit for, sometimes makes Byron sympathetic. Viewers feel his pain as Mary whimpers from scene to scene, intruding on one of Byron's few tender moments when Shelley admits his fear of being buried alive. Byron takes Shelley in his arms, kisses his neck, and tries comforting him. It's a nicely lit love scene, even if between two cads, but a moaning Mary tramps into the room to spoil the magic.

Up until now, Russell had flirted in his films with male homosexuality the way a child might covet a licorice stick that his mom told him is poisoned. Now he relaxed a little more and savored the flavor, seeing if he could perhaps depict a romance between two of England's greatest poets. Russell more or less accomplishes this, but he is still unable to depict man-on-man action without hiding

Poetic Love: Percy Shelley (Julian Sands) and Lord Byron (Gabriel Byrne).

behind a female filter. This time, it is Mary, whose shock later on in the film when catching her future husband swapping saliva with the notorious author of *Childe Harold* becomes one of the many nightmares that inspire her to write the definitive horror novel.

Spall's portrayal of John Polidori (perhaps Russell's idea of a gay December queen) is also ambiguous. Despite his lack of aggression and self-esteem, he has a commanding presence. Polidori starts out looking silly, but as the story evolves he becomes another of Russell's wise fops. Though portraying him as an erotically hungry dog drooling over Byron and fondling Shelley's pecs, both Spall and

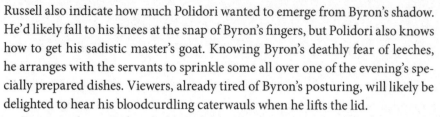

Russell also indicate how much Polidori wanted to emerge from Byron's shadow. He'd likely fall to his knees at the snap of Byron's fingers, but Polidori also knows how to get his sadistic master's goat. Knowing Byron's deathly fear of leeches, he arranges with the servants to sprinkle some all over one of the evening's specially prepared dishes. Viewers, already tired of Byron's posturing, will likely be delighted to hear his bloodcurdling caterwauls when he lifts the lid.

Existing photographs of John Polidori show a more attractive man than the homely popinjay that Spall resembles. Alex Winter plays a handsomer Polidori in the 1988 film *Haunted Summer*, which essentially tells the same story. But director Ivan Passer is too discreet about the romantic encounters between Byron and his biographer/doctor.

Spall's Polidori shows a keen perception and sensitivity that the two literary lugs who browbeat him seem to lack. In what is probably the only humanistic moment amid Russell's "Laff-in-the-Dark" approach, Polidori tries consoling Mary as they stand together by a staircase. They are just about to hold a séance, and Mary shares her fears of raising the dead. Polidori looks on her with genu-

Dr. Polidori (Timothy Spall).

ine concern, even repressed desire, as she (in many ways just as self-absorbed as Shelley) bleats on about her messy life and her premature child who died. "Shelley is too full of his tragedies to bear mine," she mutters while reminiscing about the love poems he used to write to her.

The script at various times suggests that Mary and Polidori are soul mates vexed by the same problem. In one scene, which Russell wisely keeps in long shot, Byron and Shelley are jabbering together in the foreground, a couple of philosophical gasbags. Mary and Polidori occupy the right and left ends of the screen respectively, each in mournful repose and alienated from the larger-than-life poets whom history—or at least English literature classes—would also put center stage.

Stephen Volk, who previously worked in advertising and who would go on to write the BBC cult series *Ghostwatch*, can claim *Gothic* as his first produced screenplay. Virgin Vision, which started in 1983, distributed film and video, launched a twenty-four-hour satellite music channel, and produced the 1984 version of *1984*, financed *Gothic*. Virgin's production team head Al Clark explained to *Sight and Sound* magazine in 1986 why. "It was worlds removed from the scripts that one predominantly gets sent in this country, with their literary ambience and dependence on a sort of linguistic authenticity. I felt it offered a perfect springboard to a director; the question was whom to approach. Then I saw *Crimes of Passion*."

Volk's screenplay presented a fount of possibilities, even though Russell did some predictable tweaking. He added fetishistic details: an animatronic belly dancer who slaps Shelley's hands when he gropes for her privates, a dwarf impersonating the gnome from Henri Fuseli's "Nightmare" painting who squats on Mary's chest, and of course that monstrously endowed dark knight. And as production designer, Christopher Hobbs, fresh from working with Derek Jarman on *Caravaggio*, offers sumptuous details.

Gothic also emerged in the shadow of John Landis's *Thriller* video, Wes Craven's *Nightmare*, and Dario Argento's ongoing helpings of human lasagna. But Russell, who directs every film as if it were going to be his last, packs *Gothic* with so much energy and panic that he cannibalizes his predecessors. "Russell means *Gothic* to be the last horror show," Richard Corliss wrote in his *Time* review. "Byron is Count Dracula, feeding on his guests' dreams and demons. Shelley is every weak hero, Polidori every mad doctor, Clairmont every wench whose lust turns her into a succubus. And Godwin, racked by visions of her stillborn child, becomes the cursed mothers of *The Exorcist* and *Rosemary's Baby*."

"If James Ivory had done a film about Shelley," Julian Sands continued in his *New York Times* interview, "it would be a much more lyrical and soothing piece of work, whereas Ken's treatment is much more symphonic and mesmerizing . . . James Ivory is like an Indian miniaturist, and Ken Russell is like a graffiti artist. James Ivory is like an ornithologist watching his subjects with a pair of binoculars from afar, whereas Ken Russell is a big-game hunter filming in the middle of a rhino charge."

Russell's previous two films had terrible endings, but *Gothic* makes up for this with one of his best. Mary, looking the worse for wear the next morning, descends Deodati's majestic staircase and soon ambles like a zombie through the opulent courtyard with its caged baboons and finicky servants. Byron, Polidori, Shelley, and Clairmont are physically restored and look even happy. "There are no ghosts in daylight," Byron assures her. "You'll get used to our nights at Deodati—a little indulgence to heighten our existence on this miserable earth.

Nights of the mind and the imagination, nothing more." Precisely because of the sardonic undertones that keep it from lapsing into "sappiness," this final scene is Russell's most successful stab at an optimistic ending: in the sense that horror might lurk around the corner, but there are those bright, clean, and diurnal moments when people can still endure, even laugh, in the face of inevitable death. While *Gothic* closes with at least a semblance of the world put back together again, Mary now reigns as the mistress of the macabre as she explains to Byron, Percy, Polidori, and Claire her tale of a creature haunting its mad creator to the grave. Volk wanted the movie to begin and end with Mary Shelley as an old woman looking back and telling *Gothic*'s story from her angle. But Russell opted to frame the story with tourists past and present. As circa late 1980s

sightseers pose for photos on the Deodati grounds, a voice on a bullhorn (sounding much like Spall) sums up how all of the characters (including the Shelleys' subsequent children) met their ends. The camera moves from the tourist cruise boat to a deformed newborn drowned under Lake Leman: Mary Shelley's nightmare incubating in the sea.

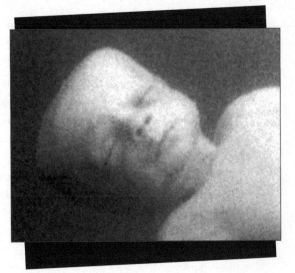

SALOME'S SALAMI

"**A**s close as two testicles." That is how Oscar Wilde describes his relationship to his boyfriend Lord Alfred "Bosie" Douglas in the opening scene of Ken Russell's *Salome's Last Dance*. But history knows otherwise. Around the time the film's story takes place, Wilde's love life was not quite so cozy. They fought over many matters, including Bosie's extravagant hotel restaurant bills; the rough, dirty, and blackmailing blokes they lusted after; and Bosie's faulty English translation of the play *Salome*, which Wilde originally wrote in French.

In the meantime, Bosie's father, the boxing enthusiast and Marquess of Queensbury, was already plagued over stories that his older son shot himself over a homosexual scandal. The idea of his younger son and Wilde traipsing about London as a couple and flaunting what Bosie described in a poem as "the love that dare not speak its name" was enough to make him declare war. One evening in 1895, he left a calling card at a playwrights' club Wilde attended. On it he scribbled, "To Oscar Wilde, posing as a somdomite [sic]." From thereon, Wilde's reputation (at least among his contemporaries) plummeted.

The irascible and vain Bosie, a glutton for both Wilde's affection and funds, got so furious at his dad that he, like Lady Macbeth goading her husband's fall from grace, urged Wilde to sue for libel. Wilde went along with the plan for a while; then the evidence against him mounted: names and addresses of gamy lads whom Wilde solicited, letters from Wilde to Bosie, and even passages from Wilde's own works, which painted for witch hunt–hungry Victorians the face of a "pederast." Realizing he'd lose, he withdrew the suit only to get slapped with indecency charges and forced back into court.

Convicted, Wilde endured two years hard labor, and the two testicles also parted ways. Bosie oddly escaped punishment, but he did petition the queen on Wilde's behalf to no avail. Wilde nonetheless felt alienated from him and documented his ill feelings in a letter he wrote in prison to Bosie that would later evolve into the famous work *De Profundis*: "While you were with me you were the absolute ruin of my art, and in allowing you to stand persistently between Art and myself I give myself shame and blame in the fullest degree."

After his release, Wilde (despite the protests of his wife, who tried forgiving him) had halfhearted reunions with Bosie in Naples and later in Paris. But Wilde's ailing body eclipsed his broken heart; he finally succumbed to encephalitic meningitis on November 30, 1900. Bosie, despite being despised by Mrs. Wilde and most of Wilde's friends, did show up as one of the mourners at Wilde's grave.

Russell turns this real-life tragedy about transgression and emotional betrayal into a speculative scenario, as Wilde watches a world premiere of *Salome* in one of London's notorious brothels. To draw the audience into Wilde's age of notoriety, Russell has the production take place three years before Queensbury's offense. It's November 5, 1892—Wilde's birthday but also Guy Fawkes Day, when bands of Brits ignite fireworks and burn effigies of the man who once plotted to free England by burning down the houses of Parliament. Wilde, like Fawkes, would also prove to be a sacrificial subject, so Russell practically delivers him to the morality carnivores. He has him attend this contraband production of his play just after the Lord Chamberlain banned it because of some cobweb-collecting English law against staged Biblical portrayals.

Wilde once planned to stage *Salome* with a peg-legged Sarah Bernhardt performing the "Dance of the Seven Veils" in the title role, but in *Salome's Last Dance*, he has to settle for a production that Alfred Taylor (Stratford Johns), the real-life brothel proprietor, assembles with his "clients and courtesans alike" (both male and female) to play many of the parts. Taylor also reserves the role of the obese and obsessed King Herod for himself. A haughty actress named Lady Alice (Glenda Jackson) deigns to walk across these tainted footlights for the eye-batting part of Herodias. Meanwhile, Bosie (Douglas Hodge) escorts Wilde (Nickolas Grace) into the establishment but soon retires to the basement: there he preens for the role of John the Baptist and likely sneaks some nooky with the bootblack set to play Herodias's page.

∎

Russell's affinity for the Wilde side of art and ethics had already surfaced when he explored Debussy, a musician allied with the French Symbolists, who basked among books filled with jeweled allusions and floral turns of phrase. As a filmmaker overcome by both image and melody, Russell also found congenial Wilde's intellectual mentor Walter Pater, the grandfather of nineteenth-century aestheticism, who wrote about how "all art aspires to the condition of music."

And he appreciated many of the works that predated and likely influenced the play. Chief among them was J. K. Huysmans's 1884 novel *Against Nature* (or *Against the Grain*) whose narrator celebrates the beauty of artificial gems and tapestries but is especially fond of Gustave Moreau's *Salome* painting, with its "concentrated gaze and the fixed eyes of a sleepwalker." Havelock Ellis in his introduction to Huysmans's book describes the so-called decadent style: "vague and most elusive in the outlines of form, listening to translate the subtle confidences of neurosis, the dying confessions of passion grown depraved, and the strange hallucinations of the obsession which is turning to madness."

Writers like Huysmans and artists like Moreau had such an impact on Wilde's interpretation of the New Testament story that he wrote the play in French (with some help from Debussy's patron Pierre Louÿs). Suspecting that British censors would give him trouble, Wilde facetiously told his compeer Robert Ross, "I have one instrument that I know I can command, and that is the English language." It is no wonder that Wilde allegedly revised much of Bosie's English translation to suit his standards.

●

That a movie as literary and idiosyncratic as *Salome's Last Dance* got made at all has much to do with Russell's temporary turn of good fortune after Vestron Video profited from American VHS sales of *Gothic*. As a result, its subsidiary Vestron Pictures (which also made a killing on the 1987 romance *Dirty Dancing*) was impressed enough to offer Russell a three-movie deal. *Salome's Last Dance* would be the first (followed by *The Lair of the White Worm* and *The Rainbow*).

When he started this project, Russell had a tradition of less outré screen Wildes to overcome. Gregory Ratoff's *Oscar Wilde* and Ken Hughes's *The Trials of Oscar Wilde* (both released in 1960) had great lead actors—Robert Morley and Peter Finch, respectively—but the scripts smothered the subject's sexuality with euphemistic perfume and sickly appeals to "family values." In contrast, Russell shows obvious sympathies for *Salome*'s author, whom he regards as one of England's greatest scribes, and his historical role as a sexual outlaw and martyr. He fleshes out Wilde's erotic and aesthetic predilections by presenting the film in a simultaneously airy-fairy and tawdry atmosphere. In doing so, Russell validates an epigram Wilde penned in *Phrases and Philosophies for the Use of the Young*: "The first duty in life is to be as artificial as possible."

●

The part of Salome, the persnickety princess of Judea, goes to one of Taylor's chambermaids, a sickly waif simply named Rose (Imogen Millais-Scott). When planning his own production, Wilde specified that Salome should be "green like a curious and poisonous lizard," but in Russell's version, she's a near-sighted near-albino who dresses in pale blue and appears to be at once eighteen and eighty years old.

Russell also adds an extra veil to the play by having Wilde watch it along with the viewer. As Russell tells it, this metanarrative innovation was borne out of a tightfisted business arrangement. Robert Littman promised Vestron that Russell could make the film for under a million dollars. To deliver on this, Russell figured that filming a play within a low-budget play could scale back costs and add complexity. This approach also implies some factual odds, since it all takes place in the kind of mostly male brothel Wilde would have visited.

Jackson, known for her more subdued and naturalistic roles, seems to relish every second as Herod's overly made up and bitchy harridan; Hodge, whose forte is Shakespeare, is a properly snippy Douglas and a jittery prophet. Grace, who made a big impression with his role as Anthony Blanche in *Brideshead Revisited*, is not as big and gangly as Wilde, but he sports his green carnation, sips champagne, and sputters aphorisms in an offhanded manner that Russell imagines Wilde would have done. "The moon rising in a jewel box of deepest night could not be more exquisitely displayed," he exclaims with a rolling *r* as he compliments Taylor's stagecraft.

Since Wilde wrote *Salome* in the spirit of the French Symbolists, artist Aubrey Beardsley got inspired to make some outlandish illustrations. He probably wanted to tease its author by including Wilde's puffy face peeping down from the heavens in a picture titled *The Woman in the Moon*. In a likely homage to Beardsley, the ads for *Salome's Last Dance* also cleverly put Johns's Herod inside the moon as he ogles at Salome munching on a banana.

Russell shows off Beardsley's drawings during the opening credits as Wilde gazes through a picture book. The play then begins with Bosie as John the Baptist, stuck behind another variation on Russell's iron bars. A lively selection from Grieg's *Peer Gynt* sprinkles into the soundtrack, as a gang of dominatrices in black leather taunts him with fist-shaped spears. Just as in *The Boy Friend*, Russell loves to expose the cheap artifice that goes into making an amateur stage play. Bosie's Baptist keeps getting lifted and lowered in a dumbwaiter, while any blood that's shed consists of thick plastic slabs.

•

Up until now, Russell would make Hitchcock-style cameos. Here, he indulges his past actorly aspirations with a vengeance—and in a double role. He is a dodgy court photographer named Kenneth who also helps with the play's special effects. But as Wilde's Cappadocian, he utters such memorable lines (apparently unique to Vivian Russell's translation of Wilde's French) as, "Is Herodias the one with the red eyes, the ruby lips, the ruby hips, and the red rubies?" Russell claims to have modeled both parts on Sir Donald Wolfit, the temperamental Shakespearean actor whom Russell calls "the greatest ham in English theater."

Regardless of the lower budget, Russell offers sumptuous and at times overwhelming set designs; the hues are so deep and rich—the rose petals redder than red—that nature's dreary color scheme outside the theater seems unsatisfying. Anachronisms also abound: Herodias smokes cigarettes against the moonlight like some film noir floozy, while Salome plays up the Lolita angle by feasting on strawberry sundaes and heart-etched lollipops. The film

Russell impersonates Doctor Caligari as King Herod's palace photographer.

also owes its visual appeal to Christopher Hobbs's set designs and production designer Michael Buchanan, who was the art director on Jarman's *Caravaggio*. Though each has a different cinematographer—Mike Southon on *Gothic* and Harvey Harrison on *Salome*—both films appear to simulate the old, super-saturated Technicolor of Michael Powell and Emeric Pressburger's *Black Narcissus*.

Critics who snarl at excess are guaranteed a tizzy with the cast's extras alone: a harem of spear-toting, topless slave girls with golden nipples; campy Nazarenes who primp as Herod's paranoia heightens; and a quarrelsome trio of Hassidic Jews made up of dwarfs who argue over whether the prophet Elijah is the only one who has seen God. Russell really flips the bird to the fainthearted when a drunken Roman soldier erupts with what Rabelais once referred to in *Gargantua and Pantagruel* as a "gutful of quavers, semiquavers, and demisemi quavers of rectal harmony."

With his metaplay approach, Russell is free to imply parallels between Herod's lust for Salome and Wilde's interest in a nubile lad playing Herodias's golden page-boy (Russell Lee Nash). As Beardsley makes manifest in his sardonically titled illustration *A Platonic Lament*, the pageboy is also enamored with the doomed Young Syrian (Warren Saire) who, in turn, can't keep his eyes off Salome. The Syrian is so stricken that he stabs himself when he knows he can't have her, leaving a trail of fake blood and a noxious omen for Herod to slip on. Johns, another Shakespearean actor, who also starred in the 1960s BBC police series *Z Cars*, steals the show as the rotund Tetrarch destined to lock Biblical horns with his Lolitaish stepdaughter. At the same time, John the Baptist keeps spewing prophesies of doom and won't stop insulting Herod's wife.

Shooting at Elstree Studios, with the symphonic backing of Richard Cooke and the London Philharmonic Orchestra, Russell also overrode any nagging musical copyrights by taking some of the public domain's best melodies: the alternately brooding and sprightly sounds of Claude Debussy, Edvard Grieg, Jacques Ibert, and Erik Satie compose the story's mood music.

Ibert's *Ports of Call* signals Salome's demands for the Prophet's kiss, as she keeps him in chains, tries seducing him with words, and gets her dominatrix servants to whip him each time he rejects her: "Your mouth is like a band of scarlet around an ivory tower. It is like a pomegranate cut by an ivory knife . . . It is like the bow of the king of Persia, which is painted vermilion with horns of

coral. There is nothing in the world as red as your mouth. Let me kiss your mouth."

"Never," he snaps. "Daughter of Babylon! Daughter of Sodom! Never!"

Instead of a kiss, Salome gets a face full of the prophet's phlegm. Regardless, she licks it with glee, knowing her revenge will be even sweeter as his badly whipped body gets carried back down the dumbwaiter.

Salome (Imogen Millais-Scott) taunts John the Baptist (Douglas Hodge).

Though Russell uses Grieg's stately "In the Hall of the Mountain King" from *Peer Gynt* for her blue light soundtrack, Salome gives Herod a crude "Dance of the Seven Veils" that also bends the genders. Millais-Scott, frail after suffering from a virus that left her with weak vision and muscles, needed a double. Russell out-Wilded Wilde by finding a male dancer about Millais-Scott's height for the intense belly and rump gyrations. As the seven veils start coming off, Russell focuses on the obviously male tush that makes Herod gush. As Grieg's theme intensifies, Russell's sleight-of-hand editing between Salome and the boy also gets more aggressive. Then, the climax: Wilde is behind a pillar making out with the pageboy while a terrified Herod gets a quick glimpse of two Salomes:

Herodias (Glenda Jackson) strikes a film noir pose.

one whose praises he had sung and one who is hung. Herod winces at the sight, but his portrayer Alfred Taylor, who was sometimes Wilde's procurer and sat right alongside him in the dock of the Old Bailey when both got sentenced for "indecency," would have relished the surprise. However, Herod's queasy reaction to Salome's salami could also be Russell projecting himself into another phallic psychodrama.

Up until now, Stratford Johns has been having a ball with the material, vying with Russell for the Sir Donald Wolfit steal-the-scenery award. But with Satie's *Gymnopédie #2* lilting in the background, he has his poignant moments, as his Herod vainly tries talking Salome out of her end of the bargain to get the Baptist's head on a silver platter. One hundred priceless white peacocks, rare amber goblets that change color to detect poison, "bangles garnished with carbuncles and jade from the city of Euphrates," and half his kingdom are not enough to sway her. Herod finally sighs and accepts the inevitable. Soon, all that rises from the dumbwaiter is the Prophet from the neck up.

Russell also wedges in some insidious connections between Salome's betrayal of John the Baptist and Bosie

King Herod (Stratford Johns) tries reneging on his bargain with the princess of Judea.

Douglas's betrayal of Wilde when he goaded him into filing his disastrous libel suit. Russell makes Bosie even nastier: he too likes the golden pageboy and, in a jealous fit, rats to the police so that they raid the brothel. Wilde gets charged with "gross sexual indecency and the corruption of minors." Taylor and even Lady Alice also get hauled into the Black Maria.

●

While working on *Salome's Last Dance*, Russell got an offer from a German company to stage a production of Strauss's opera based on Wilde's play—but in a version that was closer to Russell's movie. The production, performed at the Opera House in Bonn, got mixed responses. Years later, Russell brought Salome back into his novel *Mike and Gaby's Space Gospel*, claiming to have modeled her this time on Elizabeth Taylor in *National Velvet* and Jodie Foster in *Taxi Driver*.

In the *New York Times*, Vincent Canby welcomed *Salome's Last Dance*'s impish lunacy: "With his gifts for going too far, and with his almost childlike view of decadence (a blue-painted nipple here, a bare buttocks there, sometimes even a quick shot of full-frontal nudity!), Mr. Russell possesses just the right mixture of innocence, passion, and theatrical intelligence the job requires."

Those expecting a high-toned, "upright" rendering of an Oscar Wilde classic need only heed Wilde's words at the end of the film as he congratulates Alfred Taylor's production: "The casting was nigh on perfect, I've always admired the talent here but never more so than tonight. Your Herod out-Heroded Herod . . . Inspired, my dear Alfred, absolutely inspired. I was delighted to find that I'd written yet another comedy."

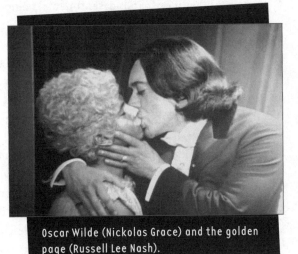

Oscar Wilde (Nickolas Grace) and the golden page (Russell Lee Nash).

THE SERPENT IN THE RAINBOW

"**D**elights in outraging our sensibilities"; "a psychologist of the uglier emotions"; "a thoroughly vicious work full of chaos and bad taste"; "crazy pursuit of novelty, decadence, and death"; "hatred, contempt, rage, disgust, despair, and mockery serve as models for his moods"; "should be banned on the grounds of indecency"; "ideas as pretentious as they are bizarre"; "erratic and erotic spasms of ugliness"; and "a sentimental voluptuary wallowing in nature."

Ken Russell's little daughter Molly hissed this venomous litany when playing the part of his wife in the 1989 autobiopic *A British Picture: Portrait of an Enfant Terrible*. Russell's even littler son Rupert, who portrays his dad at various life stages, looks discouraged and dragged into darkness as Mrs. Russell reads aloud one bad review after another. But she finishes her tongue-lashing by offering a rainbow of sorts at the end of the storm, assuring him that these are not reviews of him and his movies but of Bartók, Debussy, Delius, Elgar, Prokofiev, and several of the other composers he'd always admired and whose biographies he'd filmed.

Now, Russell was at least assured that he was "a sentimental voluptuary" in good company. Around this time, he was twitting his critics by offering two films that went to opposite directions. He continued to torture his prudish detractors with *The Lair of the White Worm* (1988), a voluptuous comedy of vipers, but he soon disappointed some of his hardier and kinkier fans with *The Rainbow* (1989), a sentimental and at times downright sappy journey back to D. H. Lawrence country.

•

Fourteen years after publishing *Dracula*, Bram Stoker lay crippled and mangy from Bright's disease. He went mad with visions of serpents taking over both

278

his mind and the world but managed to work out these obsessions with his final novel, *The Lair of the White Worm*.

Stoker got the idea for the story after learning of a former Roman settlement in England, where coins bearing a snake-wrapped crucifix were unearthed centuries later. With part-Christian, part-pagan themes, Stoker spun a tale of giant, slimy creatures lurking in an underground cavern, worshipped by vampires that terrorize the local village in their search for sacrificial victims.

Russell practically rewrites the story, paring down the number of characters and eliminating the Voodoo-practicing African slave Oolanga altogether. Instead, he turns *Lair* into a horror genre spoof that is too gruesome and ambiguous to be pure comedy. Russell also blurs the fantasy with some fact. He relished another chance to comb England's archives by retrieving from the Cecil Sharp House—which contains the sheet music to just about every folk song composed in the British Isles—a nineteenth-century folk tune called "The Lambton Worm." He has a Celtic rock band perform it at an annual celebration, where the glib lord of the manor Lord James D'Ampton (Hugh Grant) serves such culinary marvels as "pickled earthworms in aspic."

After *Gothic* and *Salome's Last Dance*, Russell took a break from "period pieces" to bring Stoker's Victorian setting into the present day. Angus Flint (Peter Capaldi), a Scottish archeology student, digs up a prehistoric skull from the former site of a thousand-year-old convent. In the process, he reawakens the curse of the D'Ampton Worm, named after a British soldier who allegedly slew the fabled beast in ancient times. Two orphaned girls, Mary (Sammi Davis) and Eve (Catherine Oxenberg) Trent, who live on the settlement where the skull surfaces, get roped into a nexus of evil as they trace their parents' recent disappearance to the Worm cult.

Grant, who'd just wooed audiences in James Ivory's *Maurice*, plays D'Ampton as a pedantic and often-pompous charmer who helps Flint uncover the mystery. But he starts losing his smooth facade when he falls for Lady Sylvia Marsh (Amanda Donohoe), the story's villain, who worships the pagan god Dionin and wants the skull for her dark rites.

•

Revamping much of Stoker's tale, Russell also gets a bit autobiographical. His hometown of Southampton is the former site of the Roman Clausentum settlement; today, excavations similar to those that Angus dredges up in the movie are still on display in the town's historical museums. And by filming much of the story in D. H. Lawrence's old stomping grounds of Derbyshire, Russell reinforces the sense of local pallor that adds to *Lair*'s idiosyncratically British atmosphere. The entire yarn often seems as if a dotty, old, and salacious English auntie is telling it from an attic where her more prim relatives have exiled her.

The theme of a monster lurking about an English countryside and the towns-folk's prim response has surfaced in past British horrors. *The Secret of the Loch*, which made such an impression on the young Ken, is one of these early cinema treasures that contrasts the monster's threat with the quirky pub habitués who "keep the cozy on the pot" while havoc crashes into their otherwise tepid world. And no matter how dire the circumstances, a matronly figure often pops in and out of the story to say something like, "While we're still alive, we might as well

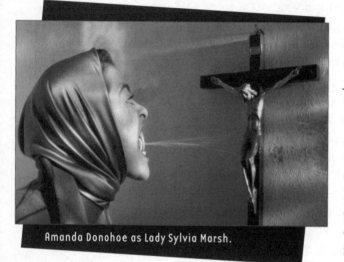

Amanda Donohoe as Lady Sylvia Marsh.

have a cup of tea." This actual line comes from David MacDonald's 1954 sci-fi offering, *Devil Girl from Mars*, whose female alien Nyah somewhat resembles Lady Sylvia. But instead of a flying saucer, *Lair*'s Lady Sylvia drives a silvery, phallic, E-Type Jag as she slithers on wheels about the countryside looking for fresh blood.

Donohoe's character exudes a sophisticated and jaded poise that is out of place in the Peak District provinces. But her alien presence also lets the audience focus on the nutty townspeople and their befuddled reactions to her. This allows Russell to populate the spoof with good English character actors that give the script some backbone. Among them is Paul Brooke, who plays the inquisitive codger cop P. C. Erny with a disconcertingly lazy eye. He ends up having Lady Sylvia suck blood from his leg when a snake on her property bites him. Another is Stratford Johns who, after out-Heroding Herod in *Salome's Last Dance*, appears as James D'Ampton's eccentric valet Peters. He has dry wit and eyes that perversely twinkle whenever his master instructs him how to help send the demons back to hell.

The exchanges between Donohoe and Grant, however, are among the funniest moments, displaying the urbane wit of a Noel Coward play. James drops by Temple House, a former Roman shrine where Lady Sylvia now stays, to introduce himself and check out her "trouble with a snake." Together, they get delectably droll. "Oh, and you're going to uphold family tradition and slay the beastie. How incredibly romantic," she tells him. To get them in the mood, Russell even played for them a recording of the Noel Coward and Gertrude Lawrence dialogue from *Private Lives*, so that they could gaze over their snifters of brandy and engage in a similar comedy-of-manners badinage.

> James: Do you have children?
> Lady Sylvia: Only when there are no men around.

> Lady Sylvia: Some people enjoy playing themselves at cards or even chess. My passion is "Snakes and Ladders."
> James: Playing with one's self can't be much fun, surely.

Lady Sylvia also lifts a "wicked line" from Oscar Wilde's *The Importance of Being Earnest*: "To lose one parent may be regarded as a misfortune; to lose both looks like carelessness." James doesn't seem amused when she's so glib about the Trent tragedy, but his morally superior air also makes him the kind of British "hero" who elicits more smirks than admiration. He hides behind a patriarchal shell to assure his minions that he can set all the god-awful situations right.

Lair is somewhat political as well: Lord James reflects the last remnants of a dead empire, with allusions to a class war raging during the Thatcher days. D'Ampton and Lady Sylvia are ghosts of the old aristocracy, while Flint and the Trents are the commoners who have to take matters into their own hands when James sometimes seems to flounder.

Later, when he ventures with the others into a vast cave to track down the monster, James D'Ampton keeps his upper lip stiff while pausing to assess the matter over sandwiches and tea. Once he's wise to Lady Sylvia's game, he plays an old 78 of Turkish charmer music from his dad's "North African collection" to drive her and her mutations out from hiding. His response when he finds the record has been stolen is consistently lukewarm: "I think we probably have another reptile loose on the premises."

∎

At times, *Lair* registers an emotional flat line, but its slow and sneaky pacing have an inner logic. Russell intended the film's rhythm to approximate the deliberate stealth of a winding reptile, moving sinuously from one character and scene to the next with baleful intent. Stanislas Syrewicz's original music is also suitably eerie throughout. The result is a sometimes ponderous, sometimes funny, but consistently creepy tale, where an otherwise bland English setting seems booby-trapped. This is where even a common garden hose or a Hoover vacuum cleaning attachment can startle.

And then there is James D'Ampton's daft dream—Russell's Freudian attempt to splay the story's ambiguous clues. After staring at a painting on his bedroom wall depicting a forebear slaying the dragon by Stone Rigg Canyon, the place where the monster suppos-

Excavation Party (Sammi Davis, Hugh Grant, Peter Capaldi, Catherine Oxenberg). The Stone Rigg Cavern suggests the interior of the White Worm's skull.

edly dwelt and whose offspring might still lurk, D'Ampton dreams he is in an Air Force uniform, walking through the painting, into the cave, and onto an airplane with serpentine contours. There, he greets all of the female characters dressed as flight attendants, who string him along with serpentine leads. A mishmash of metaphors surrounds him: snaky cords on a seat belt that end up constricting him, a noxious green liqueur that Lady Sylvia tries forcing down his throat, female legs that undulate around the cabin's corners like roused cobras, and a cheeky moment when D'Ampton looks up from his snake-shaped crossword puzzle, metaphorically lifting his pen, to watch Lady

Eve and Mary Trent's mom (Imogen Claire) after Lord D'Ampton bisects her with the family sword when she returns from the dead.

Sylvia and Eve wrestle in the first-class aisle. The Trent sisters' dad (Christopher Gable), who has been sitting alongside his wife in a zombie trance, suddenly rises and leads D'Ampton out through the plane's rear end and to the Stone Rigg Cavern. There, he finds a pocket watch that Mr. Trent left behind before vanishing. Once awake, D'Ampton interprets his nightmare: his exit from the plane's posterior alludes to the pocket watch that apparently exited from the D'Ampton Worm's digestive system after Mr. Trent got devoured. Assuming that the monster still lurks where it had eaten, D'Ampton corrals Eve, Mary, and Angus to join him on a Stone Rigg Canyon expedition.

•

Lair is relatively chaste for a Russell film, since there's no sex or even petting between the principal characters. The sisters stay relatively innocent. Eve remains a virgin while Mary (whose boyfriend got killed in a motorcycle crash) stays unattached. As far as their association with Angus and James goes, the girls take it no further than a spotless kiss. They all remain what Mary describes as "good friends in the old-fashioned sense."

There is, however, James's horny dream. And there is the part when Eve hallucinates that Roman soldiers are raping her while a phallic serpent coils around Christ's crucifix. There's also the bit when Mary envisions dildo-strapped vampire amazons defiling her, not to mention when Lady Sylvia spews orgasmic venom on the Trents' family crucifix while making off with Angus's skull, or when she captures Eve and probes her with a fourteen-inch ivory phallic symbol—which Russell claims is a replica of the intimidating devices Malaysian pygmies once used to fool others into thinking they were bigger men. Russell also depicts intergenerational abuse with unprecedented extremes: Lady Sylvia seduces the hapless and underage Kevin (Chris Pitt), a boy scout she rescues from the rain, persuades to get naked into a bath with the promise of a good meal and more, and whose anaconda she bites before drowning him when the doorbell makes his sacrifice inconvenient.

The time at last arrives for the D'Ampton Worm to emerge when Lady Sylvia manages to trap Eve, Mary, and Angus in a dungeon beneath Temple House. Russell and special effects designer Geoff Portas fashioned a creature that slithers from the Temple pit with awesome jaws cobbled together from a

Lady Sylvia offs Kevin, the hapless boy scout (Chris Pitt).

Volkswagen Beetle's front end. Flint saves Eve just in time, making sure Lady Sylvia is the serpent's dinner before throwing in a grenade for its dessert.

When the explosion occurs, and at a point when the plotline truly crinkles, a self-satisfied James stares down on high from Stone Rigg Canyon, sipping tea along with his mates who helped him smoke the worm out of hibernation. Why this happens is unclear. He only succeeds in pushing the serpent toward his pals; for all he knows, they could have all been blown up. The story, in a sense, becomes a spotty British variation on a Hardy Boys mystery: the gals return home intact, and the guys congratulate each other for saving the day. But whatever once passed for "normal" in the village is no more.

If viewers turn the sound off while watching Angus and James sit together to chat at the Trents' farm when the mayhem is supposedly over, *Lair* looks as if it could drift into a man-to-man romance. "Christ, have I a tale to tell *you!*" Angus says to James while staring at him intently. A dark romance might really happen soon.

In the final scene, Angus calls a hospital research lab to discover that what he thought was an antidote for snakebites is only a serum for arthritis relief. Earlier, James bisected the Trents' mom when she showed up as one of the vicious undead, but Russell slyly implies that she had enough time to chomp James's leg: he is likely also infected with the tainted blood.

Lady Sylvia (Amanda Donohoe) makes the ultimate sacrifice.

As they drive off together into the twilight, James suggests they stop to "get a bite," to which Angus grins and says, "Why not?" But the screen goes black, the credits scroll up, and the viewers' homoerotic imaginations are left dangling. (The final shots also call to mind the ending of David Cronenberg's *The Brood*, when a dad is about to confront his mutating daughter, who sits beside him in the car and bares marks that look similar to the snake bites on Angus Flint's knee).

Despite all the relentless exposition in the dialogue, critics tended to find *Lair*'s plot befuddling. There are times when Russell seems to purposely leave logical gaps to keep viewers mystified. The *Washington Post*'s Richard Harrington's response is typical but at least thoughtful: "There's permanent duality in the Russell/Stoker universe—Christian and pagan, violent and bucolic, earnest and decadent, real and surreal—and if you have a hard time figuring it all out, don't worry. So did Russell, who, once again, seems to have overindulged in diabolic steroids."

Through the years, *The Lair of the White Worm* has amassed a cult, thanks to repeated airings on the Sci-Fi Channel. There, it became a mystifying oddity amid cable television's more predictable fare—an eye-opener for those who previously knew nothing about Russell or his films. Legends also tell of *Lair* parties in places like Los Angeles, where revelers dress as their favorite characters. As years pass, the film's absurdity gets more intriguing, its strange and sealed world—with its stunning photography and meticulously assembled set designs—gets more inviting. *Lair* is fascinating for being simultaneously inane, confounding, and as hypnotic as an adder's stare.

•

In his 1989 adaptation of D. H. Lawrence's *The Rainbow*, Russell goes from playing games with his reptilian fears to rekindling his saddest childhood memory: his cousin Marion's death (he dedicates this film to her). Lawrence's novel follows several generations of Brangwens, but Russell focuses on the final third section—all about Ursula (Sammi Davis). In her, he sees Marion's pluck and frustrated idealism. To relate her story, Russell opts for a subdued film that he might have hoped would charm the vipers that otherwise panned him for being too bizarre and dark.

"Whatever else it is," Lawrence wrote of this work, "it is a voyage of discovery toward the real and eternal land." Russell shared Lawrence's surface optimism but for some reason avoided Lawrence's impending sense of nihilism that goes along with Ursula's quest to break out of her bounds. Still, even Russell's version, which he cowrote with his then-wife Vivian, must have registered "gloomy" on the mood scale when producers balked. "I offered the screenplay to David Puttnam," Russell told the *New York Times* in 1989, "who thought it was a bit of a downer and that Ursula was a pain in the neck."

In the film, Ursula still hisses at a world that thwarts her ambitions. But Russell is much kinder to the lesbian relationship she develops with her swimming instructor, Winifred Inger (Amanda Donohoe). Lawrence judged it as "perverted," but Russell implies this is one of the happier chapters in Ursula's life—that is, before Winifred betrays her and rules of the "norm" start hindering her.

Lawrence has Ursula reject Winfred and even take sadistic delight in matching up her manipulative and mercenary Uncle Henry (David Hemmings) with the woman she finally perceives as "clayey, inert, unquickened flesh, that reminded her of the great prehistoric lizards." Russell, in contrast, has Winifred marry Uncle Henry, despite Ursula's jealous protests.

Winifred turns out to be a turncoat. She seduces Ursula with wondrous thoughts of Sapphic romance and then rubs her nose into the fetid "facts of life." She starts by having Ursula pose for a lecherous sod of a painter (Dudley Sutton)—a character Russell added—who concentrates more on the brush stroke nuances of Ursula's bare rump crack and gets livid when she refuses to let him spank her.

Much like Lady Sylvia in *Lair*, Donohoe's Winifred is a foxy and witty dynamo amid a cluster of dullards. She is especially engaging as she astounds Ursula with her early twentieth-century suffragist views, likening men to "serpents trying to swallow themselves because they are hungry." Her bitter advice to Ursula about love is just as strident: "The best you ever get from a man is passion; even that can't last."

Oddly, Russell intended the part of Uncle Henry for Elton John. Elton would have had a great opportunity to play against type, but Russell claims Elton hemmed, hawed, and drove him up the wall until Hemmings, who did a great job as the drug-addled Samuel Taylor Coleridge in *Rime of the Ancient Mariner*, proved game for the difficult role of a man who comes across as suave and powerful but never likable.

●

Judging from *Women in Love* and Russell's version of *Lady Chatterley*, D. H. Lawrence has a way of taming Russell. But back when he published *The Rainbow* in 1915, Lawrence's torrid sex scenes outraged the decency sentries. A group called the Public Morality Council sought to prosecute Lawrence and his book for being "a mass of obscenity of thought, idea, and action throughout." And like a heretic, his literary "voyage of discovery" got ceremoniously burned.

Russell surprisingly is much more restrained than Lawrence. He doesn't give Ursula enough visual metaphors to illustrate the inner rage. Part of this is not his fault; his producers edited out more elaborate details in a scene when she glares into the moon for ungodly inspiration while her boyfriend Anton Skrebensky (Paul McGann) deflowers her with the grace of a yak. She seems to hate every moment of their first encounter and can't even look at him when it's over.

In Lawrence's version, Ursula reduces Skrebensky to a shell of a man; the more he loves her, the more she recoils. At times, Ursula sounds like a vampire. When describing one of their erotic encounters, Lawrence presents Skrebensky as a Mina to Ursula's Dracula:

> But hard and fierce she had fastened upon him, cold as the moon
> and burning as a fierce salt. Till gradually his warm, soft iron

yielded, and she was there fierce, corrosive, seething with his destruction, seething like some cruel, corrosive salt around the last substance of his being, destroying him, destroying him in the kiss. And her soul crystallized with triumph, and his soul was dissolved with agony and annihilation. So she held him there, the victim, consumed, annihilated. She had triumphed: he was not any more.

•

All along, *The Rainbow* had been hyped as the calmer Ken Russell. Even Carl Davis, known also for his original new music for silent films, provides a score with a more middle-of-the-road, John Williams style that Russell might otherwise deem maudlin.

Even so, Russell's plot gets more engrossing when Ursula establishes some independence by becoming an elementary schoolteacher. Judith Paris has an eccentric role as the officious and sadistic Miss Harby, the headmaster's sister, who pounds madly on the piano as the students make their daily marches to their desks. She also watches through the classroom widow while the students take advantage of Ursula's kindness. Ursula learns to tackle the brats before they find out she's so sensitive and chew her to pieces.

Russell reverts to his impish best when Ursula bites back. She tries mollifying the little bastards with reason but inevitably resorts to corporal punishment. Here it comes: another moment of Russellscopic catharsis as Ursula pins a boy, who'd previously thrown stones at her and kicked her, down on the floor before thrashing him over and over again with a cane. The child is so hateful that the thwacking sounds are downright sensuous. This fit of temper seems so authentic because Davis got a bit too involved in her motivation. She confessed misgivings to the *New York Times*: "I remember accidentally hitting the boy on the wrist and was in floods of tears because I thought I had really hurt him."

For the sake of continuity and perhaps some emotional refuge, Russell packs this prequel to *Women in Love* with some of the latter's cast and crew. Glenda Jackson is now Ursula's mom: strict, bitter, and often shrewish as she steers her rebellious daughter toward domestic drudgery. Christopher Gable is also back, now as Ursula's dad. He is kind enough to appease his little girl's imagination by spreading a rainbow pattern of jam on a piece of bread, but he's a damp dishrag when pointing to the real rainbow and telling her, "You can't have it, my duckie; it's not for catching."

What's missing is the Shirley Russell costume touch, which might have made the film on a par with *Women in Love* for smarter period flair. But cinematographer Billy Williams helps atone for this loss as he fluctuates his style from the dingy confines of the state-run schoolroom to the actual color-treated rainbow. Vit Wagner of the *Toronto Star* claimed in a 1989 review that the rainbow looked as if it were "ripped off the side of an ice cream wagon and taped on the camera lens." It is a high-gloss moment, apparently without any of the "shampoo commercial" irony Russell displayed in some of his past films. Russell also resorts to the kind of supersentimental ending that he'd probably ridicule any other director for executing. *The Rainbow*, as Caryn James writes in the *New York Times*, "is Mr. Russell's most lyrical and conventional film in years. The softness provides its appeal and ultimately its greatest flaw."

•

"Every summer we used to go to this place called Highcliff," Russell reminisces about the free spirit who inspired his boyhood and once saved him from a glaring adder. "There were bungalows around a field, and you went down a steep cliff to the beach. We had marvelous adventures. She was a sort of ideal character. She was like a boy and a girl at the same time, fantastically beautiful. She was too good to live, practically . . . and she didn't."

Lawrence closes his novel by describing Ursula's rainbow as "the earth's new architecture, the old, brittle corruption of houses and factories swept away, the world built up in a living fabric of Truth, fitting to the overarching Heaven." And for a few moments, Russell used his lens to glance back to when he and Marion would swim, play croquet, lament over soggy cucumber sandwiches, and dance to a 78 record of Cicely Courtneidge singing, "We'll All Go Riding on a Rainbow." But Marion had her sight set on "a new land far away" and had no time to fret about snakes—or tripwires.

MOLL FLOUNDERS

"Whenever I hear this magnificent symphony," Ken Russell writes about his impressions of Vaughan Williams's *Symphonia Antarctica*, "I get the image of icy indifference and feel the wind of vicious criticism that is cold enough to freeze the spirit and make all our goals—no matter how misconceived—unachievable."

That empty, chilly feeling Russell refers to is not unlike the insolent void Ursula Brangwen experienced in D. H. Lawrence's *The Rainbow* as she faced a classroom full of future drones. Russell also shares Anton Skrebensky's terror of nothingness when he realizes Ursula will never love him, and he "found himself struggling amid an ashen-dry, cold world of rigidity, dead walls and mechanical traffic, and creeping, specter-like people."

Russell can sometimes turn this anomie into a wry joke when looking back on the quixotic visions he failed to get on film—projects almost as astonishing as his successes. And a good place to start is a less-than-satisfying encounter he had with a legend from the glory days of Italy's Cinecittà Studios.

•

Sophia Loren was prim and proper as she faced Russell, sizing up the man who proposed to direct her as the lead in a biopic about the opera diva Maria Callas. The project had so much promise: "Russell to Write, Helm Callas Biopic," *Variety* blared on October 2, 1982. Russell had already scouted choice sites throughout Italy, looking for palazzos and canals along Venice as well as spots in Milan and Rome. He also thought of ways to get the best indoor lighting to capture the grandeur of La Scala.

In the beginning, Loren was keen and invited Russell and Vivian over to discuss the script. She was staying at her California ranch at the time; her husband, the famed producer Carlo Ponti, greeted and took them on a tour of the manor. Russell recalls, "We saw acres of parched earth and scraggy trees and the biggest private swimming pool we'd ever set eyes on—actually two pools linked by a man-made waterfall. It was very Roman and would not have been out of place at Cinecittà on a film set of Caesar's Palace. It wouldn't have been out of place in Caesar's Palace, Las Vegas, either."

Carlo and Sophia sported smiles that Russell likened to "the size of a slice of watermelon." And once Carlo left his wife alone with Ken and Vivian, Sophia (over coffee in very small cups) started going over all of the details she didn't like in the script. Russell and Vivian wanted to portray Callas warts and all: this included her temper tantrums, her use of vulgar language, and, worst of all, her saucy attitude toward her husband, the Italian industrialist Giovanni Battista Meneghini. Loren took umbrage over a scene in which Callas tries avoiding the throng of paparazzi and journalists after she pulls another of her notorious stage walkouts. Meneghini looks to her for suggestions on handling the crowd, and Callas shouts back, "Tell them you can't get it up."

Well, Loren insisted Callas would never have dealt her husband, especially an Italian husband, such a blow to his manhood, even as a joke. Russell and Vivian kept their respectful silence, wondering how to get out of this pickle since the script alterations she'd requested were unthinkable. "Further discussion was cut short," Russell recalls, "by Sophia glancing at her watch and running off to put on the pasta for Ponti's lunch."

As the Russells took a jumbo jet back to London, they thought about how defensive Sophia was about Callas's sausage sarcasm. Being twenty-something years apart themselves, Ken and Vivian ruminated over the age discrepancy between Callas and the decades older Meneghini, as well as the vast years between Sophia and Carlo. Vivian surmised, "Too close to home for comfort."

Shortly before Ms. Loren's rebuff, Russell also brushed with musical greatness in another misbegotten script. *The Beethoven Secret* was to star Anthony Hopkins as Beethoven, along with Glenda Jackson and Jodie Foster as two of the composer's mystery girls. The intrigue would have centered on an anonymous love letter found inside a secret desk compartment the day after he dies. But money proved more elusive than the mystery sender, even when Russell was close to shooting.

•

In 1982, years before Madonna joined Antonio Banderas for a forgettable adaptation of Andrew Lloyd Webber's *Evita*, Russell diligently worked on his version. But casting Eva Peron proved a lost labor. After Paramount Pictures purchased the rights, Russell worked three months on a script and took pains looking for

European locations and scheduling screen tests. Robert Stigwood was back in Russell's life as a producer. Composer Andrew Lloyd Webber and librettist Tim Rice planned to cast Elaine Paige (who originated the stage role). But Russell thought that "although there is no doubt that across the footlights her performance brought tears to the eyes, the eye of the camera proved to be made of sterner stuff." This opinion made him a pariah among his colleagues.

With no definite plans yet to cast Paige, Russell almost threw up his hands while auditioning the cavalcade of what he called "Evita clones, each doing an interpretation of 'Another Suitcase in Another Hall.'" It was another screen test and another dud, another lady in gold lamé and blonde wig and another letdown. He was at least sure that pop singer David Essex would make a charming Che Guevara.

Webber and Rice were still intent on using Paige. But even after she tried again and again with the same makeup and wig and the same lights shining ever harder to make her into the Argentine dragon lady, Russell didn't buy into the consensus.

Wanting a female lead with balls, he thought of Barbra Streisand, who was in the process of making *Yentl*. The thought of Russell and Streisand sharing the same project and the same soundstage evokes horror stories that might make even the fiasco with Paddy Chayefsky seem tame. But he'd attempted to work with her once before, to no avail, in the early 1970s for his other unmade masterpiece on the life of Sarah Bernhardt.

The negotiations with Streisand didn't go far. They at least got to her treating him to a chilly dinner and being, according to Russell, munificent enough to fulfill Russell's wish for some wine by ordering *half* a bottle and downing most of it herself. Russell claimed Streisand also tried draining his brain to the dregs on matters of camera lighting, crane shots, and zooms. But since, as he realized in retrospect, "a Jewish princess playing a Catholic whore" was a nonstarter, Russell thought of another 1970s screen icon: Liza Minnelli.

Russell claims that Rice and Stigwood had reservations about the *Cabaret* harlot, but that Andrew Lloyd Webber was more open-minded. After almost a year of wigs, warbling, and rejections, Minnelli seemed the solution. For the audition, she managed to grab hold of the damned blonde wig but couldn't slip into the lamé in time. But as far as Russell was concerned, Saint Bernadette had arrived from Lourdes at the eleventh hour:

> So Liza sang in her jeans and T-shirt, and when she didn't know
> the words she improvised, soaring above obstacles that would have
> floored most aspirants to produce a performance so charismatic,
> so charged, so inspired, that she totally transcended the sentimen-

tality and superficial glamour of the stagy, two dimensional character and turned her into a vibrant woman of flesh and blood who
had clawed her way out of the slums and slept her way to the top
to possess the very soul of a nation. . . . And when she reached her
climax with an orgasmic "I'm coming," so was everyone else in the
place: man, woman, dog.

Russell was still basking in the afterglow when Stigwood summoned him to
his luxury confines, having him transported by speedboat to a private hideaway.
As the 70 mph ride clashed with the gushing winds, Russell literally fell on his
face during the journey: a bad sign. Hitting land, he got escorted to a guest bungalow. But to meet his host, he had to walk along the palatial estate replete with
columns, manicured lawns, and pool. The suntanned and self-assured Stigwood
glued his eyes to several television news broadcasts at once before greeting him.
Stigwood then terrorized him by showing the holes on his estate where humongous spider crabs dwelt and mated. After such niceties, Russell finally focused
Stigwood's attention on the test video he brought along of Liza's performance.

Stigwood gave no ready decision. Russell had to wait until he left L.A. and
jetted back to Heathrow, where he was handed a message: "I opened the folded
paper bearing my name scribbled in pencil. The message consisted of two
words: 'Elaine Paige.' I immediately phoned my agent, who brushed aside my
protestations. . . . I couldn't believe it. I'd been set up. I'd been humored. It was
always going to be Elaine Paige. My dreams of coming up with an alternative
Evita were just dreams."

Over a bottle of Beaujolais, Russell ruminated over two paths: either be a
whore, brave Stigwood's insult, and try for a long-awaited hit; or be an idealist, keep his impoverished pride, and quit. The idealist prevailed and phoned
his disappointed agent. But as soon as he said no, another Hollywood honcho
offered another seduction.

Russell recalls Sherry Lansing inviting him back to Hollywood for a power
lunch. On his return, he was astonished at the royal treatment. Lansing was
all smiles and seduction, thinking that Russell wasn't serious about bowing
out. To show her enthusiasm, she took out a magnum of champagne to seal the
deal. Russell licked his chops before telling her straight out that he did not want
Elaine Paige or anything more to do with *Evita*. Not missing a beat, Lansing
grabbed the champagne and stuck it back into the refrigerator. "'What are you
doing?' I said, raising my voice at the sight of my lunchtime tipple being locked
away. 'We've nothing to celebrate now, have we?' she said, icily."

For all those dying to make the project, Russell became the persona non
grata. "Russell was an insane choice," Tim Rice later griped to the *New York*

Times, "and would have wrecked the film if he had gotten his hands on it. I was relieved when he got the boot." But Rice could not have been pleased to see how many years the project languished—with such directors as Richard Attenborough, Herbert Ross, and Oliver Stone flying in and then flagging out after debates about money, contract negotiations with pushy stars, and political upheavals in Argentina that made authentic shooting locations tricky.

●

Of the many Russell projects that started with the best and looniest intentions but got nowhere, *Moll Flanders* offers his most picaresque adventure. This was the mid-1980s: Bob Guccione, the *Penthouse* potentate who glamorized nudie photos through gossamer photography but grossed out the world with *Caligula*, planned what was supposed to be a bold, censor-free interpretation of Daniel Defoe's novel.

Perhaps aware of Guccione's vast holdings and penchant for ostentatious gold chains, Russell envisioned a film with a grand budget. But once again he wandered into a political minefield disguised as luxury's lair: Guccione's Rome hotel suite. Not since his encounter with Sophia Loren in L.A. did Russell endure so much Italian-style hospitality.

Guccione commissioned a script and, noticing the director's zeal at finding lucrative work, enticed him even more by treating him to what Russell remembers as "a mysterious car ride to the edge of the city." A Guccione assistant, whom Russell describes as "a slim, baggy-eyed man in a slouch hat," led him to the basement of a big and apparently abandoned apartment block.

The baggy-eyed escort, in a role similar to Elisha Cook Jr. as the haunted house tour guide in some William Castle production, unlocked the entrance to a tomb-like enclosure. Russell, wary of unlocked compartments—spooky houses where snakes, elephant trunks, Robert Stigwood's spider crabs, and other monsters might jump out—approached this wild side of Guccione's contractual courtship with suspicion; he followed nonetheless. Inside the vault and along poorly lit corridors, the baggy-eyed Elisha Cook Jr. clone switched on floodlights to expose an archive of props that included the sex machines Guccione planned for a film about Catherine the Great.

"Nothing was normal," Russell recalls as if terrified by an unsightly alter ego staring back at him. "Everything was exaggerated to the nth degree. A corpse hanging from a tree that Catherine saw as a child was magnified into a tree the size of a church with dozens of corpses hanging from its branches. Death was a recurring theme. There was an infernal plague pit dominated by a skeleton a hundred feet high pounding a giant drum to the rhythm of which countless infected couples fornicated around the perimeter of the pit, only to be pitched into the flames as they climaxed."

Russell and Guccione: could Britain's enfant terrible and America's soft-focus porn prince really be fated for an unholy match? Both waged their respective pubic wars by pushing the sexual edge further; both quaked before the Meese Commission's crackdown on what it perceived as pornography. But for Russell, Guccione looked less like a confrere and more like a frat house bully subjecting him to a hazing, a rite of passage that would seal a Faustian bargain. On the surface, the occasion was a blood ritual to bring Defoe's story about the eighteenth-century London prostitute up to date with some welcome kinkiness. Perhaps a scene of Defoe's riled skeleton twisting in its crypt might have been a good addition to the screenplay Guccione now commissioned Russell to write.

The trade papers gobbled news items about the search for the ideal Moll. Guccione combed England for girls with centerfold dimensions and required, to the ire of Actors' Equity, no previous stage or screen experience. Equity threatened hell on Earth if Moll ended up a non-union scab. Fortunately, as Russell recalls, Equity's contestants proved beautiful and sporting enough to submit to an audition: naked and over the knees of some masked man pretending to yank splinters from their buttocks. Alas, the Moll who stood out among the throng was cardless; Equity refused to grant her the coveted screen moment that would elevate her from a calendar nudie to a star.

When England's union proved unmovable, and Guccione insisted on the Moll of his choice, Russell suggested they look to Ireland for the film's locale. But Equity had jurisdiction there as well. Danger loomed as Guccione's mood got darker. Russell sensed trouble when, once back in the States, Guccione invited him for another pasta powwow, this time at his New York Penthouse Palace.

A surveillance camera recorded Russell's entrance; vicious guard dogs lunged toward him as he hobbled through the art-adorned marble halls. One of Guccione's servants led him to what Russell remembers as "the blackest room I have ever seen. Even the furnishings and fittings were black, and on the black walls hung the black and white erotic art of Aubrey Beardsley. I felt right at home. Its atmosphere of 1890s decadence was redolent of the Oscar Wilde room in L'Hôtel Paris, where I had once spent a debauched weekend with Oliver Reed."

The lure of a mirrored bed, a canopied ceiling, dinner at a marble banquet hall, and a Penthouse Pet in a black miniskirt plopped on his lap couldn't shake Russell from anticipating demands he could not meet. Guccione sat looking satisfied as he insisted that the Pets adorning the dinner table be allowed to run free through *Moll Flanders*'s scenery. Russell felt more blindsided than titillated: "My mind raced as a dozen heaving breasts threatened to tumble out of their dresses into steaming plates of fettuccine Alfredo."

A conference with the *Penthouse* board of directors in Guccione's "Georgian Room" the following day yielded more questions than answers. Everyone suggested locations from Paris to Copenhagen. But Guccione, showing signs of impatience with the whole project, felt a bit of a bounce after receiving a genuine Toulouse-Lautrec oil for a mere bagatelle of around $2 million. Reinvigorated, he suggested that the production go to Italy.

As soon as Russell flew to the Continent to find Italian approximations of English countrysides, Guccione sent a lawyer, someone who looked so much the part of a hatchet man that Russell nicknamed him "Geronimo." Geronimo started barking orders, sacking Russell's prized assistant, cameraman, editor, and costume designer. Russell persevered and went back to England, partly to find some authentic military duds for the soldier characters. But Guccione was also in London and beckoned Russell to enter the British version of the Penthouse Palace to hear more bad news. Equity, aware that that unknown calendar nudie was still up for the lead, got the International Federation of Actors to impose a worldwide *Moll Flanders* boycott.

With no location spot, no union support, legal threats, no actors officially contracted, and a script that Russell claims Guccione was rewriting on the sly, Russell couldn't be expected to digest pasta properly while discussing *Moll's* fate. He listened to Guccione and pals fondly exchange lore about New York mob warfare; he also looked at the now-beleaguered and weary calendar nude who registered with every facial muscle how much she wanted out.

"The next time I saw Guccione," Russell recalls (and recoils), "was in court a year after he had closed down the production and laid the blame on my shoulders. He claimed the *Moll Flanders* folly had cost him over a million dollars. He wanted his money back—from me. If I had him typecast as an outlaw, then perhaps he had me cast as the fall guy—on the film that never was."

●

By 1987, Russell needed a legal hero and found Richard Golub, a successful and media-friendly attorney who decided to study law after watching Robert Taylor as the mouthpiece who defends mob hoods in Nicholas Ray's 1958 film *Party Girl*. But he also entertained hopes of being a pop singer after watching Elvis go from serving time for manslaughter to being a hip-swiveling teenage idol in *Jailhouse Rock*.

Trial after trial, the handsome Golub won over jurors, partly with his slick talking style and sartorial finesse—shiny cuff links and shoes and suits from Saville Row—but also by convincing the jurors that Guccione had nothing on the man he tried to dispossess. Cleared of all charges, Russell went directly to prison. That is, Russell and a crew went to the actual site of Sing Sing—on a Sunday no less—to film a rock video. This was Russell's way of defraying some of his exorbitant legal costs, helping bolster Golub's dream of becoming a music video celeb.

Golub, who fancied himself another in the growing scion of Caucasian rap artists, had already done a number called "I Am Your Lawyer." Now, with Russell's MTV-era panache, he made the 1987 video "Dancing for Justice." The scenario has Golub's character forsake the law books to take up the "Good Book," becoming another of those evangelizing fanatics Russell loves to parody. Lording over Sing Sing's roof, Golub offers rhymes of wisdom to the reprobates:

> *Children, you're on death row, or you're doin' time,*
> *You're serving the Man for a bogus crime,*
> *You can't make a local telephone call,*
> *You've been installed like a piece of carpet, wall to wall.*

As Golub's preacher tells the cons that he can help get them free, Russell also shows up in the video as a robed judge who shakes his booty while gazing down through an iron grating. The prisoners too are shot through Russell's trademark prison bars filter as they grind their hips Elvis-style. As the guards twirl their truncheons, and another inmate wiggles his bum to the beat while pissing in the bowl, lots and lots of hands reach out through the bars toward a leather temptress shackled just beyond their reach.

Though the setting is authentic, Russell and Golub were forbidden to use real inmates. This was all for the best, since Russell found the prisoners and the prison atmosphere "more frightening than the gorilla house at the zoo." Actors masquerading as cons donned striped clothes, wielded axes, and languished over rock piles. Golub had the same sense of exuberance about the production as Russell: "We had these two beautiful girls in garter belts chained to the bars of the windows," Golub told the *New York Post*. "The prisoners were going ape." Golub ends the video as a combination Elmer Gantry and Samson, freeing all the prisoners while appearing to collect legal fees as they go. Russell also served his time, engorged Golub's ego, got absolved of all of Guccione's charges, and was free to fret over other yet another frustrated ambition.

•

As he went into postproduction on *The Rainbow*, Russell started preproduction on *All-American Murder*. Again, he paired up with screenwriter Barry Sandler. It was to be his next Vestron project: another lampoon on middle-class America.

This time the setting was to be a college campus, where several homicides occur. According to Russell, they included "death by incineration, electrocution, punctuation, compactation, copulation, and strangulation."

At the time, Russell stayed in Los Angeles at a hacienda-style villa on Outpost Drive in the Hollywood Hills, where Bela Lugosi supposedly lived. There, he held several casting sessions that included Jeff Goldblum and Linda Grey, but according to Sandler, Russell wanted Ann-Margret. When he found his ideal shooting spot, the University of Southern California campus, he got into snags with the authorities. They looked at the script and recoiled at the prospect of copycat killings.

Catholicism came to the rescue again when the Jesuits of Marymount College proved friendlier to having its holy grounds transformed into a slaughter haven. But just as the Lord stepped in, Mammon rained on the parade. Vestron, once so benevolent, was now losing money. Russell, Sandler, and the others involved in preparing the film got pink slips. The Vestron pullout even affected *The Rainbow*, which was already hitting theaters: suddenly its advertising budget evaporated. Worse, Russell never had a chance to make his planned sequel: *Revenge of the White Worm*.

This is when Russell once again got disgusted with Los Angeles. He packed his bags and flew back home to work with Melvyn Bragg for the *South Bank Show*: this time on his filmed autobiography. *A British Picture: Portrait of an Enfant Terrible* aired on the London Weekend Television network on October 15, 1989, consisting mostly of Russell's child son Rupert playing his dad in various guises: from the time Ken showed silent movies in his garage, to the drag shows he put on at the navy college, and through the highs and lows of a career with more misbegotten dreams in store.

29

FROM WHITE WORMS TO BLUE BALLS

In the 1990 film *The Russia House*, Ken Russell plays Walter, an eccentric and sometimes besotted British Intelligence agent. He is a misfit among his stiff, dark suited, and relatively humorless coworkers in this perestroika-era Cold War intrigue based on a John LeCarré novel. Despite leads from Sean Connery and Michelle Pfeiffer, the film profits more from the novelty that Russell adds (his first part as a supporting actor) whenever his character pops into the narrative. He is a combination of tipsy fop and oddball professor, sporting red plaid pants, guzzling beer, popping champagne corks, and flaunting a wonderfully high-strung speaking manner; in short, he's essentially being Ken Russell.

And Russell seems to have fun when taking command of the scenes, emerging as the agent with the biggest balls, at least ideologically. On the prospects of the British cooperating with the Russians in the spirit of perestroika, Walter morphs from a kindly fruitcake to a vituperative Cold Warrior: "Because this year it suits them to roll over on their backs and play nice doggie? Because this year they're on the floor anyway? You ninny! All the more reason to spy the living daylights out of them. Kick 'em in the balls every time they get to their knees!"

After making such a splash in the beginning, Walter disappears through a big chunk of the story and reappears at the end, pores over his Scotch on the rocks, and asks, "What about Russell?" Walter refers to a rather slippery American agent (played by Roy Scheider) who eels in and out of the plot, but the question could also be Russell inserting his autobiographical commentary. The film arrived right around the time the Soviet Union collapsed, and the Western world experienced geopolitical shifts. At the same time Russell entered a strange and ultimately unsatisfying decade that, like an unresolved spy story, led him down blind alleys and left him clueless. Anatomically put, the 1990s offered Russell the fits, starts, and frustrations of a creative orgasm that never happened. "I can't even remember what happened in the 1990s," he told the *Observer* in 2001. "Did anything happen? It's a total gap."

•

Russell started showing signs of S&M fatigue in 1989. He'd made so many movies depicting Nazis, nuns, neurotic composers, and whores in physical and psychological bondage. His 1989 music video was for "It's All Coming Back to Me Now" by rock producer Jim Steinman's all-girl group, Pandora's Box, and the song is in many ways a rehash of images and themes from his "Nessun Dorma" segment from *Aria*. This time, a woman's near-death experience is set amid operatic excesses and black leather. In a simulated city engulfed by an apocalyptic blaze, British vocalist Elaine Caswell sings and participates in a ritual to celebrate the song's "nights of sacred pleasure." All of this transpires inside a vast Pinewood Studios soundstage that is stocked with gravestones, motorcycles, pythons, and dancers (allegedly from the London production of *Cats*) strapped in chaps, studded bras, and spiked codpieces. Though the black and white evokes classic horror films, the results look more like a quick work for hire: lots of surface flash and heterosexual kinkiness that come nowhere near the heartfelt "perversions" that Russell accomplished in previous work.

Tales of black-leather bondage were simply old hat for a director who had already been more excessive than most mainstream directors when portraying pain. He needed something subtler, starker, more chaste, and fraught with sexual frustration. In his 1990 television drama *The Strange Affliction of Anton Bruckner*, which he made for Melvyn Bragg's *South Bank Show*, Russell paid homage to the quaint, lower budget BBC biopics of his past.

Bruckner was an obsessive man who, according to his biographer Derek Watson, suffered three nervous breakdowns and whose neuroses forced him to adopt a life of celibacy. To make the environment suit the man, Russell cast Bruckner (Peter MacKriel) in an immaculately white sanitarium, depending on the kindness of his comely nurse Gretel (Catherine Nielsen) and the equally comely male assistant Hans (Carsten Norgaard). And for the story's requisite bouts of suffering, Russell has Hans and Gretel spoon-feed Bruckner broth before attempting to cure his obsessive-compulsive disorders by immersing him in nasty, ice cold baths.

Nurse Gretel takes a maternal turn and, in an act of charity, disrobes to join Bruckner in his hospital bed. She tries sating his unsatisfied desire to see a naked lady, but when she cradles him, he relives the trauma that led to his affliction: sadistic fellow classmates putting a blindfold on him and locking him in a room with some strange girl. The boys' taunting giggles shatter him so much that he tries blocking out the humiliating memories by counting steps, boats, and practically everything in sight.

"People ask me what I think was really wrong with Bruckner," Russell says years after making the film in an interview with John C. Tibbetts, "what the hell was his 'numeromania,' this mania for counting things? I suggest in the film that it was a sexual thing; that he had been 'set up' in some pub with a loose woman and everybody got drunk, and he was ill prepared to deal with the situation. It was a distasteful encounter for him, and it didn't do him any good. The only way he could connect with reality was to treat it as a mass of data, as something to list and count and itemize."

●

Russell moved from a frustrated celibate's sanitized asylum to a glossy Roaring Twenties New York City penthouse when he dramatized Dorothy Parker's story "Dusk Before Fireworks," a short he contributed to an HBO television anthology called *Men and Women: Stories of Seduction*. There's still sexual frustration in the air, only this time, the tension is between a loquacious Molly Ringwald trying to ignite the romantic sparks and an unctuous, womanizing Peter Weller whose phone won't stop ringing.

Billy Williams's glossy cinematography captures the ambiance of martini glasses, flapper fashions, and windows looking out on a metropolitan skyline, although neither actor seems inspired while spouting the urbane lines. Russell would have been content to settle for the false elegance and call it a day job, but when the producers changed his intended soundtrack of period band music to a lusher Marvin Hamlisch score, he sniffed at the decision and skipped out on the premiere.

The too-precious world of penthouses and urban glamour was never Russell's forte anyway. He bristled at Garry Marshall's 1990 film *Pretty Woman*, which portrayed a hooker's life as so many enchanted evenings. And since anger often fuels his muse, Russell embarked on a project that he hoped would expose the oldest profession's putrid underbelly, even if it meant revisiting the sleazy pavements he'd already pounded in *Crimes of Passion*.

Russell intended the 1991 *Whore*, his first of only two feature films in the entire decade, to shine a rude light over Marshall's gauze. Adapting David Hines's play *Bondage*, he coscripted with Deborah Dalton a story about the daily grind of a prostitute who, far from swooning in the lap dance of luxury, is a whipping girl for male aggression. "They don't want sex," she complains of her johns. "They want revenge."

Switching the setting from London to Los Angeles, Russell casts Theresa Russell as Liz, the star harlot who spends much of the film staring into the camera and giving a monologue about the johns that practically defecate on her and the pimp who harasses and tries to kill her. Men are apparently her nemesis, except for a kind soul (Jack Nance) who saves her after she's gangbanged in a van, dumped, and left for dead on a dirt road.

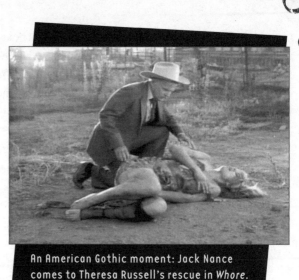

An American Gothic moment: Jack Nance comes to Theresa Russell's rescue in *Whore*.

There's Charlie (Frank Smith), an old man fixated on the sensation of Liz's whip thrashing against his prune flesh, even after he has a stroke; she also encounters a diminutive East Indian (Sanjay Chandani) who pops into the story from time to time on his motorbike to brag about his "very stout member" but refuses to wear a "rubber thing." Liz also strikes up a close friendship with Katie (Elizabeth Moorehead), but Russell does not let it conclude with the kind of lesbian bond he depicted in *The Rainbow*.

Liz also finds a confidante in Rasta (Antonio Fargas), a Jamaican street urchin who gets her out of a jam or two and becomes Liz's sounding board when she spouts off about her troubled days. Though often coming across as a witless sidekick, Rasta is among the very few sympathetic male characters. Most of the guys are cads—like her beer-guzzling husband Bill (Jason Saucier). He initially appears as a handsome and kindly chump, but he ends up a floundering cheat who can hold neither a job, his adulterous wanderlust, nor his liquor. One memorable scene of domestic dreck has him coming home with lipstick on his cheek and a conniving smile as Liz waits for him at the dinner table. But he ruins the mood by spewing vomit, which looks too much like ranch dressing, all over his salad.

Whore is most notable for a protracted scene lasting roughly twelve minutes. It's a fine example of parallel editing. Liz cries to Rasta about her squalid circumstances, while the camera keeps cutting to her pimp Blake (Benjamin Mouton) as he looks into the camera and gives his side of the story. Driving along the boulevards, he shares a cynical worldview that sounds at times frightfully convincing and sincere, even though viewers already know he's committing misogynistic atrocities and expect him to get his comeuppance.

According to Leonard Pollack, who was back as Russell's costume designer, Theresa Russell (who had earned a reputation as a high priestess of doom for all of the macabre roles she played for her husband Nicolas Roeg's later films) was Trimark Pictures' first choice. But at one point, she backed out of the project. Pollack recalls the somewhat circuitous preproduction politics that followed:

> Ken asked if I could think of a replacement. Holly Hunter came to mind. Ken didn't know her work and asked if I could find him something to see. I got him *Texas Cheerleader*. He agreed that she would be a much better street whore than Theresa. From my understanding, Holly got a script, and word got back that she wanted to meet with Russell. A meeting was set up early evening, but before that was to take place, Theresa's people called back, said she'd reconsidered, and would do it for a half a million dollars. The studio agreed, and the film certainly suffered, due to about a third of the funds going to just one player. It would have been a totally different film with Holly Hunter. But who listens to costume designers any more?

Leonard Pollack's sketch for an unused scene in *Whore*, when Russell was to play a bordello madam. (Art by and courtesy of Leonard Pollack)

Russell had other plans for *Whore* that sadly never made it to celluloid. As Pollack recalls, "In a scene where Liz works in a brothel, Ken wanted to play the madam. I designed his costume, but money got in the way—namely the star's salary. It ended up an unused idea, but if you look at my sketches, you could imagine how outlandish the whole effect could have been." Ken does sneak in a less flamboyant but still comical cameo as a snooty waiter at some high-toned restaurant who takes umbrage at having to refer to Liz's pimp as "sir."

When released to theaters with an NC-17 rating, *Whore* was scandalous to some—it was banned in Ireland—but for many jaded, post-1980s Americans, it wasn't arousing or shocking enough.

"*Whore* isn't pornographic," Vincent Canby complained in the *New York Times*. "It's not much of anything." An R-rated version got shorn of some dirty words, vomiting, and vicious coital thrusts; some truncations even bore the title *If You Can't Say It, Just See It*. But even the unrated video versions lack *Crimes of Passion*'s perverse intensity. This time around, Russell seemed as alienated and prostituted as the slut whose daily life his camera chronicles. Most likely, the L.A. atmosphere got the best of him: he was out of his element, especially with American actors who did not share his sense of British dottiness or irony.

•

Fortunately, Russell got a chance to breathe again at England's Pinewood Studios. There, he reunited with some of his old British cronies via an HBO production entitled *Prisoner of Honor*, a tightly woven 1991 film about the Dreyfus Affair. Included in the cast are Kenneth Colley as the real-life Captain Alfred Dreyfus, convicted of treason for being a German agent and finally acquitted in part because of Emile Zola's (Martin Friend) efforts. Judith Paris shows up as Dreyfus's beleaguered wife, Christopher Logue is her attorney Fernand Labori,

Oliver Reed as General de Boisdeffre in *Prisoner of Honor*—his final Russell screen role.

Imogen Claire performs a fascistic dance number on behalf of "France, the Fatherland," and Murray Melvin has a cameo as a prosecuting attorney. Russell's frequent set designer Paul Dufficey appears as a sketch artist, commissioned to paint a portrait of a comically pompous General de Boisdeffre, whom Oliver Reed plays with hammy abandon in what would be his last Russell screen performance.

"I think British cinema lost its way with the romantic neo-baroque of Roeg or Ken Russell," director Lindsay Anderson once grumbled in a late 1980s interview. But Russell apparently forgave this fatuous assertion, or at least knew a good crank when he saw one, when casting him as the grouchy minister of war. The only piece of miscasting is Richard Dreyfuss, who also coproduced the film. He is somewhat stiff as Colonel Georges Picquart, the attorney who flouts peer pressure and a public rife with Jew-baiters by going to Dreyfus's defense. Dreyfuss is the only major cast member who pulls a consistent straight face; the others players seem in on Russell's attempts to turn a dire piece of history into a wry comedy about how haughty and incompetent both the French and German authorities were in the events leading up to and during Dreyfus's trial.

Russell also tries quirking up the history: memories of *Mahler* arise when children sing anti-Semitic lyrics to "Frere Jacques"; there's some gender-bending fun when Major Ferdinand Esterhazy (Patrick Ryecart), the real traitor who's also the movie's narrator, goes to a bordello full of male prostitutes played by both men and women. There's also a kinky, anti-Semitic cabaret show, with Dreyfus portrayed as a vampire biting into a shiksa's neck.

●

As he filmed Dreyfus fending off fiends and languishing on Devil's Island, Russell was again fighting demons on the domestic front. For years, he had forged an artistic bond with wife Vivian, sharing idyllic days at Coombe Cottage in the Lake District. "I spent our time there teaching her how to become a photographer," he later griped to the *Guardian*'s Stephen Armstrong. "As soon as she was a master, she said, right, I don't need you any more, you can fuck off." In 1991, they divorced.

For a man with a sometimes bilious temper, Russell at least managed to find a matrimonial replacement in a relatively short time. In the summer of 1992, Russell married actress and dancer Hetty Baynes, who was already pregnant with another scion of the Russell bloodline. She was funny, vivacious, did great Marilyn Monroe impressions, and seemed eccentric enough to play in some of Russell's subsequent films, usually as either bimbos or wry seductresses.

Ken fell in love when casting Hetty for a flirty part in a *South Bank Show* movie he made about another British romantic composer, *The Secret Life of Arnold Bax*. The film begs for autobiographical cross-references as Russell explores not only Bax's music but also his sentimental misgivings, frustrated love life, and weakness for a younger piece of what the British rudely call "crumpet." Russell felt that he both resembled and identified with the composer so much that he should perform the title role, with a bearing that is the antithesis of Walter in *The Russia House*. Here, Russell is very subdued; other than constantly bending the elbow with brandy and muttering droll witticisms, he's a bit stiff and generally underwhelming.

This was also Glenda Jackson's final role, before she entered another kind of theater of the absurd as a Labour Party representative in the House of Commons. She plays Bax's girlfriend, the famous British pianist Harriet Cohen, for whom Bax composed most of his piano pieces. Jackson makes sure she strides out of her profession in style as she plays the high-toned harridan, flying into a rage when discovering that Bax has been seeing another woman: "What am I, your public whore? What has she ever done for you? Did she promote your music when the very mention of your name was guaranteed to empty every concert hall in the civilized world?"

As Arnold Bax, Russell portrayed a man who would take his lover's rage to heart and reform his wandering ways; as Ken Russell, he chose to embrace his new love with the zeal of a newborn adolescent. When he and Hetty got married, Russell staged their wedding ceremony beneath a Dorset beach cliff. Still, he didn't abandon all caution: he also took out an insurance policy against the event of an unexpected tidal wave. The service involved a ritual of the four elements as Ken and Hetty made vows beside a hefty lighted candle, and an officiator sprinkled them with earth, water, and incense.

∎

Relationships, and their frequent fallout, were still on Russell's mind in 1992, when he made *The Mystery of Dr. Martinu* for BBC-2. Still enamored by impressionistic history, he subtitled it "A Revelation by Ken Russell." The story is about the Czech composer Bohuslav Martinu (Patrick Ryecart) and his bonds with his wife Charlotte (Shauna Baird), his mistress Slava (Hannah King), and his psychiatrist Professor Mirisch (Martin Friend). Russell constructs it as a psychological sleuthing exercise as Martinu searches for remnants of his identity. Amid several curiosity-rousing images—Martinu's hand covered with ants, deaf mutes carousing at a seashore, and a young girl signaling him from a lighthouse—Russell focuses (with likely a few autobiographical overtones) on the composer's mental breakdown sometime in the late 1940s.

∎

In December 1992, while staging a live production of Gilbert and Sullivan's 1884 operetta *Princess Ida* for the English National Opera, Russell explored the battle of the sexes through blank verse. Rosemary Joshua played the title role as the princess trying to escape from the patriarchal authority of her father King Gama and the prince to whom she's betrothed. She retreats with fellow female rebels to Castle Adamant, where she forms a women's university to teach maidens the perils of loving men.

Russell's version is set in what was then the future world of 2002. Much of the action takes place at "Buck'n'Yen" Palace, at a time when American and Japanese interests have overwhelmed Britain's economy. Instead of Castle Adamant, the princess teaches at the Tower of London, where men are put on racks and their intestines exposed. Lady Psyche, the princess's humanities professor, appears as a *Crimes of Passion*–style virago, clad in black leather while brandishing a whip. For brazen choreography, Russell has *Altered States*–style ape-men dance up a lampoon on Darwin.

Audiences alternately booed and cheered *Princess Ida*, as Russell again took liberties that the operetta's creators might have found more amusing than the all-too-literal critics. Richard Traubner wailed against Russell's production in *Opera News*, disgusted by seeing "a nastily pruned script and a host of visual diversions, such as guardsmen's busbies with enormous ears, corgi skateboards, the 'Ye Olde Cuppa Tea' ride, King Gama as a Japanese Sushi-King magnate, his sons with Rising Sun hot-pants on bicycles, and a pastel-pearlie chorus swaying left and right."

●

Connie Chatterley (Joely Richardson) rides the dark horse of passion in Russell's BBC production of *Lady Chatterley*.

While he enjoyed portraying couples at war on film and now on the stage, Russell was savoring domestic bliss while he could. He cast Baynes again in 1993, this time as Connie Chatterley's bon vivant sister Hilda in *Lady Chatterley*—a drawn out, two-part made-for-BBC yarn for which Russell culled parts from all three versions of Lawrence's novel. It had lots of gratuitous plot but enough coitus—particularly a rear-entry scene between Lady Chatterley (Joely Richardson) and her rugged but sensitive lover Oliver Mellors (Sean Bean)—to curdle the tea and crumpets of British bluenoses.

Although Richardson is nowhere near as intense as her mother Vanessa Redgrave, she complements James Wilby, an engaging actor who, with dignified petulance, plays her war-impaired and sexually impotent husband Sir Clifford. Russell also gobbles scenery as Connie's eccentric uncle, Sir Michael Reid. His highpoint occurs when he dresses as Henry VIII at a costume party picnic on his estate. As Uncle Reid tipples and jabbers about representational art, a cavalcade of costumed sprites traipse across the background, including someone in a black bird costume—an obvious homage to Louis XIII's featured Protestant in *The Devils*.

Lady Chatterley's best moment, however, is a dream scene that occurs earlier in the story: Lady Chatterley rides the dark horse of passion, along a path adorned with naked male soldiers covered in ivy. For years, Derek Jarman had made cinematic nods to Russell in some of his films, but in this instance of male idolatry bordering on camp, Russell returns the favor.

■

Baynes emerged as a comically seductive character again in *The Insatiable Mrs. Kirsch*, a 1993 short Russell did for an anthology called *Erotic Tales*. She plays a comely blonde for whom a gutter-minded novelist (Simon Shepherd) develops a randy infatuation. But as he observes her and sees eroticism in her every movement, his imagination goes awry. The woman hums in her room at a Dorset seaside inn, but the writer, who listens from outside her door, thinks it's the sound of her vibrator.

When directing *Ken Russell's Treasure Island*, which aired on Channel Four on Christmas Eve, 1995, Russell had Baynes portray Long Jane Silver, a feminized update of Robert Louis Stevenson's evil sea thug. Even with an artificial leg, Baynes's pirate dances, sings, and still manages to balance a stuffed parrot on her shoulder. "In research for the film," Russell told the *Globe and Mail*, "I read about there being lady pirates and thought it was rather sexist of Stevenson to have an all-male cast of pirates." *Ken Russell's Treasure Island* is more notable for Russell's filming it on a Hi-8 camcorder. For him, this was a new and more economical beginning.

■

Russell continued with his cherished stories about misguided musical geniuses and their often-unfulfilled desires. In 1995, he made another installment of the *South Bank Show* called *Classic Widows*, a tribute to four women who share three qualities: "love of their late husbands, devotion to their music, and guts." Russell intersperses the works of the four composers—Sir William Walton, Bernard Stevens, Benjamin Frankel, and Humphrey Searle—while interviewing their usually discontented widows as they try to preserve their husbands' legacies.

While spreading the gospel of Sir William's music to the press, wife Susana Walton gabs on the telephone and talks about conquering her nail-biting habit. Susana also performs: glaring into the camera in a blue-feathered hat, eyes wide, and teeth gritting. She sings "Long Steel Grass" from Walton's *Facade* while two tango dancers (one played by Baynes) accent her controlled hysteria. Bertha Stevens tries organizing a Bernard revival, freely discussing her husband's Communist past, his *Liberation Symphony*, and his music's "tingle factor." Benjamin Frankel's widow Xenia, the most low-key of the four, sits in her Edwardian House in London, recalling how Frankel wrote his Sixth Symphony while hospitalized, and how he died almost penniless from a cerebral thrombosis. Fiona Searle is the saltiest of the four. She gets animated while summarizing Humphrey's accomplishments that range from an opera based on *Hamlet* to music for the British sci-fi series *Dr. Who*. Russell heightens the drama by fixing a close-up on Fiona's angry face as she rages over the public's indifference. Looking straight into the camera, she cries, "Ken, what the fuck do we do about it?"

Russell empathized with Fiona Searle's aggravation, especially that same year when he wondered "what the fuck" he was going to do about finding a studio to back a project based on a screenplay he wrote about another of his idols: the Russian composer Alexander Scriabin. Scriabin composed mystical symphonic poems to complement his interest in Helena Blavatsky's theosophical writings. Russell wanted to film the composer's dream of performing his final work, which he intended to call *Mysterium*, while dying in the Himalayas. Scriabin planned a seven-day event: bells would dangle from the sky, numinous scents would waft through the air, and a naked cast of thousands would dance, sing, and court the cosmos—all the while, a swooning orchestra's melodies would ascend with the sunrise and plummet with the sunset.

The potential backers apparently envisioned only a mystical haze of burnt money when they estimated the millions required to transpose Scriabin's high-octane orgasm to celluloid. Therefore, Russell's plans to film Scriabin's dissonant climax succumbed to blue balls. But someone at the BBC suggested Russell turn his cinematically impossible dream into a broadcast. In June 1995, BBC Radio 3 aired Russell's first radio play: *The Death of Alexander Scriabin*, speculating on an actual 1914 meeting in Moscow between the composer and occult legend Aleister Crowley. The show featured James Wilby as Scriabin and Oliver Reed as Crowley. "As a fruitily theatrical Crowley," Martin Hoyle wrote in the *Financial Times*, "Oliver Reed began as Noel Coward with laryngitis and progressed to Lady Bracknell."

Russell's reveries were still mystical when he and Baynes traveled to Israel to interpret the life and exploits of paranormalist Uri Geller. The 1996 movie

Mindbender starts with a disclaimer about how "the following events are true and are interpreted through the artistic eye of Ken Russell" and proceeds with a budget that is obviously low and a cast consisting almost entirely of Israeli natives who spout their lines with astounding American accents.

As Uri, the handsome but leaden Ishai Golan drags the narrative down. However, Terence Stamp as Joe Hartman, the man who tries harnessing Geller's talents, helps buoy the plot along. Baynes is Hartman's sensuous wife Kitti, who applies lots of makeup, takes mud baths, and has occasional moments of temper.

But Russell seems to have gotten bored with his subject going into the project and appears more interested in culling sensuous imagery out of Israel's landscape. He makes another of his trademark contrasts between the untamed mineral world and the man-made objects emerging from it when young Uri (Erez Atar) holds a shiny silver bullet against the craggy Tel Aviv sands and transforms it into a ring. Russell has another favorite theme: the abusive father. In one scene, Uri's dad (Rafi Tabor) corners his son among a bunch of tailor's dummies and starts belting him. Uri also has bad dreams that include his dad disco-dancing with a harlot under a giant Daliesque clock and shellfish littered along a tank-tracked beach that turn into detonated landmines.

The script involves Uri and some future wife, but he has a more profound relationship with his pal Shipi (Idan Alterman), who works like a faithful spouse to galvanize the Geller legend. It's another of Russell's half-assed probes into true male bonding that doesn't go far. Shipi does get somewhat captivating during a petulant snit when he gets tired of Uri ordering him around; he takes his frustrations out on a banana by stroking it before chomping it down.

Even after Uri travels to Australia, mans the airwaves at the Olympics Stadium studio in Sydney, and pleads for the world to psychokinetically join him in thwarting the trajectory of a Communist Chinese nuclear missile, the story's climax gets stilted when the soundtrack plays Elton John's "Rocket Man" and the closing credits end. Suddenly, the real Uri Geller shows up with all the strained zeal of an infomercial host, asking viewers to literally reach out to him by placing their hands against his on the television screen and letting his power mend their appliances and souls. Even with this self-promotional coda, Geller expressed some displeasure with Russell's results.

But by 1996, Russell was through with Catholicism and, therefore, not inclined to believe that a mere messianic mortal like Geller could right any mounting wrongs. The world was changing so much for Ken Russell. All the movie industry money that used to come his way had all but dried up. And his memories were getting grayer. People he'd worked with, younger than he, were passing away—at least three from AIDS: Anthony Perkins in 1992, Rudolf Nureyev in 1993, and Derek Jarman the following year. A hefty portion of his fan base, consisting primarily of a gay intelligentsia nurtured on 1960s and '70s repertory movies, was also either fading away or forgetting.

Russell's Mum also died from pneumonia in the early 1980s and Dad passed on in 1985—both in state institutions. Even though Dad wished to be cremated, Russell's brother Ray took the liberty to make sure they were both interred side by side in a predictable Church of England funeral. Thinking about Mum and Dad's underground reunion, a ritualistic gesture he at first thought "a touch macabre," Russell mulled more and more over how to dispose of his own carcass when his time arrived. By now, he felt more inclined to flame away on a pyre, preferably at the Derwentwater shores.

Sometime in 1996, he momentarily relinquished such pagan thoughts when he claims to have encountered Roman Catholic apparitions—visions not from a spontaneous re-conversion but from a stroke. "It was an extraordinary experience," he told the *Times* (London) in 1999. "A terrible noise in my head like a million volts of electricity. I thought I was dying, and I believed I saw the Virgin Mary and child floating up in a corner of the room. I think that when God decides your number's up, he just presses the abort button."

∎

Failing health also portended a faltering domestic life, as Hetty Baynes showed the obverse of her fun side, and Russell braced for another divorce. When they were newlyweds, and she moved from her flat into Russell's three-bedroom cottage near Marylebone Road, Baynes was surprised that a man with such wild films and an equally wild reputation kept such a neat house. He was so methodical in his creative rituals, insisting on using a certain type of pen and a particular style of A4 spiral notebook to write his stories and scripts. But Russell's best screen moments involved fury after a mounting calm; why should his life be any different?

In 2000, Baynes was quoted in London's *Daily Express*: "Ken had a very short fuse. If anything wasn't up to scratch he would blow up. Anything could spark it off—a baby's toy left on the floor, the tiniest thing. . . . Mostly he was sorry afterwards. But sometimes he would not even know he'd done it. It was as if his mind had temporarily gone. People with that temperament don't have any link with reality."

Russell, of course, had his twist to the story. "We got on well to start with, but she now says I was jealous of the baby, which is nonsense," he told the *Times* (London) in 2005. "Maybe I changed or maybe the demands of a director were not what she was expecting. She smashed all my best antique crockery. We were trying to make up in a hotel when she said, 'Maybe you wish you hadn't married me?' I said, 'Yes,' which wasn't the right answer. She started screaming, and the people on both sides began knocking on the walls. After my stroke, I thought she wanted to kill me, and I escaped on a train to London."

Candid all along about the personality glitches that left him romantically abandoned, Russell now wandered again, feeling unlovable and unbankable for a couple more years. While he waited for another soul mate, he contented himself with talking to his phlegmatic dog Nipper. Russell ended up filming one of their apparently one-sided conversations in 1998: a modest documentary he made for England's Channel Four called *In Search of the English Folk Song*. It starts as Russell asks Nipper the importance of an English folk song. Getting the usual dim response, Russell goes off on a village excursion to answer his own question. Along the way, he finds various English folk artists and gets them to perform their favorites. The bill includes Donovan singing "Nirvana," Fairport Convention performing "Seventeen Come Sunday," and the Percy Grainger Chamber Orchestra doing a rendition of "Country Gardens."

In the meantime, bills, including alimony and child-support, abounded; more grunt work was in order. Russell's ordeal when filming the 1998 cable television film *Dogboys* sums up his tentative place in 1990s cinema. It's a prison drama in which Bryan Brown plays Captain Robert Brown, a sadistic warden with an ear for classical music, which he listens to on a Sony Walkman. Dean Cain (anxious to shed his Superman image from the television series *Lois and Clark*) portrays Julian Taylor, the dogged con trying to escape the hellhole that ugly and vicious German Shepherds guard.

During production, Cain was desperate to find "motivation" for the part, so he got Russell in on a four-way telephone conference with Cain's agent and a vice-president for Showtime, the cable network that finally aired it after postponing the production twice. Not knowing what to say, Russell stammered into the receiver with a bunch of ad-libs, telling Cain that his character was "an exserviceman" and "a light heavyweight champion in the Marine Corps." "I was prepared to waffle on," Russell admits in his book *Directing Film: From Pitch to Premiere*, "but Dean took the bait, hook, line, and sinker."

Bryan Brown proved more difficult. Simple ad-libs weren't enough to convince this player from down under about the wisdom of going against his good guy image. He required an elaborate history to understand why his character could be so sour. Russell finally came up with a workable explanation: "Captain

Brown was . . . good at his job and kindly. And as compensation for being a widower, he had an eighteen-year-old daughter to dote on. She was a brilliant musician on the threshold of a solo career . . . Her favored instrument was the organ, and she specialized in Bach. But her brilliant career was brought to a tragic end when she was raped and murdered by an escaped convict who also slew her pet Alsatian, which died protecting her."

A lower point for Russell, in a decade of few if any highs, occurred in May 1999, when he learned that Oliver Reed—the nutcase who used to flip him around, chase him with a steel sword, and expose his pork sword—keeled over in Malta from a heart attack. Reed got soused and didn't think twice before arm wrestling Royal Navy sailors many years his junior. But Russell saw an omen eight years before when casting Reed in *Prisoner of Honor*: "There was always an animal lurking under the surface, and the animal had either been tamed or driven out of him. It wasn't the same Oliver. He was a different man."

•

Desperate for signs of a miracle but canny about spiritual illusions, Russell tried his hand at a novel that plays havoc with both the Old and New Testaments. In 1999, he published *Mike and Gaby's Space Gospel* and filled it with enough titillation, profanity, and violence to assure an NC-17 rating if ever filmed. Straddling the fault line between religious rapture and blasphemy, he presents Mike and Gaby as robot incarnations of archangels Michael and Gabriel. But instead of peering down from the clouds with haloes and wings, they sit inside a spaceship, the *Ark 2001*, and watch from a monitor screen as humankind goes through many of the growing pains, damnations, and redemptions that the Bible stories had preordained.

Russell's sci-fi tweaking gives humans a different mission. A benevolent deity creates them as part of an experiment to determine if at least one of the species has the wherewithal to ferret out from the planet's terrain an antidote to rust, a design fault that threatens to decimate the angelic robot race. Hovering above the planet and flicking their remote controls, Mike and Gaby supervise this grand scheme, observing, manipulating, and inspiring human destiny with several miracle facsimiles. They project a "high-tech white light hologram of the Celestial City," teleport a soy version of lox and bagels for a microchip-implanted Jesus to feed his faithful, track Jesus' feet with an antigravitational device as he treads the waters of Galilee, and deploy a missile destruct system to protect him from stone-throwers. But despite their good and desperate intentions, Mike and Gaby are up against a wily Satan who keeps jamming their frequencies and fouling up the divine plans.

Russell claims he wrote the novel, which is essentially remnants of a film project Russell had planned with Derek Jarman in the 1970s, "Through the eyes of a Jewish Hollywood scriptwriter." He updated the principal players to be as faithful to what were then the current pop cultural icons.

Russell specifies that Christ resembles Peter O'Toole in David Lean's *Lawrence of Arabia*, while Pontius Pilate calls up comparisons to David Bowie's portrayal in Martin Scorsese's *The Last Temptation of Christ*. He ratchets up the absurdity by making Joseph and Mary similar to the young Dustin Hoffman and Jennifer Jones as they conceive Jesus at a "Holy Day Inn." The magi and the manger call to mind "a scene from a Marx Brothers' movie, *A Night at the Opera* to be precise—the scene where a tiny cabin is packed with the Marx Brothers and half the ship's crew."

John the Baptist, who appeared as a pale, epicene figure in *Salome's Last Dance*, is here "reminiscent of the iron-willed Clint Eastwood in *Unforgiven*." The high priest Caiaphas is a Jewish Mafia Godfather who sips Bloody Marys, evokes Frank Sinatra, and surrounds himself with a Rat Pack of Dean Martin, Peter Lawford, and Sammy Davis Jr. look-alikes in priestly garb. King Herod, on the other hand, "might have been a distant ancestor of Woody Allen—even down to the horn-rimmed glasses he used to scan the night sky for signs and omens."

The gospel gals are just as colorful. Mary Magdalene calls to mind "Mae West in *Diamond Lil*," Herod Antipas's wife Herodias is "a bit like Barbra Streisand all dolled up for the Oscars," whereas his mom Jezebel is "Barbra Streisand on a bad day." But Herod's stepdaughter, the "Royal sex slut" Salome, has "all the charm of the teenage Elizabeth Taylor in *National Velvet* and all the sexual charisma of the same star in *Cleopatra*." At a pivotal moment when Christ appears at Herod's palace, Salome gets dolled up like Jodie Foster in *Taxi Driver*, gives the Lord a swift kick in the bollocks with one of her "heavy wedge shoes," and then rapturously grovels at his feet.

Just as with *The Devils*, Russell called upon the all-forgiving Reverend Gene Phillips to scan these pages and, likely differing from most Catholic priests, perceive no trace of blasphemy. But Russell also explained higher motives to *The Herald* (London):

> What has been lost from the way the gospels were written is the colloquialisms. I've got lots of Jewish friends and I also lived in Israel for a bit, which I loved. There was a great sense of welcome to outsiders. These people were full of funny jokes and phrases; they were very colorful. But there is none of that in the Bible; characters all talk the same, if they talk at all—much of it is reported speech.

There is no slang and, of course, these people would talk in slang all the time . . . I wanted to turn the whole thing upside down. I'm not writing the Bible, just trying to humanize the characters in it so that they become more than museum pieces.

·

From the days when he tried waking the sleepy British audiences, Russell developed a cinematic and narrative technique that cut through the clutter by hitting viewers with frontal, visceral assaults. Back in the 1960s and through most of the '70s, this was shocking and artistically innovative. But in the post-MTV climate, Russell awoke one day to discover he was his worst nightmare: an unwitting inspiration for a hyper-commercial cinema style that was now selling cars and sneakers. *Tommy*'s surrealistic baked bean sequence became the norm for television ads designed to be much brasher and bolder than the blander shows they sponsored.

Even the "weird" got stabilized. Surrealistic and erotically bent directors like America's David Lynch and England's Peter Greenaway were edging out such 1970s mavericks as Russell and Roeg. They also seemed craftier in sizing up their market niche: upwardly mobile spectators who could gawk at the "bizarre" yet still feel comfortably "normal." By the time the 1990s closed with the Wachowski brothers' *The Matrix*, wider audiences felt comfortable getting pelted with trippy and violent CGI effects and even snacking on some morsels of pop philosophy. The world of feature films seemed more depressing for Russell by 2000, when a computer grafted the late Oliver Reed's head onto a body double, allowing his character Proximo in *Gladiator* to depart from the cinema pantheon with a proper death.

In short, Russell became not only unbankable but also unfashionable. For many of today's viewers, Russell's quirkiness requires too much subtext, too many asterisks and footnotes. Despite all of this intelligent irony, merciless send-ups of sacred cows, and rousing affront to entrenched tastes, he seems by current standards too eccentric, idiosyncratic, and perhaps too Romantic—in the old-fashioned English literature sense. A cadre of brave independent filmmakers might carry his torch, some might even cite him as a direct inspiration, but his kind of quirky, raunchy, yet intellectual movie rarely surfaces these days as a major studio release.

Russell's beloved England, which generally favored his work less than America, threw him a bone in 1999, when the British Film Institute listed *Women in Love* number eighty-seven in its list of the nation's top one hundred films. And even as a new century started, Russell felt forgotten or flat-out ignored, writing off the era to London's *Observer* in 2001 as "the *Daily Mail* mentality, where everything is safe and yet prurient."

In weaker moments, he blames himself, as when he later thought aloud to the *Observer*'s Euan Ferguson: "Most people think I'm dead. I don't really know what happened. Mistakes. And, whoever you are you need an agent, and mine . . . my present agent hasn't gotten me a job at all."

So Russell left the fashionable auteurs to tote their fashionable scripts in their Gucci colostomy bags; he retreated to his English haven for some millennial soul-searching.

THE LOCH NESS TRICKSTER

To literal-minded viewers, the jittery, rainbow-colored object in Ken Russell's movie *The Fall of the Louse of Usher* is just a plastic Slinky. But to Russell, and anyone keen to his obsessions, it is a penis attached to the ancient Egyptian god Osiris, who has been summoned in a séance to help solve several Edgar Allan Poe mysteries. Russell casts himself as Doctor Calahari, the patriarch of a lunatic asylum, who gapes as Osiris's gigglestick whacks and wiggles with the fury of a trapped eel against an astrological map.

Russell's Calahari (so named because of his resemblance to the Dr. Caligari of German Expressionist fame and for having a mind as vast and thorny as the Kalahari Desert) seems resigned to an unsolved mystery. He is, after all, lording over a funny farm that flouts logic and proportion. The fact that he is as crazy as his inmates helps explain why the film transpires like an imaginative geezer's wet dream.

Russell, the proud Mad Hatter of British cinema, for whom the overused expression "beautifully understated" is an oxymoron, made this Poe homage in the year 2002. He did so not from the vast studio lots to which he was once accustomed but from his home in England's New Forest district. He also directed it with a camcorder and on a budget of less than twenty thousand British pounds from his own pocket. He named the four-hundred-year-old thatched cottage that he'd converted into his studio Gorsewood (for all the gorse bushes in his area), and his cast consisted of family and friends.

While entertaining his crew with champagne and strawberry picnics, Russell relished this parallel world, this fortress of solitude from the whims of fashion that ruled London, New York, and Los Angeles. As he so proudly declared to *Reuters News* in 2003, "I'm not answerable to anyone but me. I don't have to get the script approved. I don't have the final cut taken away from me."

Russell's Gorsewood offerings pale compared to the grand-scale features of his *Tommy* days, but other directors, with plenty of laurels to rest on, had less enviable latter days. Erich von Stroheim, for example, got increasingly demoted to emasculating character roles. By the 1970s, Orson Welles could still sell his wonderful voice-overs for television shows, but he also had to pay the rent by chuckling on Dean Martin celebrity roasts and doing pissy commercials for Paul Masson wine.

Russell at least lived out a dream scenario he had way back in 1971, when he interrupted a busy shooting schedule to share with the *Evening Standard* an ambition: "What I'd really like to do would be to get my own little film unit together . . . and we could all go down to the New Forest, and maybe I'd film a story about a composer, or a Dostoevsky story, and all the unit would bring down their families, and I'd put them up in caravans or a hotel, and if it was fine we'd work, but if it rained, well, we'd just go off and have a party."

Russell's Gorsewood revels got livelier when a new character entered his playhouse. As the twenty-first century dawned, he was in his early seventies, aimless, lonely, unbankable as usual, and tired of talking to his wretched dog. Wondering again about his funeral arrangements, he contemplated how his tombstone should read. His initial version was "Okay—so I fucked up."

Still technologically savvy, Russell did exactly what a teenager desperate for a warm body would do: he reached out into the Internet and posted an ad. It read, "Unbankable film director Ken Russell seeks soul mate—mad about movies, music, and Moët et Chandon champagne." As he told the *Times* (London), "Among the one thousand replies were a witch, a millionairess, a Swansea soprano, and Elize Tribble, an American fan I'd met for ten minutes twenty-five years earlier. She worked as an usherette in an arts cinema, so she could see my films."

"The thought of you fills me with light," the then fifty-year-old Tribble replied. Both then examined their complementary astrological charts and married a year later. This fortuitous turn of events, so redolent of all those tacky Catholic miracles he'd filmed and written about, gave Russell enough renewed heart to demand a tombstone retraction. Now he wanted it to read, "Okay—so I got lucky."

When he met Elize, Russell had just finished his first Gorsewood production. *Lion's Mouth* is a short film about the rector of Stiffkey, a real-life scandalous clergyman from the 1930s who lived up to his nickname, "the prostitute's padre." In Russell's version, the rector, who has no visible actor to portray him because Russell found no one at the time fitting for the part, sleeps inside a barrel and appears as only a pair of lips singing and sermonizing. Russell tells the story as a *Citizen Kane*–style investigation, as journalist Josephine Heatherington (Diana

Laurie) interviews those who had known the man. Playing a ringmaster, Russell dons a clown costume and lures the audience to his circus, where the rector, like Androcles and still in his barrel, preaches from a cage of (in this case stuffed) lions. *Lion's Mouth* might have cute moments, but Russell still struggled with a few camcorder glitches.

Getting better with his digital devices and happy in his new matrimonial Eden, Russell dragged Elize—who already described herself as an actor, poet, and folk singer—into his Gorsewood follies. In *The Fall of the Louse of Usher*, which was a bit slicker and more ambitious with its ninety-minute format, Elize plays Madeleine, the incestuous love object of brother Roderick. She sings, dances, and overacts as required. In ghoulish white pancake makeup and a black, curly fright wig flying every which way, she perfects the Art Nouveau sybarite, especially when performing a Goth duet in a graveyard with an equally cadaverous Roderick, played by the front man for the British band Gallon Drunk, James Johnston.

Russell originally planned to film *The Fall of the Louse of Usher* with Roger Daltrey and Twiggy as the main stars. Even in this more modest, cut-rate version, however, populated by relative unknowns, Russell still proves his gift for composition and his instinct for vibrant colors. An English flower garden never looks more surreal, old gravestones never exude more sinister grandeur, and even one of his

James Johnston and Elize Russell in *The Fall of the Louse of Usher*.

trademark slow-zooms onto James Johnston's rotting teeth exposes the undiscovered beauty behind what the consensus finds hideous. He also planned the film as a series of eight ten-minute shorts downloadable from the Internet but instead marketed it as a feature DVD through Image Entertainment. By prevailing standards, the movie is disjointed and mercilessly vulgar, but it also has stunning moments. In sum, it's more engaging than just about all of *Lady Chatterley*.

Never a zealot for special effects, Russell eschews the computer-generated imagery of the post-*Matrix* malaise. While watching *Louse*, viewers can experience the rhythms of primordial lust symbolically, as inflatable dolls (icons going back to *French Dressing*) and Godzillas simulate ungodly sex acts. When asked about these excursions into blow-up bestiality, Russell told *The Indepen-dent*, "I saw these dinosaurs in a toy-shop, and I saw the sex dolls in a trash shop next door, and I thought, 'That's good therapy.'"

Amid all this low budget prurience, Russell still includes lots of alternately vulgar and witty lines—packed with references to literature, science, philosophy, and film history. Many critics who got a chance to view *Louse* at special screenings hated it, but Russell seemed to thrive on the hatred as he planned his next, even more eye-vexing foray into Gorsewood Babylon.

∎

The Gorsewood movies seemed "out of control," but still Russell tried keeping in touch with a wider audience. By 2002, Melvyn Bragg had earned the title Lord, but he still had his *South Bank Show*, which now aired on Britain's ITV-1 network. He kicked off his twenty-sixth season with Russell's *Elgar, Fantasy of a Composer on a Bicycle*—just in time to celebrate the fortieth anniversary of the acclaimed *Elgar* when it debuted on the *Monitor* series.

Russell once lamented that he wasn't able to touch on Elgar's extramarital affairs. He goes into the composer's peccadilloes in this new version, stressing also how Elgar rejected all of the jingoism that lyricists made out of his "Land of Hope and Glory." Mrs. Elgar, who was much more self-effacing in the 1962 film, now emerges with a bit more of an identity as an archeologist. In place of Edwardian hauteur, Russell now opts to reflect Elgar's penchant for physical and verbal humor as he casts James Johnston, who still looks more like a post-punk rocker than a stately composer, in the title role.

Russell has always been interested in the sex lives of the great musical masters and was bound to cast a blue light on Johannes Brahms. In 2003, he presented *Brahms Gets Laid*, a novel biography that he published as an e-book through Iain Fisher, a gentleman who runs a Russell-centric Web site called SavageMes-siah.com. Here, Russell challenges the priggish perception that Brahms was "a confirmed bachelor and a respected pillar of society" by reminding everyone that the composer "was born in the red light district of Hamburg and spent his formative years playing honky-tonk piano in every whorehouse in town." He invites his readers to "listen to the inner movements of [Brahms's] Third Symphony for a sensuality that's hard to beat. And if it's white hot passion you're after, try the opening of the First Symphony and tell me if that doesn't have balls."

∎

Though Russell has flipped his middle finger to the studio world and all of the moguls, publicists, sycophants, and pseudo-weirdoes that abused, censored, and eventually ignored him through the years, his spirit still pops into mass media's verbiage. Steve Pratt, of England's paper the *Northern Echo*, needed an analogy for Baz Luhrmann's 2001 extravaganza of swooping cameras, can-can dancers, and jarring colors: "Imagine a film directed by Ken Russell on acid, and you have an idea of the movie that is *Moulin Rouge!*" Those who thought the film vacuous might assume that Pratt was hurling an insult until he followed his Russell reference with, "I loved it!" And in a March 2002 episode of *Buffy the Vampire Slayer* entitled "Normal Again," a demon feeds Buffy a hallucinogen that makes her believe all she once assumed to be real is false. A doctor in the story declares that a "demon pet has done some number on the Slayer. Got her trippin' like a Ken Russell film festival." News of other Russell endeavors continues to surface in magazines and newspapers. "I was asked to do a script on Peter Pan for an American company, and it seemed to write itself," he told the *Observer* in 2001. "It's called *Neverland*, and the script's been accepted with no changes, which is astonishing, and I believe it could happen." It happened, but what happened? Something with that name came out, but Russell's role in Marc Foster's 2004 film about the life of Peter Pan's creator J. M. Barrie is unclear, or at least unacknowledged.

By 2002, Russell was also ready to make another feature: a scientific romance called *Charged: The Life of Nikola Tesla*, about the eccentric Serbian who immigrated to America and invented alternating current. Russell wanted to explore the relationship Tesla had with the poet Robert Johnson's wife, Katherine. But the plot's choicest part would have dramatized Tesla's feud with Thomas Edison, alleging that Edison, in his fervor to discredit Tesla, used alternating current while presiding over a public execution in 1890. Edison supposedly hoped to demonstrate AC's dangers in comparison to his own direct current. Russell told Toronto's *Daily Telegraph* that Edison "began by electrocuting dogs and cats. He used to pay boys five dollars for every dog they brought him. That wasn't satisfactory, so he decided to electrocute a condemned man. Edison administered an initial burst for seventeen seconds. When that did not work, he put the machine on for three and a half minutes until the man's backbone burst into flames and he virtually burnt to death."

No surprise when the Edison family started making public statements condemning Russell's project. "Thomas Edison was not at that execution," the inventor's great-grandson, Professor David Sloane, countered in the same *Daily Telegraph* article, "and to claim otherwise is wrong. You can only embroider so much." But Tesla's great-nephew, William Terbo, was adamant that Edison indeed "used his connections to ensure that the electric chair would be adopted as a means of execution and to ensure that it would operate using the AC system. He thought that if he could show that the current was capable of killing a man it would put people off using it."

Officials at Belgrade's Tesla Museum were especially enthusiastic about the movie plans and invited Russell as a guest of honor at the 31st Belgrade Film Festival in March 2003. There, he took some press questions and scoffed at rumors that Jack Nicholson would play Tesla, claiming the actor was "too old." Jim Carrey's name allegedly cropped up as a possible lead. *Charged* almost galvanized the world—until the Serbian president got shot, and the government's funding suddenly evaporated.

In April 2004, Russell went to Turkey to accept a Tribute to the Masters award at the 23rd International Istanbul Film Festival. Clad in a glittery jacket and shirt and holding a plate of cookies that he offered to the crowd, he pirouetted to the podium to the beat of a swing band. And just like a scene in *Tommy*, when the atmosphere abruptly shifts from sparkly and jovial to horrific and vicious, Russell couldn't resist breaking the convivial spirit by stirring up more controversy.

Mel Gibson's *The Passion of the Christ* had just been released, and Russell was bound to get questions about how the film's sadomasochistic Catholic lore compares with *The Devils*. Russell proceeded to call Gibson a "scumbag" and accused him of interpreting the Bible falsely. He augmented his rant: "He made a film on the American Revolution [*The Patriot*] and showed the British burning down a church full of women and children. We never did it!" He also used his moment of glory to share baleful thoughts about the entire movie industry: "All the film companies are owned by either Japanese or soft-drink companies or anonymous business people. Instead of three people to go through, there are three thousand—and you never get to see them."

By summer of that year, Russell also got the honor of being a "professor for the day" at the University of Wales' International Film School. There, he presented several Finest Films Awards—in the shape of gongs—to the school's budding talents. But by fall, he ended up in Southampton General Hospital. While treated for a back problem, the doctor told him he tested positive for MRSA, a staph infection resistant to penicillin and several other antibiotics. But despite a life of drinking, heavy eating, and conniptions, Russell didn't stay a convalescent for long.

•

Russell nonetheless has had to cope with shifting times. Mum, Dad, and Aunt Moo were long gone. Shirley passed away from cancer in March 2002 at age sixty-six, and his adversary Alexander Walker went a year later. Russell still has his children. Molly has done some parts in such American television shows as *Law & Order* and *Sex and the City*. Xavier has served as an editor on several of Russell's films. Alex is an artist who emulates Francis Bacon, once did a performance piece mixing archival footage with himself dressed as the corpse of Judy Garland, and is at variance with the establishment on the HIV=AIDS paradigm.

Victoria, in the meantime, has taken on her mom's role as a costume designer. She worked on the 2005 film *Color Me Kubrick*, in which her dad, who often had fun filming scenes with asylum lunatics, was happy to play one in a cameo. Directed by Brian W. Cook (Kubrick's former assistant director), it's about the true misadventures of Alan Conway (John Malkovitch), a former travel agent who makes a con man's career out of impersonating the reclusive Stanley Kubrick. By playing a mad man on the other side of the camera, Russell had the advantage of supplying a wacko perspective to wacko situations in a movie that reveals the artifice and daftness behind false identities and cinema illusions.

Filmmakers Keith Fulton and Louis Pepe may seem too young to remember Russell's days as a controversial biographer, but they adeptly cast him in *Brothers of the Head*, a 2005 mockumentary based on a Brian Aldiss's novel about conjoined twins (Harry and Luke Treadaway) who get groomed to be punk rockers. The directors, who also made the 2002 documentary *Lost in La Mancha*—about Terry Gilliam's failure to film a movie called *The Man Who Killed Don Quixote*—wanted to stress what is essentially one of Russell's conundrums: how documentary gets tangled up in fiction. Russell plays himself, pretending to shoot a film—entitled *Two Way Romeo*—within the film, which gives Aldiss's story a more surrealistic dimension.

The faux Russell movie opens the story as a sinister lawyer (Jonathan Pryce) arrives at L'Estrange Head (the so-called isle off England's eastern coast where the brothers reside), intent on selling the twins' souls with a recording contract. Fulton and Pepe capture the muddy marshland in a gothic style they imagine Russell might have filmed it: a barren landscape replete with eerie winds, shreds of matter resembling umbilical tissue dangling from tree stumps, and brief glimpses of the misshapen twins hulking in the distance. Later on, Russell explains his inclusion of a third fetus growing out of them as "a wonderful metaphor for their genius" and "the essence of their being." One of the subplots is the philosophical clash between Russell and a self-righteous cinema verité enthusiast (Tom Bower), whose "authentic" documentary dominates the film and invades the boys' lives in a much more deceitful and intrusive fashion. Deleted scenes have Russell playing along more with Fulton's and Pepe's ruse. He shares an apocryphal account of having to shut down his production (and forfeit a $50,000 investment) because Aldiss took umbrage at Russell's "flights of fancy" attitude to "real events" and threatened to sue.

Russell's gift for campy horror didn't escape the producers of the 2006 anthology *Trapped Ashes*. They invited him to Vancouver to film a segment entitled "The Girl with the Golden Breasts." In the story, Phoebe (Rachel Vetri), an aspiring Hollywood actress tries augmenting her beauty with breast implants. But instead of gel or silicon, her bosom gets stuffed with the mashed up remains of human cadavers. As a result, she finds more and bigger screen parts while also meeting a new beau. But the success story gets macabre when the boyfriend wakes up with a back full of bite marks: the breasts that changed their lives have their own plans and desires.

●

Just when audiences thought that an elder *grand-père terrible* might emerge as a statelier spokesman for the art of filmmaking, Russell made his 2006 trilogy entitled *Hot Pants: 3 Sexy Shorts*. This possibly imminent camcorder classic explores his lifelong phallic loves and loathing—all done in cheeky humor that is refreshingly deranged, unabashedly puerile, and often idiosyncratic enough to merit the equally idiosyncratic label "outsider art."

The Revenge of the Elephant Man is the first entry, involving a group of professionals from the Maryland Medical Academy (Russell with family and local friends in Halloween costumes) who commingle to celebrate Mardi Gras. Nurse Randy Ravensworth (Elize) stands before the gaggle to discuss the "strange history" of Ella (Russell's neighbor Barry Lowe), "A truly remarkable subhuman being" with an unusual appendage. Ravensworth tells of how she encountered Ella while attending to leper colony patients in Darkest Africa, escaped with him amid an elephant stampede, and whisked him back to England for further study.

Showing up to bolster Ravensworth's findings is Dr. Henry Horenstein (Russell looking hot, cranky, and pie-eyed in a brown suit), who brandishes an instructor's stick to elaborate in graphic detail the depth and width of Ella's "deformity." Ella, born with "both penis and trunk combined," is nonetheless "subject to sexual laws common to both species," a point that Nurse Ravensworth tries demonstrating by arousing the beast with a fanny-waving disco dance. The snooty and sometimes foul-mouthed onlookers watching the spectacle voice a mixture of skeptical disapproval and revulsion, responses Russell probably assumes many viewers will share if they ever get a chance to watch this curiosity. Without CGI and just a plastic toy elephant's snout coated in lubricant, Russell manages to produce a most cringe-worthy image.

Russell as Dr. Horenstein, sizing up the mystery in *The Revenge of the Elephant Man.* (Courtesy of Ken Russell)

Even his fan base might be confused and revolted. Like *The Fall of the Louse of Usher, The Revenge of the Elephant Man* (for which Russell claims Marlon Brando's performance in *The Island of Dr. Moreau* as inspiration) reflects a defiant filmmaker. If people complain about his tastelessness, he now dazzles them with more bad taste; if they gripe about his episodic plots, he confuses them even more with stories that amble in priapic dreamtime. So far, his Gorsewood output requires viewers to alter their states and approximate his viewpoint. For those intrepid enough to take the dare, there are rewards.

The second *Hot Pants* installment is *The Mystery of Mata Hari.* The legendary spy becomes an occasion for Russell to celebrate Elize's quirky beauty. She has a dual role: the infamous agent and a nun who gawks at her through the iron window bars, trying to save her soul and secretly wanting her body. The story takes place in Paris in 1917 at the VIP wing of the Lafayette Military Prison. There, Madam Mata paces, pouts, and performs fan dances as she waits to face a firing squad. Besides the horny nun, there is the even hornier jailor, whom Russell portrays with a walrus moustache. He makes an ideal dirty old man while standing behind the iron door to Mata's cell, playing with himself while watching her shimmy and strut.

Russell concludes *Hot Pants* with a return to his boyhood on the high seas. In *The Good Ship Venus*, he appears as a "venerable discharged seaman," while Elize plays the sea captain's daughter, who sings and swears along with Russell and first mates (played by Barry Lowe and Russell's ongoing film editor Michael Bradsell). Together, they warble obscene couplets about conger eels, wanking machines, and shipboard fellows in compromising positions.

•

However, just as he seems to bask in a comfort zone with his soul mate and on his own turf, Russell still rattles the connubial cage by subjecting Elize to his fevered temper and darker visions. Shortly after his split from Hetty Baynes,

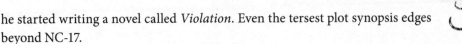

he started writing a novel called *Violation*. Even the tersest plot synopsis edges beyond NC-17.

Set some thirty years into the twenty-first century, *Violation* unravels a disturbing future, when Great Britain gets so enamored with soccer that the game becomes an official religion. The Isle of Wight is now a penal colony for any persecuted bastards who dare adhere to another faith. There's also a resident messiah, wandering in and out of the narrative, who suggests George Michael in a black Armani suit. All the while, a flying saucer hovers overhead like a menacing star of Bethlehem. There's even a passing reference to Mickey Mouse masturbating.

Elize, ever the trouper, could barely hold her stomach while helping Russell edit the *Violation* manuscript. "It's a really great satire," she told the *Independent*. "But I did sit there wondering, 'Is this what you're thinking?' Because it doesn't go with his personality at all. I was thinking, 'Where does he keep that? What piece of the brain is that in?'. . . When I read it, I think, 'This is a dangerous man.' But he's so lovely. I salute that side of him."

The first paragraph alone is a stunner, as it describes a boozer who unzips outside a bar and contemplates his "arc of golden piss" before gazing up at "a fucking great U.F.O." And at one point, the main character, a sports police captain and dominatrix, exacts revenge on the man who sodomized her as a schoolgirl. She tapes him down with his ass in the air, then impales him with a fourteen-inch rod that has "a purple knob on the end the size of a whopping, great toffee apple" and synthetic testicles engorged with hydrochloric acid.

Russell claims he wrote *Violation* as a dare. "People say I don't believe in censorship, but there should be censorship. Films harm a lot of people. This film of mine would harm a lot of people. It's meant to be censored." He had already tried daring censors, as well as grossing out even himself, years before with a script foul enough to be director-proof. The story involves the führer, Eva Braun, and a little Jewish boy who is deluded enough to think that bringing Hitler a cute furry pet for Christmas could alter human history. Russell spoke about it back in 2000 with Mark Kermode in the *Independent*: "It's a satire on Spielberg, a satire on concentration camps, a satire on schmaltz, a satire on Christmas, a satire on war movies, a satire on everything. It lasts ten minutes, and it's called *A Kitten for Hitler*. I wrote it so it would never be shown."

Striding through his eighth decade, Russell refuses to be left for roadkill on the proverbial information highway. "A trawl around the Internet," David Thomas of the *Independent* observes, "reveals hardcore pockets of Russellmania among fans who tend to be young, isolated, and weird—the very people, in short, who sometimes grow up to be creative movers and shakers. These people love the fact that Russell is over-the-top; that he has no restraint, no taste; that snooty critics turn up their noses when they see him coming."

"The land of my dreams is fraught with anxiety. My house is a desolate shell. Rain falls through shattered tiles, the roof is a gaping hole, floors have collapsed, plaster crumbles." Russell wrote these reflections about troubled sleep in his 1991 autobiography. But the words were prescient for events over a decade later when Russell's seventeenth-century New Forest cottage, in which he and Elize found sanctuary, fell to the elements one Monday morning in April 2006. Like the summerhouse that exploded in the beginning of *Mahler*, this too burst into flames. Ken, back from a doctor's appointment, saw the blaze and smoke, thought his wife was still inside, and rushed into the inferno to save her. But Elize had already fled from the bathtub to escape the black, smoky billows and ended up naked in the garden.

Press photographers soon scattered near the throng of firefighters. Russell mugged for the cameras in a hard hat, giving the thumbs-up sign to show that all was under control; he also posed, looking blindsided, beside a now-clothed Elize. A library full of vinyl and shellac records, compact discs, music sheets, stereo equipment, photographs, art works, and around eighty of Russell's handwritten scripts vanished in a flash.

Nobody ever found out what started the fire, but Russell began collaborating with the media to spin a movie-friendly story. In an eyewitness account, London's *Daily Mail* described the disaster: "A charred manuscript flutters in the breeze, wafting gently through the scorched space . . . A tarot card—the Queen of Swords—lies in a heap of thatch next to a few blackened Mahler albums. This is what remains of Ken Russell's work."

But Russell was not so bleak when the same article quoted his resolve in the face of hell's combustion. "I can't believe Ken tried to rescue me," Elize told the *Guardian* on the day after, "because he is the physical coward of the century. It proved he loved me." Russell, meanwhile, drew up a romantic scenario for London's *Daily Mail* that he would otherwise have judged as "schmaltz" had someone else concocted it: "It's not quite real somehow. It seems like one of my films. . . . My wife is the most wonderful person I have met. I thought if she is going to die, I will die trying to save her. . . . The cottage had to burn down for me to prove my love—it was probably worth it."

•

Shortly before the fire, Russell was planning to make another Gorsewood film called *Brave Tart vs. the Loch Ness Monster*, in which Elize would play what

The showdown between man and reptile from *The Secret of the Loch* (directed by Milton Rosmer, 1934).

Russell describes as "a saggy Scottish prostitute" while he assumed the role of the monster. Russell has had so many years to outgrow these primal scenes of reptilian terror but instead chooses to dwell on them until the very end, keeping the integrity of his past obsessions intact. This is why he has stayed so unique, inspiring, and exasperating all these years: he's never severed that link to his childhood nerve center. And movie history would be more enthralling with further variations on the scrotal beast that lunged at Russell from the cinema screen, sent him running in a panic along Portsmouth's High Street where Mum used to treat him to creamed teas, and past the St. Denys train station, where he watched the speeding locomotive that left him behind and alone to cultivate his daydreams and nightmares.

In his *Lair of the White Worm* audio commentary for the 2003 DVD release, Russell, with Freudian finesse once again, relived watching *The Secret of the Loch*:

> I remember the little diver they had was like one I had in my bath on Friday nights. It was a little model about six inches long, and you sucked water into him, and he went down, and you blew it up and he came up. And there was my little toy diver on the screen. And he bobbed into this cave, which looked like a cracked flower pot upside-down, standing behind an aquarium. . . . I knew the monster was coming for him. . . . And the image, ladies and gentlemen, that terrified me, and today it still haunts me in my dreams, is this image . . . of a gigantic, sixty-foot-high, plucked chicken coming round the flowerpot. . . . It's an image I hope you never encounter yourselves, because it changed my life. It made me what I am today—totally mad.

SOURCE NOTES

1. PINOCCHIO'S PECKER

Aldington, Richard. Introduction. *The Rainbow*, by D. H. Lawrence. New York: Viking Press, 1964.

Baxter, John. *An Appalling Talent: Ken Russell*. London: Michael Joseph, 1973.

Canby, Vincent. "When Too Much Is Just About Right." *New York Times*, March 30, 1975.

Collins, R., and I. Christie. "The Expense of Naturalism: Interview with Michael Powell." *The Powell & Pressburger Pages*, Monogram No. 3 (1972) www.powell-pressburger.org/Reviews/Micky/Naturalism.html.

Farber, Stephen. "A Dream Blasted by Sexual Reality." *New York Times*, February 21, 1971.

———. "'The Devils' Finds an Advocate." *New York Times*, August 15, 1971.

Gilliatt, Penelope. "Rev. of The Devils." *The New Yorker*, July 24, 1971.

Hanke, Ken. *Ken Russell's Films*. Metuchen, N.J.: The Scarecrow Press, Inc., 1984.

Katz, Ephraim. *The Film Encyclopedia*. New York: Harper & Row, 1979.

Kael, Pauline. "Genius." *The New Yorker*, January 30, 1971.

———. "Hyperbole and Narcissus." *The New Yorker*, November 18, 1972.

———. "Lust of 'Art'." *The New Yorker*, March 28, 1970.

Kroll, Jack. "Russellmania." *Newsweek*, October 20, 1975.

Powell, Dilys. "Guying the Dolls." Rev. of *The Boy Friend*. *Sunday Times* [London], February 6,1972.

Schickel, Richard. "A Past Master in the Hands of a Future One." *Life*, March 6, 1970.

2. THE LAIR OF THE BLACK MAMBA

Baxter, John. *An Appalling Talent: Ken Russell*. London: Michael Joseph, 1973.

Petty, Moira. "Ken Russell." *Times* (London), October 3, 2005.

Russell, Ken. *Altered States*. New York: Bantam Books, 1991.

———. *Directing Film: From Pitch to Premiere*. London: B.T. Bratsford, 2000.

————. *Fire Over England: The British Cinema Comes Under Friendly Fire*. London: Hutchinson, 1993.

3. THE LOST LAMOUR

Baxter, John. *An Appalling Talent: Ken Russell*. London: Michael Joseph, 1973.

Flatley, Guy. "I'm Surprised My Movies Shock People." *New York Times*, October 15, 1972.

Russell, Ken. *Altered States*. New York: Bantam Books, 1991.

Russell, Ken. Interview with Colin Wilson. *Camera Three*. CBS Television. 1973.

4. MUSIC FOR A MENTAL BREAKDOWN

Baxter, John. *An Appalling Talent: Ken Russell*. London: Michael Joseph, 1973.

Flatley, Guy. "I'm Surprised My Films Shock People." *New York Times*. October 15, 1972.

Phillips, Gene D. *Ken Russell*. Boston: Twayne Publishers, 1979.

Russell, Ken. *Altered States*. New York: Bantam Books, 1991.

————. *Fire Over England: The British Cinema Comes Under Friendly Fire*. London: Hutchinson, 1993.

Tibbetts, John C. *Composers in the Movies: Studies in Musical Biography*. New Haven: Yale University Press, 2005.

5. CATHOLIC SPACE CADETS

Aylott, Bob. "The Director's Cut." *Amateur Photographer*. June 11, 2005.

Baxter, John. *An Appalling Talent: Ken Russell*. London: Michael Joseph, 1973.

Flatley, Guy. "I'm Surprised My Films Shock People." *New York Times*, October 15, 1972.

Lloyd, Isabel. "How We Met—Melvyn Bragg & Ken Russell." *Independent*, Jan. 28, 2001.

"Peerless Knowledge of Screen's Frills." [Shirley Russell Obituary] *Australian*, March 20, 2002.

Petty, Moira. "Ken Russell." *Times* (London), October 3, 2005.

Price, Susannah. "When the Girls Came Out to Play." *Sunday Times Magazine*, March 5, 2006.

Russell, Ken. *Altered States*. New York: Bantam Books, 1991.

————. Quoted from BBC documentary, *Portrait of an Enfant Terrible*. *The South Bank Show*, London Weekend Television, originally broadcast October 15, 1989.

Wakeman, John, ed. *World Film Directors: Volume Two*. New York: The H. W. Wilson Company, 1988.

West, Jean. "The Saintly Sinner." *Herald* (London), August 14, 1999.

6. PATHOGRAPHER'S PROGRESS

Baxter, John. *An Appalling Talent: Ken Russell*. London: Michael Joseph, 1973.

Brooke, Michael. "Ken Russell on Television." *Screen Online*. British Film Institute, www.screenonline.org.uk/tv/id/1030140/index.html.

Lloyd, Isabel. "How We Met—Melvyn Bragg & Ken Russell." *Independent*, January 28, 2001.

O'Connor, John J. "TV: A Dazzling Isadora." *New York Times*, May 5, 1971.

Phillips, Gene D. *Ken Russell*. Boston: Twayne Publishers, 1979.

Rule, Vera. "Obituary—Shirley Russell." *Guardian* (London), March 22, 2002.

Russell, Ken. *Portrait of an Enfant Terrible. The South Bank Show*, London Weekend Television, originally broadcast October 15, 1989.

Schickel, Richard. "Great Lives on TV." *Harper's*, January 1971.

Tibbetts, John C. *Composers in the Movies: Studies in Musical Biography*. New Haven: Yale University Press, 2005.

7. ART WITH A CAPITAL T

Baxter, John. *An Appalling Talent: Ken Russell*. London: Michael Joseph, 1973.

O'Connor, John J. "TV: A Dazzling Isadora." *New York Times*, May 5, 1971.

Phillips, Gene D. "An Interview with Ken Russell." *Film Comment*, Fall 1970.

Russell, Ken. *Altered States*. New York: Bantam Books, 1991.

Schickel, Richard. "Great Lives on TV." *Harper's*, January 1971.

Stokes, Sewell. *Isadora: An Intimate Portrait*. London: Brentano's Ltd., 1928.

8. HEAVEN, HELL, AND A WATERFALL

Baxter, John. *An Appalling Talent: Ken Russell*. London: Michael Joseph, 1973.

Gomez, Joseph A. *Ken Russell: The Adaptor as Creator*. New York: Pergamon Press, Inc., 1977.

Prettejohn, Elizabeth. *The Art of the Pre-Raphaelites*. Princeton, NJ: Princeton University Press, 2000.

Russell, Ken. *Altered States*. New York: Bantam Books, 1991.

———. *Portrait of an Enfant Terrible*. BBC Television, 1989.

Schickel, Richard. "Great Lives on TV." *Harper's*, January 1971.

9. COLD DAYS IN PURGATORY

Baxter, John. *An Appalling Talent: Ken Russell*. London: Michael Joseph, 1973.

Billson, Anne. *My Name Is Michael Caine*. London: Muller, 1991.

Morgenstern, Joseph. "Blue Germs." *Newsweek*, January 15, 1968.

Rev. of *Billion Dollar Brain. Variety*, November 22, 1967.

Russell, Ken. *Altered States*. New York: Bantam Books, 1991.

———. *Directing Film: From Pitch to Premiere*. London: B.T. Bratsford, 2000.

———. Interview with Colin Wilson. *Camera Three*. CBS Television. 1973.

10. BLOWING BUBBLES

Baxter, John. *An Appalling Talent: Ken Russell*. London: Michael Joseph, 1973.

Caine, Michael. Interview with Terry Gross. *Fresh Air*. WHYY-FM. Philadelphia. February 7, 2003.

Coleman, John. "Writing It Again." *New Statesman*, November 14, 1969.

Gomez, Joseph A. *Ken Russell: The Adaptor as Creator*. New York: Pergamon Press, Inc., 1977.

Goodwin, Cliff. *Evil Spirits: The Life of Oliver Reed*. London: Virgin Books, 2002.

Kael, Pauline. "Lust for 'Art.'" *The New Yorker*, March 28, 1970.

Lawrence, D. H. *Women in Love*. London: Penguin Books, 1995.

Marowitz, Charles. "The Honesty of a Suburban Superstar." *New York Times*, January 19, 1975.

Nathan, David. *Glenda Jackson*. New York: Hippocrene Books, 1984.

Otterburn-Hall, William. "Men Wrestle Naked in New British Movie." *Courier-Journal & Times* (Louisville, KY), November 16, 1969.

Phillips, Gene D. *Ken Russell*. Boston: Twayne Publishers, 1979.

Robinson, David. "Trevelyan's Social History." *Sight and Sound*, Spring 1971: 70–72.

Wood, Robin. "Ken Russell." *Cinema: A Critical Dictionary, Vol. Two*. Ed. Richard Roud. New York: Viking Press, 1980.

Woodward, Ian. *Glenda Jackson: A Study in Fire and Ice*. New York: St. Martin's Press, 1985.

Zambrano, Ana Laura. "Women in Love: Counterpoint on Film." *Literature Film Quarterly* 1, January 1973.

11. SONGS OF SUPERMAN

Baxter, John. *An Appalling Talent: Ken Russell*. London: Michael Joseph, 1973.

Ede. H. S. *Savage Messiah*. London: Gordon Fraser, 1971.

Heyworth, Peter. "War Between Russell and Strauss." *Observer Review*, February 22, 1970.

Ison, Walter. "Ken Russell's Comic Strip." *Listener*, February 26, 1970.

Melly, George. "War Between Russell and Strauss." *Observer Review*, February 22, 1970.

Phillips, Gene D. "An Interview with Ken Russell." *Film Comment*, Fall 1970.

———. "Ken Russell as Adaptor." *Literature Film Quarterly* 5, 1977.

Reid, Phillipa. "Kensington Gore Comes to Cumberland." *Listener*, February 19, 1970.

Russell, Ken. Quoted from *Delius: Song of Summer*, DVD audio commentary, BFI Archive Television, 2001.

Schickel, Richard. "Great Lives on TV." *Harper's*, January 1971.

Tibbetts, John C. "Elgar's Ear: Ken Russell Talks about His Composer Biopics." *Quarterly Review of Film and Video*. Vol. 22, 2005.

12. A BUNDLE OF TORTURED NERVES

Abraham, Gerald. *Tchaikovsky: A Short Biography*. Westport, CT: Hyperion Press, Inc., 1945,1979.

Baxter, John. *An Appalling Talent: Ken Russell*. London: Michael Joseph, 1973.

Bowen, Catherine Drinker, and Barbara von Meck. *Beloved Friend: The Story of Tchaikovsky and Nadejda von Meck*. New York: Random House, 1937.

Buckley, Peter. "Savage Saviour." *Films and Filming*, October 1972.

Canby, Vincent. "Screen: Ken Russell's Study of Tchaikovsky Opens." *New York Times*, January 25, 1971.

Chamberlain, Richard. *Shattered Love: A Memoir*. New York: Regan Books, 2003.

"Director in a Caftan." *Time*, September 13, 1971.

Ebert, Roger. Rev. of *The Music Lovers*. *Chicago Sun-Times*, January 1, 1971.

Farber, Stephen. "A Dream Blasted by Sexual Reality." *New York Times*, February 21, 1971.

Flatley, Guy. "I'm Surprised My Films Shock People." *New York Times*, October 15, 1972.

Gomez, Joseph A. *Ken Russell: The Adaptor as Creator*. New York: Pergamon Press, Inc., 1977.

Gow, Gordon. "Shock Treatment." *Films and Filming*, July 1970.

Horowitz, Joseph. *The Post-Classical Predicament: Essays on Music and Society*. Boston: Northeastern University Press, 1995.

Kael, Pauline. "Genius." *The New Yorker*, January 30, 1971.

Kanfer, Stefan. "False Notes." *Time*, February 8, 1971.

Nathan, David. *Glenda Jackson*. New York: Hippocrene Books, 1984.

Reed, Rex. *People Are Crazy Here*. New York: Delacorte Press, 1974.

Russell, Ken. *Altered States*. New York: Bantam Books, 1991.

Tibbetts, John C. *Composers in the Movies: Studies in Musical Biography*. New Haven: Yale University Press, 2005.

Woodward, Ian. *Glenda Jackson: A Study in Fire and Ice*. New York: St. Martin's Press, 1985.

13. SACRILEGIOUS BITCH! *THE DEVILS*: PART ONE

Baxter, John. *An Appalling Talent: Ken Russell*. London: Michael Joseph, 1973.

Davies, Peter Maxwell. Quoted in *Hell on Earth* documentary. Dir. Paul Joyce, Film Four International, November 25, 2002.

Fiddick, Peter. "Ken Russell." *Guardian* (London), July 26, 1971.

Flatley, Guy. "Must Glenda Always Be So Neurotic?" *New York Times*, February 7, 1971.

Fremantle, Anne. Rev. of *The Devils of Loudun* by Aldous Huxley. *Saturday Review*, November 22, 1952.

Gomez, Joseph A. *Ken Russell: The Adaptor as Creator*. New York: Pergamon Press, Inc., 1977.

Goodwin, Cliff. *Evil Spirits: The Life of Oliver Reed*. London: Virgin Books, 2001.

Gow, Gordon. "Them and Us." *Films and Filming*, October 1977.

Huxley, Aldous. *The Devils of Loudun*. New York: Carroll & Graf Publishers, Inc., 1986.

Jarman, Derek. *At Your Own Risk: A Saint's Testament*. Ed. Michael Christie. Woodstock, New York: Overlook Press, 1993.

———. *Dancing Ledge*. Woodstock, New York: Overlook Press, 1993.

———. *Modern Nature*. Woodstock, New York: Overlook Press, 1994.

Macnab, Geoffrey. "Three Cuts and You're Out: Director Ken Russell remembers *The Devils* and working with Derek Jarman." *Sight and Sound*, October 1977.

Marowitz, Charles. "The Honesty of a Suburban Superstar." *New York Times*, January 19, 1975.

Redgrave, Vanessa. Quoted in *Hell on Earth* documentary. Dir. Paul Joyce, Film Four International, November 25, 2002.

Reed, Rex. *People Are Crazy Here*. New York: Delacorte Press, 1974.

Russell, Ken. *Altered States*. New York: Bantam Books, 1991.

———. Interview with Colin Wilson. *Camera Three*. CBS Television. 1973.

14. SANCTIMONIOUS WHORES! *THE DEVILS*: PART TWO

Baxter, John. *An Appalling Talent: Ken Russell*. London: Michael Joseph, 1973.

Canby, Vincent. "The Devils." *New York Times*, July 17, 1971.

Champlin, Charles. "The Games Devils Plays." *Los Angeles Times*, July 16, 1971.

Cocks, Jay. "Madhouse Notes." *Time*, July 26, 1971.

Crist, Judith. Rev. of *The Devils. New York*, July 26, 1971.

Curtiss, Thomas Quinn. "Venice Fete Cancels Public Showing of The Devils." *New York Times*, August 29, 1971.

"Director in a Caftan." *Time*, September 13, 1971.

Farber, Stephen. "'The Devils' Finds an Advocate." *New York Times*, August 15, 1971.

Fiddick, Peter. "Ken Russell." *Guardian* (London), July 26, 1971.

Flatley, Guy. "I'm Surprised My Films Shock People." *New York Times*, October 15, 1972.

Gomez, Joseph A. *Ken Russell: The Adaptor as Creator*. New York: Pergamon Press, Inc., 1977.

Goodwin, Cliff. *Evil Spirits: The Life of Oliver Reed*. London: Virgin Books, 2001.

Guarino, Ann. "*Devils* Is Anti-Religious." *New York Daily News*, July 17, 1971.

Hineline, Keith. "The Devils." *Harry* (Baltimore), 1 October 12, 1971: Cited in Rosenfeldt, Diane. *Ken Russell: A Guide to References and Resources*. Boston: G.K. Hall & Co., 1978.

Jarman, Derek. *Dancing Ledge*. Woodstock, New York: Overlook Press, 1993.

Mc Gowen, Mary. "*Devils* Is Surreal Portrait." *Iconoclast* (Dallas), September 3, 1971: Cited in Rosenfeldt, Diane. *Ken Russell: A Guide to References and Resources*. Boston: G.K. Hall & Co., 1978.

Raban, Jonathan. "Homicidal Farce." Rev. of *The Devils. New Statesman*, July 30, 1971.

Redgrave, Vanessa. *Vanessa Redgrave: An Autobiography.* New York: Random House, 1994.

Reed, Rex. *People Are Crazy Here.* New York: Delacorte Press, 1974.

Russell, Ken. *Altered States.* New York: Bantam Books, 1991.

Simon, John. "An Appalling Plague Has Been Loosed on Our Films." *New York Times*, September 19, 1971.

Sweeney, Louise. "Russell Films Devils Case." *Christian Science Monitor*, July 17, 1971.

Zimmerman, Paul D. "Over the Edge." *Newsweek*, July 26, 1971.

15. NAUGHTY, BAWDY BODIES

"Actress Dorothy Tutin Dies." *BBC News*, August 6, 2001, http://news.bbc.co.uk/1/hi/-entertainment/-arts/1475909.stm.

Baxter, John. *An Appalling Talent: Ken Russell.* London: Michael Joseph, 1973.

Buckley, Peter. "Savage Saviour." *Films and Filming*, October 1972.

Canby, Vincent. "Ken Russell's *Savage Messiah*, Biography of a Sculptor, Opens." *New York Times*, November 9, 1972.

Coleman, John. Rev. of *The Boy Friend. New Statesman*, September 15, 1972.

Crist, Judith. "Some Late Bloomers, and a Few Weeds." Rev. of *The Boy Friend. New York*, January 10, 1972.

Dawson, Jan. Rev. of *The Boy Friend. Sight and Sound*, Spring 1972.

"Director in a Caftan." Time, September 12, 1971.

Ede, H. S. *Savage Messiah.* London: Gordon Fraser, 1971.

Farber, Stephen. Rev. of *Savage Messiah. Cinema*, Spring 1972: Cited in *Ken Russell: A Guide to References and Resources*, by Diane Rosenfeldt. Boston: G.K. Hall & Co., 1978.

Gomez, *Ken Russell: The Adaptor as Creator.* New York: Pergamon Press, Inc., 1977.

Gow, Gordon. "Then and Us." *Films and Filming*, Oct. 1977.

Hughes, Robert. "Erratic Bust." Rev. of *Savage Messiah. Time*, November 20, 1972.

Jarman, Derek. *Dancing Ledge.* Woodstock, New York: Overlook Press, 1993.

Kael, Pauline. "Hyperbole and Narcissus." Rev. of *Savage Messiah. The New Yorker*, 1 November 18, 1972.

———. Rev. of *The Boy Friend. The New Yorker*, January 8, 1972.

Kahan, Saul. "Ken Russell: A Director Who Respects Artists." *Los Angeles Times* (Calendar), March 28, 1971.

"Ken Russell Panning Panners of His Pics Among London Critics." *Variety*, February 9, 1972.

Kuchwara, Michael. "1920s Fascination Sprouts 'Boy Friend.'" *Timesleader.com*, September 14, 2005.

Peake, Tony. *Derek Jarman: A Biography*. Woodstock, New York: Overlook Press, 2000.

Phillips, Gene. *Ken Russell*. Boston: Twayne Publishers, 1979.

Reed, Rex. *People Are Crazy Here*. New York: Delacorte Press, 1974.

Russell, Ken. *Altered States*. New York: Bantam Books, 1991.

———. Quoted from *The Boy Friend Souvenir Book*. New York: Souvenir Book Publishers, Inc., 1971.

"Russell: Spoofing the Spoof." *Time*, December 20, 1971.

Simon, John. Rev. of *Savage Messiah*. *New Leader*, February 7, 1972.

Siskel, Gene. Rev. of *The Boy Friend*. *Chicago Tribune*, February 7, 1972.

Walton, Tony. Quoted from *The Boy Friend Souvenir Book*. New York: Souvenir Book Publishers, Inc., 1971.

Wilson, Sandy. *I Could Be Happy*. New York: Stein and Day, 1975.

Zimmerman, Paul D. "Portrait of the Artist." Rev. of *Savage Messiah*. *Newsweek*, November 20, 1972.

16. THE COFFIN AND THE CODPIECE

Frame, Donald M. *François Rabelais: A Study*. New York: Harcourt Brace Jovanovich, 1977.

Golden, Eve. "From Stage to Screen: The Film Career of Sarah Bernhardt." *Classic Images*, www.classicimages.com/1997/june/bernhard.html.

Hamilton, J. "On a Clear Day You Can See Dolly." *Look*, December 16, 1969.

Huxley, Aldous. *Do What You Will*. Plainview, New York: Books for Libraries Press, 1975.

Jarman, Derek. *Modern Nature*. Woodstock, New York: Overlook Press, 1994.

Orwell, George. *My Country Right or Left—1940–1943: The Collected Essays, Journalism and Letters of George Orwell*. Ed. Sonia Orwell. New York: Harcourt Brace Jovanovich, 1968.

Rabelais, François. *Gargantua and Pantagruel: The Five Books*. Trans. Jacques LeClercq. New York: Heritage Press, 1942.

Rothstein, Edward. "Celebrity So Extraordinaire She Rivaled the Eiffel Tower." *New York Times*, December 2, 2005.

Russell, Ken. Letter and Film Treatment to Barbra Streisand, July 26, 1971.

Skinner, Cornelia Otis. *Madame Sarah*. Boston: Houghton Mifflin Company, 1967.

Yacowar, Maurice. "Ken Russell's Rabelais." *Literature Film Quarterly* 8, 1980.

17. MAHLER SIEG HEIL!

Alpert, Hollis. "The Murder of Mahler." *Saturday Review*, February 8, 1975.

Babel, Isaac. *The Complete Works of Isaac Babel*. Ed. Nathalie Babel. Trans. Peter Constantine. New York: W.W. Norton & Company, 2002.

Carr, Jonathan. *Mahler: A Biography*. Woodstock & New York: Overlook Press, 1998.

Coleman, John. "A Load of Symbolics." *New Statesman*, April 5, 1974.

Eder, Richard. "The Screen: Ken Russell's 'Mahler'." *New York Times*, April 5, 1976.

Hughes, Robert. "Erratic Bust." *Time*, November 20, 1972.

Mahler, Alma. *Gustav Mahler: Memories and Letters*. Ed. Donald Mitchell. Trans. Basil Creighton. New York: Viking Press, 1969.

Mitchell, Donald. Introduction. *Gustav Mahler: Memoirs and Letters*, by Alma Mahler. New York: Viking Press, 1969.

Phillips, Gene D. *Ken Russell*. Boston: Twayne Publishers, 1979.

Ritter, Naomi. "Introduction: Biographical and Historical Contexts." *Case Studies in Contemporary Criticism: Thomas Mann, Death in Venice*. Boston: Bedford Books, 1998.

Ross, Alex. "Mahlermania." *The New Yorker*, September 4, 1995.

Russell, Ken. *A British Picture: Portrait of an Enfant Terrible*. Dir. Ken Russell. South Bank Show. London Weekend Television, 1989.

———. Interview with Francine Stock. The Film Programme. BBC Radio 4. London. April 9, 2005.

———. *Directing Film: From Pitch to Premiere*. London: B.T. Bratsford, 2000.

Schonberg, Harold C. *The Great Conductors*. New York: A Fireside Book, 1967: 223.

Walter, Bruno. *Gustav Mahler*. Trans. James Galston. New York: Greystone Press, 1941.

18. A SADOMASOCHISTIC *SESAME STREET*

Ann-Margret. Interview from *Tommy*: 2- Disc Collector's Edition DVD, PrismLeisure, 2004.

Canby, Vincent. "Film: 'Tommy,' The Who's Rock Saga." *New York Times*, March 20, 1975.

Carroll, Kathleen. "The Dark Brilliance of Ken Russell." *Sunday News*, March 30, 1975.

Giuliano, Geoffrey. *Behind Blue Eyes: The Life of Pete Townshend*. New York: A Dutton Book, 1996.

Goddard, Simon. "See Me, Feel Me." *Uncut*, September 2004.

Goodwin, Cliff. *Evil Spirits: The Life of Oliver Reed*. London: Virgin Books, 2001.

Hall, William. "What the Blazes Is Ken Russell Up to Now? A Rock Opera." *New York Times*, June 23, 1974.

Hodenfield, Jan. "'Tommy' and Friends." *New York Post*, March 15, 1975.

Russell, Ken. *Altered States*. New York: Bantam Books, 1991.

———. Interview on *Russell Harty Plus*, London Weekend Television Limited, March 27, 1975, www.thewho.net/linernotes/TKAA.html.

———. Interview from *Tommy*: 2-Disc Collector's Edition DVD, Prism Leisure, 2004.

Townshend, Pete. Interview from *Tommy*: 2-Disc Collector's Edition DVD, PrismLeisure, 2004.

19. ORPHEUS EXTENDING

Care, Ross. Rev. of *Lisztomania. Film Quarterly*, Spring 1978.

Dempsey, Michael. "Ken Russell, Again." *Film Quarterly*, Winter 1977–78.

Eder, Richard. "Screen: 'Lisztomania'." *New York Times*, 1October 11, 1975.

Hanke, Ken. *Ken Russell's Films*. Metuchen, N.J.: Scarecrow Press, Inc., 1984.

Jensen, Paul M. *The Cinema of Fritz Lang*. New York: A.S. Barnes & Co., 1969.

Kael, Pauline. Rev. of *Lisztomania. The New Yorker*, November 24, 1975.

Nietzsche, Frederich. *The Gay Science. The Portable Nietzsche*. Trans. Walter Kaufman. New York: Viking Press, 1968.

Schonberg, Harold C. "Richard Wagner: Colossus of Germany." *The Lives of the Great Composers*. New York: W.W. Norton & Company, Inc., 1970.

Tibbetts, John C. *Composers in the Movies: Studies in Musical Biography*. New Haven: Yale University Press, 2005.

20. VALENTINO AND HIS DOUBLE

Chartoff, Robert. Quoted in Bland, Alexander. *The Nureyev Valentino: Portrait of a Film*. New South Wales: Cassell Australia, 1977.

Gholson, Craig. "Michelle Phillips: The Lover's Lover or Valentino's Valentine." *Interview*, July 1977.

Kael, Pauline. "The Lower Trash / The Higher Trash." *The New Yorker*, November 7, 1977.

Maslin, Janet. "Film: Vital Nureyev Upstages 'Valentino.'" *New York Times*, October 6, 1977.

———. "'Valentino' and 'Bobby Deerfield': — Where Did They Go Wrong?" *New York Times*, November 19, 1977.

Mencken, H. L. "Valentino." *The Vintage Mencken*. New York: Vintage Books, 1955.

Nureyev, Rudolf. Quoted in Bland, Alexander. *The Nureyev Valentino: Portrait of a Film*. New South Wales: Cassell Australia, 1977.

Russell, Ken. *Altered States*. New York: Bantam Books, 1991.

———. *Directing Film: From Pitch to Premiere*. London: B.T. Bratsford, 2000.

———. "Mad About the Boy." Rev. of *Valentino: A Dream of Desire* by David Bret. *The Sunday Times* (London), May 17, 1998.

Russell, Ken, and Martin Mardek. *Valentino*, Original Screenplay.

Solway, Diane. *Nureyev: His Life*. New York: William Morrow and Company, Inc., 1998.

Stuart, Otis. *Perpetual Motion: The Public and Private Lives of Rudolf Nureyev*. New York: Simon & Schuster, 1995.

Variety, January 4, 1978.

21. WAITING FOR DRACULA

Hauptfuhrer, Fred. "Wild and Woolly Ken Russell Finds the Golden Fleece Directing 'Altered States'." *People*, March 30, 1981.

McCarty, John. "Ken Russell's Dracula: Will He Ever See the Light of Day?" *Phantasma*, Spring 1988.

Petty, Moira. "Ken Russell." *Times* (London), October 3, 2005.

Russell, Ken. *Altered States*. New York: Bantam Books, 1991.

———. *Dracula*, Original Screenplay.

22. FAUST FREAKS

Buckley, Tom. "At the Movies: Ken Russell on 'Altered States' Controversy." *New York Times*, January 16, 1981.

Cagin, Seth. "Ken Russell's Altered Ego." *Soho News*, January 14, 1981.

Chayefsky, Paddy. *The Collected Works of Paddy Chayefsky: The Screenplays, Volume II: The Hospital, Network, Altered States*. New York: Applause Books, 1995.

Considine, Shaun. *Mad as Hell: The Life and Work of Paddy Chayefsky*. New York: Random House, 1994.

Corliss, Richard. "Invasion of the Mind Snatcher." *Time*, December 29, 1980.

Hauptfuhrer, Fred. "Wild and Woolly Ken Russell Finds the Golden Fleece Directing *Altered States*." *People*, March 30, 1981.

Moss, Robert F. "Paddy Chayefsky: The Agonies of a Screenwriter. *Saturday Review*, May 1981.

Rabelais, François. *Gargantua & Pantagruel: The Five Books*. Book Five. Trans. Jacques Le Clercq. New York: Heritage Press, 1942.

Russell, Ken. *Altered States*. New York: Bantam Books, 1991.

23. OPERATIC PUNKS

Corliss, Richard. "Opera for the Inoperative." *Time*, May 2, 1988.

Gruen, John. "Ken Russell Shapes a New 'Butterfly'." *New York Times*, May 22, 1983.

Il Giornale rev. of *La Bohéme*. Quoted from *New York Post*, July 24, 1984.

Jarman, Derek. *Dancing Ledge*. Woodstock, New York: Overlook Press, 1993.

Peake, Tony. *Derek Jarman: A Biography*. Woodstock, New York: Overlook Press, 2000.

Russell, Ken. *Altered States*. New York: Bantam Books, 1991.

Simon, John. Rev. of *Madame Butterfly*. *New York*, June 13, 1983.

"Spoleto Festival USA Opens Seventh Season." *New York Times*, May 21, 1983.

Walsh, Michael. "Rousing the Rake in Florence." *Time*, June 7, 1982.

24. THE DECO DILDO

Author Interview: Barry Sandler.

Barnes, Julian. Rev. of *The Planets*. *Observer* (London), June 19, 1983.

Russell, Ken. *Altered States*. New York: Bantam Books, 1991.

————. *Crimes of Passion*: DVD Audio Commentary, Anchor Bay, 2002.

————. *Directing Film: From Pitch to Premiere*. London: B.T. Bratsford, 2000.

Wakeman, John, ed. *World Film Directors: Volume Two*. New York: H.W. Wilson Company, 1988.

25. PROMETHEUS UNGAGGED

Canby, Vincent. "Film: Shelley, Byron and Friends, in 'Gothic'." *New York Times* April 10, 1987.

Corliss, Richard. "Still Crazy After All These Fears." *Time*, April 20, 1987.

Darnton, Nina. "Ken Russell Conjures 'Gothic' Tales." *New York Times*, 1 April 10, 1987.

Murray, Raymond. *Images in the Dark: An Encyclopedia of Gay and Lesbian Film and Video*. Philadelphia: TLA Publications, 1994.

Pulleine, Tim. "Russell's Romantics." *Sight and Sound*, Autumn 1986.

Russell, Ken. *Altered States*. New York: Bantam Books, 1991.

————. *Fire Over England: The British Cinema Comes Under Friendly Fire*. London: Hutchinson, 1993.

Shelley, Mary. *Frankenstein*. New York: Bantam Books, 1967.

26. SALOME'S SALAMI

Canby, Vincent. "Salome and Decadence." *New York Times*, May 6, 1988.

Ellis, Havelock. Introduction. *Against the Grain*. By J. K. Huysmans. New York: Dover Publications, Inc., 1969.

Ellmann, Richard. *Oscar Wilde*. New York: Alfred A. Knopf, 1988.

Huysmans, J.K. *Against the Grain*. New York: Dover Publications, Inc., 1969.

LeClercq, Jacques, tr. *Gargantua & Pantagruel: The Five Books*. New York: The Heritage Press, 1942.

Rickey, Carrie. "How Would You Like to Tussle with Russell?" *Village Voice*, January 21–27,1981.

Wilde, Oscar. *De Profundis*. New York: Philosophical Library, 1950.

27. THE SERPENT IN THE RAINBOW

Aldington, Richard. Introduction. *The Rainbow* by D. H. Lawrence. New York: Viking Press, 1964.

Billington, Michael. "Sammi Davis: Just Right for D. H. Lawrence." *New York Times*, April 30, 1989.

Gomez, Joseph A. *Ken Russell: The Adaptor as Creator*. New York: Pergamon Press, Inc., 1977.

Harrington, Richard. Rev. of *The Lair of the White Worm*. *Washington Post*, November 11, 1988.

James, Caryn. "Ken Russell Goes Back to Lawrence for Love." *New York Times*, May 5, 1989.

Lawrence, D. H. *The Rainbow*. New York: Viking Press, 1964.

Wagner, Kit. "Russell's Rainbow Is Weird—and Dull." *Toronto Star*, June 16, 1989.

28. MOLL FLOUNDERS

"Dance Dance Time at Sing Sing." *New York Post*, June 16, 1987.

Greenberg, James. "Is It Time Now to Cry for 'Evita'?" *New York Times*, November 19, 1989.

Lawrence, D. H. *The Rainbow*. New York: Viking Press, 1964.

Russell. Ken. *Altered States*. New York: Bantam Books, 1991.

———. *Fire Over England: The British Cinema Comes Under Friendly Fire*. London: Hutchinson, 1993.

29. FROM WHITE WORMS TO BLUE BALLS

Author Interview: Leonard Pollack.

Armstrong, Stephen. "Old Devil." *Guardian Unlimited*, October 1, 2005, http://film.guardian.co.uk/news/story/0,12589,1582595,00.html.

Canby, Vincent. "Ken Russell on a Day in "the Life." Rev. of *Whore*. *New York Times*, October 4, 1991.

Ferguson, Euan. "The Peter Pan of Shock." *Observer*, February 11, 2001.

Goodwin, Cliff. *Evil Spirits: The Life of Oliver Reed*. London: Virgin Books, 2001.

Hacker, Jonathan, and David Price. *Take Ten: Contemporary British Film Directors*. Oxford: Clarendon Press, 1991.

Hoyle, Martin. "Carry On Satanist." *Financial Times*, June 24, 1995.

"Old Devil Ken Directs His Search for a Soulmate on to the Internet." *Daily Express*, October 30, 2000.

Petty, Moira. "Ken Russell." *Times* (London), October 3, 2005.

Rabelais, François. *Gargantua & Pantagruel: The Five Books*. (Jacques LeClercq, tr.) New York: Heritage Press, 1942.

Russell, Ken. *Altered States*. New York: Bantam Books, 1991.

———. *Directing Film: From Pitch to Premiere*. London: B.T. Bratsford, 2000.

———. *Mike & Gaby's Space Gospel*. London: Warner Books, 1999.

"Russell Stages Treasure Island." *Globe and Mail* (London), November 24, 1995.

Staples, Sally. "Still an Enfant Terrible—Out for a Drink with Ken Russell." *Times* (London), December 18, 1999.

Tibbetts, John C. *Composers in the Movies: Studies in Musical Biography*. New Haven: Yale University Press, 2005.

Traubner, Richard. "Gilbert and Sullivan: *Princess Ida.*" *Opera News*, February 27, 1993.

West, Jean. "The Saintly Sinner." *Herald* (London), August 14, 1999.

30. THE LOCH NESS TRICKSTER

Clarke, Natalie. "I Was Ready to Die for My Wife . . . and She Would Have Died for Me." *Daily Mail* (London), April 13, 2006.

Davies, Barbara. "Hollywood Shed." *Mirror* (London), July 24, 2004.

Ferguson, Euan. "The Peter Pan of Shock." *Observer* February 11, 2001.

Hastings, Chris. "Edison's Family Shocked by Film: Biopic of Nikola Tesla Portrays His Rival as Sadistic and Ruthless." *Daily Telegraph* (Toronto), March 29, 2002.

Helliker, Adam. "Ken Russell Nets Wife Number Four." *Sunday Telegraph*, October 7, 2001.

"Jack Nicholson 'Too Old' to Play Scientist Nikola Tesla: Ken Russell." *Agence France-Presse* March 9, 2003.

Jordan, Mary. "Was Loch Ness Monster Actually an Elephant?" *Washington Post*, March 8, 2006.

Jury, Louise. "Ken's a Dangerous Man, but He's So Lovely." *Independent* (London), March 15, 2006.

Kermode, Mark. "The Ways and Whims of a Horny Old Devil." *Independent* (London), November 19, 2000.

Musetto, V. A. "Ken Russell's Ups and Downs." *New York Post*, May 2, 2004.

Petty, Moira. "Ken Russell" *Times* (London), October 3, 2005.

Pratt, Steve. "Imagine Ken Russell Directing on Acid." Rev. of *Moulin Rouge! The Northern Echo*, September 6, 2001.

Russell, Ken. Quoted from *The Lair of the White Worm*, DVD audio commentary, Pioneer, 2003.

———. *Violation*. Bloomington, Indiana: Author House, 2005.

"Russell Slams 'Scumbag' Gibson." *World Entertainment News Network*, April 28, 2004.

Stokes, Sewell. *Isadora: An Intimate Portrait*. London: Brentano's Ltd., 1928.

Thomas, David. "Ken Russell—Nothing's Beyond Our Ken." *Independent* (London), February 3 2001.

Wainwright, Martin. "Film Director Ken Russell Stars in Rescue Drama as Home Blazes." *Guardian* (London), April 4, 2006.

Walker, Alexander. *Hollywood UK: The British Film Industry in the Sixties*. New York: Stein and Day, 1974.

Zweynert, Astrid. "Ken Russell, the Elephant Man, and Other Scandals." *Reuters News*, November 3, 2003.

WORKS OF KEN RUSSELL

AMATEUR FILMS

Peepshow (1956)

Cameraman: M. C. Plomer; Editor: Ken Russell; Assistant Editor: Philip Jenkinson

Cast: Norman Dewhurst (Magician), Shirley Russell (Doll), with Tom Laden, Philip Evans, Terry Rhodes, Mike Shaw

Knights on Bikes: A Romance (1956)—**uncompleted**

Director: Squire Kenneth Russell; Editor: Master Philip Jenkinson

Amelia and the Angel (1957)

Story: Ken Russell and Anthony G. Evans

Costumes: Shirley Russell; Choreography: Helen May

Cast: Mercedes Quardros (Amelia), Nicolas O'Brien (Amelia's Brother), Helen May (Dancing Teacher), Elisha Manasseh (The Artist), Helen Ulman (Artist's Model)

Lourdes (1958)

TELEVISION WORK

Note: All television work until June 1965 is for the BBC Monitor *program unless otherwise noted. Telecast dates follow titles.*

Poet's London (with John Betjeman) (March 1, 1959)

Producer: Peter Newington; Commentary: John Betjeman

Gordon Jacob (March 29, 1959)

Producer: Peter Newington; Commentary: Humphrey Burton; Editor: Huw Wheldon

Guitar Craze (June 7, 1959; repeated July 24, 1960)

Variations on a Mechanical Theme (September 27, 1959)

McBryde and Colquhoun, Two Scottish Painters (October 25, 1959)

Producer: Peter Newington; Commentator: Allan McClelland; Editor: Allan Tyrer

Portrait of a Goon (Spike Milligan) (December 16, 1959)

Marie Rambert Remembers (January 17, 1960)

Producer: Peter Newington; Photography: John McGlashan

Journey into a Lost World (John Betjeman) (March 28, 1960; repeated December 15, 1964)

Producer: Peter Newington; Editor: Huw Wheldon

Cranks at Work (John Cranko) (April 24, 1960)

The Bedlington Miners' Picnic (July 3, 1960)

Shelagh Delaney's Salford (September 25, 1960)

A House in Bayswater (produced for the BBC Film Department) (December 14, 1960; repeated June 25, 1968)

Producer: Ken Russell; Screenplay: Ken Russell; Editor: Allan Tyrer; Photography: John Ray; Music: John Hotchkis

The Light Fantastic (Dancing in England) (December 18, 1960)

Script: Ron Hitchens; Editor: Allan Tyrer; Photography: Tony Leggo

Cast: Ron Hitchens (Presenter), Jim Fowell (Horn Dancer)

London Moods (November 5, 1961)

Antonio Gaudi (December 3, 1961)

Lotte Lenya Sings Kurt Weill (codirected by Humphrey Burton) (September 10, 1962; repeated August 19, 1964)

Old Battersea House (Pre-Raphaelite Museum) (June 4, 1961)

Prokofiev: Portrait of a Soviet Composer (June 18, 1961; repeated August 6, 1962)

Editor: Allan Tyrer; Introduced by Huw Wheldon; Presenter of Introduction: Michael Caine

Pop Goes the Easel (Pop Artists) (March 25, 1962)

Cameraman: Ken Higgins; Editor: Allan Tyrer; Introduced by Huw Wheldon

Cast: Peter Blake, Derek Boshier, Pauline Boty, and Peter Phillips

Preservation Man (Bruce Lacey) (May 20, 1962)

Mr. Chesher's Traction Engines (July 1, 1962)

Elgar (November 11, 1962; repeated May 16, 1963, June 26, 1966, July 16, 1968)

Producer: Humphrey Burton; Screenplay: Ken Russell; Commentary: Huw Wheldon; Cameraman: Ken Higgins; Editor: Allan Tyrer

Cast: Peter Brett (Mr. Elgar), Rowena Gregory (Mrs. Elgar), George McGrath (Sir Edward Elgar)

Watch the Birdie (David Hurn) (June 9, 1963; repeated July 15, 1964)

Lonely Shore (Archaeologist Jacquetta Hawkes) (January 14, 1964)

Associate Producers: Nancy Thomas and Humphrey Burton; Editor: Allan Tyrer; Introduced by Huw Wheldon

Bartók (May 24, 1964; repeated July 9, 1968)

Producer: David Jones; Scenario: Ken Russell; Editor: Allan Tyrer; Commentary: Huw Wheldon

Cast: Boris Ranevsky (Béla Bartók), Pauline Boty (Prostitute), Sandor Elès (Client), Peter Brett (Bluebeard), Rosalind Watkins (Judith)

The Dotty World of James Lloyd (July 5, 1964; repeated July 2, 1968)

Diary of a Nobody (produced for BBC-2) (December 12, 1964)

Producer: John McGrath; Adapted from book by George and Weedon Grossmith

Cast: Murray Melvin, Brian Murphy, Vivian Pickles, Bryan Pringle

The Debussy Film (May 18, 1965; repeated June 12, 1966)

Producer: Ken Russell; Screenplay: Ken Russell and Melvyn Bragg; Editor: Allan Tyrer; Art Nouveau Consultant: Martin Battersby

Cast: Oliver Reed (Claude Debussy), Vladek Sheybal (Director/Pierre Louÿs), Annette Robertson (Gaby), Iza Teller (Madame Bardac), Penny Service (Lily), Vernon Dobtcheff (The Actor), Jane Lumb (Saint Sebastian), Victoria Russell (Chou Chou), Verity Edmett (Zohra, the Slave Girl), Stephanie Randall (Secretary)

Always on Sunday (Henri Rousseau) (June 29, 1965; repeated July 2, 1968, June 1, 1969)

Producer: Ken Russell; Screenplay: Ken Russell and Melvyn Bragg; Editor: Larry Toft; Narrator: Oliver Reed

Cast: James Lloyd (Henri Rousseau), Annette Robertson (Alfred Jarry), Bryan Pringle (Pere Ubu), Jacqueline Cook (Mere Ubu), Roland MacLeod (Apollinaire), Iza Teller (Josephine), Dorothy-Rose Gribble (Eugénie), Sheila Van Bloemen (First Neighbor), Ann Mitchell (Second Neighbor), Joanna Rigby (Daughter), Michael Van Bloemen (Picture Dealer)

All Films from January 1966 to February 1970 are for the BBC Omnibus *program.*

Don't Shoot the Composer (Georges Delerue) (January 29, 1966)

Isadora Duncan, The Biggest Dancer in the World (September 22, 1966; repeated March 26, 1967, March 19, 1969)

Producer: Ken Russell; Scenario: Ken Russell and Sewell Stokes; Dialogue: Sewell Stokes; Choreographer: Bice Bellairs; Greek sequence: Leni Riefenstahl; Desigher: Luciana Arrighi; Costumes: Joyce Hammond; Cameramen: Dick Bush and Brian Tufano; Editors: Michael Bradsell and Roger Crittenden; Photography: Dick Bush

Cast: Vivian Pickles (Isadora Duncan); Peter Bowles (Paris Singer), Alex Jawkokimov (Sergei Yessenin), Murray Melvin (Photographer), Jeanne Le Bars (Wilma), Alita Naughton (Journalist), Sandor Elès (Bugatti)

Dante's Inferno (December 22, 1967)

Producer: Ken Russell; Commentary and Dialogue: Austin Frazer; Scenario: Austin Frazer and Ken Russell; Designer: Luciana Arrighi; Costumes: Shirley Russell (as Shirley Kingdon); Cameraman: Nat Crosby; Editors: Michael Bradsell and Roger Crittenden

Cast: Oliver Reed (Dante Gabriel Rossetti), Judith Paris (Elizabeth Siddal), Andrew Faulds (William Morris), Iza Teller (Christina Rossetti), Christopher

Logue (Algernon Charles Swinburne), Gala Mitchell (Jane Morris), Pat Ashton (Fanny Cornforth), Clive Goodwin (John Ruskin), David Jones (Charles Augustus Howell), Norman Dewhurst (Edward Burne-Jones), Tony Gray (W. M. Rossetti), Douglas Gray (Holman Hunt), Derek Boshier (John Everett Millais), Caroline Coon (Annie Miller), Janet Deuters (Emma Brown)

Song of Summer (Delius) (September 15, 1968)

Producer: Ken Russell; Script: Ken Russell and Eric Fenby; Photography: Dick Bush; Editor: Roger Crittenden; Costumes: Shirley Russell

Cast: Max Adrian (Delius), Christopher Gable (Eric Fenby), Maureen Pryor (Jelka Delius), David Collings (Percy Grainger), Geraldine Sherman (Girl Next Door), Elizabeth Ercy (Maid), Roger Worrod (Bruder), Norman Jones (Doctor), Ken Russell (Horny Priest—uncredited)

The Dance of the Seven Veils (A Comic Strip in Seven Episodes on the Life of Richard Strauss) (February 15, 1970)

Producer: Ken Russell; Scenario: Ken Russell, Henry Reed, Richard Strauss; Photography: Peter Hall; Editor: Dave King; Choreography: Terry Gilbert; Costumes: Shirley Russell

Cast: Christopher Gable (Richard Strauss); Judith Paris (Pauline Strauss), Kenneth Colley (Adolf Hitler); Vladek Sheybal (Joseph Goebbels), James Mellor (Hermann Goering), Sally Bryant (Life), Gala Mitchell (Fallen Woman), Rita Webb (Salome), Imogen Claire (Salome—dancer), Maggie Maxwell (Potiphar's Wife), Otto Diamant (Jewish Man), Dorothy Grumbar (Jewish Woman), Martin Fenwick (Baron Ochs), Anna Sharkey (Octavian), Graham Armitage (Null)

After his scandalous 1970 broadcast The Dance of the Seven Veils, *Russell was out of the British television loop until 1978. From then on, he made informative and sometimes eccentric films with a British flavor, often with the collaboration of Melvyn Bragg.*

Clouds of Glory (1978) Granada Television

Producer: Norman Swallow; Associate Producer: Diana Bramwell; Scripted by Ken Russell and Melvyn Bragg; Cinematographer: Dick Bush; Editor: Anthony Ham; Costume Designer: Shirley Russell

William and Dorothy (July 9, 1978)

Cast: David Warner (William Wordsworth), Felicity Kendal (Dorothy Wordsworth), William Hootkins (Reverend Dewey), Bridget Ashburn (Joanna Hutchinson), Freddie Fletcher (Tom Hutchinson), Thomas Henty (Jack Hutchinson),

Robin Bevan (Young William), Susan Withers (Young Dorothy), Antony Carrick (Uncle), Preston Lockwood (Dr. Carr), Trevor Wilson (John Wordsworth). Music: "Young Person's Guide to the Orchestra" and selections from the opera *Peter Grimes* by Benjamin Britten / Symphonies no. 4–7 by Ralph Vaughan Williams

The Rime of the Ancient Mariner (July 16, 1978)

Cast: David Hemmings (Samuel Taylor Coleridge), Kika Markham (Sara Coleridge), David Warner (William Wordsworth), Felicity Kendal (Dorothy Wordsworth), Ronald Letham (Thomas De Quincey), Murray Melvin (Robert Lovell), Ben Aris (Robert Southey), Imogen Claire (Specter), Peter Dodd (Hartley Coleridge), Barbara Ewing (Asra), Patricia Garwood (Edith Southey), Henry Moxon (Dr. Gillman), Iza Teller (Mrs. Gillman), Diana Mather (Mary Fricker), Annette Robertson (Servant); Music: "The Garden of Fand" by Arnold Bax

The Planets (June 12, 1983) LWT (London Weekend Television): *South Bank Show*

Music: Gustav Holst, performed by Eugene Ormandy and the Philadelphia Orchestra

Ralph Vaughan Williams (April 8, 1984) LWT: *South Bank Show*

Producer: Ken Russell; Script: Ken Russell and Ursula Vaughan Williams; Cinematographer: Mike Humphreys; Editor: Xavier Russell; Music: London Philharmonic Orchestra

Cast: Ken Russell (Himself), Ursula Vaughan Williams (Herself), Iona Brown (Herself as Violin Soloist), Peter Savidge (Himself as Vocal Soloist), John Sanders (Gloucester Cathedral Organist), Molly Russell (Herself)

Ken Russell's ABC of British Music (April 2, 1988) LWT: *South Bank Show*

Producer: Ken Russell; Executive Producer: Alan Benson; Editor: Melvyn Bragg

Cast: Ken Russell (Himself), Thomas Dolby (Himself), Rita Cullis (Herself), Evelyn Glennie (Herself), Nigel Kennedy (Himself), John Lill (Himself), Julian Lloyd Webber (Himself), Eric Parkin (Himself), The Fairer Sax (themselves)

Méphistophélès (1989) Valiant SRL

Libretto: Arrigo Boito; Costume Designer: Paul Dufficey; Conductor: Edoardo Muller; Choreographer: Richard Caceres

Cast: Paata Burchuladze (Mefistofele), Ottavio Garaventa (Faust), Adriana Morelli (Margherita), Silvana Mazzieri (Marta), Fabio Armiliato (Wagner), Josella Ligi (Elena), Laura Bocca (Pabtalis), Saverio Bambi (Nereo)

A British Picture, Portrait of an Enfant Terrible (October 15, 1989) LWT: *South Bank Show*

Producer: Ronaldo Vasconcellos; Executive Producer: Nigel Wattis
Cinematographer: Dick Bush; Editor: Xavier Russell; Costume Designer: Victoria Russell

Cast: Melvyn Bragg (Himself), Ken Russell (Himself), Molly Russell (Herself), Rupert Russell (Himself), Victoria Russell (Herself), Vivian Russell (Herself)

The Strange Affliction of Anton Bruckner (1990) LWT: *South Bank Show*

Producer: Ronaldo Vasconcellos; Associate Producer: Jeremy Bolt; Script: Ken Russell; Cinematographer: Robin Vidgeon; Editor: Brian Tagg; Costume Designer: Victoria Russell; Camera Operator (Ken Russell, as Alf Russell)

Cast: Peter Mackriel (Anton Bruckner), Catherine Neilson (Gretel), Carsten Norgaard (Hans)

Men & Women: Stories of Seduction (1990) HBO

Segment: "Dusk Before Fireworks"; Written by Dorothy Parker; Producer: William S. Gilmore; Executive Producers: Colin Callender, Ted Hartley, Jerry Offsay; Cinematographer: Billy Williams; Original Music: Marvin Hamlisch

Cast: Molly Ringwald (Kit), Peter Weller (Hobie)

Road to Mandalay (1991)

Producer: Maureen Murray; Editor: Xavier Russell

Cast: Muriel Codd or "Aunt Moo" (herself), June Codd (herself)

Prisoner of Honor (1991) **Dreyfuss/James Productions and HBO Films**

Producers: Richard Dreyfuss and Judith Rutherford James; Coproducers: Michael Bendix, Colin Callender, and Steven Nalevansky; Associate Producer: Christopher Chase; Line Producer: Ronaldo Vasconcellos; Writer: Ron Hutchinson; Cinematographer: Mike Southon; Editors: Mia Goldman, Margaret Goodspeed, and Brian Tagg; Costume Designer: Michael Jeffrey; Production Designer: Ian Whittaker; Choreographer: Anita Desmarais; Original Music: Barry Kirsch

Cast: Richard Dreyfuss (Colonel Picquart), Oliver Reed (General de Boisdeffre), Peter Firth (Major Henry), Shauna Baird (Henry's Wife), Jeremy Kemp (General de Pellieux), Brian Blessed (General Gonse), Peter Vaughan (General Mercier), Kenneth Colley (Captain Dreyfus), Judith Paris (Madame Dreyfus), Catherine Neilson (Eloise), Lindsay Anderson (War Minister), Imogen Claire (Cabaret Singer), Paul Dufficey (Sketch Artist), David Bamford (Boy Prostitute), Stephen Houghton (Male Prostitute), Martin Friend (Emile Zola), Christopher Logue (Labori), Murray Melvin (Bertillon), Nick Musker (Vampire Dreyfus), Patrick

Ryecart (Major Esterhazy), Carsten Norgaard (Colonel von Schwarzkoppen), Simon Chamberland (Cabaret Piano Player)

The Secret Life of Arnold Bax (November 22, 1992) LWT: *South Bank Show*

Producer: Maureen Murray; Script: Ken Russell; Cinematographer: Robin Vidgeon; Costume Designer: Victoria Russell; Editor: Xavier Russell; Choreographer: Hetty Baynes

Cast: Ken Russell (Sir Arnold Bax), Glenda Jackson (Harriet Cohen), Hetty Baynes (Annie), Kenneth Colley (John Ireland), Melissa Docker (Sybil Chadwick), Maureen Murray (The Manageress), Alan Arthur (The Waiter), Maurice Bush (The Doorman)

The Insatiable Mrs. Kirsch (1993) Regina Ziegler Filmproduktion

Producer: Ronaldo Vasconcellos; Executive Producer: Regina Ziegler; Associate Producers: Hartmut Köhler and Judy Tossell; Cinematographer: Hong Manley; Editor: Xavier Russell

Cast: Ken Russell (Mr. Kirsch), Hetty Baynes (Mrs. Kirsch), Simon Shepherd (Narrator)

The Mystery of Dr. Martinu (May 16, 1992) RM Associates

Editor: Xavier Russell; Costume Designer: Victoria Russell; Original Music: Bohuslav Martinu

Cast: Patrick Ryecart (Bohuslav Martinu), Hannah King (Slava), Amanda Ray-King (Czech), Melissa Docker (Voice), Tamzin Outhwaite (Girlfriend)

Lady Chatterley (June 6–27, 1993) London Film Productions and BBC

Producer: Michael Haggiag; Executive Producers: Johan Eliasch, Robert Haggiag, Barry Hanson; Associate Producers: Marina Gefter, Wendy Oberman; Line Producer: Ronaldo Vasconcellos; Based on *Lady Chatterley's Lover* by D. H. Lawrence; Screenplay: Michael Haggiag and Ken Russell; Cinematographer: Robin Vidgeon; Editors: Mick Audsley, Peter Davies, Alan Mackay, Xavier Russell; Costume Designer: Evangeline Harrison; Production Designer: James Merifield; Choreography: Hetty Baynes; Original Music: Jean Claude Petit

Cast: Joely Richardson (Lady Connie Chatterley), Sean Bean (Mellors), James Wilby (Sir Clifford Chatterley), Shirley Anne Field (Mrs. Bolton), Hetty Baynes (Hilda), Ken Russell (Sir Michael Reid), Brian Blessed (Petty Officer), Breffni McKenna (Donald Forbes), Pat Keen (Mrs. Mellors), Amanda Murray (Mrs. Draycott), P. J. Davidson (Gamekeeper), Judith Paris (Mrs. Marshall), David Sterne (Field), Melanie Hughes (Simpson), Michael Turner (Rector Asby), Ben Aris (Tommy Dukes), Molly Russell (Molly), Rupert Russell (Rupert)

Classic Widows (February 5, 1995) LWT: *South Bank Show*

Producer: Maureen Murray; Script: Melvyn Bragg; Cinematographer: Hong Manley; Editor: Xavier Russell; Choreography: Amir Hosseinpour; Camera Operator: Ken Russell (as Alf Russell); Conductor: Richard Hickox; Original Music: Benjamin Frankel, Humphrey Searle, Bernard Stevens, William Walton

Cast: Ken Russell (Himself/Interviewer), Xenia Frankel (Herself), Fiona Searle (Herself), Bertha Stevens (Herself), Susana Walton (Herself), Hetty Baynes (Dancer on "Long Steel Glass"), Fiona Cross (Performer on "Cat Variations")

Alice in Russialand (1995) Channel 4 Films

Producer: Ronaldo Vasconcellos; Editor: Xavier Russell

Cast: Hetty Baynes (Alice), Amanda Ray-King (Alice's Sister)

Ken Russell's Treasure Island (December 24, 1995) Channel 4 Films

Producer: Maureen Murray; Script: Ken Russell; Cinematographer: Hong Manley; Editor: Xavier Russell

Cast: Hetty Baynes (Long Jane Silver), Michael Elphick (Billy Bones), Gregory Hall (Jim Hawkins), Georgina Hale (Mum)

In Search of the English Folk Song (August 31, 1998) Channel 4 Films

Script: Ken Russell; Producer: Maureen Murray; Editor: Sean Mackenzie

Cast: Ken Russell (Presenter), So What ("Kick It"), Garry Fenna ("Going to Put a Bar in My Car and Drive Myself to Drink"), Bob Appleyard ("The Fawley Flame"), Lynne Fortt ("Down at Greenham Common on a Spree"), June Tabor ("The King of Rome"), Fairport Convention ("Seventeen Come Sunday"), Osibisa ("Sunshine Day"), Eliza Carthy ("Good Morning, Mr. Walker"), Chris While and the Albion Band ("Young Man Cut Down in His Prime"), Waterson Carthy ("Stars in My Crown"), Donovan ("Nirvana"), Edward II ("Shepherd's Hey"), the Percy Grainger Chamber Orchestra ("Country Gardens")

Dogboys (1998) Showtime Networks, Inc.

Producer: Ken Russell; Executive Producers: Hugh Martin, Rob Stork; Line Producer: Christopher Courtney; Cinematographer: Jamie Thompson; Editor: Xavier Russell; Production Designer: Ed Hanna; Costume Designer: Csilla Márki; Special Effects: Tim Good; Original Music: John Altman, Spencer Proffer (songs)

Cast: Bryan Brown (Captain Robert Brown), Dean Cain (Julian Taylor), Tia Carrere (D.A. Jennifer Dern), Ken James (Warden Adam Wakefield), Sean McCann (Pappy), Richard Chevolleau (Willy B.), Hardee T. Lineham (Watkins), Von

Flores (Miguel), Robbie Rox (Bull), Jody Racicot (Rego), Matthew Bennett (Carl Ewing), James Bearden (J. B. Diggs), Robert Collins (Cates), Bruce Tubbe (Bus Guard), Scott Wickware (Prison Guard #1), Billy Otis (Smitty), Rick Demas (Monster), Bernard Browne (Tower Guard), Wayne Best (Prison Guard #2)

Brighton Belles (2001) BBC-2 Southern Eye Series

Elgar: Fantasy of a Composer on a Bicycle (September 22, 2002) LWT: South Bank Show

Costumes: Victoria Russell; Introduced by Melvyn Bragg

Cast: James Johnston (Edward Elgar), Elize Tribble (Lady Elgar)

THEATRICAL FEATURES

French Dressing (1963) Associate British Picture Corporation

Producer: Kenneth Harper; Associate Producer: Andrew Mitchell; Screenplay: Peter Brett, Ronald Cass, Peter Myers; Additional Dialogue: Johnny Speight; Cinematographer: Kenneth Higgins; Editor: Jack Slade; Costume Designer: Shirley Russell; Original Music: Georges Delerue; Dance Music: Brian Bennett—uncredited

Cast: James Booth (Jim), Roy Kinnear (Henry), Marisa Mell (Françoise Fayol), Alita Naughton (Judy), Bryan Pringle (The Mayor), Himself (Robert Robinson), Germaine Delbat (French Woman), Norman Pitt (Westbourne Mayor), Henry McCarty (Bridgemouth Mayor), Sandor Elès (Vladek)

Billion Dollar Brain (1967) United Artists

Producer: Harry Saltzman; Executive Producer: Andre de Toth; Screenplay: John McGrath; Based on the novel by Len Deighton; Cinematographer: Billy Williams; Editor: Alan Osbiston; Production Designer: Syd Cain; Title Designer: Maurice Binder; Costume Designer: Shirley Russell (as Shirley Kingdon); Original Music: Richard Rodney Bennett

Cast: Michael Caine (Harry Palmer), Karl Malden (Leo Newbigen), Ed Begley (General Midwinter), Oskar Homolka (Colonel Stok), Françoise Dorléac (Anya), Guy Doleman (Colonel Ross), Vladek Sheybal (Dr. Eiwort), Milo Sperber (Basil), Janos Kurutz (Latvian Gangster), Alexi Jawdokimov (Latvian Gangster), Paul Tamarin (Latvian Gangster), Iza Teller (Latvian Gangster), Mark Elwes (Birkenshaw), Stanley Caine (GPO special delivery boy), Gregg Palmer (First Dutch Businessman), John Herrington (Second Dutch Businessman), Hans De Vries (Third Dutch Businessman), Fred Griffiths (Taxi Driver), John Brandon (Jim), Tony Harwood (Macey), Donald Sutherland (Scientist at computer)

Women in Love (1969) **United Artists**

Producers: Larry Kramer and Martin Rosen; Associate Producer: Roy Baird; Screenplay: Larry Kramer; Based on the novel by D. H. Lawrence; Cinematographer: Billy Williams; Editor: Michael Bradsell; Set Dresser: Luciana Arrighi; Costume Designer: Shirley Russell; Choreography: Terry Gilbert; Original Music: Georges Delerue

Cast: Alan Bates (Rupert Birkin), Oliver Reed (Gerald Crich), Glenda Jackson (Gudrun Brangwen), Jennie Linden (Ursula Brangwen), Eleanor Bron (Hermione Roddice), Alan Webb (Thomas Crich), Catherine Willmer (Mrs. Crich), Vladek Sheybal (Loerke), Richard Heffer (Loerke's Boyfriend), Phoebe Nicholls (as Sarah Nicholls) (Winifred Crich), Sharon Gurney (Laura Crich), Christopher Gable (Tibby Lupton), Michael Gough (Tom Brangwen), Norma Shebbeare (Mrs. Brangwen), Nike Arrighi (Contessa), James Laurenson (Minister), Michael Graham Cox (Palmer)

The Music Lovers (1970) **United Artists**

Producer: Ken Russell; Executive Producer: Roy Baird; Screenplay: Melvyn Bragg; Based on *Beloved Friend* by Catherine Drinker Bowen and Barbara von Meck; Cinematographer: Douglas Slocombe; Editor: Michael Bradsell; Production Designer: Natasha Kroll; Costume Designer: Shirley Russell; Choreography: Terry Gilbert; Original Music: Peter Tchaikovsky conducted by Andre Previn

Cast: Richard Chamberlain (Peter Tchaikovsky), Glenda Jackson (Nina Milyukova), Christopher Gable (Count Anton Chiluvsky), Kenneth Colley (Modest Tchaikovsky), Max Adrian (Nicholas Rubenstein), Sabine Maydelle (Sasha Tchaikovsky), Izabella Telezynska aka Iza Teller (Madame von Meck), Maureen Pryor (Nina's Mother), Andrew Faulds (Davidov), Xavier Russell (Koyola), Joanne Brown (Olga Bredska), Ben Aris (Sadistic Hussar), Alex Brewer (Young Tchaikovsky), Victoria Russell (Tatiana), Alexander Russell (Von Meck Child), Dennis and John Myers (Von Meck Twins), Alexi Jawdokimov (Dmitri Shubelov or Rimsky-Korsakov), Consuela Chapman (Tchaikovsky's Mother), Graham Armitage (Prince Balukin), James Russell (Bobyek), Alan Dubreuil (Prince in Swan Lake), Maggie Maxwell (Queen in Swan Lake), Imogen Claire (Streetwalker—uncredited)

The Devils (1971) **Warner Bros.**

Producers: Ken Russell and Robert H. Solo; Associate Producer: Roy Baird; Screenplay: Ken Russell; Based on *The Devils of Loudun* by Aldous Huxley and *The Devils* by John Whiting; Cinematographer: David Watkin; Editor: Michael Bradsell; Production Designer: Derek Jarman; Costume Designer: Shirley Russell; Choreography: Terry Gilbert; Original Music: Peter Maxwell Davies and the Fires of London; Period Music: David Munrow and the Early Music Consort of London

Cast: Oliver Reed (Urbain Grandier), Vanessa Redgrave (Sister Jeanne), Christopher Logue (Cardinal Richelieu), Graham Armitage (King Louis XIII), Dudley Sutton (Baron de Laubardemont), Max Adrian (Ibert), Brian Murphy (Adam), Gemma Jones (Madeleine du Brou), Murray Melvin (Father Mignon), Michael Gothard (Father Barré), Georgina Hale (Philippe Trincant), John Woodvine (Magistrate Trincant), Andrew Faulds (Rangier), Kenneth Colley (Legrand), Judith Paris (Sister Agnes), Catherine Willmer (Sister Catherine), Iza Teller (Sister Iza), Maggie Maxwell (Madeleine du Brou's Mother), Twiggy (Girl Fop at Ursuline orgy—uncredited), Justin de Villeneuve (Boy Fop at Ursuline orgy—uncredited)

The Boy Friend (1971) MGM-EMI

Producer: Ken Russell; Associate Producer: Harry Benn; Screenplay: Ken Russell; Based on the musical by Sandy Wilson; Cinematographer: David Watkin; Editor: Michael Bradsell; Production Designer: Tony Walton; Costume Designer: Shirley Russell; Original Music: Peter Maxwell Davies; Original Musical Songs by Sandy Wilson; "All I Do Is Dream of You" and "You Are My Lucky Star" by Nacio Herb Brown and Arthur Freed

Cast: Twiggy (Polly Browne), Christopher Gable (Tony Brockhurst), Max Adrian (Mr. Max/Lord Hubert Brockhurst), Bryan Pringle (Percy Parkhill/Percy Browne), Murray Melvin (Alphonse), Moyra Fraser (Moyra Parkhill/Madame Dubonnet), Georgina Hale (Fay), Antonia Ellis (Maisie), Sally Bryant (Nancy), Vladek Sheybal (De Thrill), Tommy Tune (Tommy), Brian Murphy (Peter), Graham Armitage (Michael), Glenda Jackson (Rita—uncredited), Caryl Little (Dulcie), Anne Jameson (Mrs. Peter), Catherine Willmer (Catherine Max/Lady Catherine Brockhurst), Robert La Bassier (Chauffer), Barbara Windsor (Rosie/Hortense), Peter Greenwell (Pianist—uncredited), Susan Claire (Dancer—uncredited), Petra Siniawski (Dancer—uncredited)

Savage Messiah (1972) MGM-EMI

Producer: Ken Russell; Associate Producer: Harry Benn; Screenplay: Christopher Logue; Based on Savage Messiah by H. S. Ede; Cinematographer: Dick Bush; Editor: Michael Bradsell; Production Designer: Derek Jarman; Costume Designer: Shirley Russell; Original Music: Michael Garrett; Song "Two Fleas" by Dorothy Tutin

Cast: Scott Antony (Henri Gaudier), Dorothy Tutin (Sophie Brzeska), Lindsay Kemp (Angus Corky), Helen Mirren (Gosh Boyle), Michael Gough (Monsieur Gaudier), Eleanor Fazan (Madame Gaudier), John Justin (Lionel Shaw), Aubrey Richards (Mayor), Peter Vaughan (Museum Attendant), Ben Aris (Thomas Buff), Otto Diamant (Mr. Saltzman), Imogen Claire (Mavis Coldstream), Maggie Maxwell (Old Tart), Susanna East (Pippa), Judith Paris (Kate), Robert Lang (Major Boyle), Alexi Jawdokimov (Library Student), Ken Russell (Passenger in top hat getting off of train), Paul McDowell (Agitator)

Mahler (1974) **Goodtimes Enterprises**

Producer: Roy Baird; Executive Producers: David Puttnam, Sanford Lieberson; Screenplay: Ken Russell; Cinematographer: Dick Bush; Editor: Michael Bradsell; Production Designer: John Comfort; Costume Designer: Shirley Russell; Assistant Costume Designer: Leonard Pollack; Art Direction: Ian Whittaker; Choreography: Gillian Gregory; Original Music: Gustav Mahler and Richard Wagner; "Alma's Song" by Dana Gillespie; Conductor: Bernard Haitink

Cast: Robert Powell (Gustav Mahler), Georgina Hale (Alma Mahler), Lee Montague (Bernhard Mahler), Miriam Karlin (Aunt Rosa), Rosalie Crutchley (Marie Mahler), Gary Rich (Young Gustav), Richard Morant (Max), Angela Down (Justine Mahler), Antonia Ellis (Cosima Wagner), Ronald Pickup (Nick), Peter Eyre (Otto Mahler), Dana Gillespie (Anna von Mildenburg), George Coulouris (Doctor Roth), David Collings (Hugo Wolf), Arnold Yarrow (Grandfather), David Trevena (Doctor Richter), Elaine Delmar (Princess), Benny Lee (Uncle Arnold), Andrew Faulds (Doctor on Train), Otto Diamant (Professor Sladky), Michael Southgate (Alois Mahler), Kenneth Colley (Krenek), Sarah McClellan (Putzi), Claire McClellan (Glucki), Oliver Reed (Train Conductor)

Tommy (1975) **Columbia Pictures**

Producers: Ken Russell and Robert Stigwood; Executive Producers: Christopher Stamp and Beryl Vertue; Associate Producer: Harry Benn; Screenplay: Ken Russell; Based on the rock opera by Peter Townshend; Additional Material by John Entwistle and Keith Moon; Cinematographer: Dick Bush, Ronnie Taylor, and Robin Lehman (special material); Editor: Stuart Baird; Set Designer: Paul Dufficey; Set Director: Ian Whittaker; Costume Designer: Shirley Russell; Assistant Costume Designer: Leonard Pollack (uncredited); Art Direction: John Clark; Choreographer: Gillian Gregory; Sculptor: Christopher Hobbs; Music: Peter Townshend, John Entwistle, Keith Moon; "Eyesight to the Blind" by Sonny Boy Williamson; Music Editor: Terry Rawlings; Music Arrangers: Martyn Ford and Nicky Hopkins; Quintophonic Sound developed by John Mosely

Cast: Oliver Reed (Frank Hobbs), Ann-Margret (Nora Walker Hobbs), Roger Daltrey (Tommy Walker), Elton John (The Pinball Wizard), Eric Clapton (The Preacher), John Entwistle (Himself), Keith Moon (Uncle Ernie), Paul Nicholas (Cousin Kevin), Jack Nicholson (The Specialist), Robert Powell (Captain Walker), Pete Townshend (Himself), Tina Turner (The Acid Queen), Arthur Brown (The Priest), Victoria Russell (Sally Simpson), Ben Aris (Reverend Simpson), Mary Holland (Mrs. Simpson), Gary Rich (Monster Rock Musician), Dick Allan (President Black Angels), Barry Winch (Young Tommy), Eddie Stacey (Bovver Boy); Jennifer Baker (Nurse #1)—uncredited, Susan Baker (Nurse #2—uncredited), Imogen Claire (Nurse at the Specialist's Practice—uncredited), Christine Hewett (Lady in Black Beauty Chocolate Commercial—uncredited), Juliet King (The

Acid Queen's Handmaiden—uncredited), Gilliam Lefkowitz (The Acid Queen's Handmaiden—uncredited), Ken Russell (Cripple in the crowd—uncredited)

Lisztomania (1975) **Goodtimes Enterprises**

Producers: Roy Baird and David Puttnam; Screenplay: Ken Russell; Cinematographer: Peter Suschitzky; Editor: Stuart Baird; Production Designer: Philip Harrison; Costume Designer: Shirley Russell; Music: Franz Liszt and Richard Wagner; Original Music: Rick Wakeman; Lyrics to "Love's Dream," "Orpheus Song," and "Peace at Last" by Roger Daltrey

Cast: Roger Daltrey (Franz Liszt), Sara Kestelman (Princess Carolyn), Paul Nicholas (Richard Wagner), Ringo Starr (The Pope), Rick Wakeman (Thor), John Justin (Count d'Agoult), Fiona Lewis (Marie d'Agoult), Veronica Quilligan (Cosima Liszt Wagner), Nell Campbell (Olga Janina), Andrew Reilly (Hans von Bülow), David English (Captain), Imogen Claire (George Sand), Rikki Howard (Countess), David Corti (Daniel), Anulka Dzuibinska (Lola Montez), Lucy Willers (Blondine), Felicity Devonshire (Governess), Murray Melvin (Hector Berlioz), Andrew Faulds (Levi Strauss), Ken Parry (Gioacchino Rossini), Kenneth Colley (Frederick Chopin), Otto Diamant (Felix Mendelssohn), Aubrey Morris (Manager), Georgina Hale ("Most Promising Actress"—uncredited), Iza Teller ("Millionairess"—uncredited), Oliver Reed (Princess Carolyn's Servant—uncredited)

Valentino (1977) **United Artists**

Producers: Robert Chartoff, Irwin Winkler; Associate Producer: Harry Benn; Screenplay: Ken Russell and Mardik Martin; Based on the book *Valentino: An Intimate Expose of the Sheik* by Brad Steiger and Chaw Mank; Cinematographer: Peter Suschitzky; Editor: Stuart Baird; Production Designer: Philip Harrison; Set Designer: Steve Cooper; Costume Designer: Shirley Russell; Choreographer: Gillian Gregory; Special Still Photographer: Leonard Pollack; Original Music: Stanley Black; Selections from *Grand Canyon Suite* by Ferde Grofé Sr.; "There's a New Star in Heaven Tonight" sung by Richard Day-Lewis; "The Sheik of Araby" sung by Chris Ellis

Cast: Rudolf Nureyev (Rudolph Valentino), Michelle Phillips (Natacha Rambova), Leslie Caron (Alla Nazimova), Felicity Kendal (June Mathis), Huntz Hall (Jesse Lasky), David de Keyser (Joseph Schenck), Alfred Marks (Richard Rowland), William Hootkins (Mr. Fatty), Carol Kane (Fatty's Girlfriend), Seymour Cassel (George Ullman), Peter Vaughan (Rory O'Neil), Anton Diffring (Baron Long), Jennie Linden (Agnes Ayres), Bill McKinney (Sadistic Jail Cop), Don Fellows (George Melford), John Justin (Sidney Olcott), Linda Torson (Billy Streeter), June Bolton (Bianca de Saulles), Robin Clarke (as Robin Brent Clarke) (Jack de Saulles), Penelope Milford (as Penny Milford) (Lorna Sinclair), Dudley Sutton (Willie the Wanker), Anthony Dowell (Vaslav Nijinsky), Leland Palmer (Marjorie Tain), Lindsay Kemp (Frankie Campbell), John Ratzenberger (Obnoxious Newsman), Maggy Maxwell (Whore in Prison), Marcella Markham (Floozy in Chicago), Ken Russell (Rex Ingram—uncredited)

Altered States (1980) **Warner Bros. Pictures**

Producer: Howard Gottfried; Executive Producer: Daniel Melnick; Associate Producer: Stuart Baird; Screenplay: Paddy Chayefsky, credited as Sidney Aaron; Based on the novel by Paddy Chayefsky; Cinematographer: Jordan Cronenweth; Editor: Eric Jenkins; Production Designer: Richard MacDonald; Set Decorator: Thomas Roysden; Visual Effects: Robert Blalack, Bran Ferren, James Shourt; Title Designer: Richard Greenberg; Costume Designer: Ruth Myers; Original Music: John Corigliano

Cast: William Hurt (Professor Eddie Jessup), Blair Brown (Emily Jessup), Bob Balaban (Arthur Rosenberg), Charles Haid (Mason Parrish), Thaao Penghlis (Professor Eduardo), Miguel Godreau (Primal Man), Dori Brenner (Sylvia Rosenberg), Peter Brandon (Alan Hobart), Charles White-Eagle (The Brujo), Drew Barrymore (Margaret Jessup), Megan Jeffers (Grace Jessup), Jack Murdock (Hector Orteco), Francis X. McCarthy (Obispo), Deborah Baltzell (Schizophrenic Patient), Hap Lawrence (Endocrinology Fellow), John Larroquette (X-Ray Technician), Paul Larrson (Charlie Thomas, Security Guard), Olivia Michelle (Veronica)

Crimes of Passion (1984) **New World Pictures**

Producer: Barry Sandler; Coproducer: Donald P. Borchers; Executive Producer: Larry Thompson; Screenplay: Barry Sandler; Cinematographer: Dick Bush; Editor: Brian Tagg; Art Director: Stephen Marsh; Set Decorators: Christopher Amy, Gregory Melton; Special Effects: John C. Hartigan; Music: Antonín Dvořák as interpreted by Rick Wakeman; "It's a Lovely Life" sung by Maggie Bell, lyrics by Norman Gimbel; "Get Happy" by Harold Arlen and Ted Koehler

Cast: Kathleen Turner (China Blue/Joanna Crane), Anthony Perkins (Reverend Peter Shayne), John Laughlin (Bobby Grady), Annie Potts (Amy Grady), Bruce Davison (Donny Hopper), John G. Scanlon (Carl), Janice Renney (Stripper), Stephen Lee (Jerry), Pat McNamara (Frank), Christina Lange (Lisa Grady), Seth Wagerman (Jimmy Grady), Joseph Chapman (Walt Pierson), Norman Burton (Lou Bateman), Thomas Murphy (Phil Chambers), Roxanne Mayweather (Hooker #1), Donald J. Westerdale (Airline Trick), John Rose (Arthur), Louise Sorel (Claudia), Janice Kent (Patty Marshall), James Crittenden (Tom Marshall), Yvonne McCord (Sheila), Randall Brady (S&M Cop), Ian Petrella (Jimmy's Friend), Peggy Feury (Adrian), Gerald S. O'Loughlin (Ben), Molly Russell (Little Girl in Music Video—uncredited), Victoria Russell (Bride in Music Video—uncredited), Rick Wakeman (Wedding Photographer in Music Video—uncredited)

Gothic (1986) Virgin Vision

Producer: Penny Corke; Executive Producers: Al Clark, Robert Devereux; Screenplay: Stephen Volk; Cinematographer: Mike Southon; Editor: Michael Bradsell; Production Designer: Christopher Hobbs; Costume Designers: Kay Gallway, Victoria Russell; Original Music: Thomas Dolby

Cast: Gabriel Byrne (Lord Byron), Julian Sands (Percy Shelley), Natasha Richardson (Mary Shelley), Myriam Cyr (Claire Clairmont), Timothy Spall (Dr. John Polidori), Alec Mango (Murray), Andreas Wisniewski (Fletcher), Dexter Fletcher (Rushton), Pascal King (Justine), Tom Hickey (Tour Guide), Linda Coggin (Turkish Mechanical Woman), Kristine Landon-Smith (Mechanical Woman), Chris Chappel (Man in Armor), Mark Pickard (Young William), Kiran Shah (Fuseli Monster), Christine Newby (Shelley Fan), Kim Tillesley (Shelley Fan), Ken Russell (Tourist—uncredited)

Aria (1987) Virgin Vision

Segment: Puccini's "Nessun Dorma" ("None Shall Sleep") from *Turandot*. Producer: Don Boyd; Editor: Michael Bradsell; Art Director: Paul Dufficey; Choreographer: Terry Gilbert; Costume Designer: Victoria Russell

Cast: Linzi Drew (Girl in Accident), Andreas Wisniewski (Boyfriend), with Kwabena Manso, Bella Enahoro, Bunty Mathias, Angela Walker

Salome's Last Dance (1988) Vestron Pictures

Producer: Penny Corke; Coproducer: Robert Littman; Executive Producers: Dan Ireland, William J. Quigley; Associate Producer: Ronaldo Vasconcellos; Screenplay: Ken Russell; Based on Oscar Wilde's play *Salome*, translated from the French by Vivian Russell; Cinematographer: Harvey Harrison; Editor: Timothy Gee; Production Designer: Michael Buchanan; Costume Designer: Michael Arrals; Additional Designs, Jewelry, and Headresses: Michael Jeffery; Set Designer: Christopher Hobbs; Choreographer: Arlene Phillips

Cast: Glenda Jackson (Herodias/Lady Alice), Stratford Johns (Herod/Alfred Taylor), Nickolas Grace (Oscar Wilde), Douglas Hodge (John the Baptist/Lord Alfred "Bosie" Douglas), Imogen Millais-Scott (Salome/Rose), Denis Lill (Tigellenus/Chilvers), Russell Lee Nash (Pageboy), Ken Russell (as Alfred Russell) (Cappadocian/Kenneth), David Doyle (A. Nubin), Warren Saire (Young Syrian), Kenny Ireland (First Soldier), Michael Van Wijk (Second Soldier), Paul Clayton (First Nazarean), Imogen Claire (Second Nazarean), Tim Potter (Pharisee), Matthew Taylor (Sadducean), Linzi Drew (First Slave), Tina Shaw (Second Slave), Caron Anne Kelly (Third Slave), Mike Edmonds (First Jew), Willie Coppen (Second Jew), Anthony Georghiou (Third Jew), Leon Herbert (Namaan), Dougie Howes (Male Salome), Lionel Taylor (Police Sergeant), Colin Hunt (Police Constable),

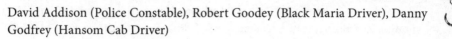

David Addison (Police Constable), Robert Goodey (Black Maria Driver), Danny Godfrey (Hansom Cab Driver)

The Lair of the White Worm (1988) Vestron Pictures

Producer: Ken Russell; Executive Producers: Dan Ireland, William J. Quigley; Line Producer: Ronaldo Vasconcellos; Screenplay: Ken Russell; Based on the novel by Bram Stoker; Cinematographer: Dick Bush; Editor: Peter Davies; Costume Designer: Michael Jeffery; Set Designer: Anne Tilby; Choreographer: Imogen Claire; Special Effects Technician: David Eltham; Special Effects Supervisor: Alan Whibley; Original Music: Stanislas Syrewicz; "The D'Ampton Worm" arranged and performed by Emilio Perez Machado and Stephen Powys, with Violinist Louise Newman; Bagpipe music arranged and performed by Ian Fleming; Harmonica music performed by Harry Pitch

Cast: Amanda Donohoe (Lady Sylvia Marsh), Hugh Grant (Lord James D'Ampton), Peter Capaldi (Angus Flint), Sammi Davis (Mary Trent), Catherine Oxenberg (Eve Trent), Stratford Johns (Peters), Paul Brooke (P. C. Erny), Imogen Claire (Dorothy Trent), Christopher Gable (Joseph Trent), Christ Pitt (Kevin), Gina McKee (Nurse Gladwell), Lloyd Peters (Jesus Christ), Jackie Russell (Snake Woman), Miranda Coe (Maids/Nuns), Linzi Drew (Maids/Nuns), Caron Anne Kelly (Maids/Nuns), Fiona O'Connor (Maids/Nuns), Caroline Pope (Maids/Nuns), Elisha Scott (Maids/Nuns), Tina Shaw (Maids/Nuns), Paul Easom (Soldier/Witchdoctor), James Hicks (Soldier/Witchdoctor), David Kiernan (Soldier/Witchdoctor), Matthew King (Soldier/Witchdoctor), Ross Murray (Soldier/Witchdoctor), Andy Norman (Soldier/Witchdoctor), Bob Smith (Soldier/Witchdoctor), Ken Russell (Village Passerby—uncredited)

The Rainbow (1989) Vestron Pictures

Producer: Ken Russell; Executive Producers: Dan Ireland, William J. Quigley; Assistant Producer: Jeremy Bolt; Line Producer: Ronaldo Vasconcellos; Screenplay: Ken Russell, Vivian Russell; Based on the novel by D. H. Lawrence; Cinematographer: Billy Williams; Editor: Peter Davies; Production Designer: Luciana Arrighi; Choreographer: Imogen Claire; Assistant Costume Designer: Stephen Miles; Original Music: Carl Davis, performed by the Symphonie Orchester Graunke

Cast: Sammi Davis (Ursula Brangwen), Amanda Donohoe (Winifred Inger), Christopher Gable (Will Brangwen), Glenda Jackson (Anna Brangwen), David Hemmings (Uncle Henry), Paul McGann (Anton Skrebensky), Dudley Sutton (MacAllister), Jim Carter (Mr. Harby), Judith Paris (Miss Harby), Kenneth Colley (Mr. Brunt), Glenda McKay (Gudrun Brangwen), Mark Owen (Jim Richards), Ralph Nossek (Vicar), Nicola Stephenson (Ethel), Molly Russell (Molly Brangwen), Rupert Russell (Rupert Brangwen), Alan Edmondson (Billy Brangwen),

Richard Platt (Chauffeur), Bernard Latham (Uncle Alfred), John Tams (Uncle Frank), Zoe Brown (Little Ursula), Amy Evans (Baby Gudrun), Sam McMullen (Winifred's Baby), Paul Reynolds (Schoolboy—uncredited)

Whore (1991) Trimark Pictures

Producers: Dan Ireland, Ronaldo Vasconcellos; Executive Producer: Mark Amin; Line Producer: Michael D. Pariser; Screenplay: Ken Russell, Deborah Dalton; Based on a play by David Hines; Cinematographer: Amir M. Mokri; Editor: Brian Tagg; Production Designer: Richard B. Lewis; Costume Designer: Leonard Pollack; Set Decorator: Amy Wells; Camera Operator: Ken Russell (as Alf Russell); Original Music: Michael Gibbs

Cast: Theresa Russell (Liz), Benjamin Mouton (Blake), Antonio Fargas (Rasta), Elizabeth Morehead (Katie), Michael Crabtree (Man in Car), John Diehl (Derelict), Robert O'Reilly (Younger Man in Car), Charles Macaulay (Older Man in Car), Jason Kristofer (Shy Kid in Van), Jack Nance (Liz's Rescuer), Sanjay Chandani (Indian without Condom), Gail McMullen (Nurse in Convalescent Home), Bob Prupas (Maître d'), Ken Russell (Snooty Waiter), Bobby Bruce (Violinist), Danny Trejo (Tattoo Artist), Jason Saucier (Bill), Amanda Goodwin (Martha), Doug MacHugh (Man in Diner), Stephanie Blake (Stripper), Barbara Eaton (Other Stripper), Alisa Christensen (Lady in Toilet), Ginger Lynn Allen (Wounded Girl), Blanche Sindelar (Theater Casher), B. J. Ward (Theater Manager), Daniel Quinn (Brutal Man), Scott David-King (Cop on Bike), Sean Fitzpatrick (Cop on Bike), Lee Arenberg (Violent John in Car), Tom Villard (Hippie), John Carlyle (Shoe Fetish Man), Scott Harte (Chris), Barbara Mallory (Rachel), Joy Baggish (Flo, the Older Whore), Jered Barclay (Dead Trick in Car), Jak Castro (Cowboy)

Tales of Erotica (1996) Regina Ziegler Filmproduktion

Segment: "The Insatiable Mrs. Kirsch" (See Television Work)

Mindbender (1996) Major Motion Pictures

Producer: Doran Eran; Executive Producers: Tal Danai, Ezra Hazel, Sefi Kiriyati; Associate Producers: André Djaoui, Ulrich Kohli; Line Producer: Dov Keren; Screenplay: Ken Russell, Yael Stern; Cinematographer: Hong Manley; Editors: John Orland, Xavier Russell; Production Designer: Jacob Turgeman; Set Decorator: Hedva Shfaram; Original Music: Bob Christianson

Cast: Ishai Golan (Uri Geller), Terence Stamp (Joe Hartman), Hetty Baynes (Kitti Hartman), Idan Alterman (Shipi), Delphine Forest (Sharon), Rachel Elner (Hanna), Rafi Tabor (Uri's Father), Aviva Yoel (Uri's Mother), Naomi Ackerman (Linda), Jack Adalist (Moti), Gilat Ankori (Glamorous Lady), Erez Atar (Young

Uri), Tami Barak (Hotel Maid), Janet Barr (Greta), Joel Eckhardt (CIA Man), Michael Greenspan (Commentator), Steve Greenstein (Don Drake), Michael Halphie (Heckler), Yochanan Harison (Dr. Zwemmer), Morris Herman (Cab Driver), Yael Horowitz (Lieutenant Jones), David Milton Johnes (U.S. Army Officer), Ulrich Kohli (Casino Manager), Jay Koller (Killer), Helen Lesnick (Uri's Father's Girlfriend), Nitza Shaul (Bitchy Teacher), Gilya Stern (Madge), Uri Geller (Himself)

Lion's Mouth (2000) A Gorsewood Production

Set Designer: Alex Russell

Cast: Diana Laurie (Josephine Heatherington), Ken Russell (Ken the Clown), Tulip Junkie (Nipply/Lion), Emma Millions (Tart/Androcles), Nipper (The Dog)

The Fall of the Louse of Usher (2001) A Gorsewood Production

Producer, Photographer, Editor, Screenplay, and Caterer: Ken Russell; Based on various stories by Edgar Allan Poe; Cinematography: Ken Russell; Séance conceived by Elize Tribble; Set Dresser: Alex Russell; Costumes: Victoria Russell, Ad Hoc, Manny of Manhattan; Masks: J'Antonio; Original Music: James Johnston; "Tolling of the Bells," Music by James Johnston, Words by E. A. Poe, Performed by Gallon Drunk; "Ligeia," Music by James Johnston, Words by Elize Tribble; "Annabelle Lee," Music by James Johnston and Elize Tribble, Words by E. A. Poe; "Fire in the Rose," Music by James Johnston, Words by Elize Tribble; "Hypnotized," Music and Words by James Johnston, Performed by Gallon Drunk

Cast: James Johnston (Roderick Usher), Elize Tribble (Madeleine Usher, Masked Mary, Mummy, Dr. Wells), Marie Findley (Nurse ABC Smith), Ken Russell (Dr. Calahari), Lesley Nunnerly (Berenice), Emma Millions (Annabelle Lee), Peter Mastin (Ernest Valdemar), Sandra Scott (Beulah von Birmingham), Barry Lowe (Dr. Glynn), Alex "Alien" Russell (Igor), Claire Cannaway (Young Lenore Usher), Sam Kitcher (Young Allan Usher), Screw (Suki Uruma), Medieval Babes (Unholy Revellers); Alex Russell, James Johnston, Barry Lowe, Roger Wilkes (Gory the Gorilla), Jackie Lowe, Ann Thomas, Neil Brookes, Leonie Brookes, Leah (Lunatics), Nipper (Black Dog)

Hot Pants: 3 Sexy Shorts (2006) A Gorsewood Production

1. "The Revenge of the Elephant Man"

Producer, Photographer, and Caterer: Ken Russell; Editor and Special Effects: Michael Bradsell; Music: Merv Greenslade, Carl Chamberlain, Mike Bradsell: "Inside Your World," Lyrics by Barry Lowe, Music by Merv Greenslade, sung by Elize Tribble; Choreography: Elize Tribble

Cast: Ken Russell (Dr. Henry Horenstein), Elize Tribble (Nurse Randy Ravensworth), Barry Lowe (Ella, the Elephant Man), The Russells (Crowd)

2. "The Mystery of Mata Hari"

Producer, Photographer, and Writer: Ken Russell; Editor: Michael Bradsell; Production Designer: H. K. A. Russell; Set Construction: Robert Harding; Costumes: Turkish Bazaar, Nottingham Novelty Shop, Mrs. Russell's Closet; "Empty Souls," Lyrics by Barry Lowe, Music by Gene Burton, Instrumental by Merv Greenslade, Vocal by Elize Tribble; Choreography: Alf and Elf Russell; Original Music: Hugo Wassermann, with the Sinfonia Rolanda

Cast: Elize Tribble (Mata Hari/Sister Claire); Ken Russell (as Henri Roussel) (The Jailer); Barry Lowe (O.C. Firing Squad)

3. "The Good Ship Venus"

Producer: Ken Russell; Editor: Michael Bradsell; Costumes: Elize Tribble; Music Arranged by Hugo Wasserman; Everything Else Supervised by Ken Russell, including slaving over a hot stove in the galley!

Cast: Performed by the Vulgar Boatmen: Cap'n "Long" Ken Russell RNVR; Barry "Deadeye" Lowe RNLJ; Mike "The Hook" Bradsell RTJM; Lisi "Mabel Black Label" Tribble RSVP

STAGED OPERAS

The Rake's Progress (1982) 45th Maggio Musicale, Florence

Composer: Igor Stravinsky; Conductor: Riccardo Chailly; Libretto: W. H. Auden and Chester Kallmann; Designer: Derek Jarman

Players: Gösta Winbergh (Tom Rakewell), Istvan Gati (Nick Shadow), Cecelia Gasdia (Anne Trulove)

Madama Butterfly (1983) Spoleto Festival, Charleston, South Carolina

Composer: Giacomo Puccini; Conductor: John Matheson; Designer: Richard MacDonald

Players: Barry McCauley (Pinkerton), Catherine Lamy (Cio-Cio San), Steven Cole (Goro), Robert Galbraith (Sharpless), Komiko Yoshii (Suzuki), Cyler Applegate/Moultrie Townsend (Butterfly's son)

The Italian Woman in Algiers (1984) Geneva Opera, Switzerland

Composer: Gioacchino Rossini

Players: John Rawnsleyn (Taddeo)

La Bohéme (1984) Macerata Festival, Italy

Composer: Giacomo Puccini; Conductor: José Collado; Designer: Richard MacDonald

Players: Cecilia Gasdia (Mimi), Elena Zilio (Musetta), Angelo Romero (Marcello), Giancarlo Ceccarini (Schaunard), Mario Luperi (Colline)

Die Soldaten (1984) English National Opera, London

Composer: Bernd-Alois Zimmermann; Conductor: Serge Baudo

Faust (1985) Vienna State Opera

Composer: Charles Gounod; Conductor: Erich Binder; Libretto: Jules Barbier and Michel Carré; Designer: Carl Toms; Choreography: Alphonse Poulin

Players: Francisco Araiza (Faust), Ruggero Raimondi (Mephistopheles), Gabriela Beňačková (Marguerite); Walton Grönroos (Valentin), Alfred Šramek (Wagner); Gabriele Sima (Siebel), Gertrude Jahn (Marthe).
DVD release: Deutsche Grammophon (2006)

Méphistophélès (1989) Grand Opera of Genoa

Composer: Arrigo Boito; Conductor: Edoardo Muller; Choreographer: Richard Caceres. Costume Designer: Paul Dufficey

Players: Paata Burchuladze (Mefistofele), Ottavio Garaventa (Faust), Adriana Morelli (Margherita), Silvana Mazzieri (Marta), Fabio Armiliato (Wagner), Josella Ligi (Elena), Laura Bocca (Pabtalis), Saverio Bambi (Nereo) (See also *Television Work*)

Princess Ida (1992) Lyon, France and also at the English National Opera (London Coliseum)

Composers: Gilbert and Sullivan; Conductor: Jane Glover; Designer: James Merifield

Players: Rosemary Joshua (Princess Ida), Anne-Marie Owens (Lady Psyche), Richard Suart/Nickolas Grace (King Gama) Mark Curtis (Hilarion), Richard Van Allan (Hildebrand), John Graham-Hall (Cyril), Geoffrey Dolton (Florian)

Salome (1993) Bonn Opera House, Germany

Composer: Richard Strauss; Designer: James Merifield

MUSIC VIDEOS

"Cry to Heaven," Elton John (1985)

"Nikita," Elton John (1985)

"The Phantom of the Opera," Sarah Brightman and Steve Harley (1986)

"Wishing You Were Somehow Here Again," Sarah Brightman (1986)

"All I Ask of You," Sarah Brightman and Cliff Richard (1986)

"Trial of the Century (Dancing for Justice)," Richard Golub (1987)

"She's So Beautiful," Cliff Richard (1988)

"It's All Coming Back to Me Now," Pandora's Box (1989)

"Diana," Bryan Adams (1993)

FILM AND TELEVISION APPEARANCES

Russell's Progress (as himself) (BBC TV) (1971)

The Kids Are Alright (as himself), dir. Jeff Stein (1979)

The Russia House (as Walter), dir. Fred Schepisi (1990)

Music of the Movies: Georges Delerue (as himself), dir. Jean-Louis Comolli (1994)

Empire of the Censors (as himself) (BBC TV), dir. Saskia Baron (1995)

i-camcorder (as himself), dir. Vic Finch (1995)

Great Composers (as himself), dir. Kriss Russman (1997)

Carry on Darkly (as himself), dir. Paul Gallagher (1998)

Turning Points (as himself), dir. Michael Le Moignan and Dean Arnett (2000)

Felicity Kendall: A Passage from India (as himself), dir. Angela O'Leary (2001)

Hell on Earth: The Desecration & Resurrection of "The Devils" (as himself) (Channel 4 TV), dir. Paul Joyce (2002)

Waking the Dead: "Final Cut" (as Gerry Raistrick) (BBC TV), (2003)

Colour Me Kubrick (as Nightgown Man), dir. Brian W. Cook (2004)

Marple: "The Moving Finger" (as Reverend Caleb Dane Calthrop) (2006)

Brothers of the Head (as himself), dir. Keith Fulton and Louis Pepe (2006)

BOOKS

Altered States (Bantam Books, 1991)

Fire over England: The British Cinema Comes Under Friendly Fire (Hutchinson, 1993)

The Lion Roars: Ken Russell on Film (Faber and Faber, 1993)

Mike & Gaby's Space Gospel (Warner Books, 1999)

Directing Film: From Pitch to Premiere (B. T. Batsford, 2000)

Brahms Gets Laid (Iain Fisher, 2003)

Violation (Author House, 2005)

Elgar: The Erotic Variations and *Delius: A Moment with Venus* (Peter Owen Ltd., 2007)

Beethoven Confidential and *Brahms Gets Laid* (Peter Owen Ltd., 2007)

INDEX

Bold page numbers denote photographs

367

INDEX

INDEX

INDEX